Identity and Experience at the India-Bangladesh Border

The effects of the Partition of India in 1947 have been more far-reaching and complex than the existing partition narratives of violence and separation reveal. The immediacy of the movement of refugees between India and the newly-formed state of Pakistan overshadowed the actual effect of the drawing of the border between the two states.

The book is an empirical study of border narratives across the India-Bangladesh border, specifically the West Bengal part of India's border with Bangladesh. It tries to move away from the perpetrator state-victim civilian framework usually used in the studies of marginal people, and looks at the kind of agencies that the border people avail themselves of. Instead of looking at the border as the periphery, the book looks at it as the line of convergence and negotiations – the 'centre of the people' who survive it every day. It shows that various social, political and economic identities converge at the borderland and are modified in unique ways by the spatial specificity of the border – thus forming a 'border identity' and a 'border consciousness'. Common sense of the civilians and the state machinery (embodied in the border guards) collide, cooperate and affect each other at the borderlands to form this unique spatial consciousness. It is the everyday survival strategies of the border people which aptly reflects this consciousness rather than any universal border theory or state-centric discourses about the borders. A bottom-up approach is of utmost importance in order to understand how a spatially unique area binds diverse other identities into a larger spatial identity of a 'border people'.

The book's relevance lies in its attempt to explore such everyday narratives across the Bengal border, while avoiding any major theorising project so as not to choke the potential of such experience-centred insights into the lives of a unique community of people. In that, it contributes towards a study of borders globally, providing potential approaches to understand border people worldwide. Based on detailed field research, this book brings a fresh approach to the study of this border. It will be of interest to researchers in the field of South Asian studies, citizenship, development, governance and border studies.

Debdatta Chowdhury is currently an Assistant Professor in Gender Studies at the Centre for Studies in Social Sciences Calcutta. Her research interests include border narratives, citizenship and migration discourses, especially across the South Asian borders. Her research interests also include feminism, caste identities, queer theories and narratives, especially in the South Asian context.

Routledge Studies in Asian Diasporas, Migrations and Mobilities

Migration, Micro-Business and Tourism in Thailand
Highlanders in the City
Alexander Trupp

Indian Immigrant Women and Work
The American Experience
Vijaya M. Ramya and Bidisha Biswas

Chinese Transnational Migration in the Age of Global Modernity
The Case of Oceania
Liangni Sally Liu

Identity and Experience at the India-Bangladesh Border
The Crisis of Belonging
Debdatta Chowdhury

For more information about this series, please visit: www.routledge.com/
Routledge-Studies-in-Asian-Diasporas-Migrations-and-Mobilities/book-series/
RSADMM

Identity and Experience at the India-Bangladesh Border
The Crisis of Belonging

Debdatta Chowdhury

LONDON AND NEW YORK

First published 2018
by Routledge
2 Park Square, Milton Park, Abingdon, Oxon OX14 4RN

and by Routledge
711 Third Avenue, New York, NY 10017

Routledge is an imprint of the Taylor & Francis Group, an informa business

© 2018 Debdatta Chowdhury

The right of Debdatta Chowdhury to be identified as author of this work
has been asserted by her in accordance with sections 77 and 78 of the
Copyright, Designs and Patents Act 1988.

All rights reserved. No part of this book may be reprinted or reproduced or
utilised in any form or by any electronic, mechanical, or other means, now
known or hereafter invented, including photocopying and recording, or in
any information storage or retrieval system, without permission in writing
from the publishers.

Trademark notice: Product or corporate names may be trademarks or
registered trademarks, and are used only for identification and explanation
without intent to infringe.

British Library Cataloguing-in-Publication Data
A catalogue record for this book is available from the British Library

Library of Congress Cataloging-in-Publication Data
A catalog record has been requested for this book

ISBN: 978-1-138-21080-6 (hbk)
ISBN: 978-1-315-29681-4 (ebk)

Typeset in Times New Roman
by Apex CoVantage, LLC

Note: The maps in this book are historical maps and they are included here for representative
purposes. The international boundaries, coastlines, denominations, and other information shown do
not necessarily imply any judgement concerning the legal status of any territory or the endorsement
or acceptance of such information. For current boundaries, readers may refer to the Survey of India
maps.

Contents

List of figures		vi
List of maps		vii
Preface		viii
Acknowledgements		x
1	Introduction	1
2	Livelihood practices: legal, illegal and the grey-zone in between	29
3	Spatial disparities: enclaves, *Chars* and disputed territories	90
4	Ethno-cultural concerns: appropriation of marginal spaces	141
5	Gendered practices: perpetrators, victims, accomplices	177
6	Conclusion	219
	Bibliography	229
	Index	239

Figures

1.1	Border pillar facing India with Bangladeshi road beyond, 2012.	10
2.1	Fencing along the South Dinajpur border, West Bengal, 2012.	32
2.2	Cattle *haat*, 2012.	52
2.3	Informal border market beside border outposts. Indian shopkeeper selling products to Bangladeshi customers, 2011.	65
3.1	Bangladeshi enclave in India, 2012.	95
3.2	Hospital in Dahagram, 2011.	118
3.3	*Tinbigha* Corridor leading to mainland Bangladesh, 2011.	119
3.4	India's border fence through which the land indicated above (*Ghoj*) passes, 2012.	127

Maps

3.1   Diagrammatic sketch map of Cooch Behar enclaves (*Chhits*).
Redrawn map. Source: District Map of Cooch Behar, Govt. of India.   91
3.2   Location of *Tinbigha*, Cooch Behar. Redrawn map. Source: Cooch
Behar District Map, Govt. of India.   114
3.3   Location map of *Tinbigha*. Redrawn map. Source: Cooch Behar
District Map, Govt. of India.   116

Preface

Cultural and linguistic difference between people is often the genesis of a cartographic border formation – an almost natural and obvious boundary-making between people speaking different tongues and observing different customs. Most of the borders in the world, be they inter-state or intra-state, have followed this logic of letting a natural boundary form where a set of socio-linguistic practices end and a new set of practices begin, often with overlapping traits along the borders. The Bengal border is a unique case, in being an imposed border, forced down upon culturally/linguistically similar people, on the basis of religious categorisations, that too mostly without a rhyme or reason. A mainland was, thus, at a stroke of a pen, transformed into a borderland – a transformation that was neither precise nor complete – resulting in a complicated border fabric. The mainstay of this book, and the study that it has been based on, is an understanding of the process of this very transformation of a mainland into a borderland and the diverse socio-cultural, political and economic narratives that it has produced in the process of this transformation. The process of the formation of a borderland can be best understood by a ripple effect where the nearest areas to the borderline are the most affected – forming the core border zone – while the farther the area is from the borderline, the lesser the impact, until the areas cease to identify themselves with the border and see themselves as mainlanders. This, pretty much, stands as the logic of calling an area a border zone or mainland.

This book aims to divest the border and the lives of its people of a certain mystery that engulfs a mainlander's idea of a border. Films, writings, reminiscences often romanticise the Bengal border as an aftermath of Partition and rarely consider the border as anything beyond an embodiment of loss, grief, separation and dystopia. A lot of seminal works on the Bengal border have gone a long way in demystifying it. But most of them have identified the border as a space of subversion and aberration – an abnormal way of life demanding constant control and rectification by the involved states. This is true of the Bengal border, but not the entire picture. Most of the existing works have also attempted at theorising the border or locating it within the larger discourses of border-making. The aim of this study is not just to demystify or de-romanticise the border but also to consciously avoid theorising the border, in order to avoid the border narratives from being enclosed within specific disciplinary frameworks. That would be an injustice to

Preface ix

the diverse strands of identity formations as experienced by the borderlanders. The aim is not to reach a conclusion or even form views, but to reveal border life as and how it is experienced by the border people. It is aimed at highlighting the lived realities of the people, to focus on their 'crisis of belonging' and how they turn the crisis in their favour in the course of their everyday survival. No single disciplinary tool can do justice to the dynamism of border life. On the contrary, it takes away the ambiguities and uniqueness that characterises this border. Statistical data or graphs have, likewise, been rarely used, in order to maintain the essence of individual experiences and perspectives, rather than objectifying and neutralising these experiences into mere statistical information.

Since the focus has been on the narratives, the language and articulation of the interviewees have been kept intact – the essence of their thoughts maintained as far as possible. The articulation has often been ambiguous, politically incorrect. But nothing has been polished or rectified while transcribing, in order to maintain the spontaneity of the responses.

A lot of varied issues have been discussed, while a lot more have been left out. Only the recurrent issues, which have spontaneously cropped up in almost all conversations (open-ended interviews), have been included. The focus has been essentially on the West Bengal-Bangladesh border and has, thus, left out India's north-eastern border with Bangladesh, because of logistical limitations (my inability to visit Bangladesh's border with India's north-east) and because of the ethno-cultural specificities of India's north-eastern states, which calls for separate in-depth study. Issues like connectivity, religious fundamentalism and terrorism along the borderland have been mentioned, but not as much as issues like these demand. That is because the interviews were meant to highlight more of the everyday lives of the border people, and less of the issues of inter-state bilateral affairs. Very recent trends across this border have also not been touched upon, limiting the discussion to September 2013, when the doctoral research was completed. A few updates have been included though, simply to place a few issues within their current contexts. The book often reads like a string of conversations, rather than a critical analysis of a cartographically sensitised space that becomes the platform for diverse identity formations. But that, precisely, brings out the everydayness of a border life, showing how surviving the border is weaved into the daily lives and practices of its people. Daily lives and practices, rather than specific events or issues per se, have, thus, formed much of the conversations. Border-making is not a one-time event, nor is it simply an issue of security, nationalistic discourses or containment of the subjects of a nation – it is a lived experience for the people who negotiate it, survive it and use it to serve their needs. Victimhood is not the only index to understand the border. Agency and appropriation are as integral to a borderlander's life. And this is what forms the crux of this book.

Acknowledgements

This work would not have seen the light of day without the infrastructural and academic support, and most importantly the studentship support of the University of Westminster. I am immensely grateful to the university for the studentship and for the help and encouragement I have received from the university staff. This dissertation would also have been unaccomplished had it not been for the excellent guidance and supervision provided by my Director of Studies, Dr Radha D'Souza. To her and to Professor Andreas Philippopoulos-Mihalopoulos, my second supervisor, I can only express a lifetime of gratitude.

I sincerely thank the institutions without which I would not have progressed: the British Library and the School of Oriental and African Studies Library, the National Library, Kolkata, especially Mr Ashim Mukhopadhyay and Mr Partha Ghosh; the Ramkrishna Mission Institute of Culture, Kolkata, the West Bengal State Archives, especially Mr Anandalal Bhattacharya; West Bengal Legislative Library; Bureau of Applied Economics and Statistics, Government of West Bengal, especially Mr Satya Bhattacharya, and the Office of Indian Census, Kolkata. I am also indebted to Shaktidas Roy, Chief Librarian, ABP Pvt. Ltd., Kolkata for providing me with useful information and helping me find the right documents. I thank the Development Research Communication and Services Centre (DRCSC), especially Ms Subhadyuti Mitra, for providing appropriate secondary material.

In a similar vein, I wish to thank the National Archives of India, Delhi, the Directorate of Archives and Libraries, Government of the People's Republic of Bangladesh and the Library support staff of the Library of the University of Dhaka. I am extremely thankful to the Asiatic Society of Bangladesh, Dhaka and especially Professor Sharifuddin Ahmed and Md. Abdul Awal Miah for not just providing me with hospitality but also relevant inputs. I fondly remember Professor Fakrul Alam of the University of Dhaka for putting me in touch with the relevant people.

Professor Subhendu Dasgupta and Professor Keya Dasgupta's support and motivation with regard to my field work cannot be expressed in words. Without the help of Mr Debiprasad Roy Chowdhury, of the Association for Protection of Democratic Rights (APDR), who helped me with field assistants in the various border areas where I worked, I would not have been able to conduct my field studies. I am deeply indebted to those APDR activists and volunteers who made my

Acknowledgements xi

field visits not just possible but safe and enjoyable. Samiran Biswas, Swapan Sanyal, Diptiman Sengupta, Krishnapada Ghosh, Subham, Sudipta, Ananda Ghosh, Abhiranjan Bhaduriand Jatiswar Bharati all deserve my sincerest gratitude. I am obliged to Binoy Krishna Mullick of Rights Jessore, Bangladesh for providing me with the necessary logistical support and field assistants during my field visits in the border districts of Bangladesh. My field visits in Bangladesh were also made possible by Rostom Ali Mondol and Sarwar Hossen.

Most of the photographs reproduced in this book are mine, and therefore they appear without acknowledgement. For the others, their sources are duly mentioned.

Without inspiration from Professor Subhas Ranjan Chakrabarty, Dr Paula Banerjee and Professor Lipi Ghosh, I would not have been able to pursue academic research. My immense gratitude to Prof. Parimal Ghosh for pushing me into turning the dissertation into a monograph and for making me believe that I can. My sincerest thanks to Rajat Kanti Sur for helping me with every kind of support for my research and for the wonderful discussions and inputs, and most importantly, for having faith in my abilities. I also thank Ishita Dey for her encouragement and inputs.

I do not have enough words to thank Tanmayee Banerjee and Sayandip Mukherjee for being my oxygen and sunshine in London. Without them, I doubt if I would have survived the grey days. Dr Devika Rangachari appeared as a life-saver at the right moment. I take complete responsibility for all the shortcomings in this monograph.

Without the freedom to work on my own research and the infrastructural support of a well-equipped office – my 'own' space – provided by the Centre for Studies in Social Sciences Calcutta, my last days of working on my book would not have been possible.

I thank Saumya and Radha Chandra for their trust in me. Last, but by no means the least, I thank my parents, my brother and Saurav for being my patient listeners, punching bags and cheerful victims of my academic zeal. Thank you for being proud of me.

1   Introduction

The effects of the Partition of India in 1947 have been way more far-reaching and complex than the existing partition narratives of violence and separation reveal. The immediacy of the movement of refugees between India and the newly-formed state of Pakistan overshadowed, for the time being, the actual effect of the drawing of the border between the two states. As communal violence and refugee exodus gradually began subsiding, the ground reality of the creation of the border started revealing itself. Partition affected almost everyone in India and Pakistan, directly or indirectly, although the effect was most strongly felt in the provinces of Punjab and Bengal, which underwent the cartographic partition. West Pakistan was carved out of Punjab and East Pakistan was carved out of Bengal. For the people who were settled and rehabilitated in the mainland territories of India and Pakistan, i.e. those not in close proximity to the newly-created border, the effect of Partition gradually began subsiding as they went about resettling their lives and livelihoods. However, for the people whose lives, homes and livelihoods were directly affected by the creation of the border, a new struggle began. The effect of Partition did not remotely subside for the people who now found themselves along the newly-created border, either by the turn of events or by choice. Partition literature (both non-fiction and fiction)[1] ended with the 'creation' of the Bengal border but rarely, if at all, ventured into discussing the border as a space where socio-cultural and spatial identities continued to be made and unmade.

In this regard, this book aims to look at the lives and some aspects of everyday practices of the people living along the India-Pakistan border, with specific focus on the West Bengal-East Pakistan border, later the Bangladesh border from 1971, in order to analyse how border identities are made, unmade and remade.

Creation of the Bengal border

The basis for the creation of the West Bengal-East Pakistan border was faulty from its inception. The drawing of the border was far from a 'clean-cut vivisection'[2] of a territory, 'executed with clinical precision'.[3] The Chairman of the Boundary Commissions and the author of the Boundary Awards, Sir Cyril Radcliffe, was a complete outsider when it came to knowledge about India and its administration. He had no prior experience in adjudicating disputes such as the ones leading to the

2 Introduction

Partition and no knowledge of the settlements in the areas to be partitioned. It was no surprise then that Radcliffe's drawing of the border on the maps was flawed.

Moreover, the basis of the Partition, as revealed from Partition votes obtained from the Bengal Legislative Assembly, seemed to bend more towards territorial considerations rather than communal aspirations, contrary to the general idea that the partition was executed on a communal basis.[4] The Bengal Legislative Assembly divided itself into two parts – one consisting of the representatives of Muslim-majority districts and the other consisting of representatives of Hindu-majority districts. The two units met at the Bengal Legislative Assembly on 20 June 1947 to indicate their views on Partition. Neither of the units, though, had any knowledge of the actual plan of the Boundary Commission nor to which state their constituencies would eventually belong when the Award was finally made.[5] From the very beginning, territorial considerations gained stronger favour with the units than the communal right to self-determination, as Joya Chatterji rightly points out.[6] This explains the meeting between the representatives of Hindu and Muslim-majority districts rather than Hindu and Muslim members 'to determine their collective communal will on what was, in its primary form, a communal question'.[7] While communal autonomy might still be achieved within a single state, i.e. without territorial separation per se, the principle of territorial autonomy demands a sovereign, bounded space which, in the case of Bengal, could only be achieved through territorial separation.[8]

The self-interest and bias of the political parties involved in the Partition Plan, namely the Congress and the Muslim League, also played significant roles in the formation of the Boundary Commissions and, hence, the final execution of the boundary plan. This was coupled with the influence of Lord Mountbatten (the then Viceroy of India) on Radcliffe in the drawing of the boundary. The immediacy of the need to finalise the boundary was stressed by Jawaharlal Nehru, member of the Indian Constituent Assembly and Prime Minister-designate, on the premise that once the Boundary Awards were finalised, India and Pakistan would sort out the rest of the disputes themselves and come to a mutually satisfactory agreement. Hence, Nehru emphasised on a make-shift border for the purpose of a quick transfer of power.[9] Along with the 'contiguity of majority areas of Muslims and Hindus', another index called the 'other factors' was also taken into account in demarcating the boundary.[10] The fact that 'other factors', however vaguely defined, played a crucial and far-reaching role in the creation of the border has been amply proved, as will be evident from subsequent chapters. Short-term gains conceived by the political parties and a rushed execution of the transfer of power by the Viceroy resulted in a territorial fabric which would have long-term effects way beyond the conception and life span of its creators.

The fact that the Boundary Commissioners were judges and the Chairman a lawyer created an impression that the Boundary Award was a matter involving 'legal expertise, resting on judicial rationality'[11] and that the 'rulings met the technical requirements of legal justice'.[12] But, as some studies of the West Bengal-Bangladesh border have shown and even this book shall reveal, socio-cultural, political and economic factors have had an overwhelming effect on the creation

Introduction 3

and evolution of the border – calling into question the legal basis and administrative concerns of the creation of the border.

That 'territory' was the most crucial factor underlying the demands of the various political parties in the Partition Plan has been proved by their conflicting claims over territory. Each party had its own reasons and interests in demanding the maximum area of Bengal to accommodate a religious majority, including the refugees (refugee exodus had already started by 1946 following the Noakhali riots),[13] and to ensure the latter's economic requirements, even if that meant laying claims over some of the other religious-majority areas. The decisive political figures behind the creation of the border had realised that the Radcliffe line would not simply 'demarcate the boundaries between two nations',[14] but would also 'shape the very contours of control and influence in the divided successor states'.[15] They had no doubts about the fact that 'the shape of the border would have implications for the future of their respective parties'.[16] Therefore, the choice and claim over space required careful consideration. Territory, thus, played a central role in the vision of the new states to be created.[17] Besides, 'the desire to preserve natural frontiers, to guarantee the military strategic unity of the new international border and aid a successful future foreign policy and the political sustenance of the new Indian nation and citizenship within it, and to ensure economic stability and social continuity' were also intertwined with the question of territory, thus, explaining the scramble for it.[18]

It would be wrong to assume that the entire public sphere was oblivious to how the border was being conceived. At least in Bengal, the Bengali public did take an interest in their political future, instead of being mere passive bystanders, as Haimanti Roy has shown.[19] 'Rather, they actively wrote to the Boundary Commission, and shared their ideas and suggestions in newspapers and journals too, feeling that it was their duty to aid the members of the Boundary Commission in making the *right* decision'.[20] With the help of census data, maps and 'details about the religious and national significance of their particular areas', they explained 'their petitions for inclusions in either western or eastern Bengal'.[21] This shows that the people, at least in Bengal, had a stake in the boundary-making though the final plan did not necessarily reflect the public opinion. This explains why the people who ended up across the border, or settled along it later, were aware of the exigencies of their territorial marginality and were, thus, fast to learn new ways of not just surviving the border, but being active beneficiaries of the possibilities that the border created. In the petitions made by the people of Bengal for inclusion in either half of the newly formed states following the Partition, concerns like religion, territory, history, patriotism played important roles. Citing Hindu archaeological heritage or birthplaces of Congress leaders as signs of patriotism, certain areas were petitioned to be included in Hindu-majority India.[22]

Despite petitions and newspaper articles, there was confusion regarding the actual distribution of territories till the Boundary Commission finally announced the plan on 17 August 1947. Eventually, the Radcliffe line created two states where the ratio of the majority to the minority population was almost exactly the same. *Thanas* (police stations) were taken as the unit for partitioning. The

4   *Introduction*

Muslim-majority districts of Murshidabad and Nadia went to West Bengal, while Hindu-majority Khulna went to Pakistan. 'The Award placed 71% of the Muslim population in East Bengal (East Pakistan) and 70.8% of the Hindu population in West Bengal'.[23] It 'assigned 36.36% of land to accommodate 35.14% of population to West Bengal, while East Bengal received 63.6% of land to accommodate 64.85% of the population. The two states had an equal proportion of majority and minority populations in a ratio of approximately 70:30'.[24] 'However, the award was inequitable in its distribution of the minority population within each area, as West Bengal contained 16% of the total Muslim population of Bengal, while East Bengal retained 42% of the total non-Muslims of undivided Bengal. The boundary divided the five districts of Nadia, Jessore, Dinajpur, Jalpaiguri and Malda'.[25] Though the Boundary Award was generally accepted without much discontent, some of the Hindu and Muslim areas (especially in Murshidabad, Nadia and Khulna) were disgruntled because of their inclusion on the wrong side of the border and for being 'shut out of their promised land'.[26] The most perturbed were, for obvious reasons, the people residing in these five districts who, now, went on to become borderland people after being traditionally mainlanders. While, later in 1950, Cooch Behar became a part of India (West Bengal), sharing its border with Bangladesh's Lalmonirhat district, its enclave question could not be resolved, resulting in statelessness of a considerable number of people, till its resolution as recently as 2015.

Complex nature of the West Bengal-Bangladesh border

As noted earlier, the border was, from the very beginning, vaguely demarcated, as it was based on outdated maps of *thana* and district boundaries. Moreover, it ran over rivers and agricultural land which were difficult to demarcate clearly except for an imaginary line. The rivers specifically posed a major problem for the border because of the seasonal nature of some of them, implying a drying-up during winter and flooding during the monsoon with disastrous effects on the demarcation as well as the security of the border. Moreover, these rivers often changed (and still do) their course, resulting in perennial confusion over disappearing and reappearing lands (*Chars*)[27] along the borderline. In the event of disputes over territories, the resolution would have to depend completely on the goodwill and co-operation of the concerned states. Confusion regarding the borderline was enhanced because of the contradictions between the *thana* maps and the settlement maps, on which the demarcation was based.[28] None of the political parties or commissioners thought it necessary to survey the land before drawing up the final borderline. It is, thus, no surprise that the border that was finally created was full of flaws and inaccuracies, the price for which has been paid ever since by the people who live along the line.

It is easy to imagine what the outcome of such a hastily-created border pushed by narrow self-interests and planned without prior ground-knowledge might have been. The Bengal landscape, therefore, saw the border running right through homes, hearths and lands, separating people from their families and livelihoods,

Introduction 5

and the towns from their hinterlands. The border, as Chatterji puts it, 'ruptured agrarian communities all along its lengths'.[29] The border also had disastrous consequences for peasant movements like *Tebhaga*,[30] cutting off *jotedars*[31] from the sharecroppers.[32] Traditional kin and associate links and economic ties were disrupted, and illegalised, and traditional practices criminalised by the creation of the international border. The communication system was heavily jeopardised, and public institutions, like administrative headquarters, hospitals and courts, were cut off from the suburbs.[33]

The Bengal border became all the more complex in nature due to the official intention of the Nehru government to keep it porous, and the regulations regarding property evacuation and compensation flexible. The Standstill Agreement in 1947 emphasised on the 'interdependence of the new nations and the need for open borders', stipulating that there would be no customs barriers or prohibitive excise taxes on goods till a long-term trade policy is framed.[34] The Inter-Dominion Conference in Calcutta in 1948 also saw the setting up of the Evacuee Management Boards on both sides of the Bengal border in order to protect the evacuee properties till their owners returned to claim them. Also, those who lived on one side of the border and worked on the other could still move freely across the border on a daily basis.[35] Even people living across the border could also move their land's produce across to their homes on the other side.[36] Water, road and rail links continued between the two parts, which benefitted India more, since its goods carriages needed to traverse East Pakistan's territory for easy communication with its north-eastern parts.

While this flexibility and porosity remained merely on paper for those migrants who settled in places far away from the border, it meant a physical practice of regular mobility for those settled near the border, as they tried to access and exercise their control over their property that was left behind on the other side.[37] This implied that even after years of the Partition and the creation of the border, the cross-border movement of people and goods was a fact, and an officially recognised one at that.[38] Yet such government policies failed to have the desired effect of a peaceful border obtained through porosity. This was largely due to conflicting ideas about the border's nature and use by the civilians and the border guards. In their zeal to protect the religious majorities and, thereby, feed into the nationalistic fervour of their respective states, the border guards and local *thana* police attempted to establish complete control over the border, thereby violating the then-official policies of porous borders and easy cross-border mobility. This led to the abuse, both physical and verbal, of those who crossed the border.[39] With the expiration of the Standstill Agreement in February 1948, customs barriers began to be implemented across the border, resulting in confusion regarding the obtaining of the permit and the fate of perishable goods. This was the beginning of an uncomfortable relation between the state, on the one hand, represented through the government policies and the border police (border guards created for the purpose), and the border civilians, on the other, that continues, unabated, till date.

But by the time the states started taking stringent measures to curb and control the fluidity, cross-border mobility and networks had become commonplace

6 *Introduction*

and integral to the lives of the border people on both sides of the Bengal border. Stringent border rules failed to stop such well-networked movements; it simply tagged such movements as illegal and criminalised the participants. The West Bengal-Bangladesh border was, thus, an interdependent borderland, characterised by symbiotic links between societies on both sides of the border, resulting in a considerable flow of economic and human resources across it.[40]

The newly-created Bengal border, thus, changed the lives, livelihoods, economies and politics of the people it directly involved itself with. 'Village politics that had, so far, revolved around the caste councils, union boards and tenancy disputes, now began to be the site where citizenship and patriotic duty were propagated, where ideological battles between nations were fought'.[41] Categories such as refugees, aliens, infiltrators attained new definitions in the post-Partition phase, with colonial subjects turning into national citizens and mainlanders turning into borderlanders. The mediations around these identities were the most strongly witnessed across the newly-created border, where refugee documents, border slips and later passports, 1952 onwards, gave dwelling and mobility a new meaning. Right from the genesis of the border, civilians and citizens across it began realising the border's 'utilitarian purposes' – for whom, the newly-acquired citizenship and other official identities were 'functional, at best and they retained old ties of wealth, kinship, and local identity even after new nationalities had been imposed on them through the documentary regime of passports and visas'.[42] In fact, it was the constant flux of migrants and refugees across the border between West Bengal and East Pakistan 'that forced India and Pakistan to craft legislations such as the passport system that ascribed nationality to their minority citizens', though the system was implemented initially in a piecemeal way and, thus, failed to stop questions from state officials to migrants regarding loyalty and national identities.[43]

It is in this context of the links between border societies that the following chapters aim to analyse certain aspects of the negotiations between the civilians themselves and between the civilians and the border guards along the West Bengal-Bangladesh border. The need to understand patterns of such negotiation in a complex border like the Bengal border not only enlightens one on the uniqueness of state-building ideologies in South Asia but also contributes in a large way to the genre of border studies in general in a global context.

Topography, habitation, livelihood, local governance, border guards, fences and zones: a brief description of the West Bengal-Bangladesh border

Topography

The stretch of Bengal (including West Bengal and Bangladesh) through which the border passes can be broadly categorised into plain land and riverine, with no natural obstacles. It is heavily populated and cultivated 'till the last inch of the border'.[44] The boundary line, in most places, is marked by border pillars.

Introduction 7

The riverine borders are of specific concern to the border guards because of the difficulty in marking the border through the rivers. Borders, in the case of rivers, are merely imaginary lines perceived as equidistant from the banks on both sides. Moreover, the changing course and flooding of the rivers also pose a challenge to border management due to the disappearing of borderlands and the reappearing of *chars* in the midst of the rivers. *Chars* are strategic locations both for control of the border by border guards on both sides, as well as for the cross-border smugglers and infiltrators who use the ambiguous location of the *chars* to operate.[45] Border rivers have, perpetually, been a cause of concern and dispute between India and Bangladesh over their sharing of waters, building of dams and maintenance of navigability. Disputes over the Farakka Barrage and the sharing of the water of the river Tista are examples of such disputes between India and Bangladesh.[46]

Habitation

The entire stretch of the West Bengal-Bangladesh border is densely populated.[47] Hence, the border passes through residential areas, cutting through houses and plots of lands. The profile of the people on both sides of the border is largely similar in terms of ethnic origin (Bengali), physical characteristics, language (*Bangla*) and culture.

Livelihood

Given the vast stretch of farmlands along the border, it is easy to understand the predominance of agriculture and agriculture-related occupations along it. Fishing constitutes the next most prominent livelihood activity due to the presence of rivers in the region. Cottage industries like *beedi*-manufacture,[48] handicrafts and gardening also contribute towards the economy of the border area, as do small-scale industries like brick-kilns, rice-mills and jute-mills. The border itself has created a vast range of livelihood opportunities for the people, including the camps of the border guards, border Land Ports (LP) as well as illegal trade. The currency of West Bengal is Indian Rupees (Rs.) and that of Bangladesh is the Bangladesh Taka (Tk.), though that does not deter nor hamper cross-border transactions, either official or unofficial, in any way.

Local governance

West Bengal (like the other 28 states in India) has its own Legislative Assembly (*Bidhan Sabha*), at the provincial level, where the various constituencies are represented through their Member of Legislative Assembly (MLA) and are represented in the House of the People (*Lok Sabha*) of the Parliament of India (*Sansad*) through Member of Parliament (MP). The districts of West Bengal also have their local three-tier governance system, consisting of the *Gram Panchayat* (at village level), the *Panchayat Samiti* (group of *Gram Panchayats*) and the *Zilla Parishad*

8   *Introduction*

(group of *Panchayat Samities*). There are local governance systems at the village, block and district levels of West Bengal consisting of elected representatives from the respective villages.

The districts of Bangladesh are represented by their elected ministers (MPs) from respective constituencies in the Parliament of Bangladesh (*Jatiyo Sansad Bhavan*). The districts also have their own local governments (*Union Parishad*) consisting of nine wards (one village is considered a single ward), each ward containing a chairman and twelve members. The number of wards in a district depends on its size.

Border guards

The origin of border guards along the West Bengal-Bangladesh border can be traced to the initiative of the Pakistani government to build a non-official military organisation called the *Ansar Bahini* in February 1948 for the purpose of guarding its borders with India,[49] though a separate paramilitary force was also formed out of the existing Eastern Frontier Rifles (EFR: formed under the colonial administration in 1920) and was renamed East Pakistan Rifles (EPR) in 1947 following the Partition. After the creation of Bangladesh as an independent state in 1971, the EPR was renamed Bangladesh Rifles (BDR). Following a coup in February 2009, the BDR underwent organisational changes and was renamed Border Guards Bangladesh (BGB). The BGB is under the administrative control of the Ministry of Home Affairs, Government of the People's Republic of Bangladesh. The BGB has its Central Headquarters in Pilkhana, Dhaka, besides its North Eastern (Sarail), North Western (Rangpur), South Eastern (Khagrachari) and South Western (Jessore) Regional Headquarters.

West Bengal also created its own semi-military frontier corps in March 1948 called the *Jatiya Rakshi Dal* (Bengal National Protection Brigade) formed of volunteers from the six border districts of Jalpaiguri, West Dinajpur, Malda, Murshidabad, Nadia and 24 Parganas. This force was administered in each district by the Magistrate, Superintendent of Police, the president of the District Congress Committee and the local Assembly Member.[50] Following the Indo-Pakistan War of 1965, the Border Security Force (BSF) was officially created as a part of the Central Armed Police Forces for the purpose of guarding its international borders. The BSF is under the administrative control of the Ministry of Home Affairs, Government of India. The BSF has its Force Headquarters at New Delhi, its Western Theatre Headquarters at Chandigarh, and its Eastern Theatre Headquarters at Kolkata. The Eastern Theatre Headquarters includes North Bengal, South Bengal and Malda Frontier of West Bengal (besides other frontiers in Assam, Tripura and Mizoram).

Both the BSF and the BGB have their respective Border Outposts (BOP) along the border. There are approximately 725 BSF BOPs (located at a distance of approximately 2–3 kilometres from each other) and 650 BGB BOPs[51] (located at a distance of approximately 5–6 kilometres from each other) along the 4096.7 kilometres-long border between India and Bangladesh, of which more than half the BSF BOPs are along the 2216.7 kilometres-long border between West Bengal and Bangladesh.

The exchange of fire between the BSF and BGB is a common occurrence along the West Bengal-Bangladesh border, especially over issues of infiltration and attacks by miscreants of the neighbouring state.[52] However, the BSF and BGB also meet at the border to discuss issues related to infiltration, smuggling or any other border-related incident that might be resolved between the border guards of the two states, without resorting to violence. Such meetings are called Flag Meetings[53] in official parlance. These meetings are usually held at a particular place on the land between the zero point (borderline) and India's border fence, which in official terms is known as No-Man's Land. Flag-bearing troupes of the border guards, led by the Company Commanders of the concerned outposts, meet to discuss the issues at hand. Meetings are also held in mid-river in riverine border areas where the BSF and BGB meet in the middle of the river at an equidistant location from both the banks on official speed boats which carry the flags of both states.

Border fence, border roads and floodlights

The Ground Rules formulated by the Military Sub-Committee of the Indian and Pakistan delegations on 20 October 1959 stipulated that: 'After an identifiable boundary line whether real or working has been demarcated, neither side will have any permanent or temporary border security forces or any other armed personnel within 150 yards on either side of this line. Also no permanent posts will be constructed till the final demarcation has been done.... If defensive works of any nature including trenches exist in the stretch of 300 yards (150 yards on each side of the working boundary) they must be destroyed or filled up'.[54] These Ground Rules were confirmed in the Joint India-Bangladesh Agreement for Border Authorities of the Two Countries in 1975.[55] Consequently, India planned and began executing the construction of a border fence (on grounds of preventing infiltration) and a border road at a distance of 150 yards (137 metres) from the 'zero point' (actual borderline), which left substantial areas of Indian farmland and homesteads (about 450 villages)[56] outside the fence.[57] These lands and houses can be accessed through gates constructed along the border fence guarded by BSF guards, on presenting identity cards at the check-posts. Whenever a person needs to cross the gates either for cultivating his land outside the fence or for moving in and out of his house across it, he needs to submit/present his identity card (Voter Cards, in most instances) to the guards or the commander at the check-post near the gate.

Bangladesh, on the other hand, objected to the construction of fences within 150 yards from the International Border (IB) on the pretext that fencing and border roads violated the guidelines of the Ground Rules.[58] Hence, Bangladesh neither has border fence nor border roads.

Till 2012, 1222 kilometres of fencing of the sanctioned 1528 kilometres had already been completed;[59] of the 1770 kilometres of border road sanctioned in West Bengal, 1616.57 kilometres had been constructed;[60] of the sanctioned 2840

10 *Introduction*

kilometres of sanctioned flood lighting along the India-Bangladesh border road, 775 kilometres had been completed (including 277 kilometres of flood lighting along West Bengal-Bangladesh border), while another 750 kilometres was in progress.[61] Construction of fences is scheduled to be completed by the end of 2018 as confirmed by the Secretary of the Border Management Division under the Ministry of Home Affairs.[62]

Border zones

The definitions of the various zones of a border region by Willem van Schendel and Michiel Baud[63] help us to understand the characteristic features of the geographical region of the West Bengal-Bangladesh border. The *border heartland* consists of the zone on the border or zones dominated by the border. Here, the social networks are directly shaped and affected by the border. The networks depend on the border for their survival and have no option but to adapt to its caprices; the *intermediate borderland* consists of the region which is affected by the border with varying intensity, from moderate to weak; and the *outer borderland* consists of those regions which feel the effect of the border at certain times and under specific circumstances.[64] It would be helpful to keep these definitions of the border zones in mind while studying the West Bengal-Bangladesh border in order to understand the effect of the border on the people and the extent of its influence on the surrounding regions.

Figure 1.1 Border pillar facing India with Bangladeshi road beyond, 2012.

Why was I drawn to this study?

In March 2008, I was working as a research associate in an organisation in Kolkata that researched issues related to refugees, migration, human rights, social justice and gender politics. I went on an official visit for two days to a border village in the border district of Nadia (West Bengal) for a survey of the situation of violence perpetrated by the BSF on the civilian[65] population living along the West Bengal border. I had certain pre-conceived notions about life in the border areas, especially along the international borders – notions pertaining to the stringency of border regulations and the patrolling of border guards. I had never been a border resident and so my knowledge about border areas was restricted to newspaper reports and a few official survey reports. Most of the existing literatures on borders pertained to dealing with them as issues of international relations and bilateral affairs between the states concerned, i.e. India and Bangladesh, and were, understandably, a simplistic narrative of diplomacy and international relations.

The works of Avtar Singh Bhasin,[66] Farooq Sobhan[67] and Garry Purcell[68] constituted literature which dealt with bilateral ties between India and Bangladesh at a purely diplomatic level, highlighting aspects of trade and economy which these states could pursue for improved relations. Narratives of (and from) the border between the two states were conspicuous by their absence in these literatures. While these works gave me a fair idea about bilateral ties between the states, they failed to highlight the local narratives of the people who negotiate the border – which was the purpose of my visit to the border village.

A brief survey of reports and articles prepared by the government officials of India and Bangladesh before the visit exposed the dearth of literature which dealt essentially with border life.[69] These reports were primarily viewing the border areas as disorderly spaces in need of stringent disciplining mechanisms and as sites in need of strengthened security apparatuses.[70] Literature prepared by the various NGOs and human rights organisations, on the other hand, emphasised more on the hapless condition of the border residents under the state machinery.[71] As part of a research organisation working on human rights and social justice, my visit was meant to serve a similar purpose, i.e. to take stock of the situation in the border village with regard to the condition of the border villages in general under the stringent presence of state machinery.

The visit served a bigger purpose than initially aimed. Apart from giving me an idea about the various instances of human rights violations of the border civilians by the border guards and the hazards associated with the daily lives of the people along the border (these formed part of my official study), the visit made me realise that the responses, perceptions and activities of the people living along the border reveal much more than meets the eye. The everyday lives and activities of the people produced a narrative which might be vastly different from the narratives of a person who lived away from the border, like myself. I was convinced that a closer study of such narratives would yield an interesting and possibly unique understanding of the border as the state's space for wielding control and as the

12 *Introduction*

civilians' space for negotiating such control mechanisms. James Scott's idea of the 'everyday forms of resistance'[72] had, in the meantime, drawn my attention to the importance of everyday narratives of people and micro-histories which constituted larger events, i.e. the Partition of India in my case. Though my ideas about the nature of these narratives and ways to obtain them were still vague, given the short length of my initial stay in the village, I came back only to go back to them.

I began learning more about the West Bengal-Bangladesh border and the India-Bangladesh border at large, apart from surveying literature on border studies in general. Eventually, my interest turned into my doctoral project.

I realised that a study of the entire India-Bangladesh border[73] would be too ambitious a project, given the limited time. So I narrowed the scope of my study down to issues which would help me analyse the border narratives in logistically feasible ways without compromising on the larger theoretical or empirical rigor. The fact that I shared the same language (*Bangla*) and similar ethnic origin/cultural traits (of being Bengali) with the majority of the people living along the West Bengal-Bangladesh border[74] was an important factor behind my decision because I could grasp their socio-cultural aspects without having to learn a new language or the cultural traits of the majority of the people.

Literature survey: preparation for field studies

The literature survey gave me a broad overview of border studies from the 1960s till about 2011, which is when I visited border areas as part of my empirical research. I understood that the study of borders had moved from being primarily a theorisation of the bordering process and understanding terminologies associated with borders[75] to being sociological and cultural studies of borders and the people who live in proximity to them.[76]

There has also been much writing on borders as geographical spaces of exclusion and the formation of peripheral subjectivities,[77] besides works studying them in the context of state and security issues.[78] These works are studies of the vulnerable nature of the border as demarcations of the state's sovereignty and how these vulnerabilities are policed by the state. The other significant contribution of these works towards border studies has been their emphasis on going beyond discursive studies of borders, and highlighting the importance of empirical studies as integral parts of methodological questions in studying these. The shift from studying borders as a straightjacketed political phenomenon to understanding them as catalysts for identity formations was also increasingly gaining pace.[79]

The existing studies either related to certain specific issues (mostly smuggling or trafficking)[80] or focussed on the deprivation of civilians from resources and basic facilities that their marginal lives entailed. The prime focus is on the victimhood of the people living across the border and their deprivation vis-à-vis the states, which was not necessarily the case, as my primary field observation hinted. Everyday narratives, in the forms of rudimentary practices of life and livelihood, culture,

Introduction   13

festivities, local politics did not find a major thrust in the existing works – van Schendel's work being the only major exception and by far, the closest indicator to what I was aiming to examine.

The aim of my study was, thus, to understand the lives of the people living on both sides of the West Bengal-Bangladesh border, including civilians and border guards, and to understand if their narratives did, in fact, reproduce and reinterpret the border. My aim was also to understand if such narratives were, in any way, subversive and belligerent in nature in terms of questioning the strength of the state's sovereignty at its seams.

A study of secondary materials in the various libraries and archives in India and Bangladesh in 2010[81] formed my initial knowledge of the areas which I was to study, in terms of an idea of the changing profile of the population (from the first census of the states in the second half of the twentieth century till date) and statistical information about the economic, ethnic and religious aspects of the people whom I intended to interact with during my field visits. Newspaper reports related to the West Bengal-Bangladesh border played an important role in shaping my idea about the chosen area of study. Both national and regional newspapers from India and Bangladesh were consulted during the pre-field visit period as well as later, during analysing the field data. *Ananda Bazar Patrika*, the Bengali-daily published from Kolkata, has been the most frequently cited newspaper, due to its consistency in reporting border-related issues, at least in its district supplements, as well as its effort in addressing some border issues, otherwise neglected by official reports or other media.

Of the ten border districts in West Bengal[82] and sixteen border districts in Bangladesh,[83] I chose to focus on six border districts of West Bengal[84] and eleven border districts of Bangladesh[85] between September 2011 and March 2012. My choice was informed by the geographical peculiarities of the areas (covering land borders and riverine borders), as well as their being important areas in terms of strategic location and economy (covering Enclaves,[86]*Chars* and Border Land Ports).[87]

The structure of fieldwork consisted mainly of interviews with the people living in the border areas, including civilians involved in a wide variety of livelihood practices, and across gender, religion and caste; border guards posted along the border outposts; public figures associated with administrative offices, mainly *Panchayat* members and heads (since most of the border areas are rural in character and, hence, form parts of local village governance) and political figures.

Borders, as territorial delimitations of a state, are spaces which mark the strongest manifestations of a state's sovereignty. Thus, they are also the spaces which witness the most visible presence of state machinery in terms of border fences, border guards and surveillance mechanisms. While the people living along the border areas negotiate such state presences in their everyday lives, the borders are virtually inaccessible, if not completely out of bounds, for a person living elsewhere but wanting to visit/study the borderlands, as in my case. My interactions with the senior members of the border guards regarding my plans of field visits also indicated the sensitivity of the state towards its borders. A feeling of

14   *Introduction*

suspicion and apprehension was present throughout our conversation as they took note of my plans. The paraphernalia included obtaining consent from the ethics committee of my university for conducting field studies and convincing them of my plans for handling possible risk hazards; preparing the Questionnaire, Consent Form (CF) and Participant Information Sheets (PIS); obtaining permissions from the Headquarters of the border guards of BSF and BGB for visiting the border areas and talking to border guards (written permissions were not available); contacting key persons and field assistants in the field areas which I planned to visit; arranging for my accommodation and travel in and around my field areas and chalking out the dates for my visits. The process of setting up the scene for the actual field work to take place was tedious and bothersome. This also, in a way, made me realise the gap between institutional research procedures and actual field studies. The formalities associated with institutional research procedures often fail to address or gauge the complexities of lived reality, especially when it comes to sensitised places like the borders. They often fail to see the everyday survival negotiations from their straightjacketed viewpoints. These gaps became visible to me even before I started my field visits. My experiences during my field visits only confirmed my apprehensions about the gap. Having gone through the ordeal of preparing for my field work, I set out on the much-awaited experience. Equipped with a recorder, a notepad and the pertinent field documents, I went about interacting with the people living along the West Bengal-Bangladesh border.

Choice of experience-centred narratives

The border narratives obtained in the course of the interviews have turned out to be powerful texts, amply reflecting the ways that the border space is re-interpreted in the everyday lives of its inhabitants. The narratives bear possibilities of questioning the sovereign nature of the state, though the narratives themselves are open to interpretations in various different ways. The narratives obtained through the interviews have been mostly *experience-centred*,[88] though *event-centred* narratives have also been recorded from time to time. Given the vast scope of interpretation that the narratives created, it has often been difficult for me to logically interpret or analyse the data. Yet I sincerely believe that the everyday life experiences of the narratives (which is what the narratives mostly consisted of) have been the nearest credible expressions of reality – as constructed by the narrators – the border people themselves. Experience-centred narratives often 'vary drastically over time, and across circumstances within which one lives, where a single phenomenon may produce very different stories, even from the same person'.[89] This explains the challenge I faced in accommodating contradictory responses, while, at the same time, being true to their spontaneous nature. But despite such challenges, the choice of experience-centred narratives of the border people was driven by their human nature and their capacity to 're-present experience, reconstituting it as well as expressing it'.[90] Their capacity to 'display transformation' has helped me highlight the evolution of border narratives expressed by the border people over a period of six decades.

Introduction   15

Field studies

The idea was to cover many categories of people across caste, religion, gender and livelihood so as not to restrict myself to a particular strand of narrative. Accordingly, I did not chalk out focus groups for my interviews and deliberately kept the questionnaire open-ended.[91] Apart from some fundamental questions related to the identity (name, age, religion, caste, gender, profession) of the person, the conversations were left to follow their own path, though roughly centring on certain larger issues which I had planned beforehand.[92] The aim was to provoke various kinds of outcomes from the conversations and not restrict them to a set pattern of responses.

The experience of carrying out the actual field work was far more exciting and challenging than I had imagined it would be. Getting access to the border areas, interacting with the local people (sometimes as individuals, sometimes in a group), interacting with the border guards, staying in the residences of the local civilians or in a tourist lodge in the border area, moving from one area to another in the private vehicles of the local people (mostly motorbikes and sometimes bicycles) and sometimes in hired cars as well: none of these activities turned out to be trouble-free, and understandably so. To travel around the border areas alone and as a woman, to be ferried around the place on a bike/bicycle driven by a man,[93] having to answer the border guards every now and then about my identity and purpose of visit,[94] being prevented from visiting certain areas of the border by them on the grounds of 'security issues', and getting them to speak to me were some of the recurrent troubles throughout the visits. To add to that was the expanse of area that I had planned to cover on both sides of this border within a limited period of six months.

Carrying out fieldwork in sensitised areas such as the borders, especially international ones, posed several challenges in not just interacting with the local civilians or the border guards, but also on deciding the ways of data collection, since organised settings for carrying out interviews were often not available.[95] Recording every response or using recorders was often not possible or even welcomed. This made the process of data collection and data storage difficult. Field diaries played important roles in filling these gaps. Besides being used for noting down the details of the places and circumstances of the interviews, they were often used for jotting down entire interviews as well.

Briefly put, the fieldwork enriched me not simply as a researcher but, more importantly, as a person, as it helped me know myself better. I learnt my own capacities, drawbacks, stamina and, often, the lack of it, during the process. I returned with a huge amount of field data and a larger amount of questions than what I had set out with.

The open-ended interactions brought out certain responses which I had least expected, which provided new dimensions to my study. In the course of the field work, the responses which I gathered fell into thematic clusters reaffirming not just the resilience of analytical categories in contemporary sociological discourses, but also the fact that these themes reflected the border narratives in their most spontaneous forms. Conversations around those themes seemed to have emerged, almost automatically, in every interaction. Likewise, the process of categorising

16 *Introduction*

my data into themes or chapters became easy, with some of the recurrent issues forming chapters in themselves – themes which, I felt, had not found resonance in earlier work on the West Bengal-Bangladesh border.[96]

I noticed a pattern in the responses of my interviewees that was characterised by the overwhelming presence of the reality of the border in their lives. Many of the issues which formed parts of the interviews were no more unique to the border than to any other non-border area, either in Bangladesh or in India. However, what was noticeable was the recurrence of the border, both as a spatial and a socio-cultural unit, in the responses regarding such issues. Worth noticing was also the fact that some of the concerns common to any other place in India and Bangladesh changed its nature and form when experienced or perceived in the light of the border. The responses also suggested (a hint of which I had borne with me right from my first interaction with the border people) that the people living along the border have their own ways of perceiving and interpreting its reality. The (re)interpretations are neither necessarily engineered by the state, nor are they necessarily signs of victimhood of the people. This is not to suggest that victimisation is absent along the border, but is meant to draw attention to the complex relation between the state and the border people which might not always be addressed through the straightjacketed binaries of the perpetrator-state and victimised-civilians.

Such perceptions create a common platform of identity formation for the people who negotiate their existence as border people – including the civilians as well as the border guards. The responses of the border guards and their spontaneous answers to some of my random curiosities revealed the irony of their situation – uncomfortably wedged between their duties as representatives of the state at the borders and their everyday negotiations with the reality of border life. In the process of living along the border over a period of time (ranging from six months to a few years depending on the terms of their posting), the border guards undergo similar hazards as the civilians do, albeit in different versions. But the reality of surviving the border is a hard reality for both. *Border life*, thus, makes the border guards more a *border people*, often overshadowing their roles as representatives and spokespersons of the states concerned. It is the overarching presence of the spatial uniqueness of the border and the everyday negotiations of the civilians and the border guards which form the fundamental content of what I choose to call *border narratives*.

Border narratives contribute towards the understanding of the negotiations between the border people and border laws and regulations. Many aspects of the West Bengal-Bangladesh border, including the undercurrents of violence and cross-border smuggling practices, have been consequences of the very laws designed to contain and control it. Having been affected by the Partition and the consequent creation of the border, the people who eventually became the border people have devised ways of negotiating the laws and regulations which were devised to control them – through violation, re-interpretation and reproduction.

While the basic idea and knowledge about the West Bengal-Bangladesh border was premised on the existing secondary materials (census reports, survey reports,

Introduction 17

newspaper reports) and literature, my understanding of this border as a socio-spatial process required me to look at the border lives myself as an active observer and as a direct communicator with the border people. Analysis of the interviews cleared my thoughts with regards to the re-interpretation and reproduction of the border space by the people who negotiate it every day. It also highlighted the pattern of psyche, i.e. a particular mind-set or mental make-up, in the people that expressed itself spontaneously but persistently, nevertheless, in their responses. Newspaper reports were used in support for some of my arguments as well as in highlighting the recurrence of some of the border-related issues in the narratives. In the process of understanding the responses, some of my pre-conceived ideas about the West Bengal-Bangladesh border changed considerably. The more difficult parts of analysing the data were:

- Narrowing down the relevant data, i.e. deciding the importance of one set of data over another, largely because of the overwhelming amount of data collected.
- Interpreting and analysing contradictions in the responses of the interviewees in support of my argument.

Methods of tackling such difficulties were, interestingly, found in the data themselves. I could recognise that there was an internal logic to the narratives. This logic bound the smaller socio-cultural narratives into a larger spatial narrative, though some of the responses in the narratives seemed contradictory on the surface. From here, the field data started shaping up into a thesis.

Theoretical discourses dealing with spatiality and subalternity in the context of the omnipresence of the state machinery vis-à-vis the marginal people (geographical marginality as seen from the state's perspective) seemed to form the basic tools of analysis. While ideas pertaining to spatial reproduction have been used to understand how the border space becomes the platform for convergence and conflict of a state and its subjects,[97] the idea of 'everyday forms of resistance' has helped me realise the importance of everyday experiences in understanding larger structures of state formation, identity creation and the point at which the two cross paths. Works by scholars of subaltern studies[98] provided the necessary understanding of subalternity in the context of Indian social, political, economic and cultural discourses. The idea of subalternity has been used here more as a form or set of practices by which people find alternative ways to access resources and gain agency to establish identities. It has been used to define the practices which the border people – the civilians and the border guards alike – have devised to not just survive their marginality but, often, to gain from it. The idea of a *thirdspace*[99] has been, specifically, helpful to that end. The idea has been evoked here to look beyond the use of the borderland as simply the space for the exercise of the state's unquestioned sovereignty or as the space for the complete subjugation of the subjects, and to look at the border as a space where the two meet, collide, communicate. The concept of the *thirdspace* gives shape to the ideological conflict between the border as a line of containment for a people and a line of convergence of two.

18   *Introduction*

Focus of the argument

Everyday forms of negotiation which the border people produce over the years crystallise into a pattern of consciousness characterised by a common psyche among the people which is not necessarily consciously designed. The consciousness is spatially-driven, i.e. affected by the specific socio-cultural features of the borderland and the kind of life it exposes its inhabitants to. The social, political or economic narratives which constitute borderland narratives are not necessarily unique to the borderland in terms of their structural form. What they are unique in is the spatial specificity that they obtain in the borderland areas as well as giving a sensitivity to the event in terms of its occurrence across an international border.

The term 'border consciousness' has been adapted from Gloria Anzaldua's concept of 'Mestiza consciousness', which she describes as a specific form of consciousness resulting from hybrid ethnicities of people born out of mixed parentage between the US and Mexico.[100] While people belonging to such hybrid ethnicities can mostly be found along the US-Mexico border, she uses the Mestiza or border consciousness as more of a social consciousness – born out of social marginalisation that these people of hybrid ethnicities (and also alternate sexualities) face. I have used the concept of border consciousness as more of a spatial consciousness in analysing how the specificity and the reality of surviving the border bind all those who live along it.

Spatial consciousness in the context of the border differs from spatial consciousness witnessed elsewhere; for example, in spaces where a specific social/ethnic/religious/gendered community comes together. In such instances, it is the coming together of the community in a ghetto that eventually produces the spatial consciousness. But in the case of borderlands, as exemplified by the West Bengal-Bangladesh border, it is the specificity of the space itself that produces the consciousness across socio-culturally diverse people. Examples of such spatial consciousness, whereby a specific form of spatial zone forms a common platform for such a diverse people, are rare.

Since this study is primarily based on empirical study, the methodological challenge lay in justifying such claims, purely through the process of analysis of the field data. The recurrence of the spatial disposition of the borderland in the responses of my interviewees, including the border guards, helped me give shape to my understanding of the border consciousness. In fact, the varied nature of my interviewees, in terms of their socio-political, economic and professional locations, helped me realise that the borderland engulfs all those living along and across it, into forming a border culture – a border milieu. Some of the more recent works on the Bengal border and South Asian borders, at large,[101] as well as some of the contemporary debates on state sovereignty and globalisation, helped me give shape to my ideas.

Debates on globalisation have emphasised the imminent possibilities of a borderless world,[102] especially in the context of economic interaction between states and the increasing flexibility of border rules in some parts of the globe. These literatures have focused on the need for states and business corporations to adapt to globalisation and the borderless world.[103] Yet studies by some scholars of border studies have, in fact, emphasised the significance of borders amidst such debates on borderlessness.[104] While it is a fact that the blurring of boundaries has, indeed, been a significant feature of economic interaction around the world from the mid-twentieth century, it is also worth keeping in mind that such economic interaction has found more relevance in certain parts of the world like Western Europe, where inter-state borders increasingly became irrelevant with the free movement of the inhabitants of the European Union.[105] While the borders of the EU became much more interdependent and integrated, those of others like India and Pakistan (also Israel and Palestine) hardened and became increasingly alienated.[106] Moreover, the increasing stringency of immigration regulations highlights a contradictory trend – that of making the borders of states non-flexible like never before. Movement of people across a border has been far more problematic than the movement of wealth around the globe.

Some of the recent works on the West Bengal-Bangladesh border have studied the distortive nature of the border narratives of the border people in the context of the various cross-border practices that they practice. According to Reece Jones (2012), these border practices challenge the state sovereignty by refusing the existence of either India or Bangladesh along the border and where the presence of either India or Bangladesh is disregarded by the border people.[107] My understanding of the border narratives of the West Bengal-Bangladesh border digresses from Jones' understanding, in terms of the perception of the border residents about the bordered spaces. My field study suggests that these border narratives do indeed challenge the sovereignty of the states concerned, i.e. India and Bangladesh, at their boundaries. But the nature of the contest is not through the blurring of the border through cross-border practices but, in fact, by making it more visible and real. The border, thus, becomes a space where both states meet, i.e. a space of *both* India and Bangladesh, contrary to the 'neither India nor Bangladesh' discourse suggested by Jones.[108] Moreover, Jones' idea of borderlands as spaces of 'refusal' indicates a conscious decision on the part of the border people to refuse and in the process, challenge the state. My study suggests that the everyday forms of re-interpretation and reproduction of the border space are not an organised or planned narrative of refusal of the state as suggested by Jones, but rather rudimentary narratives of survival well within the hegemonic structure and model of the state machinery, reflective of Scott's 'everyday forms of resistance'.[109] The convergence of states at its border, lived through its people and their livelihoods, is a bigger ideological deterrent to the role of the 'state as a container'.[110] The dominant presence of the states as the all-encompassing sovereign power at its border is highlighted in the official journals of BSF, where 'suggestions to improve border domination' are integral to their vision.[111] Re-interpretation and appropriation of the borderland by its inhabitants comes as a threat to the territorial imperative of the concerned states, questioning the basic premise of Partition and territorial redistribution. Moreover, continued existence of cross-border practices, as is characteristic of the West Bengal-Bangladesh border, question the control regime of the state. Such 'horizontally articulated rhizomatic linkages among states' put the vertically scaled 'hierarchical conceptions of political spaces' to test.[112]

20 *Introduction*

Globalisation and capital flows perform a similar function of blurring borders and questioning the role of the 'state as the container'. But the official movement of people across states with valid documents, the flow of capital through investments, and the everyday movements of people and goods across the border mostly through illegal means, must not be confused.[113] While there has been an increasing flexibility of borders in some parts of the world and a growth of global money through computer and telecommunication technologies,[114] which hint at an apparent blurring of borders, the reality hints at a re-interpretation and reproduction of the border (rather than blurring or even refusal), making it all the more visible and significant in the backdrop of debates regarding a borderless world. Gearoid O Tuathail (1999) rightly observes: 'The development of borderless worlds does not contradict but actually hastens the simultaneous development of ever more bordered worlds'.[115] Border narratives provide discerning ways of analysing cross-border practices which are neither universal nor planetary, despite constituting long-distance networks across borders.[116] They also provide hints to questions as to who the benefiters and promoters of borderlessness are. They reveal that the people who survive along the border and depend on it for their livelihoods rarely, if at all, are champions of borderlessness.[117]

Responses gathered from interviews revealed that border lives do not necessarily fit into the paradigm of 'a space of expropriation, peripheral subjectivity and a platform for claiming inclusion'.[118] They are also a space for redefining notions of citizenship, legality, licit/illicitness, to suit the needs of the ones who inhabit the space, including the border guards. An interesting observation was that the role of the border guards is often plagued by deceptiveness. While it seems that as representatives of the state, they administer and control the border space, 'in practice, however, they substitute another space for it, one that is first economic and social, and then political. They believe they are obeying something in their heads – a representation (of the country, etc.). In fact, they are establishing an order – their own'.[119] And it is through this *re-ordering* of the border that the border guards re-interpret the border differently from the order of the state.

Chapter 1 will look at some of the aspects of livelihood practices along the India-Bangladesh border – practices which are directly or indirectly dependent on the border. Some of them are traditional practices (i.e. existing from pre-border days), which have been affected by the creation of the border in 1947. Others are border-induced. This chapter will establish how the spatial uniqueness of the borderland affects both traditional and non-traditional livelihood practices to form a larger spatial narrative, characterised by the overwhelming presence of the borderland milieu in the lives of the border people – both civilians and border guards. The discussion, in this chapter, on livelihood practices across the India-Bangladesh border will also feed into the larger framework of border consciousness, including discussions on community identities/links versus a state-imposed control mechanism.

Chapter 2 will look at certain geographical specificities, like enclaves, *Chars* (pocket-lands), *Ghoj* (protruding lands) and other disputed territories along the India-Bangladesh border in the light of their strategic significance of being located

Introduction 21

across an international border and how their geographical uniqueness affects both the lives of the people and security concerns of the states. Discussion on the recently-exchanged enclaves between India and Bangladesh will form the main thrust of the chapter, including the historical background leading to the formation of these enclaves, followed by a discussion on the six decades of negligence and destitution which the enclave-inhabitants faced, the movement for their exchange that its inhabitants have tirelessly carried on, the significance and politics behind the recent exchange and finally what this exchange holds for its inhabitants in the future. Discussions in this chapter will form the second strand of narrative in the larger framework of spatial consciousness to be established in the conclusion, especially in the context of narratives and counter-narratives of citizenship status revolving around these enclave dwellers.

Chapter 3 will look at how spatial marginality affects the socio-cultural identities of the 'border people', like caste, religion, language, ethnicity. It will take up 'caste' as the main parameter of cultural identity to be discussed in this chapter, though language, religion, ethnicity will be no less important. This chapter will be important in establishing my basic argument that the centrifugal pull of the socio-cultural identities questions the states' attempt at homogenising the border and establishing an organised control-mechanism across their borders. Discussions on 'community links' vis-à-vis 'spatial consciousness' will be integral to this chapter.

Chapter 4 will look at various forms of interaction between the civilian border people and the border guards along the India-Bangladesh border through gender discourses. The interaction between the male, female and other gendered categories of civilians, and the largely male border guards, throws light on certain gendered aspects, which are both physical and social in nature. These gendered narratives are doubly affected for simultaneously being part of border narratives. At one level, it will highlight the need to see the gendered nature of every other socio-cultural, political or economic narrative in the context of border studies by highlighting how gender issues have cropped up in the preceding chapters as 'parts' of other socio-political issues, justifying in the process the need to have a separate chapter on gendered practices across the India-Bangladesh border. At another level, it will contribute towards the larger discussion on socio-cultural identities vis-à-vis state-induced universalistic homogenising identities as seen across this border.

Flexible approach

The spontaneous narratives of lived experiences of the border people, and flexible approaches to methodological and theoretical questions, have helped me understand the complex nature of border life at the West Bengal-Bangladesh border. They helped me reveal the multi-dimensional narratives which are produced by the border people – narratives which accommodate religious, social, political and economic factors and yet cut across all these strands to create a psyche that has its foundation in the unique spatiality of the borderland. An interdisciplinary approach towards analysis of the narratives, bringing together discourses on state

22 *Introduction*

theories, space, geography and subaltern studies, has helped me in explicating the complex yet interesting web of relations laid out along this border. That the fruitfulness of research lies not in 'proving the correctness of a hypothesis'[120] but in 'finding out something'[121] has been amply qualified by my own research trajectory.

As Maria Tamboukou explains, narratives constitute realities and shape the social, rather than being determined by it.[122] Border narratives, as revealed in the following chapters, do indeed shape other social narratives into a spatial narrative to produce a psyche that binds the narrators together.

Notes

1 Following are some of the more important non-fictional and fictional works on the Partition of India, and specifically Bengal: *Non-Fiction* – Samaddar, R. (Ed.). (1997) *Reflections on Partition in the East*. New Delhi: Vikas Publishing House; Butalia, U. (1998) *The Other Side of Silence: Voices from the Partition of India*. New Delhi, London: Penguin; Kaul, S. (Ed.). (2001) *The Partitions of Memory: The Afterlife of the Divisions of India*. New Delhi: Permanent Black; Chatterji, J. (1994) *Bengal Divided: Hindu Communalism and Partition, 1932–1947*. Cambridge: Cambridge University Press; Menon, R. and Bhasin, K. (1998) *Borders and Boundaries: Women in India's Partition*. New Delhi: Kali for Women; Chatterji, J. (February 1999) The Fashioning of a Frontier: The Radcliffe Line and Bengal's Border Landscape, 1947–52. *Modern Asian Studies*. 33(1). pp. 185–242; Talbot, I. and Singh, G. (Eds.). (1999) *Region and Partition: Bengal, Punjab and the Partition of the Subcontinent*. Karachi: Oxford University Press; Fraser, B. (2006) *Bengal Partition Stories: An Unclosed Chapter* (trs. Sheila Sen Gupta). London: Anthem; Pandey, G. (2001) *Remembering Partition: Violence, Nationalism and History in India*. Cambridge: Cambridge University Press; Ahmed, I. (Ed.). (2002) *Memories of a Genocidal Partition: The Haunting Tales of Victims, Witnesses and Perpetrators*. Colombo: Regional Centre for Strategic Studies; Chatterji, J. (2007) *The Spoils of Partition: Bengal and India, 1947–1967*. Cambridge: Cambridge University Press; Sengupta, D. (2016) *The Partition of Bengal: Fragile Borders and New Identities*. New Delhi: Cambridge University Press; *Fiction* – Zaman, N. (1999) *A Divided Legacy: The Partition in Selected Novels of India, Pakistan, and Bangladesh*. Dhaka: The University Press Limited; Bandyopadhyay, A. (1971) *Nilkantha Pakhir Khonje*. Calcutta: Karuna Prakashan; Ganguli, S. (1988) *Purba Pashchim*. Calcutta: Ananda Publishers; Sengupta, M. (2003) *Bishadbriksha*. Kolkata: Subarnarekha; Sikdar, S. (2008) *Dayamayeer Katha*. Kolkata: Gangchil.
2 Chatterji, 1999, p. 186.
3 Ibid.
4 Ibid. pp. 188–189.
5 Ibid. p. 189.
6 Ibid.
7 Ibid.
8 Ibid. p. 190; Jinnah's two-nation theory, in fact, was not a territorial concept but a demand for parity between Hindu and Muslim representation in the soon-to-be-formed government of independent India. Jalal, A. (1985) *The Sole Spokesman: Jinnah, the Muslim League and the Demand for Pakistan*. Cambridge: Cambridge University Press.
9 Chatterji, 1999, pp. 191–193.
10 Ibid. p. 196.
11 Ibid. p. 197.
12 Ibid.

Introduction 23

13 The Noakhali Riot was a communal riot that broke out in the Noakhali district of the Chittagong division of the eastern part of Bengal in October 1946 following the decision to partition Bengal on religious grounds. The then undivided district of Noakhali, with 80.57% Muslims and 19.31% Hindus, became the hotbed for a communal breakout, where Hindu lives and properties came under attack from the Muslims, and included forceful conversions of Hindus to Islam. Mohandas K. Gandhi camped in Noakhali and toured the district for four months in an effort to restore peace, though with little positive outcome. A majority of the survivors of the riot migrated to West Bengal, Tripura and Assam.
14 Chatterji, 1999, p. 212.
15 Ibid.
16 Ibid.
17 Ibid. pp. 199–202.
18 Roy, H. (2012) *Partitioned Lives: Migrants, Refugees, Citizens in India and Pakistan, 1947–1965*. New Delhi: Oxford University Press. p. 43.
19 Ibid. p. 40.
20 Ibid.
21 Ibid.
22 Ibid. p. 41.
23 Chatterji, 1999, pp. 215–216.
24 Roy, 2012, p. 46.
25 Ibid. pp. 46, 48.
26 Chatterji, 1999, pp. 217–219.
27 *Char* is the Bengali term used for a strip of land which appears on the riverbed when the river deposits silt or changes course. The *Chars* along the riverine borders gain strategic importance due to their location on the border and, hence, become reasons for dispute between the states on both sides of the border who claim control over the *Char*. *Chars* became a perennial source of dispute between India and Pakistan, given the formation of new *Chars* every year due to the changing course and flooding of the rivers. The idea of treating the *Chars* as 'no-man's land' did not work out well for either of the states, given that these often housed entire villages who had lost lands to river erosion and had, thus, re-settled on the *Chars* when they happened to appear mid-river. Many such *Chars* had actually to pay the price for being located along the borderline, when its people had to prove their allegiance to either India or Pakistan as the situation demanded. A lot of the *Char* residents lost their lives to cross-border firing between the border guards and the police.
28 Chatterji, 1999, pp. 220–222.
29 Ibid. p. 226.
30 The *Tebhaga* movement was a militant campaign of the peasants (mainly tenants or sharecroppers) led by the Kishan Sabha (peasant front of the Communist Party of India) in Bengal in 1946, where the peasants demanded that only one-third (*Tebhaga*) of the harvest be given to the landlord as his share instead of the existing rule of giving half the produce. In many areas, the movement became violent, forcing the *zamindars* to flee their villages. For detailed knowledge of *Tebhaga*, see Chattopadhyay, K. (1986) *Tebhaga Andolaner Itihas*. Kolkata: Progressive Publishers.
31 *Jotedars* were the tenants of the revenue-collecting *zamindars* and *taluqdars* in Bengal, who owned sizeable portions of village lands and cultivated their broad acres with the help of sharecroppers, tenants-at-will and hired labourers. Ray, R.K. and Ray, R. (1975) Zamindars and Jotedars: A Study of Rural Politics in Bengal. *Modern Asian Studies*. 9(1). p. 82.
32 Chatterji, 1999, p. 226.
33 Ibid. p. 230.
34 Roy, 2012, p. 62.
35 Ibid. p. 62.

24 *Introduction*

36 Ibid. pp. 62–63.
37 Chatterji, 1999, pp. 232–233.
38 Ibid. p. 232.
39 Ibid. p. 233.
40 Martinez, O. (1994) *Border People: Life and Society in the U.S.-Mexico Borderlands.* Tucson: University of Arizona Press. pp. 5–10. Besides the model of interdependent borderlands, the other three models of borderlands suggested by Martinez are alienated borderlands: where animosity between the two sides of the border prevents any kind of cross-border interchange; coexistent borderlands: where despite unfriendly relations, a minimum cross-border exchange exists; and integrated borderlands: where all barriers to movement of economic and human resources have been abolished.
41 Chatterji, 1999, p. 241.
42 Roy, 2012, p. 10.
43 Ibid. p. 11.
44 Jamwal, N.S. (January–March 2004) Border Management: Dilemma of Guarding the India-Bangladesh Border. *Strategic Analysis.* 28(1). p. 8.
45 Ibid.
46 Roy, A. (6 May 2012) Bangladesher arthamantri ke shangey niyei Dhakaye Pranab. *Ananda Bazar Patrika.* [Online] Available from: www.anandabazar.com/archive/1120506/6bdesh2.html. [Last accessed: 17 September 2013]; Staff Reporter. (9 May 2012) Tista o Chhitmahal chukti niye fer chap dilen Dipu. *Ananda Bazar Patrika.* [Online] Available from: www.anandabazar.com/9bdesh3.html. [Last accessed: 17 September 2013]; Staff Reporter. (10 May 2012) Farakkar gate bodol. *Ananda Bazar Patrika.* [Online] Available from: www.anandabazar.com/archive/1120510/10mur4.html. [Last accessed: 17 September 2013].
47 The population density of West Bengal is 1029 per sq. kms, according to the Census of 2011. The population densities for the border districts, according to their ranks in descending order, are as follows: North 24 Parganas-2463, Murshidabad-1334, Nadia-1316, Maldah-1071, North Dinajpur-956, Cooch Behar-833, South 24 Parganas-819, South Dinajpur-753, Jalpaiguri-621, Darjeeling-585. *Census of India 2011.* Ministry of Home Affairs, Government of India. According to the 2011 Census, the population density of Bangladesh is an average of 964, with the density in its border districts (with West Bengal) as follows: Kushtia-1207, Nilphamari-1162, Rajshahi-1069, Jessore-1068, Lalmonirhat-1006, Chapai Nawabganj-960, Chuadanga-954, Joypurhat-942, Meherpur-910, Jhenaidah-895, Kurigram-893, Dinajpur-864, Thakurgaon-762, Naogaon-750, Panchagarh-696, Satkhira-511. *Bangladesh Bureau of Statistics,* Ministry of Planning, Government of the People's Republic of Bangladesh.
48 *Beedi* is a thin, Indian cigarette filled with tobacco flake, and wrapped in a *tendu* leaf tied with a string at one end. It is widely popular in South Asia and parts of the Middle East – the cheap price being one of the major reasons for its popularity. *Beedi* consumption outpaces that of conventional cigarettes, though they are more harmful than the latter. Due to restrictions on factoryregulations, *beedi* production over the years became a cottage-industry with a home-based women's workforce predominantly employed in *beedi* rolling, while males continue to be employed in all aspects of *beedi* production.
49 Chatterji, 1999, p. 236.
50 Ibid. p. 238.
51 Jamwal, 2004, p. 9.
52 Staff Reporter. (30 October 2009) BSF-BDR guli binimoy. *Ananda Bazar Patrika.* [Online] Available from: www.anandabazar.com/archive/1091030/30south11.htm. [Last accessed: 17 September 2013].
53 Staff Reporter. (3 November 2009) Simantarakshi der flag meeting Raninagar e. *Ananda Bazar Patrika.* [Online] Available from: www.anandabazar.com/archive/1091103/3mur6.htm. [Last accessed: 17 September 2013].

Introduction   25

54 Bhasin, A.S. (Ed.). (2003) *India-Bangladesh Relations: Documents, 1971–2002*, Volume 5. New Delhi: Geetika Publishers. p. 2738.
55 Ibid. pp. 1902–1907.
56 Van Schendel, W. (2005) *The Bengal Borderland: Beyond State and Nation in South Asia*. London: Anthem. p. 213.
57 Jamwal, 2004, p. 30.
58 Ibid.; Agreed Minutes of the 4th Meeting of the Indo-Bangladesh Joint Working Group (JWG), Dhaka, October 20 1997. In Bhasin, A.S. (Ed.). (2003) *India-Bangladesh Relations: Documents, 1971–2002*, Volume 1. New Delhi: Geetika Publishers. p. 446.
59 Out of the total 3436.59 kilometres of sanctioned fencing in India (including West Bengal, Assam, Meghalaya, Tripura, Mizoram), 2760.12 kilometres had been completed by 2012.
60 Out of a total 4426.11 kilometres of border roads sanctioned in India (including West Bengal, Assam, Meghalaya, Tripura, Mizoram), 3605.20 kilometres had been constructed by 2012.
61 *Management of Indo-Bangladesh Border*. Available from: http://mha.nic.in/pdfs/BM_MAN-IN-BANG(E).pdf.
62 PTI. (25 June 2016). Indo-Bangla Border Fencing Work to Finish by 2017. *The Indian Express*. [Online] Available from: http://indianexpress.com/article/india/india-news-india/indo-bangla-border-fencing-work-to-finish-by-2017-2875548/. [Last accessed: 24 July 2017].
63 Van Schendel, W. and Baud, M. (1997) Toward a Comparative History of Borderlands. *Journal of World History*. 8(2). pp. 221–222.
64 Ibid.
65 The people who live at the border areas, i.e. those common people who are not the official border guards or who do not belong to the police/military force in any way, are generally called 'civilians'. This term has become part of the everyday vocabulary of both the civilians themselves as well as the border guards all along the West Bengal-Bangladesh border.
66 Bhasin, A.S. (Ed.). (2003) *India-Bangladesh Relations: Documents, 1971–2002*. New Delhi: Geetika Publishers.
67 Sobhan, F. (Ed.). (2005) *Dynamics of Bangladesh-India Relations: Dialogues of Young Journalists Across the Border*. Dhaka: The University Press Limited.
68 Purcell, G. (2006) *India-Bangladesh Bilateral Trade and Potential Free Trade Agreement*. Dhaka: World Bank Office.
69 For example, Jamwal, 2004, pp. 5–36.
70 For an idea on how the state (mis)reads border activities, see Samaddar, R. (1999) *The Marginal Nation: Transborder Migration from Bangladesh to West Bengal*. New Delhi: Sage.
71 Reports prepared by organisations such as *Odhikar* (www.odhikar.org) and Human Rights Watch (www.hrw.org) exemplify such literature.
72 Scott, J. (1985). *Weapons of the Weak: Everyday Forms of Peasant Resistance*. New Haven, London: Yale University Press.
73 Bangladesh shares its border with West Bengal, Assam, Meghalaya, Tripura and Mizoram in India.
74 A stretch of 2216.7 kilometres.
75 Prescott, J.R.V. (1968) *The Geography of State Policies*. London: Hutchinson & Co; Prescott, J.R.V. (1978) *Boundaries and Frontiers*. London: Croom Helm.
76 Donnan, H. and Wilson, T.M. (Eds.). (1994) *Border Approaches: Anthropological Perspectives on Frontiers*. Lanham, London: University Press of America; Donnan, H. and Wilson, T.M. (Eds.). (1998) *Border Identities: Nation and State at International Frontiers*. Cambridge, New York: Cambridge University Press; Donnan, H. and Wilson, T.M. (1999) *Borders: Frontiers of Identity, Nation and State*. Oxford: Berg; Martinez, O.J. (1994) *Border People: Life and Society in the US-Mexico Borderlands*. Tuscon: University of Arizona Press.

26 *Introduction*

77 Aggarwal, R. (2004) *Beyond Lines of Control: Performance and Politics on the Disputed Borders of Ladakh, India.* Durham: Duke University Press; Kumar Rajaram, P. and Grundy-Warr, C. (Eds.). (2007) *Borderscapes: Hidden Geographies and Politics at Territory's Edge.* Minneapolis: University of Minnesota Press; Eilenberg, M. (2010) Negotiating Autonomy at the Margins of the State: The Dynamics of Elite Politics in the Borderland of West Kalimantan, Indonesia. *South East Asia Research.* 17(2). pp. 201–227.

78 Samaddar, R. (1999) *The Marginal Nation: Transborder Migration from Bangladesh to West Bengal.* New Delhi: Sage; Van Schendel, W. (2005) *The Bengal Borderland: Beyond State and Nation in South Asia.* London: Anthem; Van Schendel, W. and Abraham, I. (Eds.). (2005) *Illicit Flows and Criminal Things: States, Borders, and the Other Side of Globalisation.* Bloomington: University of Indiana Press; Coleman, M. (2009) What Counts as the Politics and Practice of Security, and Where? Devolution and Immigrant Insecurity after 9/11. *Annals of the Association of American Geographers.* 99(5). pp. 904–913; Jones, R. (2009) Geopolitical Boundary Narratives, the Global War on Terror and Border Fencing in India. *Transactions of the Institute of British Geographers.* 34. pp. 290–304.

79 Asiwaju, A.I. (Ed.). (1985) *Partitioned Africans: Ethnic Relations across Africa's International Boundaries, 1884–1984.* London: C. Hurst & Co; Anzaldua, G. (1987) *Borderlands/La frontera: The New Mestiza.* San Francisco: Aunt Lute Books; Sahlins, P. (1998) State Formation and National Identity in the Catalan Borderlands during the Eighteenth and Nineteenth Centuries. In: Wilson, T.M. and Donnan, H. (Eds.). *Border Identities.* Cambridge: Cambridge University Press. pp. 31–61; Stokes, M. (1998) Imagining 'the South': Hybridity, Heterotopias and Arabesk on the Turkish-Syrian Border. In: Wilson, T.M. and Donnan, H. (Eds.). *Border Identities.* pp. 263–288. Cambridge: Cambridge University Press.

80 Van Schendel, W. and Abraham, I. (Eds.). (2005) *Illicit Flows and Criminal Things: States, Borders, and the Other Side of Globalisation.* Bloomington: University of Indiana Press; Banerjee, P. and Basu Ray Chaudhury, A. (Eds.). (2011) *Women in Indian Borderlands.* New Delhi: Sage.

81 National Archives, New Delhi, India; National Library, Kolkata, India; Bureau of Applied Economics and Statistics, Department of Planning, Government of West Bengal, India; Census of India Regional Office, Kolkata; Ramkrishna Mission Institute of Culture, Kolkata, India; West Bengal State Archives, Kolkata, India; Dhaka University Library, Bangladesh; National Archives, Dhaka, Bangladesh; National Library, Dhaka, Bangladesh.

82 Cooch Behar, Jalpaiguri, Darjeeling, North Dinajpur, South Dinajpur, Malda, Murshidabad, Nadia, North 24 Parganas, South 24 Parganas.

83 Kurigram, Lalmonirhat, Nilphamari, Panchagarh, Thakurgaon, Dinajpur, Jaypurhat, Naogaon, Nawabganj, Rajshahi, Kushtia, Meherpur, Chuadanga, Jhenaidah, Jessore, Satkhira.

84 Cooch Behar, North Dinajpur, South Dinajpur, Murshidabad, Nadia, North 24 Parganas.

85 Kurigram, Lalmonirhat, Panchgarh, Thakurgaon, Rajshahi, Kushtia, Nilphamari, Chuadanga, Jhenaidah, Jessore, Satkhira.

86 Enclaves are pockets of land surrounded completely by territories of the neighbouring state. The West Bengal-Bangladesh border enclaves are examples of a unique territorial configuration, not to be found anywhere else in the world (discussed in Chapter 2).

87 Discussed in Chapter 1.

88 Andrews, M., Squire, C. and Tamboukou, M. (2009) *Doing Narrative Research.* London: Sage. p. 5.

89 Ibid. pp. 5–6.

90 Squire, C. (2009) From Experience-Centred to Socioculturally-Oriented Approaches to Narrative. In Andrews, Squire and Tamboukou, 2009, p. 48.

Introduction 27

91 The total number of interviews conducted during the first phase of my field work in 2011–12 was 137. For details of the interviewees, see Appendix 2. The names of my interviewees have been anonymised (unless specified otherwise) to protect their identities; later in 2016, 20 interviews were conducted in Jalpaiguri and Cooch Behar.

92 For the structure of the questionnaire, see Appendix 1.

93 This was often a cause of considerable embarrassment for the man doing it, given that I was not of his family relation.

94 The border guards often did not seem to be satisfied by my answers and continued being suspicious of my purpose.

95 Situations were often not conducive for a formal set-up of the interviews or going through the formalities of Consent Forms, Participant Information Sheets, etc. Many of the interviews were impromptu and quick. Some of the informal conversations turned into interviews eventually, with no prior preparation.

96 Aspects related to some of the themes such as gender, caste and livelihood practices (besides illegal cross-border practices) along the West Bengal-Bangladesh border have not been studied by Willem van Schendel, Ranabir Samaddar or Paula Banerjee – researchers who have worked extensively in this area.

97 Lefebvre, H. (1991) *The Production of Space* (trs. Donald Nicholson-Smith). Oxford: Basil Blackwell; Soja, E. (1989). *Postmodern Geographies: The Reassertion of Space in Critical Social Theory*. London, New York: Verso; Soja, E. (1996) *Thirdspace*. Cambridge, MA: Blackwell.

98 Guha, R. (1988) *Selected Subaltern Studies*. Oxford: Oxford University Press; Guha, R. (1997) *A Subaltern Studies Reader, 1986–1995*. Minneapolis: University of Minnesota Press; Amin, S. and Chakraborty, D. (1996) *Subaltern Studies IX: Writings on South Asian History and Society*. New Delhi: Oxford University Press; Chatterjee, P. (2004) *The Politics of the Governed: Reflections on Popular Politics in Most of the World*. New York, Chichester, West Sussex: Columbia University Press; Chakravorty, S., Milevska, S. and Barlow, T.E. (2006) *Conversations with Gayatri Chakraborty Spivak*. London: Seagull Books.

99 Soja, 1989, 1996.

100 Anzaldua, 1987; For further understanding of Anzaldua's concept of Mestiza consciousness, see Feghali, Z. (2011) Re-Articulating the New Mestiza. *Journal of International Women's Studies*. Special Issue. 12(2). pp. 61–74; Aigner-Varoz, E. (Summer 2000) Metaphors of a Mestiza Consciousness: Anzaldua's Borderlands/La Frontera. *Melus*. 25(2). pp. 47–62.

101 Kalir, B. and Sur, M. (Eds.). (2013). *Transnational Flows and Permissive Polities: Ethnographies of Human Mobilities in Asia*. Amsterdam: Amsterdam University Press; Roy, H. (2012). *Partitioned Lives: Migrants, Refugees, Citizens in India and Pakistan, 1947–1965*. New Delhi: Oxford University Press; Misra, S. (2011). *Becoming a Borderland: The Politics of Space and Identity in Colonial Northeastern India*. New Delhi: Routledge; More recent ones which helped me with insightful understanding of the Bengal/South Asian borders are Gellner, D. (2014). *Borderland Lives in Northern South Asia*. New Delhi: Orient Blackswan; Cons, J. (2016). *Sensitive Space: Fragmented Territory at the India-Bangladesh Border*. Seattle and London: University of Washington Press.

102 Ohmae, K. (1990) *The Borderless World*. New York: Harper Collins; Shapiro, M. and Alker, H. (Eds.). (1996) *Challenging Boundaries: Global Flows, Territorial Identities*. Minneapolis: University of Minnesota Press.

103 Ohmae, 1990; Ohmae, K. (1995) *The End of the Nation State*. New York: Free Press.

104 Newman, D. (2002) Boundaries. In Agnew J., Mitchell, K. and Toal, G. (Eds.). *A Companion to Political Geography*. Oxford: Blackwell. pp. 123–137; Newman, D. (2006) The Lines that Continue to Separate Us: Borders in a Borderless World. *Progress in Human Geography*. 30(2). pp. 1–19; Newman, D. and Paasi, A. (1998) Fences and Neighbours in

28 *Introduction*

the Post-Modern World: Boundary Narratives in Political Geography. *Progress in Human Geography*. 22(2). pp. 186–207; Paasi, A. (1996) *Territories, Boundaries and Consciousness*. New York: John Wiley & Sons Ltd; Paasi, A. (1998) Boundaries as Social Processes: Territoriality in the World of Flows. *Geopolitics*. 3(1). pp. 69–88; Paasi, A. (2005) The Changing Discourses on Political Boundaries: Mapping the Backgrounds, Contents and Contexts. In Van Houtum, H., Kramsch, O. and Zierhoffer, W. (Eds.). *B/ordering Space*. Aldershot: Ashgate. pp. 17–32; Yeung, H. (1998) Capital, State and Space: Contesting the Borderless World. *Transactions of the Institute of British Geographers*. 23(3). pp. 291–310.

105 Newman, 2006, pp. 171–186.

106 Van Schendel, 2005, p. 372.

107 Jones, R. (2012) Spaces of Refusal: Rethinking Sovereign Power and Resistance at the Border. *Annals of the Association of American Geographers*. 102(3). pp. 685–699.

108 Ibid.

109 Scott, J. (1986). Everyday Forms of Peasant Resistance. In: Scott, J. and Tria Kerkvliet, B.J. (Eds.). *Everyday Forms of Peasant Resistance in South-East Asia*. Library of Peasant Studies, No. 9. London: Frank Cass & Co.

110 Taylor, P.F. (2003) The State as Container: Territoriality in the Modern World-System. In Brenner, N., Jessop, B., Jones, M. and Macleod, G. (Eds.). *State/Space: A Reader*. Malden, Oxford: Blackwell. p. 101; Walker, R.B.J. (1993) *Inside/Outside: International Relations as Political Theory*. Cambridge: Cambridge University Press.

111 *Uttar Vang Prahari Samachar Patrika*. (March 2012). 4(11).

112 Brenner, N., Jessop, B., Jones, M. and Macleod, G. (2003) Introduction. In Brenner, Jessop, Jones and Macleod, 2003, pp. 14–15.

113 Glassman, J. (August 1999) State Power Beyond the 'Territorial Trap': The Internationalisation of the State. *Political Geography*. 18(6). pp. 669–696.

114 Taylor, 2003, pp. 109–110.

115 Tuathail, G.O. (1999) Borderless Worlds? Problematising Discourses of Deterritorialisation. *Geopolitics*. 4(2). p. 143.

116 Cooper, F. (2001) What Is the Concept of Globalisation Good For? An African Historian's Perspective. *African Affairs*. 100. p. 189.

117 My field interviews also hint at similar responses from the border inhabitants. On being asked about their views on a borderless world/borderless Bengal, none of them thought doing away with the border was a positive idea, because their lives had become completely dependent on the existence of the border – directly or indirectly.

118 Cons, J. (2012) Narrating Boundaries: Framing and Contesting Suffering, Community, and Belonging in Enclaves Along the India-Bangladesh Border. *Political Geography*. Elsevier. pp. 1–10. [Online] Available from: http://dx.doi.org/10.1016/j.polgeo.2012.06.004. [Accessed: 14 June 2013].

119 Lefebvre, H. (2003) Space and the State. In Brenner, Jessop, Jones and Macleod, 2003, p. 87.

120 Clark, R.S. (1977) *Fundamentals of Criminal Justice Research*. New York: Lexington Books. p. 34.

121 Ibid.

122 Andrews, Squire and Tamboukou, 2009, p. 15.

2 Livelihood practices

Legal, illegal and the grey-zone in between

Introduction

In this chapter, I wish to look at the diverse forms of livelihood practices seen across the West Bengal-Bangladesh border. In doing so, I wish to use 'common sense' as a discursive concept – both from the point of view of the border-control mechanisms of the state and the ways in which the border people negotiate such control regimes. Democratic common sense,[1] as the 'superiority of the many to the few', has often been recognised by scholars as a platform on which 'communal political life' or 'real democracy' thrives. Common sense has widely been believed to be 'certain basic, largely unquestioned notions (that) were common to common people simply because of their common natures and experiences. That included observation of the world around them and communication with one another'.[2] Many of the livelihood practices which we see across the said border conform to this idea of common sense having stemmed from 'common experiences' of having to survive the border every day. On the other hand, common sense, as 'democracy's popular face' might work in opposition to its constitutional face – a 'perennial threat' vis-à-vis the state.[3] The borders are, perhaps, the best place to see how this happens, where the popular forms of common sense are often in conflict with the state machinery. In such cases, common sense, used as a structural or constitutive censorship, is made instrumental by the state to dominate and 'keep in line' its people to exclude outlying voices as deviants. In such cases, common sense perceptions of statehood propounded by the states threaten the citizenship statuses of its people and render some of their everyday practices as illicit – driven by criminal tendencies. I hope to delve into such diverse ideas of common sense in the following part through a discussion of the livelihood practices across the West Bengal-Bangladesh border.

The Bengal border has been unique in more than one way right from its inception, in the haphazard ways by which it was conceived and drawn, followed by its physical execution along the length of more than 2000 kilometres – running amidst courtyards, cutting across agricultural fields, disrupting communication links and community networks at large. Compared to the immediate confusion and violence that the formation of the border resulted in, the long-term consequences it had on

30 *Livelihood practices*

the lives and livelihoods of the people who settled along and across the border seem to be more impactful. While considering themselves as 'border people', the border dwellers have, in fact, made the border the 'centre' of their existence and often, the main source of their livelihoods – legally and/or illegally. Talking to these people, wanting to understand their ways of negotiation has been my job and passion for the last few years. The kind of responses which have emerged from these interactions have been intriguing, to say the least, and often at odds with my understandings and conclusions. It has, often, been a challenge for me to accommodate these responses within a clear analytical framework, or even categorise their everyday practices as everyday livelihoods, responses to situations or simply criminal acts.

The basis for the creation of the West Bengal-East Pakistan (later Bangladesh) border was faulty from its inception, as has been mentioned earlier – hastily drawn to make it run across homes, hearths, lands – cutting people off from their families and livelihoods, towns from hinterlands. Traditional kin and associate links and economic ties were disrupted, and illegalised, and traditional practices criminalised by the creation of the international border. The communication system was heavily jeopardised, and public institutions, like administrative headquarters, hospitals and courts, were cut off from the suburbs.

The initial policy of the Nehru government to keep the border porous posed yet another complication. This had stronger implications for those who settled near the border, as they tried to access and exercise their control over their property that was left behind on the other side. This implied that even after years of the Partition and the creation of the border, the cross-border movement of people and goods was a fact, and an officially recognised one at that. Yet such government policies failed to have the desired effect of a peaceful border obtained through porosity because the border police in charge of controlling the border interpreted the meaning of the border in their own terms. They violated the official policies of porous borders and physically abused (and even killed) the border crossers. This was the root of an uncomfortable relation between the state, on the one hand, represented through the government policies, and the border police and the border civilians, on the other, that continues till date in modified versions all along the West Bengal-Bangladesh border.

By the time porosity threatened India and Bangladesh with security concerns and the states took steps to stop cross-border movements, the latter had become commonplace and integral to the lives of the border people on both sides. Stringent border rules failed to stop such well-networked movements; it simply tagged such movements illegal and tagged the people involved as trespassers and criminals.

So, from its very genesis, the West Bengal-Bangladesh border has been an interdependent borderland – characterised by symbiotic links between societies on both sides, resulting in a considerable flow of economic and human resources across it. The various narratives which evolve across this border give birth to a 'border community'.

Livelihood practices 31

It is in the light of certain aspects of the livelihood practices of the West Bengal-Bangladesh border that the life-cycle of the border will be understood – from being a porous one in its initial years to witnessing a materiality through barbed wires and border guards and an increasing shift towards zero-tolerance policies with regard to activities which the concerned states consider a 'nuisance'.

While the logic of statehood renders the state responsible to secure its borders as markers of its sovereignty and as a container of its subjects, the ideological and material manifestation of this logic gives rise to a complex relation between the state and its border people. In the process, the pattern of consciousness or common sense that the border people are seen to develop works itself out in two phases: firstly, and in the initial phase, in terms of negotiating with the fact that the definition of the 'local' has changed. What used to be local is now on the other side of the borderline, and next-door neighbours are now separated by an international border, it is no longer possible to move around freely, mobility will be controlled and gauged and citizenship status will, now, need to be proved every now and then. And secondly, in terms of gradually coming to terms with the fact that the border is here to stay, is a reality in their lives and that they will, now, have to redesign their lives and livelihood practices around the border. 'Making use of the border' is the culmination of this thought pattern.

A brief description of some of the evolving patterns of livelihood practices along this border will help in understanding how the border becomes a zone where common senses meet.

Agriculture

The predominant means of livelihood in India is agriculture, which provides for more than 70% of the population. The rural areas of India are dependent almost entirely on agriculture-related livelihoods.[4] Most of the post-1947 migrant peasant communities crossing the West Bengal-Bangladesh border settled along it and took up agriculture as an obvious occupation. While their traditional agricultural skill was one reason for the choice, the topography of extensive farmland along the border[5] was another reason. Most of the original inhabitants of the areas which became the border areas after partition were already pursuing agriculture-related livelihoods.[6] This implied that agriculture-related livelihoods became, and still are, the predominant means of livelihood along the West Bengal-Bangladesh border.

The predominance of these livelihoods is characteristic of almost all the rural areas of India and Bangladesh.[7] Yet the nature of some of the aspects of these livelihood practices attains a unique feature in the context of their performance along the border. These features make agriculture-related livelihoods along the West Bengal-Bangladesh border different from their non-border version. The creation of the border caused complications for the farmers by separating most from their farmlands on the other side of the border and making border-crossing and negotiating with the border guards a part of their regular practice.[8]

32 *Livelihood practices*

Figure 2.1 Fencing along the South Dinajpur border, West Bengal, 2012.

Crisis of the 'fenced-out' lands

As mentioned in the Introduction, the regulations of the Ground Rules followed by India's decision to fence its borders left large parts of lands (both residential villages and cultivated land) outside the fence.[9] The issue of being fenced-out has, over the years, been the most persistent crisis for the people living and earning a livelihood on the West Bengal side of the West Bengal-Bangladesh border.

The farmers require official attestation from local administrative heads and subsequent permission from the BSF of the fact that they live and/or cultivate their lands or work as agricultural labourers outside the fence. They receive cards of different colours (farmers get red cards, agricultural labourers get yellow) for the purpose.[10] The attestation needs to be provided by the *Panchayat*[11] head. Submitting the attested documents along with proof of his identity (mostly voter cards) to the BSF constables at the fence gates every morning constitutes the daily routine of a farmer.[12] The gates are opened for the farmers to access their lands at certain scheduled times of the day.[13] This implies that the farmers' access to fenced-out lands depends on the border regulations and whims of the BSF. 'Only if the documents are considered sufficiently valid by the BSF, will they let us pass through the gate. Otherwise they do not accept them, even if it is in order', says Rashid Hossein while complaining about how the farmers live and work according to the whims of the border guards.[14] The farmers are also required to attest to names of other possible male members of the family (son, brother or a male relative) who might need to attend work in the fenced-out lands in the absence of the farmer himself.[15] Women are, most often, not allowed to cross the fence at all, even if they need to take food to the male members working in the fenced-out land.[16]

Livelihood practices   33

There are restrictions on the cattle, tools and other agriculture-related products (seeds, fertilisers) which a farmer can carry to his land outside the fence. The type and number/amount of such items also require attestation from the *Panchayat* official and cannot be violated under any means. The BSFs often have the last word in matters of disputes regarding such regulations.[17] 'We have to work in the fields according to their (BSF's) whims. They are creating problems regarding our agricultural tools, fertilisers. They do not let us carry more than 5 kilograms of fertiliser and in these cases, permissions from *Panchayat* members do not help',[18]says Balaram Mahato, who cultivates lands outside the fence. The measures are meant for preventing smuggling across the border, explains a BSF official: 'The tendency to carry more than what is required outside the fence and illegally sell the extra amount to the Bangladeshis on the other side of the fence is rampant among the border population'.[19]

The process of submission of documents at the gate, followed by entrance to the lands, one at a time, delays the farmers' work schedule. This, specifically, becomes a serious concern in the summer months, since farmers have to work late in the afternoons in the scorching heat.[20] Moreover, once past the gate, the farmers cannot come back even if they need to and have to wait for the next opening slot. Incidents of farmers falling sick during work and not being able to access a doctor because they have been fenced out for that while, or even of farmers being hit by hailstorms at work and unable to run to a shelter because of being fenced out, are common.[21]

Negotiating the fence is as hazardous for agricultural labourers as it is for owners of farmlands outside the fence. The latter often employ agricultural labourers to cultivate their lands. The labourers are often not local residents of the border areas and, thus, not accustomed to border regulations. They are apprehensive about submitting their voter cards to the BSF for fear of them being misplaced.[22] Being dependent on the whims of the BSF affects the labourers as well, who are often seen to be engaged in other forms of livelihood practices to support their meagre earnings as agricultural labourers. However, the gate restrictions prohibit them from utilising their time. 'Even if the labourers finish their work, they have to wait in the field for hours till the gate reopens on the next scheduled time',[23] says Imtiaz, a farmer cultivating fenced-out land.

For those whose homesteads have been left outside the fence, living by and surviving the border has become a challenge in itself. The scheduled timings for the opening of the fence gates are in no way made flexible for them, implying that they also have to abide by the timings like the farmers. Access to schools, colleges, hospitals, relatives, friends and any other basic amenities depends on the opening of the gates at scheduled timings. Registering their names at the BSF checkposts near the gates is a daily routine for them as well. The villages outside the fence lack every civic amenity, which forces the inhabitants of the fenced-out lands to cross the gate for every little need.[24] Incidents of death, for not being able to cross the gate and access a doctor, are not rare.[25]

The anxiety of being fenced out rings loud in the responses of the people who negotiate the fence every day. 'There is a feeling of being imprisoned when we

34   *Livelihood practices*

are on that side of the fence, when we cannot enter the gates even if we want to. We want the gates to be left open all day so that we can move in and out freely',[26] says Animesh. Given the confinement of the people outside the fence for about 20 hours every day, such responses make perfect sense and are indications of how the process of double-bordering affected by the fence has affected the perceptions of the farmers, like inside-outside, free-imprisoned.

It is important to keep in mind that this ordeal of negotiating border fences by the farmers is to move within their own state and not across an international border. The construction of the fence has re-defined the spatial perception of what constitutes the border, acting, in a way, as a second border between two territorial locations – the 'inside' and the 'outside' of the fence. 'An Indian is devoid of the freedom to move around freely at the borders', is how Narendranath Ghosh expresses his anguish,[27] when explaining the irony of having to prove one's identity when moving around in one's own country in the border areas, let alone crossing the borders. Neil Brenner's idea of a 'scalar structuration'[28] helps us in understanding the re-interpretation of the scales of the border space by civilians as well as border guards, where the creation of the border followed by the construction of the fence has redefined the sense of inclusion-exclusion for the people who negotiate state apparatuses at the border everyday.[29]

The demand for shifting the fence and the BSF outposts to the 'zero point' rings loud in most of the responses. 'The BSF must be posted at the zero point … they must man the actual border',[30] says Samsuddin. The phrase 'actual border' indicates the perceptions of *double-bordering* that the fence has led to.

The theft of crops or attack on farmers by miscreants on the fenced-out lands is a common occurrence along the West Bengal-Bangladesh border.[31] Once the gates close for the day, the crops on these lands lie unattended and exposed to theft by miscreants from the Bangladesh side.[32] Despite the farmers being witness to such thefts, the BSF constables prohibit them from accessing their lands and stopping the theft. Complaints to the BSF officials regarding such occurrences rarely bear fruit,[33] as they cite reasons of jurisdictional complications in justifying their inactivity. According to the BSF officers, such occurrences are not under their jurisdiction since the theft is by foreign nationals, i.e. Bangladeshis, and that, too, outside the fence and, hence, outside the realm of their control.[34] Officially, the land between the 'zero point' and the border fence is Indian territory, by virtue of being located within the territorial delimitations of the state. But the construction of the fence has virtually turned these lands into no-man's lands – unguarded by Indian border guards and vulnerable to criminal activities by miscreants from Bangladesh.[35] The crisis of fenced-out territories is common to the entire stretch of India's border with Bangladesh, including the north-eastern border states of Assam, Meghalaya and Tripura.[36]

Interestingly, responses confirming the decrease in the number of burglaries in homes inside the fence are also not rare. This implies that while the fence safeguards the houses inside the fence from 'Bangladeshi burglars', it also exposes the fenced-out lands and homes to the same miscreants.[37] Ambivalent feelings regarding the fence are discernible among the respondents. Kuddus Rahman expresses his concern in the following way: 'Let there be fencing. We do not have

Livelihood practices 35

a problem with that. They have to do whatever it takes for the security of India. But our humble request is to let the farmers work in their fields without problem. And BSF is the main obstacle to this end'.[38]

Recorded cases of trespassing have noticeably increased after the fencing. This does not necessarily suggest that the actual number of trespassing incidents has increased, but only that the presence of the gates now makes the movement of people more visible and easy to locate, unlike the previous unfenced border where unhindered movement across the border often went unnoticed and, hence, unrecorded. The following response from a Bangladeshi interviewee, Md. Zia-ul Haq, explains how the fence has made the border more visible and cross-border movement more traceable than it was previously:

> There are a large number of Indian convicts in Dinajpur jail in Bangladesh. Most of them are convicted of illegal infiltration. Some of them might have crossed over to the Bangladesh side for agriculture. Some of them have been caught from their own land in India. From 2005 onwards, the number of Indian convicts in Dinajpur jail has increased. Most of these convicts used to be set free before the fence had been constructed. After the fencing, the number of officially-convicted trespassers has increased. Many of them are Indian farmers who mistakenly cross over to the Bangladeshi side without an official document. Many of them are afraid to go back in fear of being apprehended by the BSF. So they surrender to BGB and are, then, sent back to India through Flag Meetings between the BSF and the BGB.[39]

The issue of the violation of fencing rules by the BSF has been one of the more important issues regarding fencing.[40] 'The rule of leaving a 150 yards gap between the 'zero point' and the fence is not being observed everywhere. Often the fences are constructed way inside the villages, at a distance of more than 200 yards from the 'zero point'. The fence should at least be moved to its stipulated position. And still after that the land that will be fenced out should be taken over by the government against a compensation to the farmers who lose their land', says Pranabesh, a farmer with 'fenced-out' farmlands.[41]

Demands for exchanging the 'fenced-out' lands in return for compensation from the government are frequent in the responses of the farmers owning lands outside the fence. In some parts of the north-west frontier provinces in India, including provinces like Rajasthan and Punjab, government compensation for fenced-out lands is already in place, where the government pays a fixed amount of Rs. 3000–4000 to farmers who have their lands outside the fence, irrespective of the yield. While the government of West Bengal is aware of such a scheme, no definite policy has yet been designed.[42] 'We have requested government officials to look into this possibility of compensation. In spite of assurances, no such policy has been, so far, announced', says Hirak Kanti Munshi, secretary to the local committee of a political party at Balurghat in South Dinajpur district (West Bengal).[43] And rows between the civilians and the BSF over required permission to move across the fence gates continue, despite protests and meetings regarding possible solutions.[44]

36 *Livelihood practices*

Legal consequences of fencing

The fence violates some of the aspects of the Indian Constitution, specifically aspects of Article 19 and 21. Article 19(1) says that all citizens of India shall have the right (d) to move throughout the territory of India and (e) to reside and settle in any part of the territory of India. The state can only make reasonable restriction of the right in the interest of the general public or for the protection of the interest of any scheduled tribe [Article 19(5)]. The fence violates Article 19(1) of the Constitution by restricting the movement and settlement of people outside it, in spite of the fact that it is neither in public interest nor are the lands outside it tribal areas (i.e. not officially designated). The issue of security cited by India as a reason for fencing does not hold good for two reasons: one, unless there is a state of emergency, martial law or war, such construction in the name of security is a violation of the fundamental rights of Indian citizens; two, even after the construction of the fence on security grounds, India is unable to prevent or even trace illegal Bangladeshi infiltrators into its territory.

Article 21 of the Indian Constitution ensures the life and personal liberty of its citizens. Yet by preventing them from pursuing livelihoods (and, hence, life), by denying the citizens their access to basic amenities and by illegally confining the citizens outside the fence for 20 hours every day, the latter is a serious violation of some of the basic rights of Indian citizens.

The Right to Property (Article 300-A) is also being violated by depriving the citizens of free access to their property outside the fence, rendering the property valueless, and also by depriving them of any compensation for such forceful devaluation of their property through the construction of the fence.

Effect of the border on the nature of cultivation along it

The whole stretch of the West Bengal-Bangladesh border boasts of fertile land fed by a number of rivers, making this belt and almost the whole length of the border zone a highly cultivable territory, with a three-crop record in one year.[45] Apart from the usual food crops such as paddy, wheat, lentils and mustard, and cash crops such as jute, a variety of fruit cultivation is also practiced by the cultivators.

Certain crops that are harmful to the health of the farmers and also have addictive features, such as tobacco and poppy,[46] are also seen to have increased along the border because they constitute profitable smuggling items.

> *Poppy:* Poppy cultivation is illegal in West Bengal,[47] though that has not stopped cultivators from growing it due to its high profitability. Out of the seven districts in West Bengal where poppy cultivation has been reported, four are border districts – Nadia, Murshidabad, Malda and South Dinajpur (the other three being Bardhaman, Hooghly and Birbhum).[48] According to the police, an organised criminal network is encouraging poppy cultivation by offering greater profit margins to cultivators. As newspaper reports suggest, thousands of acres[49] of poppy plantations have been burned down through government initiatives in January 2011 (January being the

time of harvest). In January 2012, about 340 acres were burnt down, while another 3000 acres were still being cultivated illegally.[50] The role of the border becomes clear in the explanation given by a section of the police department with regard to the failure in completely preventing poppy cultivation. According to them, while most of the poppy plantations are traced with the help of satellites, a major portion lying near the border or on the *Chars*/enclaves cannot be detected due to satellite restrictions in border areas. Sometimes poppy plantations are also surrounded by other plantations to escape detection. No amount of warning, awareness programmes or legal steps have succeeded in preventing the illegal cultivation of poppy, especially along the border.[51]

Tobacco: The cultivation of tobacco is yet another widespread occurrence along the West Bengal-Bangladesh border despite the harmful effects of tobacco plantation on the cultivators. There are no official restrictions on tobacco plantation, either in India or Bangladesh, to act as a deterrent in this case. But cultivating tobacco has its share of hazards. 'Green Tobacco Sickness'[52] and lung problems are some of the hazards associated with it. Tobacco companies around the world encourage its cultivation, especially in developing countries, and the government subsidies add to the problem. Poor farmers fall prey to such inducements. West Bengal is an important area for tobacco cultivation – Cooch Behar, Jalpaiguri, Malda and Murshidabad being the most widely-cultivated districts, apart from other areas, including Nadia.[53] All the five above-mentioned districts happen to be border districts in West Bengal.

Cannabis: Cannabis[54] production has also been on the rise in the border district of Cooch Behar because of high profits[55] and, more importantly, the district's close proximity to the 'Siliguri Corridor'[56] that caters to the neighbouring states of Bangladesh, besides Nepal, Bhutan and Tibet. The riverbeds or the kitchen gardens of the local inhabitants of Cooch Behar, a border district in West Bengal, are being used for cannabis production, making Cooch Behar a flourishing cannabis-producing district.[57] The Siliguri Corridor takes care of the merchandising of the product. Despite the police destroying truckloads of cannabis or burning produce in the field, cannabis cultivation continues in full swing, much like poppy cultivation[58] – drawing attention to the territorial importance of the border in the context of the nature of cultivation.

Labourers

Agricultural labourers

Though working as agricultural labourers is an important source of livelihood along the West Bengal-Bangladesh border, it is clearly not sufficient to provide for the entire population living along it. 'My husband works as a labourer in other people's jute cultivations where his job is to bring the harvest from the field and

38 *Livelihood practices*

then to wash and dry them. The whole job fetches him a meagre sum of Rs. 120 a day. Do you think a whole family can survive on that? It is like being a daily-wage worker. There is no income on the days when there is no work',[59] says Rupali Mahato.

Labourers moving to other parts of the country or abroad

The lack of alternative livelihood opportunities at the border drives the border civilians to other non-border and affluent areas in search of their livelihood, both in India and Bangladesh.[60] 'We do not have any industry at this border, which is why more than 50% of the population goes abroad as labourers', says Ranjit.[61] Male civilians are more prone to migration to non-border areas as labourers in factories.[62] In recent times, MGNREGA (Mahatma Gandhi National Rural Employment Guarantee Act 2005)[63] is taking initiatives, through various employment schemes, to hold back people in their own areas and to prevent migration to faraway places as labourers. 'But through NREGA, at best 50 to 70 people can be employed at a time, but not 500 to 700',[64] says Animesh. The indication is clear. The West Bengal-Bangladesh border areas are ill-equipped in providing enough livelihood opportunities to their inhabitants.

The other avenues of labour for the border people include working as labourers in brick-kilns and rice-mills, and as porters at the Border Land Ports. Engaging more people, especially young men looking for livelihood opportunities, as labourers in these places might help reduce their engagement in cross-border smuggling activities, feels Hirak Kanti Munshi.[65]

Brick-kilns

In the southern part of West Bengal, especially in the border district of the North 24 Parganas, more than 400 brick-kilns[66] have mushroomed over the years due to the presence of rivers in the district. West Bengal shares a substantial area of riverine borders with Bangladesh, making the border area suitable for the growth of brick-kilns. The sand deposition left by the rivers on their banks acts as raw materials for the brick-kiln industries[67] and, hence, these kilns develop along the banks of rivers. The landless labourers, including a large number of migrant labourers not just from within India but also from Bangladesh (who cross the border to work in these kilns), depend largely on the seasonal occupation that these kilns provide.[68] The labourers from Bangladesh are mostly illegal migrants, who cross the border without passports and start working in these kilns on a seasonal basis. The demand for cheap labour pushes the owners of these kilns to adopt 'unofficial' means of employing labourers. The illegal migrant labourers from Bangladesh do not find any official recognition. What they do find is a means of livelihood on a seasonal basis. Most of them go back to Bangladesh once the brick-making season is over. But many of them stay back and eventually mix with the local Bengali population of West Bengal to look for other avenues of livelihood.

Livelihood practices 39

'The brick-kilns have increased a lot in the last few years. We are extremely dependent on the kilns. The womenfolk also work there', says Md. Tafikul Islam.[69] In the absence of large-scale industries in the border areas, brick-kilns provide employment opportunities, even if seasonally, to a large number of people living along the borders. 'There is nothing like an industry here. We just have the brick-kilns in this area. Otherwise, livelihood here means agriculture', says Riazul Mondol.[70]

Amidst the lack of employment opportunities and the increasing involvement of border people with illegal means of earning, the brick-kilns have almost become life-savers, as responses from the border civilians indicate. The stretch between Lalgola (Murshidabad) and Basirhat (North 24 Parganas) along the West Bengal-Bangladesh border is especially lined by such brick-kilns, many of them illegal and without official license, given the vast area of riverine borders in this stretch.[71]

Yet the narrative of the brick-kilns has its share of irony as well. While the brick-kilns have provided better livelihood opportunities in the border areas, they have also driven many of their labourers into smuggling practices. The labourers use their income from these brick-kilns in smuggling, informs Kalipada Ghosh, a human-rights activist working with the labourers of the brick-kilns.[72] Border regulations affect the brick-kiln labourers in other ways as well, including the need to present voter cards to the BSF when required, and restrictions on working after 6PM. This implies that the labourers are unable to earn the wage that labourers in non-border brick-kilns make by loading bricks on to trucks in the evening.[73]

Rice-mills

Rice-mills had once constituted an important source of livelihood for the areas which now constitute the border districts of South Dinajpur (West Bengal) and Dinajpur (Bangladesh). While raw paddy came from the farmlands of Dinajpur, the rice-mills were mostly located in the western part of the district (which, after Partition, became a part of West Bengal). The few remaining rice-mills in South Dinajpur (West Bengal) stand testimony to the immense impact that the Partition of Bengal in 1947 had on the flourishing economy of the region. The now-decadent rice-mills were once flourishing industries and catalysts in the process of the growth of the districts, which are now the border districts.[74] Gourab Sarkar, a businessman in Hili, explains it in the following way:

> After the partition, the hinterland for these mills was cut off from the mills, having been located on the other side of the border. Many of the rice-mills here shifted to the places which produced the raw materials, leaving Hili (the headquarters of South Dinajpur) barren. Increase in the carrying cost of raw paddy resulted in this shift. The mills, therefore, moved nearer to the hinterland.[75]

Jute shares a similar trajectory, as Haimanti Roy reminds us, when the Partition separated the jute-growing East Bengal from its manufacturing area along the banks of Hooghly and its market in Calcutta.[76]

40   *Livelihood practices*

These districts had their heyday during the flourishing of these mills and, eventually, went into decadence after the Partition – followed by the closure of the rice-mills. Just as brick-kilns make themselves visible in every narrative of the people of the southern part of the West Bengal-Bangladesh border, so do rice-mills in those of the northern part of the border – the difference being in the tone of loss and frustration in the latter, due to the degenerate state of the rice-mills. Both the rice-mill industry and the brick-kiln industry have been affected by the creation of the West Bengal-Bangladesh border in a negative and positive way, respectively. While the brick-kilns are a positive product of the riverine borders, the rice-mills reveal the negative impact that the creation of the border had on some traditional industries. Rues Hirak Kanti Munshi:

> Earlier the mills engaged a lot of people. Now, there are just two of these mills left, which do not suffice for the demand for livelihood of the people of this area. After the Partition, the process of giving out licenses for trading in raw materials have become more stringent, and has almost stopped, in order to avoid misuse of the licenses through illegal trading. This has led to the closure of a number of rice-mills. As a result, many people are going away to other places for work.[77]

The stringency of the border resulted in the downfall of Hili as a commercial hub by increasing the communication hazards between it and Kolkata (the headquarters of West Bengal). Laments Gourab:

> The railways could pass through the eastern parts of Bengal which later became Bangladesh, to cut short the travel time between Kolkata and Hili. Partition has increased the travel time between the two, forcing the trains to take a longer route. Most of the major railway services halted at Hili because it was an important destination. Hili was then the most flourishing business centre after Kolkata, since neither Siliguri nor Balurghat had emerged as business towns back then. In Hili alone, there were fifteen rice-mills, making Hili not just the most important commercial hub in north Bengal but also the gateway to the north-east – a role that Siliguri now plays.[78]

There have been renewed efforts in recent times to re-establish railway links via Bangladesh between commercial hubs of the northern part of West Bengal and its major railway stations.[79] These efforts complete the circle of the journey of border narratives, beginning from the disruption and illegalisation of links to their being re-established.

Land Ports

Coolies in Land Ports

The land ports along the West Bengal-Bangladesh border provide a range of livelihood opportunities to the border population, in both legitimate and illegitimate forms. Hili (West Bengal)-Bangla Hili (Bangladesh) and Petrapole (West Bengal)-Benapole

Livelihood practices 41

(Bangladesh) form the two most important Land Ports along the West Bengal-Bangladesh border, though other check posts also function as ports or are being developed as Land Ports in order to reduce the load on these two existing ones.

One of the important means of involvement for the border people that these ports offer is in the form of labourers. A substantial number of them are required for loading and unloading the trucks. It is mostly the local population living near the border that works as full-time or part-time _coolies_ (labourers) in these ports.[80]

While the Land Ports provide a good livelihood opportunity to the border population, they also have their flip side like all the other livelihood practices along the border. Those along the West Bengal-Bangladesh border are also important sites of smuggling, contrary to the idea that Land Ports ought to be under strict surveillance and, hence, are unfavourable for illegal activities. It is, in fact, under the surveillance mechanisms of the border forces at these ports that illegal practices thrive the most.[81]

The _coolies_ are not just the ones most prone to getting involved in activities like working as carriers for smuggling contraband items across the borders, but also the worst victims of the same by getting addicted to the drugs they smuggle. A number of families are affected by this whereby male members of the families fall prey to drug networks and, eventually, addiction, while working as _coolies_ in one of these border ports.[82]

Traders at the Land Ports

Bangladesh shares about 40 border points with India, including the Land Ports (LP) and Land Customs Stations (LCS), of which less than 15 are active.[83] In terms of legal trading, a wide range of produce – natural and otherwise – moves between the two states of India and Bangladesh through border ports, constituting about 60% of the total trade between the two states.[84] The largest trading point between India and Bangladesh is the Land Port (LP) of Benapole-Petrapole between the Jessore district of Bangladesh and the North 24 Parganas district of West Bengal, respectively. Other important Land Ports, especially between Bangladesh and West Bengal, are Sonamasjid-Mehdipur, Hili-Bangla Hili, Birol-Radhikapur, Banglabandha-Phulbari, Burimari-Chengrabandha and Bhomra-Ghojadanga.[85] The enormity of trade through these Land Ports ensures the involvement of a substantial number of people, including labourers and traders from local areas and other cities/towns,[86] customs officials and a whole array of people in official and non-official capacities.

Both in terms of the variety of traded products as well as infrastructure, Benapole-Petrapole port scores over Hili.[87] This explains the widespread occurrence of illegal cross-border activities in Hili, including bribes paid to border guards.[88]

Currency-exchange counters, restaurants and shops at the Land Ports

Currency-exchange counters

The Land Ports provide other livelihood opportunities as well. The currency-exchange counters, which exchange Bangladeshi Taka for Indian Rupees and vice

42 *Livelihood practices*

versa, constitute an important livelihood opportunity in the Land Port areas along the West Bengal-Bangladesh border. The counters double-up as tourist agents in arranging for accommodation and travel for tourists who travel to India and Bangladesh through these ports. Mornings are the busiest times for the counters due to restrictions in border areas on any kind of official work late in the evenings.[89]

Subodh Majumdar, who has been working in a currency-exchange counter at the Petrapole border for over a decade now, explains the flip side of the system:

> There are hardly any checks on the number of people travelling across the border. If someone intends to stay back for some illegal intentions, he/she simply has to destroy his/her passport and that will destroy all proofs of his/her existence. When they enter, they provide an Indian address of the place where they will be staying. But no one checks the validity of the address. Most of them (Bangladeshis) have relatives on this side. They come, put up in their relatives' place, gradually buy land and property here and settle here for good. They just send back their passports to Bangladesh via someone. The border forces or police do not keep an eye on the people, until they are specifically suspicious about someone, in which case, the matter goes to the court. Otherwise, they (Bangladeshis) eventually obtain voter cards and settle here once and for all.[90]

Restaurants

Restaurants[91] form yet another important source of livelihood in and around the border Land Ports along the West Bengal-Bangladesh border. The sheer number of such eating joints in and around the ports indicates the prospect of having restaurants in such busy areas. 'There are less residential houses here and more restaurants and counters. Thousands of people come here every day, where will they have their food? It is these restaurants and counters which make the border so buzzing', says Apurba Kumar Biswas, a resident of the Petrapole border area.[92] These restaurants, apart from serving the tourists, traders, labourers and all those who live and work at the border, act as a source of livelihood for hundreds of people as well.

Though these counters or restaurants might seem minor livelihood opportunities compared to the enormity of the large-scale trading that takes place at these ports, they are no less important. In fact, as far as engaging the local population at the border is concerned, they largely score over the big trading businesses. Unlike the traders, the people employed in these counters and restaurants are essentially local people whose lives, over the years, have come to depend on the border.

Border shops

The ownership of small shops in these port areas also constitutes another border-dependent livelihood option along the West Bengal-Bangladesh border. These depend mostly on 'side-trading' – a co-lateral occurrence from the large assignments of trade that the ports witness everyday. A small part of the trade assignments is channelised into the local shops, which sell these items at lower prices than their actual market prices. The items enter the country legally as part of a larger consignment and then find their way into the small shops dotting the border Land Ports, while the rest of the consignment travels to other parts of the country. The items sold in these shops mostly include cigarettes, spices, small electronic goods, chocolates, juices and snacks. The border guards, as well as the police and customs officials, are aware of their functioning.[93]

Office of the border guards

The office of the border guards, apart from providing livelihood to the border guards themselves, provides livelihood opportunities to the local civilians as well. Some of the local border population, though miniscule in number, are either engaged as assistants in the auctioning of smuggled items or as *purohits* (priest) in the shrines inside the camps (this is specific to the BSF on the West Bengal border since a majority of them have shrines devoted to Hindu gods/goddesses). People engaged in one or the other activity inside the camps often end up playing mediators between the local civilians and the border guards.[94] But their role as mediators depends on the discretion of the border guards, whose general feeling of distrust towards the local population prevents them from mingling with the border civilians.

In recent times, BSF has started recruiting local youths from border areas into BSF services, providing yet another livelihood option for the border civilians.[95]

Fishing

West Bengal and Bangladesh share 200 kilometres of a riverine border,[96] of which Ichamati, Padma and Tista are the most important border rivers. While these rivers as borders, ironically, attain significance more as catalysts for smuggling, they are also important for promoting fishing as a livelihood option for the people on both their sides.[97] However, border regulations affect riverine borders as much as they do land borders, influencing the livelihood options of the people along them.[98]

Moreover, the sense of insecurity associated with border life in general also looms large in the responses of the civilians. 'There is always the fear of being shot by the BSF. If someone moves a bit to the other side of the river during fishing, BSF gets hold of them and beats them up',[99] says Jahangir, a fisherman in Kalindi river. The borderline, running along the river, is an imaginary line – seen at an equidistant point from either bank. It is, in fact, difficult *not* to violate the borderline when one is in the river since gauging the distance to the bank from the river is far more difficult than it is from the bank. The irony of imagining a riverine border has also been expressed by the border guards themselves, besides the fishermen and civilians affected by it. The anxiety of the border guards in controlling riverine borders is palpable in poems written by the guards themselves, where they write about the impossibility of 'drawing lines on water'.[100]

44 *Livelihood practices*

Livelihoods not directly related to the border

Some of the other livelihood practices seen in the border areas, such as tailoring, *beedi*-making, owning a band-party and so on, though not directly related to the border, are nevertheless affected by it. If nothing else, the general sense of insecurity haunts the people engaged in these livelihoods as much as those in other border-related occupations.

Beedi-making

Beedi manufacturing is a 20 billion revenue-yielding industry in India that involves more than 10 million organised people and another 30 million people in the unorganised sector. The unorganised workforce in the *beedi* industry includes about 20 million marginal labourers, 6 million farmers, 4 million registered *beedi* rollers and another 1 million involved in plucking *tendu* leaves (the leaves used for making *beedi*). Women constitute 75% of the total workforce, which is almost essentially a rural one.[101]

The areas along the West Bengal-Bangladesh border, being essentially rural in character, also see involvement of a substantial number of their people in the *beedi*-making industry. The involvement is especially in the form of an unorganised workforce, including pluckers and rollers. Women constitute the major portion of the workforce, more so because of restrictions and insecurities involved in their movement in border areas.[102] In the northern parts of the West Bengal-Bangladesh border, the closure of the rice-mills has triggered the large-scale involvement of local civilians in *beedi*-making.[103] The creation of the border catalysed the closure of the rice-mills which, in turn, encouraged the emergence of *beedi*-making as an important alternative livelihood practice.

Tailoring

Proximity to a city or an affluent town encourages the emergence of certain livelihood practices. Understandably, certain professions have emerged in those parts of the West Bengal-Bangladesh border which are in close proximity to Kolkata. The district of North 24 Parganas, being the closest border area to Kolkata,[104] has witnessed the emergence of certain livelihood practices, such as tailoring, which depends for its market upon Kolkata. Basirhat is one such border town in this district which has seen the large-scale emergence of the tailoring business in the last couple of decades.[105] This explains the concentration of a huge number of tailoring shops/factories in and around the border areas of Basirhat. Though these occupations are not directly related to the West Bengal-Bangladesh border, they are integral to narratives of border livelihoods along it.

Other options

The fluctuating prices of agricultural produce, coupled with restrictions in using the fenced-out lands, compel the border dwellers to look for alternative livelihood options. While some of these alternatives are related to or dependent on the border, others are not. Moreover, the seasonal nature of agriculture also renders the cultivators jobless at certain times, when they look for other options. Running band-parties[106] or even working as domestic help[107] constitute such alternative means of livelihoods. But the essentially unaffluent nature of the border areas implies that such alternative means of livelihoods often fail to provide sufficient earnings.[108]

Illegal livelihood practices

The creation of the West Bengal-Bangladesh border in 1947 followed by the deployment of border guards and, finally, the beginning of the construction of the fence in 1986 has affected traditional livelihood practices in these parts. The border has also resulted in the evolution of some livelihood practices never seen before in the areas which now constitute the border. Both kinds of influences of the border on livelihood practices are seen in the legal and illegal practices prevalent, at present, along it. While some of the traditional practices have been illegalised by the creation of the border, some illegal practices have been a result of the creation of the border itself. The emergence of cross-border smuggling practices along it also has its roots in the 'confused policy' of India and East Pakistan following the Partition, regarding the commodities which could be allowed to move across the border legally. This confusion 'created a space for the emergence of smuggling as a thriving enterprise in the border areas, usually with the connivance of the border police'.[109] Livelihood concerns figured even in the border-making process during the Partition, when editorials expressed the need to have a substantial territory of Bengal awarded to West Bengal because 'it seems certain that sooner or later the Hindus of East Bengal will have to be accommodated in West Bengal and provided with honest means of livelihood'.[110] Smuggling was sought to be equated with 'anti-national' and 'unpatriotic' conduct and local youths were trained into private militias along the border districts of Darjeeling, Jalpaiguri, West Dinajpur, Malda, Murshidabad, Nadia, and 24 Parganas to 'protect frontiers of West Bengal from any aggression by evil minded persons'.[111]

The geographical expanse of smuggling practices along the border in terms of the area covered and the range of contraband items crossing it indicate that cross-border smuggling practices are integral to the understanding of not just livelihood practices but the characteristic features of the West Bengal-Bangladesh border in general.

From drugs (like heroin, marijuana, cough syrups, syringes, hormone-stimulating drugs and alcohols) to domestic and household necessities (crops, spices, utensils, cattle and fish), from turtles[112] (even Monitor Lizards)[113] and skeletons[114] to cooking oil, petrol, diesel, metals, from electronic goods (phone sets, calculators) to luxury items (cloths, perfumes, junk jewelry), from gold/silver, fake currency notes and mobile phone SIM cards to newspapers – every conceivable item is being smuggled across the West Bengal-Bangladesh border, despite the patrolling

46   *Livelihood practices*

border guards and the surveillance mechanisms at work.[115] This also indicates a possible involvement of the border guards in such practices. Categorised as 'kacha bebsha' (perishables) and 'pakka bebsha'(high value and contraband), the goods are, likewise, smuggled through appropriate means.[116]

Some points along the West Bengal-Bangladesh border have attained specific strategic importance for cross-border smuggling practices, like Hili (between the South Dinajpur district of West Bengal and Dinajpur district of Bangladesh), Petrapole-Benapole (between North 24 Parganas district of West Bengal and Jessore district of Bangladesh),[117] and areas like Phulbari-Banglabandhu, Changrabandha-Burimari, South Gitaldaha-Mogolhat, Raiganj-Ranipukur, Bagdha-Ansolia, Krishnanagar-Jadabpur and Bashirhat-Bhomra.[118] Such illegal livelihood practices have, over years of their functioning, not just become characteristic of the West Bengal-Bangladesh border but also an integral part of the economy that runs along it.

Drugs

Cough Syrup: The smuggling of drugs, especially the cough syrup called Phensidyl,[119] is the most commonly known practice in this border, besides that of heroin (like Jamtala, Khalidpur in Bongaon)[120] and marijuana.[121] Phensidyl is manufactured by a well-known pharmaceutical company in India from where it is distributed mostly to the north-eastern parts of India and West Bengal.[122] 'In addition, empty Phensidyl bottles are refilled with higher narcotic content, repackaged as "Phensidyl Plus" and smuggled back into Bangladesh',[123] where they are acquired by addicts at a cheap price (the price for a 100ml bottle of smuggled Phensidyl in Bangladesh amounts to Tk. 500[124] and is acquired in India for Rs. 150,[125] though the official market price for a 100ml Phensidyl bottle in India is Rs. 75 and Rs. 40.78 for a 50ml bottle).[126] Large consignments of Phensidyl bottles have been reportedly seized along the India-Bangladesh border and still continue to be seized on a regular basis by the border guards.[127]

Heroin/Hashish: Heroin has been mostly reported as sourced from the 'Golden Crescent',[128] through India into Bangladesh.[129] Along the stretch of the West Bengal-Bangladesh border, the Benapole-Petrapole, Hili-Bangla Hili and Gede-Darshana borders are the most prone to drug-trafficking.[130] Other informal and small-scale drug-trafficking routes along this stretch include Phulbari-Banglabandhu, Changrabandha-Burimari, South Gitaldaha-Mogolhat, Raiganj-Ranipukur, Bagdha-Ansolia, Krishnanagar-Jadabpur, and Bashirhat-Bhomra.[131] The smuggling of heroin as well as other drugs is executed through conceivable and inconceivable ways, within tool boxes of bullock carts, the folds of women's *sarees*, underground canals (built to drain excess rain water) and boats,[132] besides trucks carrying agricultural products, fabrics and, as a journalist in a local newspaper in Dinajpur informed me, even hidden inside the death-beds of corpses taken for cremation or burial.[133] Smuggling through underground canals is difficult to trace since it is easy to mistake the act of smuggling for routine agricultural

Livelihood practices 47

practices such as draining water from the fields by farmers. It is only below the culverts that such acts of smuggling can be traced as such.[134] Innovations in use of tunnels make it even more difficult for the border forces to keep track of the latest methods. Underground secret tunnels, made by smugglers exclusively for the purpose, in the comparatively isolated border areas like those of Dinajpur, have been a cause of anxiety for the officials. Abandoned tea gardens are being chosen for the purpose, away from the well-surveillanced check posts and border outposts of border guards.[135]

The latest addition to smuggling vehicles has been Toto (the battery-driven three-wheeled vehicle vying mostly in suburban areas of West Bengal), which carries drugs and addiction syrups under crates of mangoes and loads of potatoes. The viability of such methods is proved by the fact that large consignments of cough syrups have been confiscated recently by the police in and around various border areas in Nadia and Murshidabad districts in West Bengal.[136] The seemingly unassuming vehicle, the Toto, has been the newest addition to the usual list of smuggling vehicles such as trucks or even VIP cars with redlights.[137] Ambulances and cars with fake 'Police' and 'Press' stickers are also in use along the border areas for smuggling cough syrups or hashish.[138]

The problem with tackling heroin production has been that the main component of heroin – Acetic Anhydride[139] – is used for making medicinal drugs (e.g. Aspirin), besides leather, fabrics and paper, because of which the production of this chemical cannot be banned.[140] Incidences of hashish[141] smuggling inside plastic capsules have been recently reported. Hashish is packed inside capsules that look like ordinary medicine and is smuggled across the border from India (mostly from the border districts of Siliguri and Jalpaiguri in West Bengal) to Bangladesh.[142] Heroin, hashish and marijuana (*ganja*) are also regularly seized by the border guards, though the actual amount which is successfully smuggled is much more than the amount seized.[143] Snake poison has been one of the more frequently smuggled drugs in recent times, due to the vigilance on other, more common drugs, like the ones mentioned above. With 'rave parties' on the rise in various Indian cities, snake poison has replaced or joined heroin/hashish as a trendy addiction, especially among the youth. Seizure of snake poison in the border districts of Nadia in West Bengal, worth crores, indicates its growing demand. That most of the confiscated poison is contained in similar France-made containers indicate a single source for the same, that, police forces guess, could be part of a global drug network.[144]

'Both the sides are affected by drug smuggling. But it still persists due to the profit it brings and because the BSF officials are also involved in it',[145] laments Narendranath Ghosh, a resident of Karimpur. The closure of the border region to the general civilians after 5PM every day helps the smugglers in getting their way. It helps the latter as well as the border guards to operate unhindered, without the fear of being exposed,[146] says another border resident.

The BSF, the BGB or the police can rarely lay their hands on the contractors of these trades. It is the carrier, known as *dhoor* in local parlance, who mostly gets caught by the border guards.[147] Carriers are usually local border civilians.[148] Any

48   *Livelihood practices*

person capable of carrying any amount of weight, irrespective of gender or age, can earn as a *dhoor*. I was witness to scenes of smuggling on the Bangladesh side of the Hili border (Dinajpur) during one of my field visits, where children ranging from 7/8 years of age to boys in their mid-twenties were running on the roofs of a moving train carrying sacks of Phensidyl bottles and jumping from moving trains onto the other side of the border, the railway line being located within a few yards from it.[149]

The *dhoors* are assigned the 'job' by the manager of the smuggling network, locally known as the 'lineman', who is responsible for maintaining the liaison between the carriers and the border guards.[150] The linemen are often locally-known faces, but are hardly reported to the border guards or the police. Fear of life threats from them is a reason cited by the local civilians, who witness such practices and know the lineman as well.[151] But the more important reason cited by the locals themselves is that of attracting the unwanted attention of the border guards. Since a substantial number of local civilians are directly or indirectly involved in illegal cross-border practices, they are also dependent on the lineman for the smooth operation of these.[152]

Moreover, the border guards are often the direct profiteers of such practices. They depend on the skills of the linemen for the smooth execution of cross-border smuggling. These reasons make the linemen indispensable to both the border civilians and border guards.[153] This explains the power that they wield in the border areas. 'Here, the power and influence of the linemen is more than any political leader or *Panchayat* head. This can happen only in a border area', says Gourab Sarkar, a trader at the Hili Land Port.[154] Support from the political parties in power is also a reason for the growing influence and affluence of the linemen, says Kuddus Rahman, chairman of the local committee of the political party in power in West Bengal, hinting towards the misdeeds of the previous government.[155]

The prospect of instant money drives the essentially poor and often unemployed border civilians into such smuggling networks and this trend is the same on both sides of the border.[156] Moreover, the carriers often fall prey to addiction themselves and are unable to avoid drug smuggling jobs out of desperation.[157] The addiction of the carrier ruins him/her in the long run, leaves them incapable of earning a livelihood, eventually ruining the whole family. Subodh Burman was arrested by the BGB during the early hours of dawn near the Mohorapara area in Hili while smuggling 278 bottles of Phensidyl across the border. The bottles were being carried by him to the contractor's house for which he would have been paid Tk. 350 for each bottle. He was a farmer by occupation and his family consisted of his wife and little daughter.[158] Carriers are often deceived by linemen into being victimised by the border guards and the police, while the former wash their hands off the whole operation.[159]

Illegal human crossings

Illegal human border-crossings constitute yet another form of cross-border practice along the West Bengal-Bangladesh border, where the *dhoors* help people cross

Livelihood practices 49

the border illegally, without a passport.[160] Its riverine borders,[161] especially those between Satkhira (Bangladesh) and North 24 Parganas (West Bengal), are prone to illegal human crossings,[162] besides being strategic locations for the smuggling of contraband items as well.[163] The Dinajpur border between West Bengal and Bangladesh is another such point.[164] With increasing surveillance mechanisms along the riverine and unfenced borders, a greater number of such crossings are being operated along the fenced areas, according to the statistics given by the BSF.[165] Hari, an agent helping Bangladeshi people to cross over into West Bengal, informs me that such illegal crossings generally take place at night. 'Here, BSF does not fire',[166] he assures.

In fact, some policies of the concerned states, especially the ones related to travel tax, encourage these illegal border-crossings. The unaffordable rates of travel tax imposed by both India and Bangladesh,[167] coupled with the hazards and expenditure of obtaining passports, drive the poor local civilians into illegal ways of crossing the border by paying a much smaller amount to the brokers or *dhoors*. It is not always necessarily the poor who cross the border illegally. People also tend to cross the border for better economic prospects, and this variety almost always entails crossing from Bangladesh to India. They also cross as part of smuggling networks, as would be evident from the nature of involvement or activity of the convicts arrested by the police and BSF.[168] Centres and agents providing fake documents, like voter cards, adhar cards, ration cards, passports, to the illegal migrants abound all along the West Bengal-Bangladesh border. Spending anything between Rs. 500 and Rs. 1500 could fetch an illegal migrant the necessary documents to be able to settle, atleast temporarily, anywhere in the country that they have entered.[169] Often, the poor, ill-informed, helpless migrants are made to believe that the documents are real, leading them to police harassments, later, when they provide the same for official purposes. Providing fake documents for a sum of money has become rampant all along this border.[170]

'Some people also cross the river along with the smuggled cattle',[171] informs a witness. The co-operation of the local population with the illegal border crossers[172] as well as the common language (*Bangla*) of the illegal crossers and the legal residents are often the reasons for the failure of the border guards or the local police in tracking down this illegal movement.[173]

Illegal or unauthorised border-crossing also involves the state personnel, where such officials cross the border illegally to either take stock of situations or probe into an incident or occurrence.[174] 'We knew that sneaking into Bangladesh will be a risky decision. But we were determined to know what is going on there. People who were coming here told us their tales of plight. That's why we took the risk',[175] said an official of the Border Intelligence Corps (BIC), following reports of attacks on Hindu minorities under the Khaleda Zia government across the Bangladesh border in the Satkhira, Kaligunj and Khulna areas of Bangladesh in 2001. These acts of unauthorised border-crossing make the border guards as much a part of the narrative of contesting the sovereign delimitations of a state as the border civilians, rendering them an integral part of the border culture.

50 *Livelihood practices*

Cattle

Cattle smuggling (or 'trade', as the participants would prefer to call it) across the West Bengal-Bangladesh border is almost always a one-way occurrence where cattle are procured from provinces like Rajasthan, Punjab, Himachal Pradesh, Haryana, Uttarakhand, Madhya Pradesh, Utter Pradesh and Bihar in India and smuggled into Bangladesh, mostly through Murshidabad and the North and South 24 Parganas districts of West Bengal,[176] apart from the Nadia and North Bengal border.[177] The cattle are stocked in herds at strategic locations near the border from where they are made to cross the border with the help of a lineman.

The transportation of cattle within India is in violation of Article 55 of the Transport of Animals Rules, 1978, which prohibits carrying more than 10 adult cattle or 15 calves on broad gauge and more than 4 adult cattle or 6 calves on narrow gauge.[178] The traders carry as many as 300 cattle in each wagon while transporting them from one province to another in India.[179]

The export ban on cattle trade imposed by India is a major factor for the flourishing of its illegal version. While the demand for beef in Bangladesh is not met by its limited supply, India has a cattle surplus due to its low demand for beef.[180] The Rs. 2000 crore meat industry in Bangladesh keeps the demand for cattle high.[181] The 'official' number of seized cattle indicates the expanse of the trade since it does not point out the actual number of cattle successfully smuggled across the border.[182] The demand-supply imbalance in West Bengal and Bangladesh also explains the increase in cattle smuggling during such festivals as *Eid*. The demand for cattle in Bangladesh increases during *Eid*, especially during *Eid-e-Qurban* or *Eid al-Bakr*[183] when cattle smugglers in West Bengal make quick money by smuggling cattle into Bangladesh. The volume of trade, in such cases, increases all the more if *Eid* happens to be celebrated around festivals like *Durga Puja*[184] in West Bengal (as was the case in 2011 and 2012[185]).[186]

The demand-supply equation ensures that cattle worth between Rs. 500 and Rs. 3000 fetches anything between Rs. 20,000 and Rs. 40,000 in Bangladesh.[187] The cattle trade from India (West Bengal, Assam, Tripura and Meghalaya) to Bangladesh is worth \$500 million annually[188] – an indication of its enormity. Anywhere between 5000 and 15,000 cows cross everyday,[189] while other estimates put the range between 20,000 and 25,000, which is worth \$81,000.[190] The profits for cattle smuggling are substantial. The price of a cow worth Rs. 500 in Haryana (India) becomes five times higher on entering West Bengal. At the West Bengal border, it could become as high as Rs. 5000,[191] which is then shared by the contractor, carrier, lineman (often they are the same person in the case of cattle smuggling) and the border guards on both sides.[192] The nature of increase in the price of a cow, not just between the two provinces within India but within a single province (from a non-border to a border area), indicates the effect that the border has on such illegal livelihood practices.

> *The Indian perspective*: The flourishing of the cattle trade across the West Bengal-Bangladesh border has its roots in the ban on cattle slaughter and cattle export imposed by India. Article 48 of the Indian Constitution bans the slaughter of

Livelihood practices 51

cattle on terms of agricultural needs and animal husbandry. Yet with the mechanisation of agriculture following India's independence in 1947, the need for cattle in agriculture decreased. Ban on slaughter and exports resulted in surplus cattle in India. With the creation of Bangladesh in 1971, possibilities of cattle trade opened up between the two states. The issue of cattle trade has always been a sensitive issue in India due to the religious baggage that the cow carries in this Hindu-majority state.[193] With the increasing shift towards an orthodox, almost fundamentalist Hindu stricture in India under the current government, the issue of cattle trade has become all the more sensitive, negating any remote possibility of legalising the trade, which, many feel could have been a solution to the illegal transaction. Under the current Indian government, possibilities of legalising cattle trade have become an impossibility anymore. The West Bengal government, under its current regime, has also been against cattle smuggling, more due to concerns over the functioning of a parallel economy at the border rather than communal concerns.[194]

The Bangladesh perspective: The legalisation of cattle trade in Bangladesh in 1993 turned a cattle 'smuggler' into a cattle 'trader' on its border. The payment of Tk. 500 (Rs. 383) as Customs charges to the BGB on the Bangladesh border make the trade official.[195] Bangladesh also profits from the bone and leather collected from the slaughtered cattle in its leather and ceramic industries, besides its major export of beef.[196] It is, therefore, natural that it does not take any step towards curbing such cross-border practices since cattle trade is directly linked to Bangladesh's economy and food security.[197] The Bangladesh government as well as the BGB are aware of the profits that Bangladesh reaps from the cross-border cattle trade.[198]

Years of operation have established contractual links between cattle smugglers on both sides.[199] While the creation of the border disrupted or adversely affected traditional ties and livelihood practices in the border areas between West Bengal and Bangladesh, it also created new links. The 'cross-border' aspect is common to both the broken (and illegalised) traditional links and the new (illegal) links.

'Earlier, the Bangladeshis would have to move into the Indian side of the border to bring the cattle. But now, with the help of the BSF, the Indians themselves bring the cattle to a certain point across the border. The BSF officials do not otherwise say anything, except for rare cases of their seizing a couple of cows, to show that they are doing their job honestly',[200] says Ismail, indicating the role that border guards play in this border trade.

The border markets or *haats* (local term for markets) are located on the corresponding side of the Bangladesh border where the cattle are stocked immediately after crossing it. Traders come from all over Bangladesh, from as far as Sylhet, Cox's Bazar and Teknaf to as near as Satkhira, Khulna and Jessore, to deal in cattle.[201] They come with trucks, load them with their purchases (generally 15–25 cows per truck)[202] and head off to markets where they sell the cattle to other local buyers within Bangladesh. 'The cows are marked according to their assigned serial numbers (depending on the consignment number of the contractor). The

52 *Livelihood practices*

Figure 2.2 Cattle *haat*, 2012.

locals are appointed as labourers for loading the cows on to the trucks',[203] says Alamgir, a cattle trader. The cattle trade, thus, creates co-lateral livelihood opportunities for the border civilians, besides their obvious involvement as traders.

The cattle *haats* act as wholesale markets, supplying the demands of innumerable local shops/markets across Bangladesh, like the *haats* in Matila and Lebutola[204] or Putkhali[205] in Jessore. Each of these wholesale markets witnesses dealings worth thousands of Indian Rupees and Bangladesh Taka each day, adding up to huge transactions for both the states of India and Bangladesh. The auctioning of seized cattle by the BSF contributes towards the cattle trade, since the bidders are mostly smugglers who re-smuggle the cattle at high prices.[206]

The relation between the cattle traders and the border guards on both sides is generally dictated by the unstated rules of the trade and is, hence, harmonious, especially on the Bangladesh border. A cattle trader at Kaikhali border, Satkhira (Bangladesh), in explaining the cattle trade network across the West Bengal-Bangladesh border, says:

> Those who smuggle cattle generally do not indulge in smuggling other things, because they share a good rapport with the BGB and, understandably, do not want to ruin that rapport by smuggling other things. Cattle smuggling is not a crime to them (the BGB), while smuggling Phensidyl is, any day, a far more harmful act. That is immoral. Cattle smuggling is as much a part of legal business as is any other legally traded item.[207]

The presence of BSF and BGB camps in front of the cattle *haats* along the border is ample proof of the unstated understanding.[208]

Livelihood practices   53

This does not suggest that other contraband items are not smuggled together with cattle or in return for it. Drugs, spices, fake currency notes or even firearms constitute items which are often smuggled along with or in return for cattle.[209]

The wholesale cattle *haats* are a thriving economy in themselves, complete with shops catering to every need of the traders. The items sold at the shops range between food, tea,[210] toiletries, clothes, tyres, petrol and anything that a trader, having travelled from afar for an overnight journey might need. Initially, the local civilians would rent out rooms to these traders, who would reach the market in the evening, stay overnight near the market at one of these guest accommodations, complete their transactions early the next morning, and start on their way back. Recently, some private guest accommodations have been built by the locals and the committee of traders who are in charge of the overall trade operations for accommodating the traders.[211] These *haats* are run by the locals, who look after the various departments of the transactions – complete with an organised committee of members, presidents and secretaries.[212] From *lungis*[213] to toothbrushes, from petrol to tyres, from rice and beef curry to tea and biscuits – cattle markets are a self-sustained economy, thriving along the West Bengal-Bangladesh border.

'Everyday the revenue from cattle businesses amounts to about Tk. 50,000',[214] informs one of the members of the syndicate incharge of the cattle *haat* at Putkhali. He also reveals that the reason behind the flourishing of cattle trade at particular points along the border is the 'security' that those points offer – indicating hassle-free trade. 'The other borders cannot provide this security',[215] is how he phrases his concern, unaware of how he redefined the concept of security and illegality by talking about unofficial security for an officially illegal business. The cattle trade, thus, provides livelihood opportunities to a substantial number of border people, including the civilians and the guards, without a legal recognition, especially from India. The irony is well-expressed in a response from one of the local traders: 'Tendencies towards other kinds of crimes have diminished significantly because the cattle businesses have improved the over-all economy of the area'[216] – indicating how the spatial specificity of the border creates its own socio-economic narrative, which is often beyond the comprehension or even control of the state.

Instances of violence towards the smugglers by the border guards, especially the BSF on the West Bengal border, are not rare.[217] Cattle trade-related violence is often the result of such situations where the credibility of the BSF is under question or where its general efficiency at the borders is questioned.[218] They also result from disputes over payment between the trader and border guards.

However, such risks do not deter smugglers from trading in cattle. 'The smugglers are daring and have a don't-care attitude. Border life has made them daring', says a BGB official at Hakimpur in Dinajpur district (Bangladesh).[219] Moreover, restrictions on using lethal weapons by the BSF[220] have catalysed cross-border cattle smuggling like never before.[221] The number of attacks on BSF constables in instances of clashes between them and the cattle smugglers[222] indicate that borders are, indeed, the toughest hurdles for states when it comes to establishing control over its territories.[223]

54   *Livelihood practices*

Frequent skirmishes between the smugglers and border guards[224] followed by violent abuse and the deaths of both have led to considerations of legalisation of the cattle trade.[225] The border guards, especially the higher officials of the BSF, are keen to see the cattle trade legalised through the lifting of the export ban by India in order to curb both smuggling and violence.[226] Till a point, the Indian government chose to ignore the issue of cattle smuggling for fear of hampering bilateral relations with Bangladesh. In the current scenario, the agenda of the state is clearer – it wants cattle trade stopped. The BSF, however, is concerned because it knows how border economy works. BSF clearly sees the profit that cattle trade brings to its participants, most of whom are, in fact, Hindus. The lucrative business of cattle smuggling goes beyond communal concerns for the traders. With stricter vigilance on such trading, cattle smuggling has taken more violent turns in many places, with smugglers turning to communal clashes to divert the attention of the police and BSF towards maintaining law and order rather than curbing cattle trade.[227] The desperation of the smugglers to continue cattle smuggling amidst increasing restrictions is also borne by the innovations made to smuggle cattle across borders, to avoid being detected and things turning violent. Vegetable baskets loaded onto unassuming vehicles carrying cattle in them are the most recent ways of cattle smuggling, where a full-sized cow, legs tied up, is held down in a vegetable basket with vegetables covering it on top. Police and BSF in Bongaon border area in the South 24 Parganas, after becoming aware of such methods, have started thorough checks of all vegetable carriers to detect cattle. Carrying cattle in large trucks has, in fact, substantially decreased after such innovative yet unassuming ways have been devised, informs BSF officials.[228] Horse smuggling has also been a recent addition to the smuggling list, either for consumption or for use in racing,[229] though cattle remains the most lucrative and, thus, obvious.

BSF and police try spreading awareness regarding cattle smuggling, especially among the local villagers who rarely have a stake in the trade. The women of the villages are especially encouraged to stand against cattle trading, with police and BSF officials holding awareness camps to talk to local civilians on possible ways to curb smuggling.[230] The issue of trampling of crops by cattle on their way to being led towards the border by the smugglers is brought up by the police and BSF as a context to rouse local villagers against the smugglers, given the increasing number of complaints lodged recently against such destruction of crops by the cattle.

Firearms

The smuggling of firearms is not uncommon along the West Bengal-Bangladesh border, with the border guards themselves confessing such occurrences.[231] 'Firearms are mostly smuggled in along with the cattle, especially in the Putkhali border area',[232] confesses a BGB official at Benapole. The North Dinajpur district is also an important transit for firearm-smuggling networks between West Bengal and Bangladesh, as reports of the seizure of firearms are not rare in the area.[233] In fact, reports hint at an increasing number of firearm smugglers operating in various pockets of the West Bengal-Bangladesh border, including the districts of

Livelihood practices 55

Kushtia, Jhenaidah, Chuadanga, Meherpur, Satkhira and Jessore on the Bangladesh side, and the adjoining districts of Murshidabad, Nadia, North 24 Parganas and South 24 Parganas on the West Bengal side.[234]

Factories in the border district of Murshidabad in West Bengal have been reported to be manufacturing these arms in villages which are at a distance of about three kilometres from the Bangladesh border. The cheap price of firearms (pipe-gun, one-shooter gun, musket rifle and revolver) made in West Bengal (as well as in other parts of India) and their easy availability increases their demand in neighbouring Bangladesh.[235] In fact West Bengal's border districts of Murshidabad, Malda and 24 Parganas, in recent years, are almost on the verge of replacing Bihar's Munger district as the hub of manufacturing illegal firearms. Manufacturers from Bihar have set up factories in these areas for lucrative cross-border arms trade, supplying 7mm pistols for Rs. 15–20,000 each and making crores in return.[236]

Reports confirm the confession of the border guards that firearms are often smuggled in consignments of fruits, eggs, rice, vegetables and other items of daily need, which mostly go unchecked by them. 'Good relations' between the border guards and the smugglers is often the reason cited for such exemptions. About 50% of these illegal firearms serve the leaders and cadres of political parties,[237] while the names of the leaders of these parties are also often found on the list of people directly related to firearm smuggling.[238] Reports of increasing deaths by firearms in Bangladesh can be traced back to the availability of smuggled firearms, mostly procured from India, through the West Bengal border.[239]

Buyers also include the terrorist organisations that use these arms to train their members.[240] Some of the arrested cadres confessed to being involved in cross-border cattle trade, while being actively involved in smuggling guns and ammunitions for terrorist groups.[241] Small-arms, locally named as *Belgharia*, *Moyur* and *Chhakka*, are being smuggled into Bangladesh through the south-western frontier, which shares the border with Murshidabad, Nadia, and the North 24 Parganas and South 24 Parganas districts of West Bengal, suggest reports.[242] The firearms cost anything 'between Tk. 25,000 to over Tk. 0.1 million. Unsuspecting low income people are often used as carriers of the smuggled firearms',[243] the report says.

Fake currency notes

The smuggling of Fake Indian Currency Notes (FICN) has increasingly become rampant across the West Bengal-Bangladesh border, especially with the flourishing of cattle trade. Cattle traders are often paid in fake currencies (cattle worth Rs. 4000 is paid for by Rs. 10,000 worth fake currencies by the Bangladeshi smuggler), which is then circulated in India.[244] Fake currency notes worth thousands are often reported to be seized from smugglers, while thousands of them are successfully distributed across the states in innumerable markets and shops.[245] Farmers crossing the fence for cultivating their farmlands outside it are often seen to be involved in smuggling fake currencies.[246] Fake currency notes worth Rs. 43,81,000 in 2011 and Rs. 15,82,000 till August 2012 have reportedly been

56 Livelihood practices

seized in India.[247] The nexus between FICN, firearms and terrorist organisations is, increasingly, becoming a matter of concern for both India and Bangladesh.[248]

FCN has taken a new turn in the post-demonitisation period by the current BJP government in India November 2016 onwards. With a gap of about a couple of weeks after the demonitisation announcement, FCN is back in the Indian market with offset Rs. 2000 notes being successfully circulated from their manufacturing centres in the border areas as also making space for the ones being smuggled into West Bengal from Bangladesh.[249]Unavailability of new currency notes in the post-demonitisation phase has led to the increasing market for FCN, with more advanced techniques being used to print FCN as well as new areas being identified from which to operate FCN smuggling. The disputed border areas and *Chars*, where border vigilance is comparatively sparse, are being used as platforms for manufacturing and smuggling FCN.[250] Bangladesh has fast caught up with the demonitisation crisis situation in India and has started manufacturing new notes to be fed into the Indian market. The amount of FCN being confiscated daily across the West Bengal-Bangladesh border stands testimony to the demands for FCN in the Indian market as well as the profit that such risky business entails.[251] Setting up of technologically advanced FCN printing machines in Bangladesh also stems from the fact that FCN worth hundreds of thousands, travelling from Karachi in Pakistan to Bangladesh via Dubai has been confiscated at the Bangladesh airport and Chittagong port in recent times. Manufacturing FCN in Bangladesh makes it economically viable as well as less risky for the smugglers to smuggle them across the border into West Bengal and India, at large. The initiatives of setting up FCN printing units in Bangladesh is largely helped by Pakistani intelligence agency ISI, suspects India's National Intelligence Agency (NIA).[252] NIA has also unearthed underground rooms full of FCNs in Bangladesh's Chapainababgunj area, where most of the new FCN printing machines also happen to have been traced.[253]

The Malda border in West Bengal has been especially under the scanner for being the most active border region in terms of FCN smuggling. Kaliachak and Vishnabnagar areas of Malda district have, recently, been the hub of FCN smuggling, given the easy access across its riverine border and the yet-unfenced border areas. The main traders also happen to have their operations from these areas in Malda. In 2016 alone, police and BSF have confiscated FCN worth 1,47,70,500 along the south Bengal border areas, having nabbed 19 convicts.[254] Recurrence of FCN smuggling in Malda has been a constant source of anxiety for both the police and BSF as well as the other traders and businessmen who see their legal trades being threatened by such illegal trading.[255] What concerns the businessmen and BSF more is the fact that the legal trades are often misused by smugglers to smuggle FCN across borders, as has been the case with convicts held for smuggling FCN across the Malda border in the guise of a *coolie* working in the Land Border checkpost at Mehdipur.[256] In fact, cases of FCN smugglers entering India with valid passports have also been reported, causing much anxiety among the police and border forces, who feel misuse of official documents in smuggling is a direct threat to the security structure of both India and Bangladesh.[257]

Livelihood practices 57

But FCN smugglers take much effort to maintain the local and cross-border FCN smuggling network created over the years, fearing that a low phase in FCN trading might drive away these local links to other occupations. In the absence of a new consignment of FCN in the post-demonitisation phase in the early months of 2017, the FCN smugglers ensured circulation of low-quality FCNs from Malda just to keep the network running.[258] Use of official documents and legal trading networks are part of this desperate effort to continue the age-old network.

Chargesheets are difficult to provide against the smugglers for want of proofs. Consignments of FCN are often thrown across the fence in small packages in areas where vigilance is comparatively sparse. Despite knowledge of probable offenders, the border forces or the police are often not able to provide substantial evidence of their involvement.[259]

Currency coins

Currency coins (known as *Rejki* in smuggling lingo) adding up to thousands have recently been reported as being smuggled across the West Bengal-Bangladesh border. The process involves procuring currency coins from across West Bengal and smuggling them across the border into Bangladesh. In Bangladesh, these coins are made into metal blades. Local foundries or ferro-alloy factories along the West Bengal border also melt coins into metal sheets before smuggling them to Bangladesh. Re. 1, Rs. 2 and Rs. 5 coins are mostly used for the purpose. While melting a Re. 1 coin makes about four blades, melting Rs. 5 produces anything between five and seven blades – indicating the profits made by the coin smugglers. This explains why drivers of public vehicles, small-scale traders and even women homemakers in and around Kolkata have been reported to be involved in smuggling coins.[260] Metal smuggling in the form of coins has been the recent addition to the already vast range of cross-border smuggling practices along the West Bengal-Bangladesh border. It has a direct effect on the circulation and unavailability of currency coins in other non-border areas of West Bengal.[261]

Bullion

Bullion smuggling in various forms has been rampant along this border for quite sometime now, especially in the form of gold bars/biscuits.[262] Silver smuggling has, recently, been added to the list of frequently smuggled items. With fences having made cattle smuggling difficult, packaged silver thrown across the fences has become an easier smuggling method. Bangladeshi silver, as also gold, generally cheaper than their Indian counterparts, are being smuggled into India in packets of about 20 kilograms across Chowdhuryhat, Gitaldaha, Shitai, Mekhligunj border areas in North Bengal (Cooch Behar, Siliguri).[263] The involvement of clearing agents in bullion smuggling, working in the Customs department at the border checkposts, indicate the return that the risky business of bullion smuggling involves.[264] Newer ways of bullion smuggling, like plating metallic frames of luggage with gold (which are otherwise meant to be made of aluminium), are being

58 *Livelihood practices*

deployed to continue the trade, as age-old ways are becoming easily trackable by Customs officials and border forces.[265]

Items of daily necessity

Besides the riskier and more expansive trading in drugs, cattle, firearms or fake currencies, the people living along the West Bengal-Bangladesh border survive on smuggling items of daily necessity, from a few litres of petrol/diesel to a few kilograms of spices, vegetables and eggs[266] to a few utensils, electronic items, clothing, tools, audio-visual disks and so on. The Bhomra border in the Satkhira district of Jessore (Bangladesh) is an intriguing study in informal smuggling transactions over the stretch of the unfenced border. Bhomra is a Land Port between Satkhira (Bangladesh) and North 24 Parganas (West Bengal), which is used for trading in vegetables, cement, zip shutters, fish, etc. between India and Bangladesh.[267] But that does not stop the local civilian population from indulging in the small-scale smuggling of household items like spices, onion and garlic, apart from Phensidyl.[268] There is a narrow canal flowing along the Bhomra border which acts as a meeting point for women from both sides of the border.[269] These women smuggle in/out items like spices or even cooking ware, in return for a small amount of money. Some of them sell the smuggled spices or vegetables to other households in the village.[270] The seasonal nature of agriculture, coupled with the fluctuating prices of crops, ensures a steady demand for such items.

Newspapers are smuggled across the border despite the availability of both locally-published as well as national newspapers along the whole length of the West Bengal-Bangladesh border. Some of the major Indian newspapers are smuggled into Bangladesh for Tk. 20–25 and vice-versa. Alok Sengupta, resident of Dinhata, says:

> Money transaction for the newspapers is done through recharge of mobile phones. The smuggler on one side tops up the SIM card of his counterpart on the other side with the amount payable for the smuggled newspapers. This 'talktime' in his phone is used by the smuggler to contact his counterpart for further deals involving more newspapers, cattle, etc. ensuring that newspaper smuggling is executed with no direct transaction of money.[271]

Smuggling of motorbikes is on the rise given the combination of size and profit that bikes ensure, compared to other lighter or heavier vehicles as items of smuggling. The male smugglers pillion ride female sex workers, disguised as their wives and drive the bike upto the border, where the vehicles are hidden among the crop fields to be smuggled on a boat across the river to Bangladesh at an opportune moment. Sometimes, the entire vehicle is dismembered and packed in a bag/ container to be ferried across the border. India-made motorbikes fetch double their price from Bangladesh, making them a lucrative smuggling item, especially along the riverine border areas between 24 Parganas district (West Bengal) and Jessore, Satkhira districts (Bangladesh).[272]

Livelihood practices 59

The nature of the smuggled items indicates that cross-border smuggling is not always necessarily linked to global smuggling networks, as some studies on such practices indicate. They show instead that such cross-border practices become rudimentary ways of living and earning for the people living along the border. The border people learn to put the reality of the border to the best of their interest, irrespective of its legal/illegal nature. Over the years, smuggling practices come to be seen as an integral part of livelihood practice along the border.[273]

Parbati Mohanto gives a vivid description of not just the process of cross-border smuggling practices along the West Bengal-Bangladesh border but also the nature of relations between the smugglers and border guards. 'This is our job and is like any other job that people do. We don't think there is anything wrong with it', begins Parbati, herself a regular smuggler in the Hili border area.[274]

'We work as *dholai*[275] for contractors and have to pay the BSF Rs. 150 for every trip that we make across the border. Some of the BSF constables are kind enough not to take any money from us. But some are greedy and do not spare us a rupee…. We get Rs. 15 for smuggling a single goat. A few days back garlic was in much demand, for which we got Rs. 3 per kilogram. We had to pay the BSF Rs. 2, which left us with a profit of Re.1. Generally, our Bangladeshi counterpart throws the sacks of items to this side of the border. We carry the sacks in turn to another place. The BSF officials know all about it. They allow us to carry 1–2 quintals at a time and dump them at a safe place, from where these sacks are then distributed to other local markets, like Maburghat, Trimohini, etc. The *Mahajans* (contractors) take half of the total transaction amount. All the people in this village are engaged in this job. This is our profession…. If we need to use cycles for carrying the items to and from the border, the *Mahajan* pays Rs. 60 to the border guards and Rs. 10 extra to the person who carries them. The border guards allow the cycles to pass at an opportune moment. The higher officials of the BSF might not know about these practices. It is the guards patrolling the border who mostly engage in it. Even they need money. We understand their situation. Sometimes we cook some good food for them because the food in the camp is not good. They buy the meat and we cook it with spices…. When a new battalion comes, they try to be strict about these things. Instances of heated arguments are not rare in those phases. But gradually we develop a rapport with them…. In fact we feel sad when the battalions are transferred. They help us do our work by making us aware if the situation at the border is tense or by suggesting safe smuggling routes…. The BSF constables keep their share of the money either inside their sticks or their boots, or even in a hole that they dig into the ground from where they collect the money later. Even they have fear of being caught by their seniors. And once a case is filed against them, they have to pay a heavy fine from their salary.[276]

If poverty of the civilians is an important reason for their involvement in such practices, the fee structures of the border guards (both BSF and BGB),[277] in a way,

60 *Livelihood practices*

explain their involvement in the practices as well, given the meagre salary that the constables of BSF and BGB get. The constables are also often the only earning members of their families. Earning an extra amount of cash helps them financially as much as it helps the border civilians to support their meagre income from agriculture or other livelihood options (if at all). This makes the border guards an integral part of the everyday survival narratives of the border and no less part of the border culture than the civilians.

Whenever the situation at the border becomes tense, smuggling is checked for a while, which makes life for these people extremely hard, due to their complete dependence on these practices. 'In those times, we have to resort to whatever we had earlier earned and so have to be careful about our expenditures',[278] says Parbati. The predominance of the linemen in this particular area is weak compared to other border areas because of the absence of the fence. Linemen, explains Parbati, attain importance in the fenced areas because the need to co-ordinate cross-border movements is higher in them. In unfenced areas such as this village, the transaction takes place directly between the contractors, carriers and the border guards.[279] The vulnerability of the unfenced areas and the villages close to the IB (International Border) on either side in terms of smuggling are also highlighted in the records of the BSF.[280]

A stretch of the border near the Ghunapara-Dhumron village where this interview took place has yet not been fenced. On being asked how this stretch remained unfenced, Parbati explained how the local MLA of the Left Front agreed to arrange for the prevention of fencing in that area after the local people pleaded with him: 'He came and asked us what to do. We said that this is a poor area. If you fence the border, how will we earn a living? So he looked into the matter and prevented fencing. That has been a great help to us'.[281] When she was asked what alternatives the local people had in case the area was fenced someday, she said with a grin:

> If the border is fenced someday, we will find other ways to carry on our work. Do the fenced areas lack smuggling practices? Just as an animal finds its food under any circumstances, even we will do the same. God has given us brain, so I am sure we will find a way. In fact, then the guards at the gates will help us find other ways.[282]

This conversation provides a fair idea about the *modus operandi* of small-scale cross-border smuggling practices involving the civilians and border guards, as well as the nature of involvement of the latter in such practices, especially in the unfenced stretches of the border. Similar narratives of cross-border transactions with the co-operation of the border guards are common along the entire stretch of the Bengal border, as Malini Sur's experiences testify.[283]

The construction of the fence has, in fact, played an important role in the labelling of certain practices as 'illegal' in official terms. Even after the creation of the border in 1947, the unhindered movement of people and items between West Bengal and Bangladesh existed without being officially illegalised. The construction of the fence has made such movements visible and, thus, officially illegal.[284]

This explains the heavy concentration of smuggling practices in the remaining of the unfenced areas along the West Bengal-Bangladesh border, like the 40-kms. Changrabandha border area between Cooch Behar and Lalmonirhat districts of West Bengal and Bangladesh respectively. Land acquisition issues have prevented construction of fences and has, likewise, become a haven for smuggling and transit point for miscreants.[285]

While the construction of the fence, as a decision of the Indian state, has illegalised these cross-border practices, the border guards are the ones who actually negotiate the fence and the cross-border movements everyday. Their ways of negotiation with these practices gives us an idea that the border guards, inspite of being the representatives of the state, interpret the border and the fence in ways which are acceptable, and often profitable, for them. The essentially poor local civilians along the border are often seen to survive on smuggling things as basic as dry leaves, which earn them a mere Rs. 20–30 a day. The border guards consciously overlook such practices on humanitarian grounds.[286] 'We spare the poor people',[287] says a BGB official at Benapole, while talking about how small-scale smuggling forms the only resort for the poor local people along the border.

Obstacles in curbing smuggling

Responses from the border guards, especially the senior commanders in the camps, do not, however, point to the involvement of the constables as the main reason for their failure to curb cross-border smuggling. Rather, the lack of manpower and the failure of surveillance mechanisms are cited as reasons. According to a BSF official, the distance between the border checkposts needs to be reduced and searchlights need to be immediately fitted along the fence: 'Government does not implement it, nor do the smugglers let the implementation take place'.[288] Such responses indicate, yet again, that inspite of being representations of the state at the borders, the border guards become enmeshed in the border culture that eventually affects their perceptions, actions and negotiations with the border civilians and their ways of life. The responses clearly indicate the vulnerable position that the double-role of the border guards thrust them into – one, as the representative of the state and the other, as an integral part of the border culture. Such spontaneous responses bring out their lived experience.

Natural environmental conditions, like foggy days or dark nights, make surveillance more difficult for the patrolling constables.[289] Winters pose a huge threat to the border guards because the available equipment like binoculars, SST (searchlights) or night-vision cameras fail to fight the dense fog.[290] The thick cover of clothing which the people wear in winter makes it easier for smugglers to hide smuggled goods. The folds of *sarees*[291] worn by women and the jackets worn by men are used for this purpose. Specialised jackets with numerous pockets have lately been seen to be used by smugglers to smuggle Phensidyl and have come to be known as 'Dyl Jackets' in local jargon.[292] Winters also mean that the water levels of the rivers reduce considerably, making it easier for the smugglers to cross them.[293]

62 *Livelihood practices*

Nature and flow of contraband products

The nature and flow of contraband items across the West Bengal-Bangladesh border indicate that the border economy has its own logic and pattern of functioning, and has no necessary connection with the larger economic scenario of either India or Bangladesh. Other than cattle, drugs and fake currencies, most of the smuggled items circulate locally in the border areas. Eggs, spices, dairy products, toiletries, cigarettes, newspapers and SIM cards for mobile phones constitute such items.[294] Most of the items of regular use are manufactured on both sides of the West Bengal-Bangladesh border. Thus, the flow of items depends on the demand for a particular variety or quality of an item on a particular side of the border.[295]

The Public Distribution System (PDS) on the West Bengal side of the border also plays an important role in the smuggling of items of daily use. The PDS system in India ensures the distribution of items like sugar, wheat, rice, etc. to villagers at subsidised rates. The PDS shops are generally not located inside the villages, which means that local salesmen carry the items from the PDS shops or godown to villages along the border. The salesmen are required to show a chit to the BSF mentioning the quantities of the items carried. While the quantities are required to be specified, there are no specifications on the number of trips that a salesman can make to the border villages. Invariably, the salesmen make a number of trips in a day, selling quantities of items far exceeding the required amount for the population of that village. The excess amount thus collected is smuggled across the border to Bangladesh at opportune moments, mostly at nights.[296]

Everyday narratives of such cross-border flows give a more comprehensive idea about the state of things than the biased state-centric discourses. The state-centric discourses on cross-border flows tend to ignore what leaves the state, focusing only on what enters it; ignore the role of consumer demands that decide the nature and direction of the flows of contraband items; ignore the perceptions of the local people regarding the legality-illegality of transacting in certain goods or even the illegal nature of certain practices; and ignore the role of the state itself in facilitating such flows and the benefits that these bring to the state.[297] Thus, the everyday survival narratives of the border people are lost in the larger discourses of security and border control of the state in the context of these cross-border smuggling practices.

Gendered aspect of the nature of involvement in smuggling

A careful observation of the nature of smuggling suggests that there are clear categorisations regarding the forms and items of smuggling between men, women and even children. Women are mostly involved in smuggling light-weight items, including Phensidyl, spices, food items or even household items of everyday use.[298] The clothing of the women (mostly *sarees*) helps them carry these small and light items within their drapes.[299] The lack of women border guards makes it even easier for them to operate.[300] Moreover, instances of sexual favours offered by women or demanded of women by the border guards[301] in a number of instances also indicate the gendered aspect of livelihood practices along the West Bengal-Bangladesh border.[302]

Men mostly perform smuggling practices which involve carrying or moving heavy items or acts which involve physical strain, such as running, climbing or crossing high barriers.[303] This does not, however, mean that men are not involved in smuggling light items such as drugs or items of daily use. But practices which demand physical strength almost exclusively involve them. This explains the large-scale involvement of men in cattle smuggling, especially along the riverine borders.[304]

Often, the male members of families are seen to be in charge of 'managing' the execution of the smuggling, while the women and children execute the operation. The reasons cited for such *modus operandi* is the sympathy that border guards often show towards women and children.[305] Malini Sur reminds us that this gendered nature of cross-border practices, especially illegal ones, could be seen even during the early years of the Bengal border's coming into existence, when the border guards moved between permissiveness and control/deportation towards the smugglers depending on whether they were men or women.[306]

Children are involved in cross-border smuggling practices from a very young age along the West Bengal-Bangladesh border. While the items smuggled by them are mostly lightweight items such as drugs, fruits and spices, they often assist their mothers or other female members of their families in executing the strenuous part of the operation, like running across the border or getting aboard trains. The Hili border is an example where children aged anything between 7/8 years to their mid-twenties are seen running on the roofs of moving trains, carrying sacks of Phensidyl bottles and jumping from these trains on to the other side of the border.[307] Dropouts from schools are common in the West Bengal-Bangladesh border areas due to the involvement of children in illegal activities from a young age. The prospect of instant earnings drives the children into such activities. Their guardians, constituted mostly of poor farmers or labourers, are rarely seen to prohibit their children from getting involved in smuggling.[308]

The involvement of transgender individuals and *hijras*[309] in cross-border smuggling in certain parts of the West Bengal-Bangladesh border[310] cannot be overlooked if one has to understand livelihood practices along it. The fact that a substantial number of *hijras* are involved in smuggling[311] clearly suggests that they utilise their unique gendered status to earn a living. They mostly work as *dhoors* in smuggling drugs, while themselves falling prey to addictions most of the time.[312] One round-trip across the border fetches them around Tk. 200, while the sacks may contain drugs worth Tk. 50,000 to 60,000.[313] The *hijra* status helps them escape the abuse faced by other male or female smugglers.[314] The fact that they are 'neither male, nor female' keeps the border guards at bay as they feel that 'handling *hijras*' questions their dignity.[315] Humanitarian grounds are, however, cited as the real reasons by the border guards for allowing the *hijras* to continue smuggling.[316] The prospect for a *hijra* involved in cross-border smuggling in these parts of the West Bengal-Bangladesh border has become highly profitable, which explains men undergoing emasculation operations or even disguising themselves as *hijras* to earn a living.[317]

64 *Livelihood practices*

The involvement of physically disabled people, including children, is also not rare in cross-border smuggling practices along the West Bengal-Bangladesh border. 'They make use of their disability to carry on the smuggling. They carry light things like marijuana, heroin, etc. But the guards leave them because of their disability',[318] says a BGB official at Hili, indicating the similarity in attitudes of the border guards towards both the disabled and the *hijra* smugglers. The involvement of around 25 physically disabled people, including men and women, in and around the Hili port area indicates that physical disability, like the *hijra* status, is utilised by the border civilians to earn and survive on the border. Recent reports of confiscation of bullion and cough syrups from disabled people in Nadia and Murshidabad border areas indicate that this practice of using disabled people and children in smuggling is, indeed, a viable practice, though the border guards have increasingly become more vigilant. 'It is risky to trust anyone unnecessarily in the border areas', says a BSF jawan on duty.[319] Border is, indeed, a place where trust is an unnecessary and risky affair and mistrust is the way of life.

Prospects for formalisation of border markets

The formalisation and legalisation of the already existing border markets along the West Bengal-Bangladesh border have been suggested both by civilians as well as border guards as a measure to curb illegal cross-border practices. This is also an indication of how the creation of the border has affected traditional links, local village markets being one of them,[320] and has created new, mostly illegal ties (cattle smuggling networks, for example). 'If cattle trading is legalised and these *haats* are officialised, the propensity for smuggling will automatically be checked', says Ranjit, the local *Panchayat* head of Jamalpur.[321] Many senior officials among the border guards admit the prospect and necessity for the legalisation of *haats*, especially the cattle *haats*. 'We all have to think about it seriously. It is not a problem that can be solved by policing', says a BSF official.[322] In fact, the BSF has been sending proposals for such 'open *haats*' along the border to the government of India, confirmed the BSF IG of the Malda frontier.[323] The use of the word 'open', interestingly, stands in contradiction to the idea of the border as a closed 'container' as envisioned by the state. It also highlights the failure of state policing and regulations in gauging or negotiating the uniqueness of the border, as admitted by the border guards themselves. So far, India's north-eastern border with Bangladesh has seen a number of border *haats* in operation and more are likely to come up soon.[324] The ease in cross-border legal trade transactions in these *haats* make the necessity for the same along the West Bengal border all the more obvious.

Certain areas in the North and South Dinajpur border with Bangladesh's Dinajpur district, and the Malda border with Bangladesh's Joypurhat and Naogaon districts, have been identified as viable places for border *haats* since these are some of the areas which still remain unfenced. Allowing the people from both sides of the border to trade in these *haats* with valid passports for a specified time is what the BSF suggests. Not only will these *haats* cater to the daily needs of the

Figure 2.3 Informal border market beside border outposts. Indian shopkeeper selling products to Bangladeshi customers, 2011.

locals, they will also reduce the life risks of both the smugglers and border guards, besides 'contributing towards the revenue of both the governments'.[325] Amidst debates on the need and viability of these border *haats*, the government of West Bengal has approved four locations along the West Bengal-Bangladesh border as freetrade zones, where traders from both states can sell their products.[326] The markets will be located 'on' the international border, said B. D. Sharma, Additional DG, BSF. 'Half of the area will be on the Indian side and the remaining in Bangladeshi territory. It will be an enclosed space with gates on either side. All infrastructures such as banks will be set up', he informed.[327] Bangladesh has also been planning to build Special Economic Zones (SEZs) along its borders with India in order to encourage cross-border trade within the legal framework of the state.[328] Such suggestions indicate the state's desperate attempt to negotiate its borders within the structures of state machinery (transaction in the *haats* with passports). They also indicate the role that borders play in questioning the state's role as the container of socio-political relations.

The existing border *haats* are currently havens for the smugglers to negotiate their deals, which can only be prevented if they are regularised and trading in certain items is legalised. 'A *haat* is organised near the border every Sunday where these smugglers come for making deals. You can easily identify them from

66 *Livelihood practices*

their suspicious body-language. Even the BSF knows them',[329] says a civilian in Balurghat, implying that these *haats* could be put to better use for the civilians if only they were officialised by the state.

I have been witness to such illegal but flourishing border *haats* providing both cattle and other products such as juices, snacks, chocolates and biscuits on my field visits to border areas between North 24 Parganas-Jessore and Burimari-Changrabandha, respectively.[330] In some of the regular border *haats*, the fear of persecution by border guards looms large among the local civilians, simply because of the 'illegal' aspect of the whole operation.[331]

The prospect of meeting relatives and friends from across the border is also evident in the responses of the civilians,[332] besides that of being able to trade without fear. The way the existing border *haats* flourish during festivities, such as *Durga Puja* and *Eid*, stands proof of their prospects once properly organised. Many of these *haats* were in existence much before the creation of the border but have lost much of their glory and significance after the Partition.[333] The ones which still function are plagued by illegal transactions. Thus, *haats* are a natural culmination of not just the exchange of various products across the border but also of cross-border cultural ties that the border people on both sides share, besides having great potential for contributing towards the economies of both India and Bangladesh. Traditional *haats*, which have been de-legitimised by the state-building agendas of India and Bangladesh, need to be re-legitimised for the people along the border to live and earn without fear.

Conclusion

The Partition of Bengal in 1947 did not merely create territorial boundaries but also disrupted traditional ties. The border 'breached the notions of the moral economy'[334] of the people by restricting their movements and rupturing traditional socio-economic links. Clearly, defining and establishing complete control of the borders became political compulsions for both India and East Pakistan, and, later, Bangladesh, in order to establish unquestionable sovereignty over their respective territories. The process of the creation of the West Bengal-Bangladesh border has to be understood from two perspectives. On the one hand, borders were cartographically marked by the states (despite territorial disputes over certain parts), border guards and surveillance mechanisms deployed, and, eventually, border fences constructed (by India) to check the porousness of the borders. On the other hand, the partitioned people negotiated the creation of the border in two ways. Traditional links broken by the border were re-established, albeit with an 'illegal' tag from the respective states. And new links were established as outcomes of the border itself, most of which were again, illegalised by the states concerned.

The effect of the creation of the border on livelihood practices, as discussed above, might be understood through Van Schendel's concept of three levels of scales, which he describes in the following ways: *scales-we-almost-lost*, indicating a pre-border web of relations that has weakened but not vanished; *state-scale*, indicating the web of relations that the state created through the creation

Livelihood practices 67

of the border; and *border-induced scales*, indicating the web of relations created by the border itself.[335] The study of various aspects of livelihood practices along the West Bengal-Bangladesh border gives us a fair idea about the various patterns of livelihood practices which have been affected and created by it. Disruption of traditional livelihoods, the officially-recognised livelihoods created by the border and the co-lateral (mostly illegal) livelihoods created by it become clear in the light of Van Schendel's framework of scales.

Effects of the border on the role of the states, border guards and civilians

In the context of livelihood practices, a study of the roles of the concerned states, the border guards as representations of the states and the border civilians reveals a complex pattern of operation. Apart from establishing border Land Ports and a few small-scale (brick-kilns, rice-mills) and cottage industries (*beedi*) along the border, the role of India and Bangladesh in the context of the livelihood practices of their border people has been mostly negative. Regulations and restrictions related to movement along and across the border have affected the lives of civilians in adverse ways. The construction of the fence has been a double jeopardy.

The border guards as representatives of the states were deployed for guarding and protecting the border. Lethal and non-lethal weapons, surveillance mechanisms and border outposts are the more visible forms of enactment of the role of the state's representative by the border guards. The abuse of people violating the regulations of the border by the border guards also forms a visible form of enactment of their duties.

The civilians, affected by the border and often victimised by the border guards, learnt to negotiate their spatial identity, i.e. the identity of the people of the borderland. They modified existing livelihood practices and produced new ones where the border could be put to their best interests. Negotiating regulations related to the crossing of the fence for cultivation or fishing in the riverine borders and resorting to cottage industries are examples of the effect of the border on traditional livelihood practices. The civilians also resorted to new livelihood practices created by the border, including engagement as traders, labourers, counter owners or shopkeepers at border Land Ports, and assisting or serving border guards in camps. But the most significant change brought about by the border in the livelihood practices of the people of these parts was the creation of exchange patterns across the border, considered illegal by the state but of potential to the economic interests of the border civilians. Engaging in illegal cultivation, engaging as illegal workforce (brick-kilns) and engaging in cross-border illegal trade constitute such practices and exchange patterns.

All these livelihood practices have become integral to border life in the last six decades of their operation along the West Bengal-Bangladesh border. Interestingly, the role of the border guards in the livelihood narratives of this border is seen to have two aspects. While the more visible aspect is that of the protection of the territorial sanctity of the border by restricting the movement of people and

68   *Livelihood practices*

commodities, and increasing surveillance mechanisms,[336] the subtler aspect is the involvement of the border guards themselves in such movements. Their involvement in these practices indicates how state agents are 'drawn into cross-border politics of scale'.[337] This explains the large-scale involvement of border guards in illegal cross-border livelihood practices in heavily guarded parts of the border like Hili or Petrapole-Benapole. Their uniforms and other visible trappings of territorial discipline do not necessarily match the spatiality of their everyday relations or how they place themselves in the border milieu, as Van Schendel rightly observes.[338] The 'lure of the border' makes the border guards susceptible to practices which weaken state territoriality[339] and makes them as much a part of the border milieu as the civilians.

The study of livelihood practices along the West Bengal-Bangladesh border has, so far, highlighted the effect of border regulations on peasants and migrants, the effect of fencing on movement, and the establishment of global illegal trade networks using the topographical qualities and strategic location of the border in question.[340] Studies have also been done on the clash between statist definitions of 'legal' and local perceptions of 'licit', resulting in the illegalisation of licit ties.[341] Most of these studies have had the model of the state as the perpetrator and the border civilians as the victims as the index for understanding livelihood practices along the border. This chapter shows that there are many more complex strands of narratives beneath such linear narratives of perpetrator-victim discourses. It also shows that livelihood narratives of the West Bengal-Bangladesh border are not limited to the disruption of traditional links followed by the destitution of border civilians, but are also studies in the production of new links and the modification of old ones. A one-way linear study shows how pre-existing practices have been illegalised by the state. But the fact that the West Bengal-Bangladesh border, in the last six decades, has also seen the production of illegal practices and networks cannot be overlooked in the study of livelihood practices along it. The fact that such networks have not just been established by global traders but also by the local inhabitants of the border areas makes the study all the more significant.

The use of international borders by global smuggling networks has been a usual occurrence, globally. Nor is it a unique feature of the West Bengal-Bangladesh border. Understanding the definitions of legality/illegality by the concerned states and illegal traders, or understanding the *modus operandi* of the international networks, has been a much-explored area. This explains the abundance of studies related to drug-trading networks across the various borders of India, including those with Bangladesh.

This chapter highlights the local aspect of the creation of the border rather than the global implications. The effect of the border on the cultivation patterns of farmers, the co-lateral livelihood opportunities created by it like assisting or serving the border guards, the local economies created by Land Ports and cattle trades and the cross-border exchange of items of daily necessity constitute patterns of the localised effect of the border on the people who live along it.

Livelihood practices   69

The livelihood practices along the West Bengal border are not results of an organised or pre-planned effort. Theyare rather what James Scott phrases as 'everyday forms of resistance'.[342] The border civilians are well aware of the various nuances of the economy and the related livelihood possibilities in the border areas. They are also aware of the nature of state presence and governance in the border, what the border regulations are constituted of and most importantly, what practices are deemed to be considered legal or illegal by the states. The various practices that they engage themselves in despite knowledge of the above clearly indicate that border civilians are not always necessarily victims of statehood but beneficiaries of the same as well. Their practices are their efforts 'to work the system to their maximum advantage or minimum disadvantage, ever testing the limits of the possible'.[343] The practices are not organised and, thus, might not find a significant place in the studies related to this border. But they are, nevertheless, 'opportunistic and self-indulgent',[344] indicating that the civilians use the border to their own interest. The lack of a formal organisation in such practices does not, however, imply that there is a lack of co-ordination as well. The various patterns and networks of livelihood practices along the West Bengal-Bangladesh border clearly point towards a well co-ordinated narrative of survival, which alerts us to the fact that the practices are 'by no means merely random individual action'.[345]

Yet another significant observation is that the intentions of the practices indicate 'an accommodation with the structure of domination'.[346] This explains why the livelihood practices are not in any visible way organised efforts to deny the presence of the state at the borders but simple rudimentary ways of putting the reality of the border to use. Instead of a denial or refusal of the state machinery, the livelihood practices of the civilians operate well within the structure of the same. What, nevertheless, makes the practices unique are the ways in which the civilians re-interpret and redefine the space of the borderland to suit their survival needs and how the border guards, inspite of being representatives of the states, involve themselves in this process of redefining the border. Involvement with the various livelihood practices along the border makes the practices of the border guards more a part of its everyday life than any organised, pre-planned effort to either establish or refuse the presence of the state at the borders.

The border, as a space of separation from the neighbour, as container of its own civilians and as a space for the exercise of unquestionable sovereign power of the state is re-interpreted and, in the process, reproduced by the border people, including the civilians and the border guards. The border, thus, becomes the platform on which the clash of perceptions between the border people and the state is performed, turning the border into the *thirdspace*,[347] i.e. the everyday lived reality of the border people. The border is perceived by the state as a non-fluid space of containment and sovereign power. The border guards, despite being embodied representatives of the state, conceive the border as a space for both establishing control as well as for personal gains. The border civilians survive the reality of the border through practices and actions that suit their needs. Conflicting perceptions

70 Livelihood practices

of the border, thus, converge in the borderland, making the border the platform for the production of unique narratives.

Years of performance of such border narratives crystallise into a pattern of consciousness among everybody who negotiates the border in their daily lives. This consciousness is spatial in character, i.e. tied to the specificity of the borderland, and has been termed here as a border consciousness. This chapter provides a building block, by analysing livelihood practices, towards the establishment of the thesis that various strands of socio-economic and ethno-religious narratives converge in the border to be crystallised into a larger spatial narrative – the narrative of the borderland, and that years of performance of certain actions and perceptions turn into a pattern of consciousness – the border consciousness. The omnipresence of the border in all the actions and perceptions of the border people constitutes an integral feature of the border consciousness – right from the role of the border fence in issues of cultivation, the role of border regulations in fishing, the role that the border Land Ports play in providing livelihood opportunities, the role of small-scale industries in attracting labourers across the borders to the role that the border plays in creating illegal avenues of livelihood. The words 'Bangladeshi' and 'Indian' become almost interchangeable when it comes to responses regarding such border narratives, especially livelihood narratives, so that after a point, only the performance of the activity matters and no more the nationality. This highlights the overpowering role that the border plays in the lives of its people – in binding the people on both sides of the borderline over their status as borderlanders. While the ways of negotiation of the people with their bordered-status differs, the consciousness that they are indeed a 'border people',[348] – different from the non-border people on both sides – remains constant. This was, in fact, reflected in the response of an Indian intelligence officer, who was surprised to find 'no disorder and very little bad feeling among the people of the two dominions' during his survey of the border villages of 24 Parganas in 1950. He assessed that the self-interest of both the people of India and Pakistan had nipped any possibilities of bad feeling in the bud right in the beginning. 'They were too busy with their own smuggling of chillies, mustard oil, cloth, black pepper etc.', he observed.[349]

The study of livelihood practices along the West Bengal-Bangladesh border serves as a reminder that subalternity is not merely an inert position characterised by a lack of agency within the framework of the state machinery, but a potential consciousness that creates its own subversive narrative despite the omnipresence of the dominant state narratives. Interestingly, 'no subaltern claims subalternity'.[350] On the contrary, the subaltern makes an attempt to negotiate the vulnerable situation that he finds himself in.[351] The dynamic livelihood narratives along the West Bengal-Bangladesh border evolving into a unique border consciousness stands proof of that negotiation. The above narratives feed into the discussion of 'common sense'[352] with which I began this chapter – as a characteristic feature of the 'everyday forms' of negotiations, as ways of absorption of new ideas and techniques to adapt to new conditions of life.[353] Thus, studying livelihood practices along the West Bengal-Bangladesh border contributes towards our understanding of how such everyday forms of common sense are adapted to suit the survival needs of a spatially marginal people.

Notes

1 Rawls, J. (1971) *A Theory of Justice*. Cambridge, MA: Harvard University Press. pp. 25–28; Rawls, J. (1993) *Political Liberalism*. New York: Columbia University Press. p. 14.
2 Rosenfeld, S. (2011). *Common Sense: A Political History*. Cambridge, MA: Harvard University Press. p. 4.
3 Ibid. pp. 5–6.
4 Agriculture in South Asia. *The World Bank*. Available from: http://web.worldbank. org/WBSITE/EXTERNAL/COUNTRIES/SOUTHASIAEXT/EXTSAREGTOPAG RI/0,,contentMDK:20273764~menuPK:548214~pagePK:34004173~piPK:3400370 7~theSitePK:452766,00.html. [Accessed: 27 July 2013].
5 Jamwal, N.S. (January–March 2004) Border Management: Dilemma of Guarding the India-Bangladesh Border. *Strategic Analysis*. 28(1). pp. 5–36.
6 Chatterji, J. (February 1999) The Fashioning of a Frontier: The Radcliffe Line and Bengal's Border Landscape, 1947–52. *Modern Asian Studies*. 33(1). pp. 185–242.
7 Hossain, M. (1991) *Agriculture in Bangladesh: Performance, Problems and Prospects*. Dhaka: The University Press Limited.
8 Van Schendel, W. (2001). Working through Partition: Making a Living in the Bengal Borderlands. *IRSH*. 46. p. 402.
9 PTI. (31 January 2010) Indo-Bangla Border: Fencing Forces Thousands in No Man's Land. *Hindustan Times*. [Online] Available from: www.hindustantimes.com/india-news/newdelhi/Indo-Bangla-border-Fencing-forces-thousands-in-no-man-s-land/Article1–503736.aspx. [Last accessed: 27 July 2013]; Van Schendel, W. (2005) *The Bengal Borderland: Beyond State and Nation in South Asia*. London: Anthem. p. 213.
10 Interview with a BSF official at Asharidoho BSF camp (Murshidabad district of West Bengal, 9 November 2011).
11 *Gram Panchayats* and their counterparts in Bangladesh – the Union *Parishads*, are the local self-government units at the village and small-town levels. They consist of a head (*Pradhan* for *Panchayats*; Chairman for *Parishads*) and elected members from the area, representing a block/village/ward as the case may be. Discussed in the Introduction.
12 Interview with a BSF official at Asharidoho BSF camp (Murshidabad district of West Bengal, 9 November 2011).
13 The timings are as follows: 6–7, 9–10AM; 1–2, 4–5PM in a day.
14 Interview with Rashid Hossein, resident of Lalgola (Murshidabad district of West Bengal, 8 November 2011).
15 Interview with a BSF official at Asharidoho BSF camp (Murshidabad district of West Bengal, 9 November 2011).
16 Interview with Pranabesh, resident and farmer at Ramnagar village (Murshidabad district of West Bengal, 9 November 2011).
17 Staff Reporter. (29 March 2012) BSF ebong grambashir bibad Bagdaye. *Ananda Bazar Patrika*. [Online] Available from: www.anandabazar.com/29pgn3.html. [Last accessed: 17 September 2013].
18 Interview with Balaram Mahato, resident of Char Meghna (Nadia district of West Bengal, 21 October 2011).
19 Interview with a BSF official at Asharidoho BSF camp (Murshidabad district of West Bengal, 9 November 2011).
20 Interview with Kuddus Rahman, resident of Jaykrishnapur village, Jalangi (Murshidabad district of West Bengal, 22 October 2011).
21 Interview with Animesh, resident and farmer at Bindol (North Dinajpur district of West Bengal, 26 January 2012).
22 Ibid.
23 'আসতে দেরী হলে গেট বন্ধ হয়ে যাচ্ছে. তখন লেবার ভেতরে বসে থাকছে. আবার ২ ঘন্টা পরে যখন খুলবে তখন বেরোবে. কোম্পানি কমান্ডার তো সারাক্ষণ গেট-এর কাছে থাকে. তাও কেন আসতে দেয় না ।' (The labourer has to wait

72 *Livelihood practices*

outside the gate for hours till the gate opens again. The Company Commander is generally near the gate. But even then he does not allow us to cross the gate as we want to.) Interview with Imtiaz Mondol, resident of Mathurapur village (Nadia district of West Bengal, 22 October 2011).

24 Awasthi, A.P., Safaya, C., Sharma, D., Narula, T. and Dey, S. (2010) *Indo-Bangladesh Fence Issue*. Centre for Civil Society. Research Project by CCS Fellows. [Online] Available from: http://ccsindia.org/nolandsman/. [Accessed: 3 August 2013].

25 Saha, P. (15 May 2012) Darja kholeni BSF, mrityu ashustho mohilar. *Ananda Bazar Patrika*. [Online] Available from: www.anandabazar.com/15uttar2.html. [Last accessed: 17 September 2013].

26 Interview with Animesh, resident and farmer at Bindol (North Dinajpur district of West Bengal, 26 January 2012).

27 Interview with Narendranath Ghosh, resident of Karimpur (Nadia district of West Bengal, 24 October 2011).

28 Brenner, N. (2001) The Limits to Scale? Methodological Reflections on Scalar Structuration. *Progress in Human Geography*. 25(4). p. 592.

29 Scalar structuration as a socio-spatial process includes the convergence of varying, often conflicting scales of spatial perception by the various actors. In the case of the West Bengal-Bangladesh border, the various scalar structurations perceived by the civilians and the border guards converge over the space of the border, resulting in a complex pattern or mosaic of spatial identities.

30 'বি এস এফ-এর জিরো পয়েন্ট-এ থাকা উচিত... বি এস এফ এক্চুয়াল সীমান্তে ডিউটি করুক ।' Interview with Samsuddin Mondol, resident of Nowadpur village, Jalangi (Murshidabad district of West Bengal, 22 October 2011).

31 Staff Reporter. (29 March 2012) Petrapole shimantey fer bondho sushonghoto checkpost toirir kaj. *Ananda Bazar Patrika*. [Online] Available from: www.anandabazar.com/29pgn2.html. [Last accessed: 17 September 2013].

32 Awasthi et al., 2010.

33 Interview with Prasanta Mondol, resident of Char Meghna (Nadia district of West Bengal, 21 October 2011).

34 Interview with Imtiaz Mondol, resident of Mathurapur village (Nadia district of West Bengal, 22 October 2011).

35 'ফসল কেটে নিয়ে যায়ে বাংলাদেশীরা. এবার পাট হারিয়ে গেছে অনেক লোকেরা' (The Bangladeshi thieves steal our crops from the fenced-out lands. This year a number of farmers have lost their jute in this way.) Interview with Kuddus Rahman, resident of Jaykrishnapur village, Jalangi (Murshidabad district of West Bengal, 22 October 2011).

36 Staff Reporter. (4 March 2017). Gram protisthaponer dabi Assamey. *Ananda Bazar Patrika*. [Online] Available from: www.anandabazar.com/national/proposal-to-bring-the-villages-of-outskirts-in-the-assam-1.573814?ref=national-new-stry. [Last accessed: 6 July 2017].

37 Interview with Sabitri Mahato and Imtiaz Mondol, residents of Char Meghna and Mathurapur village, respectively (Nadia district of West Bengal, 21 and 22 October 2011 respectively).

38 'কাঁটা তার পরুক, তাতে আমাদের আপত্তি নেই. ভারতবর্ষের রক্ষার জন্য যা করে করুক. কিন্তু আমাদের আর্জি এটুকুই যেন চাষীরা মাঠে ঠিক করে চাষ করতে পারে. বি এস এফ সেই ক্ষেত্রেই বাঁধা হয়ে দাঁড়াচ্ছে ।' Interview with Kuddus Rahman, resident of Jaykrishnapur village, Jalangi (Murshidabad district of West Bengal, 22 October 2011).

39 Interview with Md. Zia-ul Haq, resident and college lecturer in Dinajpur town (Dinajpur district of Bangladesh, 8 October 2011).

40 PTI. (31 January 2010) Indo-Bangla Border: Fencing Forces Thousands in No Man's Land. *Hindustan Times*. [Online] Available from: www.hindustantimes.com/india-news/newdelhi/Indo-Bangla-border-Fencing-forces-thousands-in-no-man-s-land/Article1–503736.aspx. [Last accessed: 27 July 2013].

41 Interview with Pranabesh, resident and farmer at Ramnagar village (Murshidabad district of West Bengal, 9 November 2011).

Livelihood practices 73

42 Interview with Ranjit, resident of Jamalpur village, Hili (South Dinajpur district of West Bengal, 24 January 2012).

43 Interview with Hirak Kanti Munshi, resident of Balurghat (South Dinajpur district of West Bengal, 24 January 2012); there have been government-level talks between ministers and the BSF regarding the fence issue, but to no fruitful effect. Staff Reporter. (4 November 2009) BSF Pranab Katha: Simanta basi der jonyo udyog. *Ananda Bazar Patrika*. [Online] Available from: www.anandabazar.com/archive/1091104/4mur4. htm. [Last accessed: 17 September 2013].

44 Staff Reporter. (29 January 2017). Tar kataye bondi, khubdho grambashi. *Ananda Bazar Patrika*. [Online] Available from: www.anandabazar.com/district/nodia-murshidabbad/villagers-facing-trouble-due-to-tight-border-security-1.555688. [Last accessed: 6 July 2017].

45 Interview with a BSF official at BRC-pur BSF camp (Nadia district of West Bengal, 22 October 2011); Jamwal, 2004, p. 8.

46 The dried latex of the poppy is called opium – an addictive drug, which again can be chemically processed for making heroin – a stronger narcotic.

47 In India, only in the states of Uttar Pradesh, Madhya Pradesh and Rajasthan can poppy be cultivated legally, according to the regulations of the Central Bureau of Narcotics.

48 De Sarkar, S. (1 October 2012) Posto chash rukhtey ebar SMS-e pulishi prochar. *Ananda Bazar Patrika*. [Online] Available from: www.anandabazar.com/archive/1121001/1raj1. html. [Last accessed: 27 July 2013].

49 640 acres = 1 square mile.

50 De Sarkar, 1 October 2012, *Ananda Bazar Patrika*.

51 Ibid.

52 Green Tobacco Sickness is a form of nicotine poisoning. When wet leaves are handled, nicotine from the leaves gets absorbed by the skin and causes nausea, vomiting and dizziness.

53 Dinhata Jute Tobacco Co. *Indiamart*. Available from: www.indiamart.com/dinhata-jute/profile.html.

54 Cannabis is a genus of flowering plant and is grown mostly in Central and South Asia. Though traditionally used for fibre, oil, medicinal purposes and recreational drugs, the dried flowers are also widely used to make marijuana – a narcotic, while extracts of cannabis are used for making hashish – yet another narcotic, and hash oil.

55 15,000 square feet of cannabis production gives a return of about Rs.5,00000. Sarkar, D. (15 June 2012) Cultivation of Illegal Cannabis Flourishing in Coochbehar. *The Economic Times*. [Online] Available from: http://articles.economictimes.indiatimes. com/2012-06-15/news/32254673_1_cannabis-kitchen-garden-coochbehar-district. [Last accessed: 27 July 2013].

56 The Siliguri Corridor or Chicken's Neck has its origin in the Partition of India in 1947 and is a narrow stretch of land that connects India's north-eastern provinces to the rest of India, with the countries of Nepal and Bangladesh lying on either side of the corridor. The kingdom of Bhutan lies on the northern side of the corridor. The city of Siliguri in the state of West Bengal is the major city in this area. The city is the central node that connects Bhutan, Nepal, Sikkim, the Darjeeling hills, north-east India and the rest of India. Apart from being the hotbed of illegal infiltration, this stretch of land has also become an important corridor for narcotics and weapon trafficking.

57 About 10,0000000 square feet of agricultural land is under cannabis production in Cooch Behar, as of June 2012. Sarkar, 15 June 2012, *The Economic Times*.

58 Ibid.

59 'স্বামী অসুস্থ. এমনিতে রোজ কার রোজগার বলতে লেবার খাটে. পাট চাষ করার পর সেটা তুলে আনা, ধওয়া, এসব কাজ করে. ১২০ টাকা পাওয়া যায়ে. তাতেই গোটা একটা পরিবার চলে? চলে না. দিন মজুরির মত. যেদিন কাজ থাকে না, সেদিন রোজগার নেই।' Interview with Rupali Mahato, resident of Char Meghna (Nadia district of West Bengal, 21 October 2011).

60 Interview with Hirak Kanti Munshi, resident of Balurghat (South Dinajpur district of West Bengal, 24 January 2012).

74 Livelihood practices

61 Interview with Ranjit, resident of Jamalpur village, Hili (South Dinajpur district of West Bengal, 24 January 2012).

62 Interview with Bina Pramanik, resident of Ramjivanpur village (South Dinajpur district of West Bengal, 24 January 2012).

63 The Mahatma Gandhi National Rural Employment Guarantee Act (MGNREGA) is an Indian job guarantee scheme, enacted by legislation on 25 August 2005. The scheme provides a legal guarantee for 100 days of employment in every financial year to adult members of any rural household willing to do public work-related unskilled manual work at the statutory minimum wage of 120 (US$2.18) per day in 2009 prices. If they fail to do so, the government has to pay the salary to their homes. The law was initially called the National Rural Employment Guarantee Act (NREGA) but was renamed on 2 October 2009.

64 'এন আর ই জি এ চেষ্টা করছে তাদের এখানে ধরে রাখার. কিন্তু তাদের এক একটা প্রকল্পে ৫০-৭০ জন কে খুব বেশি হলে কাজ দিতে পারবে এক এক বারে. ৫০০-৭০০ লোক কে তো আর দেওয়া যাবে না।' Interview with Animesh, resident and farmer at Bindol (North Dinajpur district of West Bengal, 26 January 2012).

65 Interview with Hirak Kanti Munshi, resident of Balurghat (South Dinajpur district of West Bengal, 24 January 2012).

66 Cheruvari, S. (2006) Changing Lives in the Brick Kilns of West Bengal. *Report for UNICEF India.* Available from: www.unicef.org/india/child_protection_1736.htm. [Accessed: 27 July 2013].

67 Molla, H.R. (2011) Embankment of Lower Ajoy River and Its Impact on Brick-Kiln Indsutry in Central Bengal, India. *International Journal of Research in Social Sciences and Humanities.* 2(2). [Online] Available from: www.ijrssh.com/webmaster/upload/Oct_2012_Hasibur%20Rahaman%20Molla.pdf. [Accessed: 27 July 2013].

68 Cheruvari, 2006.

69 Interview with Md. Tafikul Islam, resident of Panitor border (North 24 Parganas district of West Bengal, 17 January 2012).

70 Interview with Riazul Mondol, resident of Balurghat (South Dinajpur district of West Bengal, 24 January 2012).

71 Biswas, G. and Sujauddin. (16 January 2013) Abhijoger shasti chhilo boro tikto. *Ananda Bazar Patrika.* [Online] Available from: www.anandabazar.com/16mur1.html. [Last accessed: 17 September 2013]; Biswas, G. and Mukhopadhyay, S. (17 January 2013) Policer najar kintu koda. *Ananda Bazar Patrika.* [Online] Available from: www.anandabazar.com/17mur2.html. [Last accessed: 17 September 2013].

72 Interview with Kalipada Ghosh, resident and human rights activist at Basirhat (North 24 Parganas district of West Bengal, 17 January 2012).

73 Ibid.

74 Interview with Gourab Sarkar, resident of Hili (South Dinajpur district of West Bengal, 25 January 2012).

75 Ibid.; The 'other factors' were part of the demand for territories during partition; the Muslim League had demanded the inclusion of Kolkata urban agglomeration in East Bengal, including the areas where the 'jute mills, military installations, ordnance factories, railway workshops and lines were located'. The demands were made on the grounds of East Bengal's 'economy, internal communication and defence'. Chatterji, J. (February 1999) The Fashioning of a Frontier: The Radcliffe Line and Bengal's Border Landscape, 1947–52. *Modern Asian Studies.* 33(1). pp. 198–199.

76 Roy, H. (2012). *Partitioned Lives: Migranst, Refugees, Citizens in India and Pakistan, 1947–1965.* New Delhi: Oxford University Press. p. 45.

77 'বর্ডার এলাকাতে মানুষের কিছু নেই. আছে বলতে চালকল শিল্প. এখন ভাঙ্গনের মুখে. আগে প্রচুর মানুষ করত. এখন ২ টো আছে. তাতে এখানকার সব মজুরদের রুটি রুজি হয় না. চালকল বন্ধ হয়ে যাওয়ার কারণ বর্ডার এর ফলে দু দিকের লাইসেন্স সংক্রান্ত রেস্ট্রিকশন. পাচার এর ভয় ও লাইসেন্স দেওয়া বন্ধ করে দিয়েছে বলে প্রচুর চালকল বন্ধ হয়ে গেছে. যে ২ টো চলছে. তাতে কিছু হয় না. প্রচুর লোক বাইরে যাচ্ছে।' Interview with Hirak Kanti Munshi, resident of Balurghat (South Dinajpur district of West Bengal, 24 January 2012).

78 Interview with Gourab Sarkar, resident of Hili (South Dinajpur district of West Bengal, 25 January 2012); The humiliation of being searched by Pakistani guards has

Livelihood practices 75

been cited as reason for the disappointment of those travelling between North and West Bengal via Pakistani territory after partition, besides the hazards of taking circuitous routes, and numerous changes and long waits. Chatterji, 1999, p. 230.

79 Staff Reporter. (12 February 2010) Via Bangladesh, Haldibari-Sealdah train chalu r dabi. _Ananda Bazar Patrika_. [Online] Available from: www.anandabazar.com/archive/1100212/12uttar3.htm. [Last accessed: 17 September 2013].

80 Interview with Gourab Sarkar, resident of Hili (South Dinajpur district of West Bengal, 25 January 2012).

81 Interview with Jumaira, resident of Hili border (Dinajpur district of Bangladesh, 9 October 2011).

82 'হিলি পোর্ট এ কুলি ছিল স্বামী. কুলি থাকা কালীন স্বামী হেরোইন আসক্ত হয়ে পড়ে. সংসারে খরচ দিত না. বছর ২ এক থেকে সে ধুর হিসেবে কাজ করে. বাচ্চা-সুরুজ (১২) আর ফুরুজ (১০)- এরাও যুক্ত।' (My husband was a _coolie_ at Hili port. During that time he became addicted to heroin. He stopped contributing money to the family. It's been two years that he has been working as a _dhoor_ here. My children Shuruj [12] and Furuj [10] are also involved in smuggling.) Interview with Rumela Begum, resident of Hili border area (Dinajpur district of Bangladesh, 8 October 2011).

83 Mirza, T. and Bacani, E. (2013) Addressing Hard and Soft Infrastructure Barriers to Trade in South Asia. _Asian Development Bank South Asia Working Paper Series_. No. 16. [Online] Available from: http://sasec.asia/web/images/sasec/pdf/Addressing_Infra_Barriers_to_Trade_in_SA.pdf. [Accessed: 29 July 2013].

84 Staff Reporter. (23 March 2013) Govt. to Set Up 4 New Land-Ports to Facilitate Cross-Border Trade. _The Financial Express_. [Online] Available from: www.thefinancial express-bd.com/index.php?ref=MjBfMDNfMjNfMTNfMV8yXzE2NDE0MA. [Last accessed: 29 July 2013].

85 Mirza and Bacani, 2013.

86 Interview with Jumaira, resident of Hili border (Dinajpur district of Bangladesh, 9 October 2011).

87 Mirza and Bacani, 2013.

88 Interview with Gourab Sarkar, resident of Hili (South Dinajpur district of West Bengal, 25 January 2012).

89 Interview with Subodh Majumdar, resident and employee at counter at Petrapole border area (North 24 Parganas district of West Bengal, 20 September 2011).

90 Ibid.

91 More like makeshift eating joints (like _Dhabas_ in India) serving basic meals of rice, _dal_, vegetable, fish/meat. The service is personal/casual in nature and lacks any of the formality or even the poshness of the restaurants that one comes across in big cities.

92 'এখানে বসত বাড়ি কম. রেস্টুরান্ট আর কাউন্টার বেশি. কত কোটি লোক আসে, তারা খাবে কোথায়? তাদের জন্যই বর্ডার-টা অত জমজমাট।' Interview with Apurba Kumar Biswas, resident of Petrapole border area (North 24 Parganas district of West Bengal, 20 September 2011).

93 Interview with Hasan-ul, resident of Burimari border area, Patgram (Lalmonirhat district of Bangladesh, 6 October 2011).

94 Interview with Rashid Hossein, resident of Lagola (Murshidabad district of West Bengal, 8 November 2011).

95 Staff Reporter. (25 March 2013) Daulatpurey tarunder proshikhshan BSFer. _Ananda Bazar Patrika_. [Online] Available from: www.anandabazar.com/25mur2.html. [Last accessed: 17 September 2013].

96 Jamwal, 2004, p. 8.

97 Interview with Abedin, fisherman at Kaikhali village, Shyamnagar (Satkhira district of Bangladesh, 14 February 2012).

98 'বি এস এফ মাছ ধরতে দেয় না সিকিউরিটি-র কারণে. আমাদের গরিব দেশ. মাছ ধরার ওপর জীবিকা নির্ভর করে।' (BSF often prohibits us from fishing in these rivers citing to security reasons. We are a poor country and depend heavily on fishing.) Ibid.

76 Livelihood practices

99 'এখানে বি এস এফ এর গুলি করার ভয় সবসময়. কেউ যদি মাছ ধরতে গিয়ে একটু ওদিকে চলে যায়, বি এস এফ ধরে নিয়ে গিয়ে মারে।' Interview with Jahangir, fisherman and resident of Kabilpur village, Chougachha (Jessore district of Bangladesh, 16 February 2012).

100 Composed by Nirmal Verma and Manohar Batham, *BSF*. [Online] Available from: http://bsf.nic.in/doc/archi/archi17.pdf.

101 Patel, R.P. (2000) Submission to WHOs Tobacco Free Initiative on FCTC Framework Convention on Tobacco Control. *All India Bidi Industry Federation*. Ahmedabad. [Online] Available from: www.who.int/tobacco/framework/public_hearings/F2000196.pdf. [Accessed: 29 July 2013].

102 Interview with Hirak Kanti Munshi, resident of Balurghat (South Dinajpur district of West Bengal, 24 January 2012).

103 Ibid.

104 Petrapole is at a distance of about 80 kilometres from Kolkata.

105 'এখানে টেলারিং এর কাজ খুব চলে. এখানে বেশ কিছু ছেলে আছে যারা হয়ত এক সময় কলকাতা-এ টেলারিং করত. কাজ শিখে এখন এখানে এসে টেলারিং-এর দোকান খুলেছে. এটা এখানে খুব ইউসুয়াল একটা পেশা. তারা কারখানা খোলে. মাল গুলো কলকাতা যায়. ওখানে কোনো একজন ধরা মালিক এর থেকে মাল এনে এখানে সেলাই করে আবার নিয়ে যাই।' (Tailoring is a very commonly practiced livelihood here. Many of the tailors have had their training in Kolkata and now own tailoring shops here. It is a very useful profession here. Kolkata serves as both our source for raw materials as well as markets for our products.) Interview with Bilal, resident of Basirhat (North 24 Parganas district of West Bengal, 17 January 2012).

106 Interview with Nikhil, resident of Mathurapur village (South Dinajpur district of West Bengal, 24 January 2012).

107 Interview with Julekha, resident of Raibhat village, Bowladar (Dinajpur district of Bangladesh, 9 October 2011).

108 Interview with Nikhil, resident of Mathurapur village (South Dinajpur district of West Bengal, 24 January 2012).

109 Chatterji, 1999, p. 234.

110 *Hindustan Standard*, 11 July 1947, p. 4, quoted in Roy, 2012, p. 42.

111 Roy, 2012, p. 68.

112 Staff Reporter. (26 February 2017). Malda town-e bag-bhorti kochhop udhhar, dhrito teen. *Ananda Bazar Patrika*. [Online] Available from: www.anandabazar.com/district/uttarbanga/a-full-bag-with-tortoise-has-been-recovered-from-maldah-3-arrested-1.570388. [Last accessed: 7 July 2017].

113 Staff Reporter. (27 September 2012) *Ananda Bazar Patrika*. [Online] Available from: www.anandabazar.com/archive/1120927/jibjagat.html. [Last accessed: 3 August 2013]. Monitor Lizards (Latin name: Varamus Monitor) are often used for vaccine industries for experimentation. They are also consumed in parts of southern India and Malaysia.

114 Staff Reporter. (2 February 2010) 10 ti kankaal uddhar simante. *Ananda Bazar Patrika*. [Online] Available from: www.anandabazar.com/archive/1100202/2mur5.htm. [Last accessed: 17 September 2013]; Sujauddin and Biswas, G. (5 March 2010) Simante kankaal pachare lagano hochhe kisore der. *Ananda Bazar Patrika*. [Online] Available from: www.anandabazar.com/archive/1100305/5mur1.htm. [Last accessed: 17 September 2013].

115 The total number of contraband items seized by the North Bengal Frontier of BSF while being smuggled across the border amounted to 2,80,06,460 (2009), 3,75,91,925 (2010), 4,24,28,407 (2011) and 38,31,393 (January-March 2012), out of which 98% of the seizures (including cattleheads) were of outgoing items, i.e. smuggled from West Bengal to Bangladesh. *Uttar Vang Prahari Samachar Patrika*. (December 2012). 4(14); in 2013, seizures by the North Bengal Frontier included 3,09,401 Bangladesh Taka, FICN 51,000, 60,562 bottles of cough syrup, Rs. 2,08,92,989 worth contraband products, 2330 Kg. Ganja (till July 2013), 700 gm. bullion in gold. *Uttar Vang Prahari Samachar Patrika*. (July–December 2013); in 2014, seizures by North Bengal Frontier included 27 lakh Bangladesh Taka, 44,000 FICN, 75 gm. heroin, 35

Livelihood practices 77

gm. brown sugar, 28,378 bottles of cough syrup, 3021 cattle. *Uttar Vang Prahari Samachar Patrika*. (June 2014); Between January and March 2016, South Bengal Frontier seized 15, 04,109 Bangladesh Taka, US $1700, 5 UAE Currency, Euro 162, 3.5 Kg. opium, Rs.7, 31,500 worth silver bullion. *Bagher Garjan*. (January 2016); Between July and December 2016, South Bengal Frontier seized 24,233 cattle, Rs. 28,05,184 worth contraband items, 652 Bangladesh Taka. *Bagher Garjan*. (July–December 2016).

116 Sur, M. (2012). Bamboo Baskets and Barricades: Gendered Landscapes at the India-Bangladesh Border. In Kalir, B. and Sur, M. (Eds.). *Transnational Flows and Permissive Polities: Ethnographies of Human Mobilities in Asia*. Amsterdam: Amsterdam University Press. p. 141.

117 Interview with Gourab Sarkar, resident of Hili (South Dinajpur district of West Bengal, 25 January 2012).

118 Das, P. (2012) *Drug Trafficking in India: A Case for Border Security*. IDSA Occasional Paper, No. 24. New Delhi: Institute for Defence Studies and Analysis. pp. 33–34; Changrabandha, Panisala, B S Bari, Oran and Arjun – all located along the Saniajan and Teesta rivers, are some of the more sensitive BOPs of the North Bengal Frontier of BSF in terms of cross-border smuggling. *Uttar Vang Prahari Samachar Patrika*. (March 2012). 4(11).

119 Phensidyl is a cough linctus, a liquid preparation like syrup which contains glucose in high concentration for better taste. One of its main ingredients includes codeine phosphate – mostly used as a painkiller and cough suppressant. Phensidyl is often used as a recreational narcotic and/or antidepressant, due to the higher proportion of codeine phosphate in it, as compared to other cough syrups. This is why many people in India, Nepal and Bangladesh are addicted to it. The syrup is illegal in Bangladesh but not in India, as a result of which Phensidyl is smuggled from India to Bangladesh. Myanmar is the only other place besides India where Phensidyl is produced.

120 Interview with Ujjal Ghosh, resident of Petrapole border area (North 24 Parganas district of West Bengal, 20 September 2011).

121 Das, 2012, p. 30.

122 Ibid.

123 Jain, S.K. (2006) The Spurious Drug Menace and Remedy. *Health Administrator*. 19(1). p. 33, as quoted in Das, 2012, pp. 30–31.

124 Interview with a BGB official at Goga BGB camp, Agro-Bhulot (Jessore district of Bangladesh, 15 February 2012).

125 Interview with Bijon, a journalist with a Bengali daily at Jessore town (Jessore district of Bangladesh, 16 February 2012).

126 Information given by a pharmacist in a pharmaceutical shop in Kolkata, October 2012.

127 In 2009, BGB seized 58,875 bottles of Phensidyl. Annual Report 2010, the International Narcotics Control Board, No. 27, p. 90, quoted in Das, 2012, p. 31; In the same year, BSF seized 4,18,788 bottles along the India-Bangladesh border. Annual Report 2009, Narcotics Control Bureau, No. 12, p.30, quoted in Das, 2012, p. 31; In 2011 Phensidyl bottles worth over Rs.10,00000 has been seized by the BSF. Kashyap, S.G. (5 December 2011) Smuggling Thrives as Fencing of Indo-Bangla Border Delayed. *The Indian Express*. [Online] Available from: www.indianexpress.com/news/smuggling-thrives-as-fencing-of-indobangla-border-delayed/884123/0. [Last accessed: 30 July 2013]; Between July and December 2012, 2,831 Phensidyl bottles have been seized by the North Bengal Frontier of BSF. *Uttar Vang Prahari Samachar Patrika*. (December 2012). 4(14). Between January and March 2013, 15,326 bottles of Phensidyl have been seized by the North Bengal Frontier of BSF. *Uttar Vang PrahariSamachar Patrika*. (March 2013). 5(15).

128 'Golden Crescent' is the name given to one of Asia's two principal areas of illicit opium production (the other being the 'Golden Triangle'), located at the crossroads of Central, South and Western Asia. This space overlaps three nations – Afghanistan, Iran, and

78 *Livelihood practices*

Pakistan, whose mountainous peripheries define the crescent, though only Afghanistan and Pakistan produce opium, with Iran being a consumer and trans-shipment route for the smuggled opiates. In 1991, Afghanistan became the world's primary opium producer. It now produces over 90% of the world's non-pharmaceutical-grade opium, besides being the world's largest producer of hashish.

129 Das, 2012, p. 32.
130 Ibid. p. 33.
131 Ibid. pp. 33–34.
132 Interview with a BSF official at Ramnagar BSF camp (Murshidabad district of West Bengal, 9 November 2011).
133 Interview with Bijon, a journalist with a Bengali daily in Dinajpur town (Dinajpur district of Bangladesh, 5 October 2011).
134 Biswas, G. and Sujauddin. (7 January 2013) Sheeter shimantey barchhe pachar. *Ananda Bazar Patrika*. [Online] Available from: www.anandabazar.com/archive/1130107/7mur1.html. [Last accessed: 30 July 2013].
135 Basu, A. (12 May 2017). Dinajpur shimantey chora patal pother hodish kintu chinta baralo. *Ananda Bazar Patrika*. [Online] Available from: www.anandabazar.com/bangladesh-news/high-alert-along-the-dinajpur-international-border-after-bsf-found-a-tunnel-dgtl-1.611603?ref=bangladesh-news-new-stry. [Last accessed: 7 July 2017].
136 Staff Reporter. (16 July 2017). Goti komiye Toto-tei cholchhe obadh pachar. *Ananda Bazar Patrika*. [Online] Available from: www.anandabazar.com/district/nodia-murshidabbad/smugglers-are-using-toto-for-smuggling-goods-1.643042?ref=nodia-murshidabbad-new-stry. [Last accessed: 17 July 2017].
137 Sujauddin. (4 June 2017). Aam jhuritey neshar oshudh. *Ananda Bazar Patrika*. [Online] Available from: www.anandabazar.com/district/nodia-murshidabbad/sleeping-pills-are-getting-exported-in-boxes-which-were-used-to-export-mangoes-1.622957?ref=nodia-murshidabbad-new-stry. [Last accessed: 7 July 2017].
138 Staff Reporter. (16 July 2017). Ambulance-e 100 kg. ganja. *Ananda Bazar Patrika*. [Online] Available from: www.anandabazar.com/calcutta/100-kg-cannabis-found-in-an-ambulance-1.643089?ref=hm-new-stry. [Last accessed: 17 July 2017].
139 Acetic Anhydride is used for the synthesis of heroin by the diacetylation of morphine.
140 In a recent raid in a Sealdah-bound train in West Bengal, police and customs officials found 350 kilograms of Asetic Anhydride, which, if used for heroin, can produce about 150 kilograms of the same – the price for which would be around Rs. 50, 00,000 in the Indian market. Ghosh, S. (13 October 2012). Train bahonei kanchamal eney romroma heroin-er. *Ananda Bazar Patrika*. [Online] Available from: www.anandabazar.com/archive/1121013/13raj5.html. [Last accessed: 30 July 2013].
141 Hashish, often known as 'hash', is a cannabis product and is sold either in a solid or a paste-like form. Traditionally, it has been used as a medicine and recreational drug, though currently it is illegal to consume it nearly everywhere in the world. In northern India, hashish is locally known as *charas*. Special varieties of cannabis are particularly cultivated for the production of *ganja* (marijuana) and hashish in West Bengal, Rajasthan and the Himalayas in India.
142 Ghosh, N. (3 January 2013) Capsuler ondorey chupisharey pachar hochhe hashish. *Anandabazar Bazar Patrika*. [Online] Available from: www.anandabazar.com/archive/1130103/3desh6.html. [Last accessed: 30 July 2013].
143 Between October and December 2012, 62.85 kilograms of *ganja* were seized by the South Bengal Frontier of BSF. *Bagher Garjan* (October–December 2012). 26.
144 De Sarkar, S. (26 February 2017). Fona tulchhe bisher nesha, jogan dichhe shimanto par. *Ananda Bazar Patrika*. [Online] Available from: www.anandabazar.com/calcutta/craze-for-snake-poison-intoxication-is-increasing-for-rave-parties-1.570292. [Last accessed: 7 July 2017].
145 Interview with Narendranath Ghosh, resident of Karimpur (Nadia district of West Bengal, 24 October 2011).

Livelihood practices 79

146 Interview with Kalipada Ghosh, resident of Panitor village, Basirhat (North 24 Parganas district of West Bengal, 17 January 2012).
147 Interview with Parbati Mohanto, resident of Ghunapara-Dhumron village (South Dinajpur district of West Bengal, 25 January 2012).
148 Ibid.
149 As witnessed on my visit to the Bangladesh side of Hili border, around the Hili Land Port on 8 October 2011.
150 Interview with Md. Zia-ul Haq, resident and lecturer in college at Dinajpur town (Dinajpur district of Bangladesh, 8 October 2011).
151 Interview with Parbati Mohanto, resident of Ghunapara-Dhumron village (South Dinajpur district of West Bengal, 25 January 2012).
152 Interview with Md. Zia-ul Haq, resident and lecturer in college at Dinajpur town (Dinajpur district of Bangladesh, 8 October 2011).
153 Ibid.
154 Interview with Gourab Sarkar, resident and trader at Hili border area (South Dinajpur district of West Bengal, 25 January 2012).
155 Interview with Kuddus Rahman, resident of Jaykrishnapur village, Jalangi (Murshidabad district of West Bengal, 22 October 2011).
156 *Bagher Garjan* (October–December 2012). 26.
157 'The main reason behind their involvement is making fast money, besides, obviously, the addiction itself. A whole day's labour earns them Rs.150 whereas a couple of (smuggling) trips earn them Rs.300. Half the people have, thus, moved to other places for work. The remaining earn through smuggling'. Interview with a BSF official at Shikarpur BSF camp (Nadia district of West Bengal, 21 October 2011).
158 As noted in a conversation with the convict and the BGB officials by me at the Bamdebpur BGB Camp at Hili (Dinajpur district of Bangladesh, 9 October 2011).
159 Interview with Rashid Hossein, resident of Lalgola (Murshidabad district of West Bengal, 8 November 2011).
160 Interview with Bibek, resident of Debhata village (Satkhira district of Bangladesh, 12 February 2012).
161 West Bengal shares a riverine border with Bangladesh along the Ichamati and Kalindi rivers. The Mathabhanga River originates from the right bank of the Padma, at Munshiganj in the Kushtia district of Bangladesh. It bifurcates near Majidia in Nadia district in West Bengal (India), creating two rivers, Ichamati and Churni. After traversing a length of 19.5 kilometres in India, the Ichamati enters Bangladesh near Mubarakpur. It flows for 35.5 kilometres in Bangladesh and again enters India at Duttaphulia in Nadia district. It forms the international border between India and Bangladesh for 21 kilometres from Angrail to Kalanchi, and again from Goalpara to the Kalindi-Raimangal outfall into the Bay of Bengal. The Ichamati breaks up into several distributaries below Hingalganj in North 24 Parganas, of which Kalindi is a major one, besides Raimangal, Bidya, Jhilla and Jamuna. The Kalindi River forms the riverine border between the North 24 Parganas district in West Bengal and the Satkhira district in Bangladesh.
162 Interview with a BGB official at New Sripur BGB camp (Satkhira district of Bangladesh, 12 February 2012).
163 *Uttar Vang Prahari Samachar Patrika.* (March 2012). 4(11).
164 *Uttar Vang Prahari Samachar Patrika.* (March 2013). 5(15).
165 *Uttar Vang Prahari Samachar Patrika.* (December 2012). 4(14).
166 "মানুষ পারাপার হয় রাতে, কালিন্দী নদীর ওপর দিয়ে. এখানে বি এস এফ গুলি করে না." Interview with Hari, resident and *dhoor* in Kaikhali village, Shyamnagar (Satkhira district of Bangladesh, 14 February 2012).
167 Momin, S.M. (7 September 2003) Illegal Border Crossing-Benapole Style. *The Independent.*
168 Staff Reporter. (26 May 2017). Petrapole-e dhrito Bangladeshi mohila. *Ananda Bazar Patrika.* [Online] Available from: www.anandabazar.com/district/dhaksinbanga/

80 *Livelihood practices*

north-south-24-paraganas/bangladeshi-woman-arrested-1.618443?ref=north-south-24-paraganas-new-stry. [Last accessed: 13 July 2017].

169 Staff Reporter. (17 June 2017). Bhuo parichaypotro tairir nalish, greftar teen. *Ananda Bazar Patrika.* [Online] Available from: www.anandabazar.com/district/dhaksinbanga/north-south-24-paraganas/complaint-of-making-fake-identity-cards-1.629560?ref=north-south-24-paraganas-new-stry. [Last accessed: 18 July 2017].

170 Basu, A. (25 June 2017). Bangladeshider thokanor jaal chakra Gaighata-e. *Ananda Bazar Patrika.* [Online] Available from: www.anandabazar.com/bangladesh-news/fraud-racket-targeting-bangladeshis-foiled-in-north-24-parganas-bng-dgtl-1.633659?ref=bangladesh-news-ft-stry. [Last accessed: 18 July 2017].

171 'রাতে কিছু গরু আসে, গরুর পিঠে বসে বা লেজ ধরে সাতরে লোক-ও চলে আসে।' (The cattle are smuggled at night. People sit on those cattle or hold on to their tails and cross the river.) Interview with Niru, resident of Durmukhhali village, Shyamnagar (Satkhira district of Bangladesh, 14 February 2012).

172 Interview with Biplab Ganguly (original name), Officer-in-Charge of Murutia Police Station (Nadia district of West Bengal, 22 October 2011).

173 Interview with a BSF official at Asharidoho BSF camp, (Murshidabad district of West Bengal, 9 November 2011).

174 Staff Reporter. (2 November 2001) Border-Cross for Influx Insight. *The Telegraph.* [Online] Available from: www.telegraphindia.com/archives/archive.html. [Last accessed: 30 August 2013].

175 Ibid.

176 Bhattacharjee, J. (July 2013) India-Bangladesh Border Management: The Challenge of Cattle Smuggling. *Special Report, Observer Research Foundation.* (1). p. 3.

177 Staff Reporter. (22 June 2017). Goru pacharer nalish BJP-r. *Ananda Bazar Patrika.* [Online] Available from: www.anandabazar.com/district/uttarbanga/bjp-wrote-a-letter-to-home-ministry-alleging-that-bsf-and-police-are-engaged-in-cow-smuggling-1.632041?ref=uttarbanga-new-stry. [Last accessed: 11 July 2017].

178 Transport of Animals Rules 1978. Available from: http://pashudhanharyana.gov.in/html/pdf%20&%20downloads/AH%20Acts/15_The%20Transport%20of%20animals%20rules,%201978.pdf. [Accessed: 31 July 2013].

179 Bhattacharjee, 2013, p. 3.

180 Ibid.

181 Tiwary, D. (1 December 2012) Legalise Cattle Smuggling on Bangladesh Border: BSF Chief. *The Times of India.* [Online] Available from: http://articles.timesofindia.indiatimes.com/2012-12-01/india/35530471_1_bsf-men-bangladesh-border-indo-bangla-border. [Last accessed: 31 July 2013].

182 In 2010, 1,01,381 were seized and 287 persons arrested for smuggling; in 2011, the numbers were 1,35,291 and 411 respectively; in 2012, the numbers were 1,20,724 and 395 respectively; between January and February 2013, the numbers were 22,627 and 55, respectively. Ministry of Home Affairs, March 2013; between July and December 2012, 3624 cattles have been seized by the North Bengal Frontier of BSF. *Uttar Vang Prahari Samachar Patrika.* (December 2012). 4(14); Beween October 2012 and March 2013, 4048 cattles have been seized by the North Bengal Frontier of BSF. *Uttar Vang Prahari Samachar Patrika.* (March 2013). 5(15).

183 *Eid al-Bakr* is one of the two *Eid* celebrations of Muslims wordwide, the other being *Eid al-Fitr.* Sacrifice of cattle is integral to the rituals of *Eid al-Bakr* or *Bakrid* and, thus, increases the demand for cattle in Bangladesh, given that it is a Muslim-majority state.

184 *Durga Puja* is the largest religious festival of the Bengali Hindus of West Bengal.

185 In 2011, *Eid al-Bakr* was on the 5th and 6th of November, while *Durga Puja* was between 3rd and 6th of October. In 2012, *Eid al-Bakr* was on the 25th and 26th of October, while *Durga Puja* was between 21st and 24th October. In 2017 again, *Eid al-Bakr* was on 2 September while Durga Puja was on 27 September.

Livelihood practices 81

186 *Uttar Vang Prahari Samachar Patrika.* (March 2012). 4(11).
187 Burman, P. (12 April 2012) Battle of Cattle at Indo-Bangla Border. *Headlines India.* [Online] Available from: http://headlinesindia.mapsofindia.com/special-reports/battle-of-cattle-at-indo-bangla-border.html. [Last accessed: 31 July 2013].
188 Bhattacharjee, 2013, p. 3.
189 Interview with Alamgir, resident and cattle trader in Putkhali village, Sharsha (Jessore district of Bangladesh, 15 February 2012).
190 Chowdhury, S.T. (7 February 2012) A Border Too Far for Bangladesh. *Asia Times Online.* [Online] Available from: www.atimes.com/atimes/South_Asia/NB07Df01. html. [Last accessed: 31 July 2013].
191 Bhattacharjee, 2013, p. 3.
192 Interview with Md. Ismail, resident and cattle trader in Matila village, Maheshpur (Jhenaidah district of Bangladesh, 11 February 2012).
193 Bhattacharjee, 2013, p. 5.
194 Basu, N. and Maitra, S. (31 May 2017). Goru pachar niye nojordarir barta. *Ananda Bazar Patrika.* [Online] Available from: www.anandabazar.com/state/this-is-my-first-and-last-warning-not-a-single-cow-trafficking-will-be-done-cm-1.621083?ref=hm-new-stry. [Last accessed: 11 July 2017].
195 Bhattacharjee, 2013, p. 6.
196 Ibid.
197 The New Horizon. (29 January 2012) *The Endless Blood.* [Online] Available from: http://horizonspeaks.wordpress.com/2012/01/29/the-endless-blood/. [Accessed: 31 July 2013]; *Uttar Vang Prahari Samachar Patrika.* (March 2012). 4(11).
198 'বাংলাদেশের জন্য উপকার বলেই গরু টা বাঁধা দিছি না ।' (We do not prevent the cattle trade because it helps Bangladesh's economy.) Interview with a BGB official at Goga BGB camp, Sharsha (Jessore district of Bangladesh, 15 February 2012).
199 Interview with Asif, resident and cattle trader at Kaikhali village, Shyamnagar (Satkhira district of Bangladesh, 14 February 2012).
200 'আগে বাংলাদেশীদের ওদিকে ঢুকে নিয়ে আসতে হত. এখন বি এস এফ এর সহযোগিতায়ে ইন্ডিয়ান রাই দিয়ে যায়. বি এস এফ এমনিতে কিছু বলে না. মাঝে মাঝে এক আধজন কে ধরে দেখানোর জন্য যে তারা কাজ করছে ।' Interview with Md. Ismail, resident and cattle trader in Matila village, Maheshpur (Jhenaidah district of Bangladesh, 11 February 2012).
201 Interview with Alamgir, resident and cattle trader at Putkhali village, Sharsha (Jessore district of Bangladesh, 15 February 2012).
202 Ibid.
203 Ibid.
204 Interview with Md. Ismail, resident and trader at Matila village, Maheshpur (Jhenaidah district of Bangladesh, 11 February 2012).
205 I visited the Putkhali *haat*, Sharsha (Jessore district of Bangladesh) on 15 February 2012 as part of my field visit in Bangladesh.
206 Bhattacharjee, 2013, p. 4.
207 'যারা গরু পাচার করে, তারা সাধারণত অন্য কিছু পাচার করে না. তাদের বক্তব্য যে তাদের বি জি বি-র সাথে ভালো সম্পর্ক. বাজে জিনিস পাচার করে এই সম্ভাব টা নষ্ট করবে কেন? গরু পাচার এদের কাছে অপরাধ নয়. ফেন্সি পাচার কিন্তু ভীষণ অপরাধ. ওটা ইম্মরাল. গরু পাচার টা বৈধ পাচার এর মধ্যেই পড়ে ।' Interview with Asif, resident and cattle trader at Kaikhali village, Shyamnagar (Satkhira district of Bangladesh, 14 February 2012).
208 Interview with Tofazzal, resident and trader at Agro-Bhulot village, Sharsha (Jessore district of Bangladesh, 15 February 2012); Witnessed during my field visit to the cattle *haat* at Kaikhali village, Shyamnagar (Satkhira district of Bangladesh, 14 February 2012).
209 'ফেন্সি আসে, অস্ত্র আসে. গরুর সাথে এলে আলাদা করে চেকিং হয় না.' (Phensidyl and firearms are smuggled in. If they are smuggled with cattle, then they are spared the checking.) Interview with a BGB official at Goga BGB camp, Sharsha (Jessore district of Bangladesh, 15 February 2012).
210 As witnessed during my field visit to Matila village, Maheshpur (Jhenaidah district of Bangladesh, 11 February 2012).

82   *Livelihood practices*

211   Interview with Alamgir, resident and trader at Putkhali village, Sharsha (Jessore district of Bangladesh, 15 February 2012).
212   Ibid.
213   The *lungi* is a traditional garment worn around the waist in Indonesia, Bangladesh, India, Sri Lanka, Burma, Brunei, Malaysia, Singapore, the Horn of Africa and the southern Arabian Peninsula. It is particularly popular in regions where the heat and humidity create an unpleasant climate for trousers. In Bangladesh, it is the most commonlyworn dress of men, though not normally worn on formal occasions. In India, it is also a common form of dress in certain states, though the custom and practice of wearing *lungis* in India varies from state to state.
214   Interview with Alamgir, resident and trader at Putkhali village, Sharsha (Jessore district of Bangladesh, 15 February 2012).
215   Ibid.
216   Ibid.
217   Interview with Javed, resident and trader at Khanjiya village, Debhata (Satkhira district of Bangladesh, 12 February 2012).
218   Interview with Rashid Hossein, resident of Lalgola (Murshidabad district of West Bengal, 8 November 2011).
219   Interview with a BGB official at Hakimpur BGB camp (Dinajpur district of Bangladesh, 9 October 2011).
220   In an effort to reduce violence along its borders, the government of India decided to arm the BSF with non-lethal weapons in 2009, following requests from BGB chiefs to prevent killings of Bangladeshis by the BSF on the India-Bangladesh border. The BSF, under this regulation, is to use pump-action guns with rubber bullets in the first-fire and challenge-fire rounds. Firing from regular guns would be the last resort. PTI. (22 May 2011) BSF to Use 'Non-Lethal' Weapons Along Indo-Bangla Border. *Zeenews.com*. [Online] Available from: http://zeenews.india.com/news/delhi/bsf-to-use-non-lethal-weapons-along-indo-bangla-border_707946.html. [Last accessed: 24 July 2013].
221   Interview with a BSF official at Shikarpur BSF camp (Nadia district of West Bengal, 21 October 2011).
222   Tiwary, D. (1 December 2012) Legalise Cattle Smuggling on Bangladesh Border: BSF Chief. *The Times of India*. [Online] Available from: http://articles.timesofindia. indiatimes.com/2012-12-01/india/35530471_1_bsf-men-bangladesh-border-indo-bangla-border. [Last accessed: 31 July 2013].
223   Chowdhury, K. (16 February 2017). Goru pachar niye gulir lorai shimante. *Ananda Bazar Patrika*. [Online] Available from: www.anandabazar.com/district/uttarbanga/ fight-with-guns-in-border-for-cow-trafficking-1.565158#. [Last accessed: 11 July 2017].
224   Staff Reporter. (31 January 2017). Guli-kande obhijuktoder khonj shuru BSF-er. *Ananda Bazar Patrika*. [Online] Available from: www.anandabazar.com/district/ uttarbanga/bsf-starts-searching-five-suspects-1.556695#. [Last accessed: 11 July 2017].
225   Interview with Gourab Sarkar, resident of Hili (South Dinajpur district of West Bengal, 25 January 2012).
226   Tiwary, 1 December 2012, *The Times of India*.
227   Ghatak, S. (10 July 2017). Pachar komtei nishanaye police. *Ananda Bazar Patrika*. [Online] Available from: www.anandabazar.com/state/attack-on-police-started-when-police-stopped-trafficking-1.640321?ref=state-new-stry. [Last accessed: 11 July 2017].
228   Maitro, S. (7 February 2017). Goru pacharer notun fikir shobjir jhuri. *Ananda Bazar Patrika*. [Online] Available from: www.anandabazar.com/district/dhaksinbanga/north-south-24-paraganas/cow-trafficking-continues-in-district-1.560195#. [Last accessed: 11 July 2017].
229   Staff Reporter. (24 March 2017). Shimante dhora porlo ghora. *Ananda Bazar Patrika*. [Online] Available from: www.anandabazar.com/district/dhaksinbanga/north-south-

Livelihood practices 83

24-paraganas/horse-been-captured-from-border-1.585351?ref=north-south-24-paraganas-new-stry. [Last accessed: 11 July 2017].
230 Staff Reporter. (13 May 2017). Goru pachar bondhe ekkatta gayer bodhura. *Ananda Bazar Patrika*. [Online] Available from: www.anandabazar.com/district/dhaksinbanga/north-south-24-paraganas/housewives-of-bongaon-united-against-cow-trafficking-1.611838?ref=north-south-24-paraganas-new-stry. [Last accessed: 11 July 2017].
231 Ten airguns were seized at the Gobrabil Chowki on 9 October 2012 by the ACP Party of the 26 Battalion of the South Bengal Frontier of BSF. On 27 October of the same year, one 'desi' revolver and two rounds of 315 bore were seized by the 40 battalion of the South Bengal Frontier of BSF at Petrapole. *Bagher Garjan*. (October–December 2012). 26.
232 Interview with a BGB official at Benapole BGB camp (Jessore district of Bangladesh, 15 February 2012).
233 Staff Reporter. (30 May 2012) Agneyastro shoho dhrito. *Ananda Bazar Patrika*. [Online] Available from: www.anandabazar.com/archive/1120530/30uttar6.html. [Last accessed: 31 July 2013].
234 Staff Reporter. (11 September 2013) CPM-er shabhapati khuney tapta Hasnabad. *Ananda Bazar Patrika*. [Online] Available from: www.anandabazar.com/11pgn2.html. [Last accessed: 11 September 2013].
235 Staff Reporter. (19 February 2012) Cadres Buying Smuggled Small Arms: Intel Report. *The Financial Express*. [Online] Available from: www.thefinancialexpress-bd.com/more.php?news_id=120706&date=2012-02-19. [Last accessed: 31 July 2013].
236 Ghatak, S. (8 June 2017). Rajyo jure oboidho astra karkhana, jachhe opareo. *Ananda Bazar Patrika*. [Online] Available from: www.anandabazar.com/state/illegal-arms-factory-across-the-state-1.625033?ref=hm-new-stry. [Last accessed: 9 July 2017].
237 Staff Reporter, 19 February 2012, *The Financial Express*.
238 Pakistan Defence. (2012) *Arms Smuggling, Trading Trouble*. [Online] Available from: www.defence.pk/forums/bangladesh-defence/90052-arms-smuggling-trading-double.html. [Accessed: 31 July 2013].
239 Staff Reporter, 19 February 2012, *The Financial Express*.
240 Nandi Majumdar, A. (26 August 2009) Bangladesh Route for Arms Smuggling. *India Today* [Online] Available from: http://indiatoday.intoday.in/story/Bangladesh+route+for+arms+smuggling/1/58592.html. [Last accessed: 12 September 2013].
241 Mishra, M. (3 October 2008) Llegal Cattle Trade Funding Terror. *The Times of India*. [Online] Available from: http://articles.timesofindia.indiatimes.com/2008-10-03/india/27943404_1_terror-funding-cattle-trade-india-bangladesh-border. [Last accessed: 31 July 2013]; Mohan, V. (11 April 2013) National Investigation Agency Files Charge-Sheet against Three for Raising Terror Fund. *The Times of India*. [Online] Available from: http://articles.timesofindia.indiatimes.com/2013-04-11/delhi/38462199_1_high-quality-ficn-fake-indian-currency-notes-malda. [Last accessed: 31 July 2013].
242 Staff Reporter, 19 February 2012, *The Financial Express*.
243 Ibid.
244 Bhattacharjee, 2013, p. 4.
245 Staff Reporter. (1 October 2012) Goru pacharer haat dhore jaal noter amdani eparey. *Ananda Bazar Patrika*. [Online] Available from: www.anandabazar.com/archive/1121001/1bdesh1.html. [Last accessed: 31 July 2013]; FICN worth Rs. 1, 00000 have been seized from Mohangunj on 26 October 2012 by the 130 battalion of the South Bengal Frontier of BSF. *Bagher Garjan*. (October–December 2012). 26; FICN worth Rs.9, 00,000 have been seized by the BSF on the Malda border on 24 August 2013. Tiwary, D. (25 August 2013) FICN Seized. *The Times of India*. [Online] Available from: http://timesofindia.indiatimes.com/FICN-seized/speednewsbytopic/keyid-881955. cms. [Last accessed: 7 September 2013]; FICN worth Rs.10, 00000 have been seized by the 125 battalion of BSF in Malda on 3 September 2013. IBNS (4 September 2013) Fake Indian Currency Notes worth Rs 10 lakhs seized by BSF. *News Wala*. [Online]

84 *Livelihood practices*

Available from: www.newswala.com/India-National-News/Fake-Indian-Currency-Notes-worth-Rs-10-lakhs-seized-by-BSF-45911.html. [Last accessed: 7 September 2013].

246 Staff Reporter, 1 October 2012, *Ananda Bazar Patrika*.

247 Ibid.

248 Ghosh, S. and Monata, A.R. (26 January 2010) Jaal note jangi jog astra byabsha, jaal e Hili r school sikshak. *Ananda Bazar Patrika*. [Online] Available from: www.anandabazar.com/archive/1100126/26raj1.htm. [Last accessed: 17 September 2013].

249 Shujauddin. (9 February 2017). Gondhei dhora pore gelo jaal hajari note. *Ananda Bazar Patrika*. [Online] Available from: www.anandabazar.com/district/nodia-murshidabbad/fake-2000-rupee-note-identifed-by-smell-1.561375. [Last accessed: 11 July 2017].

250 Hajra, B. (10 February 2017). Char jomine note-er chash.*Ananda Bazar Patrika*. [Online] Available from: www.anandabazar.com/district/nodia-murshidabbad/counterfeit-industry-has-ballooned-in-murshidabad-1.561848#. [Last accessed: 11 July 2017].

251 Biswas, S. (11 February 2017). Ebar notun takao jaal Bangladesh-e. *Ananda Bazar Patrika*. [Online] Available from: www.anandabazar.com/national/now-india-s-fake-currency-has-been-traced-from-bangladesh-1.562562. [Last accessed: 11 July 2017].

252 Biswas, S. (17 February 2017). Bangladesh-e jaal note chhpachhe ISI. *Ananda Bazar Patrika*. [Online] Available from: www.anandabazar.com/national/isi-making-indian-fake-notes-in-bangladesh-1.565759#. [Last accessed: 11 July 2017].

253 Biswas, S. (8 May 2017). Jakher dhan noy, pataley thore thore shajano note. *Ananda Bazar Patrika*. [Online] Available from: www.anandabazar.com/bangladesh-news/nia-visits-bangladesh-to-investigate-fake-currency-rackets-1.609495?ref=hm-ft-stry. [Last accessed: 11 July 2017].

254 Saha, A. (21 February 2017). Jaal note-e najehal jela. *Ananda Bazar Patrika*. [Online] Available from: www.anandabazar.com/district/uttarbanga/one-by-one-fake-currencies-are-found-in-malda-district-1.567789. [Last accessed: 11 July 2017].

255 Staff Reporter. (1 March 2017). Fer jaal note udhhar, atonko byabshayi moholey.*Ananda Bazar Patrika*. [Online] Available from: www.anandabazar.com/district/uttarbanga/again-fake-notes-been-rescued-panic-in-business-people-1.571884?ref=uttarbanga-new-stry#. [Last accessed: 11 July 2017]; Staff Reporter. (3 March 2017). Jaal note rukhte udyogi police. *Ananda Bazar Patrika*. [Online] Available from: www.anandabazar.com/district/uttarbanga/stringent-measures-taken-by-police-to-stop-fake-currency-1.573103?ref=uttarbanga-new-stry#. [Last accessed: 11 July 2017].

256 Staff Reporter. (6 March 2017). Khalashi sheje pacharer cheshtaye dhrito Bhutto. *Ananda Bazar Patrika*. [Online] Available from: www.anandabazar.com/district/uttarbanga/smuggler-arrested-in-malda-in-fake-currency-business-1.574830?ref=uttarbanga-new-stry. [Last accessed: 11 July 2017].

257 Staff Reporter. (1 June 2017). Passport dekhiye eshei jaal note pachar. *Ananda Bazar Patrika*. [Online] Available from: www.anandabazar.com/district/uttarbanga/1-arrested-in-connection-of-fake-notes-trafficking-1.621486?ref=uttarbanga-new-stry. [Last accessed: 11 July 2017].

258 Biswas, S. (19 March 2017). Chakra banchiye rakhtei nimno maner jaal note. *Ananda Bazar Patrika*. [Online] Available from: www.anandabazar.com/state/low-quality-fake-notes-are-getting-printed-only-to-carry-on-the-fake-currency-smuggling-1.582307?ref=hm-new-stry. [Last accessed: 11 July 2017].

259 Biswas, S. (29 May 2017). Jaal note-e jhokki chargesheet peshei. *Ananda Bazar Patrika*. [Online] Available from: www.anandabazar.com/state/nia-is-unable-to-give-charge-sheet-to-the-10-accused-bangladeshi-over-fake-currency-racket-1.620015?ref=state-new-stry#. [Last accessed: 11 July 2017].

260 Roy, D. (21 August 2012) Blade banate khuchro pachar: bajar jerbar. *Ananda Bazar Patrika*. [Online] Available from: www.anandabazar.com/archive/1120821/21raj1.html. [Last accessed: 31 July 2013].

Livelihood practices 85

261 Moitro, S. (22 August 2012) Khuchror akale jerbar Bongaon-e mushkil ashan coupon. *Ananda Bazar Patrika*. [Online] Available from: www.anandabazar.com/archive/ 1120822/22pgn2.html. [Last accessed: 31 July 2013].

262 Staff Reporter. (12 July 2017). Shonar biscuit shoho greftar dui. *Ananda Bazar Patrika*. [Online] Available from: www.anandabazar.com/district/dhaksinbanga/north-south-24-paraganas/police-arrested-2-person-with-gold-bar-1.641224?ref=north-south-24-paraganas-new-stry. [Last accessed: 17 July 2017].

263 Ghosh, N. (2 March 2017). Shimantey rupor dheeler romroma. *Ananda Bazar Patrika*. [Online] Available from: www.anandabazar.com/district/uttarbanga/silver-smuggling-have-increased-in-border-area-1.572477?ref=uttarbanga-new-stry. [Last accessed: 7 July 2017].

264 Staff Reporter. (18 June 2017). Shonar biscuit, baat shoho dhrito Clearing Agent. *Ananda Bazar Patrika*. [Online] Available from: www.anandabazar.com/district/ dhaksinbanga/north-south-24-paraganas/clearing-agent-arrested-with-gold-biscuits-1.629968?ref=north-south-24-paraganas-new-stry. [Last accessed: 9 July 2017].

265 Maitra, S. (29 June 2017). Trolley te shonar pat lagiye pachar. *Ananda Bazar Patrika*. [Online] Available from: www.anandabazar.com/district/dhaksinbanga/north-south-24-paraganas/active-gold-trafficking-cycle-at-the-border-1.635242?ref=north-south-24-paraganas-ft-stry. [Last accessed: 9 July 2017].

266 Interview with Jasimuddin Mondol, resident of Mathurapur village (Nadia district of West Bengal, 22 October 2011).

267 Interview with Bikram, Lakshmidari village, Bhomra (Satkhira district of Bangladesh, 12 February 2012).

268 Ibid.

269 As witnessed during my field visit to Lakshmidari village, Bhomra (Satkhira district of Bangladesh, 12 February 2012).

270 Interview with Bikram, Lakshmidari village, Bhomra (Satkhira district of Bangladesh, 12 February 2012).

271 Interview with Alok Sengupta, resident of Dinhata (Cooch Behar district of West Bengal, 19 March 2012).

272 Staff Reporter. (18 February 2017). Pechone jounokormi ke boshiye chole bike pachar. *Ananda Bazar Patrika*. [Online] Available from: www.anandabazar.com/dis trict/dhaksinbanga/north-south-24-paraganas/bike-trafficking-continues-in-a-new-process-1.566179. [Last accessed: 9 July 2017].

273 'বিকল্প কাজ বলতে ২ নম্বরী, এটাই পেশা হিসেবে দেখে এখানে।' (Alternative forms of livelihood means smuggling. Here, smuggling is seen as a livelihood in itself.) Interview with Ranjit, resident of Jamalpur village, Hili (South Dinajpur district of West Bengal, 24 January 2012).

274 Interview with Parbati Mohanto, resident and smuggler at Ghunapara-Dhumron village, Hili (South Dinajpur district of West Bengal, 25 January 2012).

275 *Dholai*, like *Dhoor* is yet another local term used for carriers.

276 Interview with Parbati Mohanto, resident and smuggler at Ghunapara-Dhumron village, Hili (South Dinajpur district of West Bengal, 25 January 2012).

277 The average monthly salary of a BSF constable is between Rs.8460 and Rs.9910, while that of an inspector is between Rs.11,360 and Rs.17,140, depending upon the specific ranking. Available from: www.bsf.nic.in/en/structure.html; the average monthly salary of a BGB constable is Tk.9095. Available from: www.bgb.gov.bd/ images/career/83_Batch_Carcula-1.pdf.

278 Interview with Parbati Mohanto, resident and smuggler at Ghunapara-Dhumron village, Hili (South Dinajpur district of West Bengal, 25 January 2012).

279 Ibid.

280 *Uttar Vang Prahari Samachar Patrika*. (March 2012). 4(11).

281 Interview with Parbati Mohanto, resident and smuggler at Ghunapara-Dhumron village, Hili (South Dinajpur district of West Bengal, 25 January 2012).

86 *Livelihood practices*

282 Ibid.

283 Sur, 2012, p. 141.

284 Interview with Hirak Kanti Munshi, resident of Balurghat (South Dinajpur district of West Bengal, 24 January 2012).

285 Staff Reporter. (9 March 2017). Dhorla parer shimantey barchhe pachar, udbeg. *Ananda Bazar Patrika*. [Online] Available from: www.anandabazar.com/district/uttarbanga/cow-trafficking-increased-at-dharla-1.576681?ref=uttarbanga-new-stry. [Last accessed: 7 July 2017].

286 'গরিব কাঠ কুরুনী রা অবাধে বর্ডার এর এপার অপার করে. ২০-৩০ টাকা পায় ওসব বেঁচে. বি এস এফ আটকায়ে না।' Interview with Apurba Kumar Biswas, resident of Petrapole border, Bongaon (North 24 Parganas district of West Bengal, 20 September 2011).

287 Interview with a BGB official at Benapole BGB camp (Jessore district of Bangladesh, 15 February 2012).

288 '১০০-২০০ মিটার পড়ে পড়ে পোস্ট. সার্চ লাইট নেই. সরকার লাগায়ে না. স্মাগলার রাও দেয় না লাগাতে।' (The check-posts are at a distance of 100–200 metres from each other. There are no search lights. Government does not implement it, nor do the smugglers let the implementation take place.) Interview with a BSF official at Shikarpur BSF camp (Nadia district of West Bengal, 21 October 2011).

289 Interview with a BSF official at Asharidoho BSF camp (Murshidabad district of West Bengal, 9 November 2011).

290 This also explains the increase in seizures of smuggled goods in the winter months of December, January and February along this border. *Uttar Vang Prahari Samachar Patrika*. (March 2012). 4(11).

291 *Saree* is a strip of unstitched cloth worn by women, ranging from four to nine yards in length that is draped over the body in various styles, which is native to the Indian subcontinent. It is popular in India, Bangladesh, Pakistan, Nepal, Sri Lanka, Bhutan, Burma, Malaysia and Singapore. The most common style is for the *saree* to be wrapped around the waist, with one end then draped over the shoulder, baring the midriff.

292 Biswas, G and Sujauddin. (7 January 2013) Sheeter shimante barchhe pachar, hoyerani. *Ananda Bazar Patrika*. [Online] Available from: www.anandabazar.com/archive/1130107/7mur1.html. [Last accessed: 1 August 2013].

293 Ibid.

294 Interview with Gourab Sarkar, resident and trader at Hili (South Dinajpur district of West Bengal, 25 January 2012); Interview with Alok Sengupta, resident of Dinhata (Cooch Behar district of West Bengal, 19 March 2012).

295 Interview with Subir Biswas, resident and NGO worker at Tiyor (South Dinajpur district of West Bengal, 25 January 2012); According to BSF records, the outgoing items from West Bengal to Bangladesh include cattle, Phensidyl, fertilisers, medicines and hemp, whereas incoming items mostly include Fake Indian Currency Notes (FICN), garlic and readymade garments. *Uttar Vang Prahari Samachar Patrika*. (March 2012). 4(11).

296 Jamwal, 2004, pp. 26–27.

297 Van Schendel, 2005, pp. 382–383.

298 Interview with Parbati Mohanto, resident and smuggler at Ghunapara-Dhumron village, Hili (South Dinajpur district of West Bengal, 25 January 2012).

299 Biswas and Sujauddin, 7 January 2013, *Ananda Bazar Patrika*; interview with Rumela Begum, resident and smuggler at Hili border (Dinajpur district of Bangladesh, 8 October 2011).

300 'মহিলারা ফেন্সি আনে প্রচুর. মহিলা অফিসার নেই বলে, কেউ এদের চেক করার নেই।' (Women smuggle a lot of Phensidyl. There are no women guards, so no one to check them.) Interview with Hare Krishna Mondol, village *Panchayat* member of Char Meghna (Nadia district of West Bengal, 21 October 2011).

301 Discussed in Chapter 4.

Livelihood practices   87

302 Interview with Parbati Mohanto, resident of Ghunapara-Dhumron village (South Dinajpur district of West Bengal, 25 January 2012).

303 Interview with Asif, resident and smuggler at Kaikhali village, Shyamnagar (Satkhira district of Bangladesh, 14 February 2012).

304 Interview with Asif and Hari, residents and smugglers at Kaikhali village, Shyamnagar (Stakhira district of Bangladesh, 14 February 2012).

305 Interview with a BGB official at Benapole BGB camp (Jessore district of Bangladesh, 15 February 2012).

306 Sur, 2012, pp. 127–150.

307 Witnessed during my field visit to the Hili border (Dinajpur district of Bangladesh, 8 October 2011).

308 Interview with Parbati Mohanto, resident of Ghunapara-Dhumron village (South Dinajpur district of West Bengal, 25 January 2012).

309 In the culture of the Indian sub-continent, *hijras* are regarded as a 'third gender'; most *hijras* see themselves as 'neither man nor woman'. They cannot accurately be described as 'eunuchs' or 'hermaphrodites' or 'transsexual women'. Most *hijras* were born male or 'intersex' (with ambiguous genitalia); many will have undergone a ritual emasculation operation, which includes castration. Some other individuals who identify as *hijras* were born female. Although most *hijras* wear women's clothing and adopt female mannerisms, they generally do not attempt to pass off as women. Becoming a *hijra* involves a process of initiation into a *hijra* 'family', or small group, under a guru 'teacher'. *UK Border Agency: Bangladesh, 2012.* [Online] Available from: www.ukba.homeoffice.gov.uk/sitecontent/documents/policyandlaw/coi/bangladesh/report-0912.pdf?view=Binary. [Accessed: 24 July 2013].

310 Discussed in Chapter 4.

311 Interview with Rajib, *hijra* and smuggler at Hili (Dinajpur district of Bangladesh, 8 October 2011).

312 Interview with Sheena Akhtar, *hijra* and smuggler at Hili (Dinajpur district of Bangladesh, 8 October 2011).

313 Ibid.

314 Interview with Rajib, *hijra* and smuggler at Hili (Dinajpur district of Bangladesh, 8 October 2011).

315 Interview with Sheena Akhtar, *hijra* and resident of Hili (Dinajpur district of Bangladesh, 8 October 2011).

316 Interview with a BGB official at Hili BGB camp, Hili (Dinajpur district of Bangladesh, 8 October 2011); Interview with Rajib, *hijra* and resident of Hili (Dinajpur district of Bangladesh, 8 October 2011).

317 Interview with Bijon, resident and journalist with a Bengali daily in Jessore town (Jessore district of Bangladesh, 16 February 2012).

318 Interview with a BGB official at Hili BGB camp, Hili (Dinajpur district of Bangladesh, 8 October 2011).

319 Shujauddin. (5 June 2017). Bhikhher jhulite shonar biscuit. *Ananda Bazar Patrika.* [Online] Available from: www.anandabazar.com/district/nodia-murshidabbad/physically-disabled-helping-smugglers-across-border-area-1.623490?ref=nodia-murshidabbad-ft-stry. [Last accessed: 17 July 2017].

320 The border had cut the villages off from their local markets, forcing them to cross it to purchase their 'personal supplies of salt, cloth and oil and whatever other goods they needed. The local trade on which the region depended was seriously hampered by cutting the town off from its hinterland. Chatterji, 1999, p. 228; van Schendel, 2001, p. 401.

321 Interview with Ranjit, resident and *Panchayat* head of Jamalpur village (South Dinajpur district of West Bengal, 24 January 2012).

322 Tiwary, D. (1 December 2012) Legalise Cattle Smuggling on Bangladesh Border: BSF Chief. *The Times of India.* [Online] Available from: http://articles.timesofindia.

88 *Livelihood practices*

indiatimes.com/2012-12-01/india/35530471_1_bsf-men-bangladesh-border-indo-bangla-border. [Last accessed: 1 August 2013].

323 Staff Reporter. (29 December 2012) Chorachalan thekatey shimantey 'haat' toiri. *Ananda Bazar Patrika*. [Online] Available from: www.anandabazar.com/archive/1121229/29uttar3.html. [Last accessed: 1 August 2013].

324 Basu, A. (3 May 2017). Chorachalan rukhte Bharat-Bangladesh shimante aro border haat. *Ananda Bazar Patrika*. [Online] Available from: www.anandabazar.com/bangla desh-news/more-retail-market-is-being-established-along-indo-bangladesh-border-bng-dgtl-1.606855?ref=hm-new-stry. [Last accessed: 13 July 2017].

325 Staff Reporter, 29 December 2012, *Ananda Bazar Patrika*.

326 Times News Network. (22 September 2013) Bengal Approves 4 Border Haats. *The Times of India*. [Online] Available from: http://epaper.timesofindia.com/Repository/ml.asp?Ref=VE9JS00vMjAxMy8wOS8yMiNBcjAxNjAz. [Last accessed: 23 September 2013].

327 Ibid.

328 Staff Reporter. (30 January 2013) E parey baron, o parey udyam, shimantey SEZ. *Ananda Bazar Patrika*. [Online] Available from: www.anandabazar.com/30bdesh1.html. [Last accessed: 17 September 2013].

329 'আগে রাত ১১ টার পর চোরাই হাট চালু হত. এখন কম. পুলিশ আসছে শুনলে এক ঘন্টার মধ্যে পুরো জায়গাটা কলাবাগান চাষবাসে ভর্তি হয়ে যাবে. পুলিশ এসে দেখবে চাষ জমি।' (The illegal *haats* begin from 11PM. If they are informed of police raids, they will vacate the place in an hour and make it look like a simple farmland.) Interview with Bijoy Mondol, resident of Shikarpur (Nadia district of West Bengal, 21 October 2011).

330 Field visits on 12 and 14 February 2012 and 6 October 2011, respectively.

331 Interview with Jahangir, resident and farmer at Kabilpur village, Chougachha (Jessore district of Bangladesh, 16 February 2012).

332 Interview with Banchharam Mondol, resident and ex-*Panchayat* head of Mathurapur village (Nadia district of West Bengal, 22 October 2011).

333 Staff Reporter. (4 October 2012) Utsav-e jomey uthechhey shimanter haat. *Ananda Bazar Patrika*. [Online] Available from: www.anandabazar.com/archive/1121004/4mur2.html. [Last accessed: 1 August 2013].

334 Guha, R. (1989) Saboteurs in the Forest: Colonialism and Peasant Resistance in the Indian Himalaya. In Colburn, F.D. (Ed.). *Everyday Forms of Peasant Resistance*. Armonk, London: M.E Sharpe. p. 86.

335 Van Schendel, 2005, p. 375.

336 Fencing the unfenced areas, installation of flood lights, installation of Closed Circuit (CC) cameras on the border gates along the fence, deployment of small-size hovercrafts in riverine border areas, and re-adjusting patrolling plans include some of the mechanisms of strengthening surveillance along the West Bengal-Bangladesh border. *Uttar Vang Prahari Samachar Patrika*. (March 2012). 4(11).

337 Van Schendel, 2005, p. 378.

338 Ibid. pp. 378–379.

339 Ibid. p. 379.

340 Samaddar, R. (1999) *The Marginal Nation: Transborder Migration from Bangladesh to West Bengal*. New Delhi: Sage; Van Schendel, W. (2005) *The Bengal Borderland: Beyond State and Nation in South Asia*. London: Anthem.

341 Van Schendel and Abraham, 2005.

342 Scott, J.C. (1989) Everyday Forms of Resistance. In Colburn, F.D. (Ed.). *Everyday Forms of Peasant Resistance*. Armonk, London: M.E. Sharpe.

343 Colburn, 1989. p. X.

344 Scott, 1989, p. 21.

345 Ibid. p. 23.

346 Ibid. p. 21.

347 Soja, E. (1996) *Thirdspace*. Cambridge: Blackwell.

Livelihood practices 89

348 Martinez, O.J. (1994) *Border People: Life and Society in the US-Mexico Borderlands*. Tuscon: University of Arizona Press.
349 Report on border affairs dated 20 March 1950. GB IB File No. 1238–47 (24 Parganas). Quoted in Chatterji, 1999, pp. 235–236.
350 Chakravorty, Milevska and Barlow, 2006, p. 65.
351 Ibid. pp. 65–66.
352 Gramsci, A. (1971) *Selections from the Prison Notebooks* (trs. Quintin Hoare and Geoffrey Nowell Smith). London: Lawrence and Wishart. pp. 325–343.
353 Chatterjee, P. (1989) Caste and Subaltern Consciousness. In Guha, R. (Ed.). *Subaltern Studies VI: Writings on South Asian History and Society*. New Delhi: Oxford University Press. p. 173.

3 Spatial disparities

Enclaves, *Chars* and disputed territories

Introduction

The West Bengal-Bangladesh border, from the way it was conceived and drawn, resulted in a number of convoluted territorial arrangements which left its inhabitants in a permanent limbo. The enclaves or *Chhitmahals*, as they are called in the regional parlance, were the most complicated territorial dispute that ensued, leaving a considerable number of inhabitants permanently stranded as foreigners in a neighbouring state. The *Chars* or islands along the riverine borders and the deltaic region in the southern part of the India-Bangladesh border are other such geographies where inhabitants negotiate a constant threat of being displaced and disavowed.

Enclaves

The word 'enclave' as a geopolitical entity first appeared in the diplomatic document of the Treaty of Madrid (1526).[1] An enclave has been defined as an outlying portion of a country entirely or mostly surrounded by the territory of another country.[2] The evolved geopolitical meaning of the word has currently come to mean a portion of a country separated from the mainland and surrounded by a politically alien territory.[3] The term exclave has also come to exist besides the term enclave, with a slight variation in definition. From the point of view of the state in which the pocket of land is located, it is an enclave. From the point of view of the state to which the territory belongs, it is an exclave. A political exclave is defined by G.W.S. Robinson as a part of the territory of one country entirely surrounded by the territory of another country.[4] Given the similarity in their definitions, the terms enclave and exclave are often used interchangeably. Besides standard enclaves, the two other types of enclaves located so far are counter-enclaves and counter-counter-enclaves. A counter-enclave is an enclave within an enclave, i.e. domestic territory lying within the enclave territory of another state. A counter-counter-enclave is an enclave lying within a counter-enclave, i.e. a detached part of the principal enclave lying in the counter-enclave of that enclave.[5]

In general understanding, enclaves may be accessible from the mainland through an alien or foreign territory, by land or sea. However, with increasing political

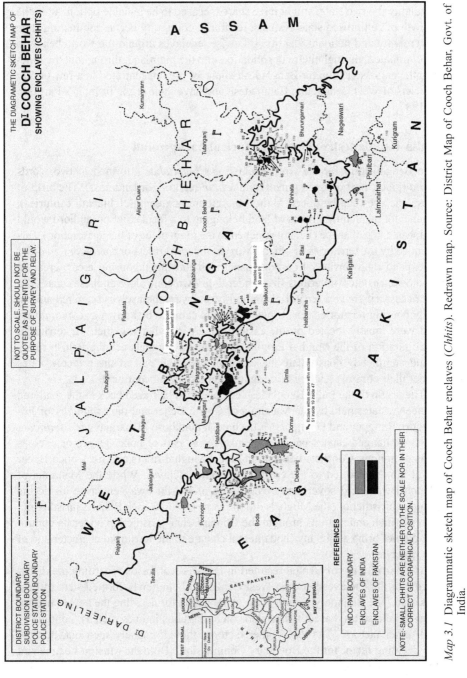

Map 3.1 Diagrammatic sketch map of Cooch Behar enclaves (*Chhits*). Redrawn map. Source: District Map of Cooch Behar, Govt. of India.

92 *Spatial disparities*

complications and the enhanced stringency of legalities associated with travelling across foreign territories, accessing enclaves by the parent states, however much cordiality the two states might have shared, ceased to be a viable option. With the growth of centralised state systems, territorial contiguity began dominating state sovereignty and national identity. Likewise, enclaves around the world began to be eliminated, through their consolidation into the mainland, throughout the nineteenth century.[6] The India-Bangladesh enclaves are concentrated in a few border districts of West Bengal and Bangladesh and have their origin in India's Partition in 1947.[7]

India-Bangladesh enclaves: historical background

The Bengali term for the word enclave is *Chhitmahal* – formed of two words *Chhit* (piece, portion or fragment) and *Mahal*(territory or landmass). The birth of these enclaves can be traced to the Mughal era (sixteenth-eighteenth centuries), when a lot of such fragments of land belonging to a local chief or landlord would be located at a distance (i.e. not attached to the main piece of his jurisdiction), surrounded by the territories of others. Most of the local rulers or *zamindars*, in order to expand their territorial control, penetrated into neighbouring areas, creating landlocked estates of various sizes under their own control. Even these estates did not necessarily have a territorial continuity and were themselves scattered among neighbouring territories. These pieces of land came to be known as *Chhitmahals* and were mostly located on the eastern fringes of what was then the territorial configuration of the Mughal Empire. Neither the Mughals nor the British rulers could completely consolidate these estates (forming part of the princely states under their control) scattered throughout the Indian subcontinent.

The origin of the India-Bangladesh enclaves can be traced back to the scattered princely estates held by the Maharaja of Cooch Behar and the *zamindars* of Jalpaiguri, Rangpur and Dinajpur. Myths have it that these Maharajas and *zamindars* often exchanged estates between themselves as part of poker games or even as gifts of honour. Conflicts between the local Mughal rulers and the Cooch Behar royal family also led to the creation of some enclaves. While the Maharaja of Cooch Behar held sovereignty over some of the far away enclaves inside the Mughal jurisdiction, the Mughals did the same within Cooch Behar's jurisdiction. Later British annexations brought the Cooch Behar jurisdiction under its control but did not bring about any fundamental change to the territorial characteristic of the enclaves.

The partitioning of Bengal resulted in renewed confusion regarding the distribution of the enclaves between West Bengal and the newly-formed state of East Pakistan. The Boundary Commission, responsible for deciding the new boundary between the states, based its decisions on ambiguous indices such as 'contiguity' and 'other factors'. The term 'other factors', though vaguely spelt out, became the deciding factor for the Boundary Commission.[8] Both the Muslim League and the National Congress based their suggestions on the 'other factors' and decided on the boundary line. It was this 'other factor' reference that was used to include

Spatial disparities 93

and/or exclude enclaves which otherwise would not have been justified by the territorial 'contiguity' factor. The boundary line itself was decided and executed in haste. Moreover, the Boundary Commission based its decision on district maps rather than field surveys,[9] which resulted in the enclaves remaining a part of a district but being located in another state.

The princely states were not immediately partitioned or set free in 1947 following the Partition. They were given time to weigh their options between joining India or Pakistan. Accordingly, in 1949, Maharaja Jagadependra Narayan of Cooch Behar merged with India following the 'Cooch Bihar Merger Agreement' on 28 August 1949.[10] According to the Agreement, all the territories belonging to the Maharaja of Cooch Behar fell under the sovereignty of India, implying that the enclaves held by Cooch Behar in the *zamindari* of Rangpur and Dinajpur formed part of India, despite being separated from the main jurisdictional area of Cooch Behar.[11] Similarly, the enclaves under the Rangpur and Dinajpur division fell under the sovereignty of Pakistan despite being surrounded on all sides by the territories of Cooch Behar (West Bengal). The geographical characteristics of the enclaves were rendered all the more complex due to the zigzag demarcation of the areas where the enclaves were situated.[12]

Interestingly, there was never any confusion about the area and demarcation of the enclaves themselves in India and Bangladesh, despite disagreements about the citizenship status of their inhabitants. The borders between British India and Cooch Behar had been clearly demarcated in 1934 through concrete pillars. Many of these pillars are still in place today, though they look different from the ones marking the India-Bangladesh border that was constructed in 1947.[13]

The districts of Cooch Behar (the areas of Haldibari, Mekhligunj, Mathabhanga, Sitalkuchi, Dinhata and Tufangunj) and Jalpaiguri in the state of West Bengal (India) host the Bangladeshi enclaves, while the Bangladeshi districts of Panchagarh (Panchagarh, Debigunj, Boda), Nilphamari (Dimla), Lalmonirhat (Lalmonirhat, Hatibandha, Patgram) and Kurigram (Kurigram, Bhurungamari, Fulbari) host the Indian enclaves.

There are a total of 162 enclaves in India and Bangladesh, including 111 Indian enclaves in Bangladesh (covering an area of 17,158 acres) and 51 Bangladeshi enclaves in India (covering an area of 7110 acres).[14] The population of the 111 Indian enclaves in Bangladesh amounts to 37,550 according to a census of the enclaves (the first ever) in July 2011, while that in the 51 Bangladeshi enclaves in India amounts to 14,310.[15] These figures give a fair idea of the enormity of the crisis, given that more than 51,000 people have been walking the tightrope between citizenship and statelessness for over six decades.

In 1951, the first attempt at enumerating the population of the enclaves was taken up by the government of Pakistan as part of its census. But the enumerators were harassed and arrested by the Indian border police when they tried to enter the enclaves and, hence, began the exclusion of the enclave dwellers from all the censuses of both the countries for the next 66 years.[16] The bigger irony, perhaps, is the fact that in the 1961 Census of Pakistan, 82 villages mentioned as 'uninhabited' actually constituted the enclaves.[17] The enlisting of the enclaves

94 *Spatial disparities*

as uninhabited territories together with the uninhabited status of the deserted villages around (deserted due to river erosion) makes the unrecognised status of the enclaves amply clear.

The partition of Bengal saw the exchange of lands between Hindus and Muslims migrating between India and East Pakistan. Though cases of planned exchange of lands were few compared to the large-scale frenzied exodus, official documents testify to such exchanges in a substantial number. Hindus from East Pakistan migrating to West Bengal exchanged their lands with the Muslims of West Bengal who migrated to East Pakistan.[18] Yet the enclave residents hardly had the choice of exchanging their lands with non-enclave lands, since that would involve exchange with foreign lands. In order to keep to the jurisdictions of their own states, the enclave inhabitants could exchange lands only with enclave inhabitants from the other side of the border. 'If there is an exchange between *Chhits* and lands of the other state, then the matter will fall under the Foreigner's Act',[19] informs Phulmoni, an enclave resident.

The trajectory of the enclave inhabitants has been somewhat similar to that of the *Namasudra* and other agricultural castes who were the last to leave their lands and so, the last to arrive in the new states after Partition.[20] Essentially peasants by occupation, enclave residents were among the last migrants to leave their original enclaves and migrate to those on the other side of the border. Such migrations continued in phases well into the 1990s. Phulmoni complains:

> Changing our jurisdictional areas, i.e. police stations, was the most that we could do. But, in any case, we had to stick to enclaves in order to be within the larger jurisdiction of our country. Many of our Muslim neighbours here in the enclaves are those who have been inhabitants of these lands for generations, and who did not migrate to East Pakistan even after Partition. They are technically Indian citizens by birth (by virtue of being inhabitants of the Indian side of the land for generations), but have been turned into Bangladeshi citizens due to this enclave status.[21]

Much of the enclave population consists of such original inhabitants, who were living in these territories for ages – long before the Partition took place. That has not ensured access to the basic facilities of their states for these people. Their politico-territorial status prevents them from accessing the minimum needs of life and livelihood.

Partition and migration, thus, affected the enclave residents in ways different from the non-enclave residents and immigrants. Change of sides did not mean change of nationality for those enclave-residents who migrated, while the nationality of those who did not migrate from their original enclaves changed. This makes the enclave narratives unique not just as a socio-spatial phenomenon but also in partition and citizenship discourses.

The construction of the fence put a complete halt to the interaction between the enclave population and their parent states. The fence made cross-border movement visible like never before and cut off the enclaves from their states. Even

Figure 3.1 Bangladeshi enclave in India, 2012.

till the early 1980s, people could travel to their own states for casting their votes or accessing some basic facilities. With the increased cross-border restrictions on mobility being put into operation between India and Bangladesh, such movements ceased.[22]

Bilateral agreements concerning the India-Bangladesh enclaves

Nehru-Noon accord (1958)

The territorial complexity of the enclaves coupled with the possibility of religious tension (between some of the Muslim-majority enclaves and their Hindu-majority neighbouring areas and vice-versa) troubled the prime ministers of both India and Pakistan – Jawaharlal Nehru and Firoz Khan Noon, respectively. Discussions regarding a decision about the enclaves began between the ministries of both countries, complemented by survey initiatives and demarcation talks. The idea of the exchange of enclaves began to appear in the public discourses of both India and Pakistan. Eventually, on 10 September 1958, an agreement was signed between Nehru and Noon for the exchange of enclaves.

The Berubari question formed the main issue of the agreement together with the question of the exchange of enclaves. In fact, there had been talks regarding the separation of the two issues, and of the enclave question to be dealt separately under the Acquired Territories (Merger) Bill, 1960. Despite objections by the West Bengal State Assembly to the separation of the Berubari question

96   *Spatial disparities*

and the enclave issue, the Acquired Territories (Merger) Act[23] was finalised in 1960. The Act provided for the 'Exchange of old Cooch Behar enclaves in Pakistan and Pakistan enclaves in India without claim to compensation for extra area going to Pakistan'.

However, amidst opposition from political parties over both the Berubari issue as well as the enclaves, the Act could not be implemented. In 1971, the Indian Supreme Court's attempt for a final implementation of the Act was overshadowed by a war crisis (leading to the formation of Bangladesh), stalling the exchange for the time being.

The Berubari Question: On 17 August 1947, the report of the Boundary Commission was presented which made Kolkata, 24 Parganas, Murshidabad and Bardhhaman districts part of West Bengal, while making Chittagong and Dhaka division, Khulna and Sylhet (except for four specific thanas) districts part of East Pakistan. The districts of Dinajpur, Malda, Nadia, Jessore and Jalpaiguri were divided between the two states. Initially, some of the areas of Jalpaiguri like Boda, Panchagarh, Tetulia, Patgram and Debigunj were under the impression that they would be part of India. Accordingly, on 15 August 1947 (before the report of the Boundary Commission was made known), they had hoisted the Indian flag in recognition of their citizenship status. But the Boundary Commission made these areas parts of East Pakistan, following which Pakistan's flag was hoisted, instead of the Indian one.

Jalpaiguri was made into an administrative district way back in 1869. The largest sub-division or mouja of Jalpaiguri district is Berubari. And when Jalpaiguri District and Union Boards were formed in 1885 and 1919 respectively, the Berubari mouja was divided into No.10 Nagar Berubari, No.11 Kharija Berubari and No.12 South Berubari. Following the partition of Bengal in 1947, Berubari Union No. 12 (area of 8.75 square miles), was described as part of West Bengal and allotted to India. But the map annexed to the Radcliffe Award, however, showed Berubari as part of East Bengal. Though the provisions of the Award specifically mentioned that in case of discrepancy between description and map, the description was to prevail. But in 1952, Pakistan alleged that the Radcliffe Award provided for the inclusion of Berubari into Pakistan and that it had been wrongly treated as part of West Bengal. Nehru and Noon signed an agreement provisioning for the Berubari Union to be horizontally divided and the lower half given to Pakistan. Political debates over this agreement took the form of a full-blown mass movement, led by Berubari Protirokhha Committee (Berubari Defence Committee). The Berubari Question became integral to the Adverse Possession question between India and East Pakistan (and later Bangladesh), and began to be dealt together with the question of the exchange of enclaves. The case was taken up in the Supreme Court, where the decision went against India's cause. The government of India, in response to the Supreme Court's decision, passed the Ninth Amendment Act of the Constitution. Hence, 'on an application made under Art.22b of the Indian Constitution, Justice Sinha issued an injunction on the State of West Bengal and the Union of India restraining them from giving effect to the proposed transfer'.

Spatial disparities   97

The Nehru-Noon Agreement, apart from including the provision for the exchange of enclaves, also returned to the Berubari Question, whereby a part of the South Berubari division would go to East Pakistan along with the other adjacent enclaves. Movement to retain the whole of South Berubari continued after the Nehru-Noon Agreement.

Indira-Mujib agreement (1974)

The struggle for the independence of East Pakistan followed by the creation of Bangladesh in 1971 renewed optimism among the people of both West Bengal and Bangladesh regarding the enclave issue. India's co-operation with Bangladesh in its liberation war was largely responsible for this optimism. Accordingly, on 16 May 1974, the Prime Ministers of India and Bangladesh – Indira Gandhi and Sheikh Mujibur Rahman, signed yet another agreement provisioning for the full exchange of the enclaves. Bangladesh dropped its claim over South Berubari in return for the possession of its largest enclave in West Bengal – Dahagram-Angarpota.

The agreement provided for the lease of land by India for use by Bangladesh (measuring 175×85 metres) as a passage between the Bangladesh mainland and the Dahagram-Angarpota enclave. This passage came to be called the *Tinbigha* Corridor.[24] The agreement was followed by protests by the people of Mekhligunj (the area of Jalpaiguri which ought to host the corridor), which delayed the final implementation of the creation of the corridor. Finally, in 1982, the matter was taken up by H. M. Ershad[25] in Bangladesh and an agreement was signed between Indira Gandhi and Ershad leasing the *Tinbigha* Corridor to Bangladesh. But it was not before 1990 that all the hurdles in the path of the implementation of the agreement could be resolved and a corridor could be built across Indian territory, connecting the Bangladeshi enclave of Dahagram-Angarpota to the mainland of Bangladesh.[26]

But the South Berubari question was yet to be resolved. A second phase of movement for the official inclusion of South Berubari in the map of India consti-tuted the mainstay of the movement this time.

Manmohan-Hasina agreement (2011)

While the *Tinbigha* Agreement signified a breakthrough in India-Bangladesh bilateral relations, it also meant that the larger enclave issue involving more than 160 other enclaves was pushed to the backseat. The *Tinbigha* Corridor overshad-owed the situation of the rest of the enclaves, who were, since 1947, in a wretched state.

In 2011, the Prime Ministers of India and Bangladesh – Manmohan Singh and Sheikh Hasina, signed yet another accord providing for the exchange of the enclaves, by which their inhabitants could continue to reside at their present location and be recognised as the citizen of the host country or else they could move to the country of their choice. The agreement took another five years to be implemented.

98 *Spatial disparities*

As for the Berubari question, the Deputy Director of Survey of West Bengal met with the members of Berubari Protirokhha Committee on 1 November 1996 to talk about the possibility of incorporating South Berubari into the map of India. Meetings between the Committee and the officials of the Border Security Forces as well as India's Home Minister Shivraj Patil took place in 2005 and 2006 respectively. Assurances kept coming from ministers in Parliament. Ministers and leaders from Bangladesh also visited South Berubari between 2007 and 2011, with the aim of a solution to the question. In the press release of 2007 of the India-Bangladesh Joint Working Group, it was decided that a 'pragmatic solution to the issue' was of utmost necessity, 'keeping in mind the spirit of Land Boundary Agreement and also in the light of ground realities'.[27] A joint survey was decided to be a step towards such pragmatic solution. Despite repeated attempts to introduce the bill regarding the question of adverse possessions like the South Berubari issue, the question remains unresolved as of yet.

Bilateral affairs between India and Bangladesh over the enclave question have, in a way, pushed the reality of the existence of enclave dwellers to the backseat, since the reality of the situation never made it to the state-level agreements. Security and economic concerns of the states have been prioritised over the destitution of the people who are the victims of state-building.

In 1948, an agreement had been signed between the East Bengal government and Cooch Behar agreeing to allow the armed forces of both sides across the other's territory in order to enter and leave the enclaves. The district officials, under the agreement, were required to have photograph identity cards. Their visits were also to be preceded by an announcement no less than fifteen days in advance. Police officials were required to be in their uniforms and unarmed. The agreement had also provided for supplying certain goods to the enclaves once a month and the collection of revenue once every six months. The agreement had not provided for the transit of people in and out of the enclaves. While state officials could transfer goods into the enclaves, the produce from the enclaves could not be transferred out, barring the enclave people from participating in the regional economy,[28] forcing them into a virtual economic blockade and criminalising their survival practices. 'If they were to survive, they had to ignore the agreement and face the peril of being defined as smugglers'.[29]

The nature and provisions of the agreements regarding the enclaves from their inception to date stand proof of the fact that the bilateral relations between states have been prioritised over the survival concerns of the people for whom these agreements were meant. The introduction of the passport and visa control systems in 1952 added to the woes. The passport system drove the enclave people into acting more against the law. In the absence of passport offices within the enclaves, the enclave people wanting to obtain a passport had to cross foreign territory illegally to reach their parent state. The parent state would have to allow them to enter without a passport. In case they somehow got through this process and obtained a passport, they had to approach the consulate of the neighbouring state for a visa to return to their enclaves. Once the visa expired, they had to go through the whole process again illegally. The passport and visa system struck the final blow

Spatial disparities 99

to the citizenship status of the enclave people, driving them into infringement of the laws of both India and Bangladesh through every little move they made.[30] With the introduction of the passport system, the collection of revenue from the enclaves by state officials also ceased since the latter now required visas to enter the enclaves.[31]

Given their unique territorial nature and absence of state apparatuses within the enclaves, it is not difficult to imagine what the lives of these enclave-dwellers entail. Law and order is conspicuous by its absence. With no access to the police, border guards or administrative institutions, the enclave people have to deal with any kind of issue – environmental, social, legal, economic or political – by themselves.

The earlier literature on enclaves had mostly looked at them from the perspective of geographical uniqueness, sovereignty, international law and issues of administration.[32] Some recent studies have attempted to look at the various strands of identity formation within the enclaves as well as negotiation between the enclave people and their neighbours,[33] but have not studied them as constitutive parts of border narratives per se. This chapter aims to look at the narratives of the India-Bangladesh enclaves as integral parts of border narratives and as an important strand in the evolution of border consciousness along the border.

Deprivation from access to basic facilities

Land documents, identity proofs and other basic amenities

The enclave population neither have formal citizenship status nor any specific document showing their status as enclave inhabitants. 'Neither do we have birth certificates, nor do we have Polio cards. We are only known as "people" (implying the deprivation from a formal citizenship)'.[34] The only document related to land that some of these people might have is an age-old one that shows that the land had been owned or rented out to one of their ancestors for cultivation by the local landowners. These land documents still act as the only continuing connection with their parent state.[35] Other than this, the enclaves do not officially belong to any police station or district.

While the district that they officially belong to does not recognise them, the district within which they are located cannot recognise them since they are a foreign territory. Nirendranath Burman, resident of a village adjoining a Bangladeshi enclave in India, while responding to questions about the condition of their enclave neighbours, says:

> The way we can claim to belong to a district, a police station, these people cannot claim any of these. They lack an identity and are foreigners in their own lands. They cannot even access the facilities of their own states due to the border fencing. They are practically left without laws or a Constitution unlike us. BSF insists that even if they have to pass over a few yards of the

100 *Spatial disparities*

neighbouring state's land while travelling from their enclaves to their states, they require a passport. We cannot help them in any way even if we want to.[36]

This also means that the people belonging to the Scheduled Castes and Tribes in the enclaves are also without a certificate documenting their caste status.[37] Their unique territorial status has resulted in the absence of even basic facilities which the official citizens of a state enjoy like schools, hospitals, police stations, etc. 'The only thing we can call our own is this air we breathe',[38] laments Md. Iqbal Ali.

Taking help from neighbours in terms of fake identities to get admission to a school or hospital in the host state is routine for the enclave dwellers. And this service includes a certain amount of expenditure as well. 'We have to pay about Tk. 500 each to the Bangladeshi *Union* member of the neighbouring village for fake birth certificates for our children, where the father's name and the name of the village of the child's birth are forged',[39] says Hafizul.

Though electric poles run through them, the enclaves themselves are deprived of electricity. The electric poles provide electricity to the neighbours on all sides, depriving the enclaves in which they are installed. 'If we try to hook current from the lines, we are threatened. Even if we want to buy electricity from them, they do not co-operate'.[40] This also means that irrigation water needs to be pumped in using diesel-engine machines in the absence of electricity. The lack of electricity implies that the enclave inhabitants have to depend on their neighbours for daily activities such as charging their mobile phones. 'We charge our phones from the houses of our neighbours, since we cannot use the electricity that runs through our *Chhits*',[41] says Kamal, resident of a Bangladeshi enclave. This has forced many of the enclave people to extend their houses into the neighbouring territories in order to acquire electricity and postal addresses in the host state.[42]

Some of the enclaves have arranged for their own drinking water facility with no help from either state. The kerosene oil, which their neighbours get at a subsidised rate at the ration shops, needs to be procured at a substantial rate for use as lighting purposes in their huts. With no citizenship documents, the enclave dwellers cannot access subsidised rations like their neighbours. 'The moon, sun, rain and air are the only things we get free here. If the Indians could, they probably would have cut off our access to these as well',[43] laments Md. Iqbal, resident of a Bangladeshi enclave in India.

The enclave dwellers have built roads themselves in the absence of any state initiatives to improve the communication system inside them. Temporary bridges have been built in some, using bamboo as their main resource. Almost all the inhabitants of that particular enclave contribute in the construction of the roads or bridges, either by providing bamboo or by providing labour. Senior enclave residents supervise the construction.[44]

Land issues

A lot of people from the surrounding areas have managed to grab land inside the enclaves in the absence of their original owners (who might have migrated elsewhere) or any state administration. They continue to live in their own state, in the vicinity of the enclave but enjoy the possession of the land inside the enclaves – lands for which they are not required to pay revenue. Moreover, in the period following Partition, the uncertainty over the future of the enclaves had reduced their land prices.[45] This was another reason behind some of the neighbouring people buying land inside the enclaves in the hope that they would eventually be merged with the host state.[46]

Some of these landowners bring landless people from other areas (mostly victims of displacement due to natural calamities like river erosion) and settle them on their lands in the enclaves as *adhiars*, who then form their own little colonies and start cultivating the land as sharecroppers. The *adhiar* families are provided with a piece of agricultural land and a piece of land for residence by the owner of the land. The yield from these lands is divided equally between the *adhiar* and the landowner. These sharecroppers are often treated as subjects of the landowner, and called *proja* (subject).[47] A new version of socio-economic subjectivity, thus, awaits these *adhiars* once they are settled inside the enclaves by the landowners – though such identities are not recognised by either of the states concerned.

Besides enjoying the yield from an unregistered and untaxed land, people having lands inside the enclaves can also use their own shallow pumps to irrigate their part of the lands, which the enclave inhabitant cannot do. The owners of these enclave lands are registered under the BPL (Below Poverty Line)[48] list in their own states since they do not officially own any land in the states of which they are citizens. They cultivate their lands inside the enclaves and reap the benefits to the full, not having to pay any revenue for the produce. 'We cannot complain for fear of threats, nor does the Indian government do anything about this',[49] says an enclave resident. This does not imply that the enclave dwellers themselves are happy about their non-revenue status. One of the respondents makes it clear when he says, 'revenue-paying has been a tradition of this country. Our forefathers paid tax (revenue) throughout their lives. Why shouldn't we pay?'[50]

Some of the neighbouring cultivators have come to own hundreds of acres of lands inside the enclaves over the years. 'The Chatterjees of Dinhata own 600–700 *bighas*[51] of agricultural land here. They bring their own agricultural labourers from outside the enclaves to work on their land. Even when they sell the land, they do it to Indians, but never to us. We are perpetually deprived of every opportunity',[52] says a visibly infuriated Kamal Debnath, inhabitant of a Bangladeshi enclave in India.

Even if the enclave dwellers try buying land from their neighbours, they often end up being defrauded by the sellers in the absence of documents and also because most of them are unable to attend the land registry process as it takes place in the nearest local administrative unit of the district under which the enclave lies, across the border. Moreover, the enclave lands have never been included in the land settlement surveys of either state since 1947, which puts these lands and their owners (both fake and real) into complete uncertainty as to the future of their possessions.[53] 'We cannot register our land holdings either in India or Bangladesh. So we write it down informally. It has no real validity and is susceptible

102 *Spatial disparities*

to manipulation in future',[54] says Bimal, resident of a Bangladeshi enclave. Nor is there any uniformity in the land registration systems of the various enclaves. The land registration documents are without any legal standing and have no validity outside the enclave.

Commercial transactions

Being completely surrounded by the territories of the host state, the enclave people have to depend on their neighbours for commercial transactions, as well as for schools, hospitals, etc. They use the *haats* of their neighbouring locality of the host state for commercial purposes; use the currency of the host state; maintain family and friendship links with the surrounding areas, including marriage ties (which are officially cross-border marriage ties), and often participate in the religious festivals of the neighbours (Hindu enclave residents in Hindu festivals and Muslim residents in mosque congregations).[55]

Adverse position of some neighbouring territories

Due to the enclaves, some areas of the host state are deprived of communication systems and electricity as the enclaves pose a barrier. These areas, bounded by the enclaves, have turned into Adversely Possessed territories themselves. The kind of infrastructure required to deal with such situations (for example, building a bridge around the enclave) might not always be economically viable. This leaves the people of such areas with little choice but to traverse the enclaves for communicating with other neighbouring villages of their own state – being forced into being 'trespassers'.[56]

Schools, hospitals

It is with the fake identity of their neighbours that the children from the enclaves are admitted into neighbouring schools.[57] The issue of having to 'pose a stranger as my husband in order to get my children admitted to school' keeps coming up in numerous responses of the women inhabitants of the enclaves.[58] Admission to hospitals operates on a similar use of fake identities.

School education, even after such a hazardous beginning, can only continue till the primary level, after which it is not possible to continue education in a high school since issues of identity are more formalised in them. Official documents, like a voter card, ration card or birth certificates, to which the enclave inhabitants do not have access, are essential for admission into government-run high schools.[59] 'In the higher classes, they are asked about their whereabouts', says Fatima Bibi in context of sending children to neighbouring schools with fake identities.[60]

Some of the enclaves have informal schools, run either by one of their own residents or sometimes volunteered by a person from the neighbouring areas.[61] These schools cannot provide any food or books to their students, unlike primary schools in the neighbouring areas where the students are entitled to free meals

Spatial disparities   103

and textbooks at the primary level. 'We cannot even pay any remuneration to the teachers who volunteer to teach in these schools',[62] laments an enclave inhabitant. The uncertainty of educational degrees, if acquired somehow, leaves the enclave people disinterested in pursuing education. With no access to the parent state and no legal access to the employment opportunities of the host state, the enclave people are left with little choice. Using fake documents to acquire government jobs poses the risk of being apprehended on verification (a process that every government job entails).[63]

Matrimonial issues and sexual violence

Despite efforts and examples of cross-border marriages between the enclave people and their neighbours in the host states, the prospect of marriage is often critical and forever hazardous for them. Finding a bride from the neighbouring areas is often difficult for the male residents of enclaves since that entails a loss of citizenship for the bride. The wife as well as the children are rendered document-less because the husband/father does not possess one.[64] 'Once one marries into the enclaves, her official documents lose validity, putting her citizenship status into peril, like the rest of the enclave population. All her previously existing documents become invalid on entering the enclave after marriage'.[65]

Women from the enclaves have another version of the crisis of marrying outside the enclaves. Fatima Bibi narrates how her daughter is being harassed by her in-laws for not being able to provide documents. 'My daughter is unable to obtain Indian citizenship because of lack of documents. Her in-laws are demanding Rs. 5000 so that they can arrange for fake documents with that money. We are poor people. Where do we get so much money?'[66] Bhabani Burman and Bimal Burman second Fatima on the plight of the women inhabitants of the enclaves who are married into neighbouring villages.[67] To ensure the acceptance of their daughters into non-enclave families, the enclave residents encourage the marriage ceremony to be held in the presence of a marriage registrar (or a priest/*kaji*)of the choice of the groom's house, arranged from the neighbouring area.[68]

Incidents of sexual harassment, including rape and molestation by both the neighbouring miscreants as well as the border guards, are not uncommon in the enclaves.[69] Lack of medical facilities within the enclaves result in complications related to childbirth, including miscarriages.[70]

Fatima narrates the irony that though her paternal house is in a village which is currently in the Rangpur district of Bangladesh, her parents could never visit her in her present address in the Bangladeshi enclave of Mashaldanga within the Cooch Behar district of West Bengal. The piece of Indian land between the Bangladesh mainland and the enclave prevents them from visiting their daughter. 'Even we cannot attend funerals of our parents for the same reason',[71] rues Fatima. Movement across the enclaves and the neighbouring areas is all the more restricted for the women of the former, given the belief of the men 'in their (women's) inability to flee from pursuers'.[72] The tragic trajectory of the enclave people rings loud in such responses. This crisis, however, fails to put a complete halt to cross-border

104 *Spatial disparities*

marriages between enclave and non-enclave residents. Incidents of women from distant places in the host state marrying into the enclaves do occur, although rarely.[73]

Religious aspect

A religious implication in the context of fake documents and identities has also been noticed in some of the responses. Md. Iqbal explains that most of the Hindu inhabitants of the enclaves have their Hindu relatives as neighbours, living in the Indian territories around them, and they provide fake documents and identities to Hindus in the enclaves, whereas the Muslim enclave dwellers need to obtain these documents through the payment of a substantial amount of cash.[74] Similar responses are heard from the Hindu residents of Indian enclaves in the Muslim-majority Bangladeshi areas.

Fatema Bibi supports Iqbal's claim that religion often plays a role in the kind of behaviour that the enclave population can expect from their neighbours: 'They behave all the more badly because we are Muslims. All the surrounding villages are Hindu, and all of us inside the *Chhit* are Muslims. If they unleash their cattle on our *Chhits* to graze, we cannot complain, or else they become violent'.[75] Irrespective of religion, the relation between the enclave population and their neighbours, in most cases, is not favourable. 'We have to interact with our neighbours. But if they behave badly, we cannot answer them back. We are always being apologetic, often unnecessarily, simply to ensure that they keep co-operating with us',[76] says Fatema.

These responses are manifestations of what Willem van Schendel phrases as the clash between citizenship, proxy citizenship and an enclave identity. In the post-Partition phase, the states of India and Pakistan 'saw themselves as being in charge of the population living in their own territory, but also of a category of people living in the territory of the other state'.[77] These groups have been termed by Van Schendel as citizens and proxy citizens, respectively. India's proxy citizens were the Hindus living in Pakistan, while Pakistan's proxy citizens were the Muslims living in India.[78] This *transterritorial*[79] aspect of nationality was often related to questions of the loyalty of proxy citizens towards their territorial nation.

The condition of the enclave people was perhaps the most complicated against the backdrop of such citizenship issues because of the location of their identity at the crossroads of being citizens, proxy citizens and enclave people.[80] Communal outbreaks in the post-Partition phases elsewhere in India or Bangladesh affected the enclave people in ways whereby the proxy citizens of the enclaves were unharmed, while the citizens of the other state were made victims of the communal violence. The dilemma in identifying themselves with either the parent state or the host state pushed the enclave people to the brink of vulnerability. Their identification as *citizens* distanced them from their neighbours and relatives outside the enclaves on whom they were economically dependent. The more the enclave people identified themselves as *proxy citizens*, the more they distanced themselves from their co-residents in the enclaves.[81] This drove them to create a third identity for themselves – that of being 'enclave people'.[82] The undercurrent of citizenship and identity issues can still be felt in the responses of the enclave people like the ones above. Religious issues related to citizenship questions still occupy an important role in the narratives of the enclave people.

The complex pattern of citizenship and proxy citizenship in the enclaves can also be understood from the recent survey of the enclave people regarding their choice of state once the exchange of enclaves comes into effect. Seven hundred forty-three out of the 14,000 Indian enclave residents (constituting 149 families) in Bangladesh expressed their desire to be rehabilitated in India, while none among the 37,000 Bangladeshi enclave residents in India expressed their desire to be rehabilitated in Bangladesh after the exchange. Interestingly, the Bangladeshi enclave residents in India have themselves started preparing for the rehabilitation of those who choose to rehabilitate from the Indian enclaves in Bangladesh instead of waiting for the Indian state or even the West Bengal government to take action. The Bangladeshi enclave residents in India have also decided to help the Indian enclave residents from Bangladesh with the necessary financial support to start their lives afresh in the Bangladeshi enclaves in India. This also indicates the desperation of the enclave residents for the execution of the exchange.[83]

Relation between the enclave residents and the Panchayat/Union

Earlier, the *Panchayat*/Union heads of the *Panchayats*/Unions to whom the enclaves officially belonged could come to the enclave for the mediation of disputes or the issuing of certificates. However, with the introduction of the passport/visa system and the enclave issue gaining political momentum in India-Bangladesh bilateral affairs, the border guards stopped allowing the same, depriving the enclave population of their last resort of communication with their parent states.

Interestingly, the *Panchayat*/Union heads of the neighbouring villages of the host state still engage in such co-operation, as and when possible, despite its illegal nature. 'We do try to help the enclave people in some ways, even though it will be considered officially illegal. We cannot do anything legally, especially for those who do not have a single document. Those having a basic document can still be helped, albeit illegally. In fact, I have arranged for many of their school admissions, livelihood opportunities as labourers outside the enclaves or even arranged for voter cards for many of them – all illegally',[84] says the Deputy-Head of the village *Panchayat* of an Indian village adjacent to a Bangladeshi enclave, but he also adds that, 'not all Indian *Panchayats* help the enclave people in the way we are trying to'[85] – indicating the inherent troubled relations between the enclave population and its neighbours.

Some of the Indian neighbours of the Bangladeshi enclaves and vice versa confirm these responses regarding the troubled relationships between the enclave inhabitants and their neighbours. 'It is true that they do not share a cordial relation with their neighbours. The Indians do abuse the enclave dwellers, though there are exceptions of course. Many of us try to co-operate with them, which is

106 *Spatial disparities*

also reflected in the relation between many of these enclave dwellers and their neighbouring villages', says Md. Ziauddin Miah.[86] Some of the responses, in fact, point towards an ambience of cordiality between the two, especially during times of festivities.[87]

Trespassing and 'push-backs'

The threat of conviction for trespassing is omnipresent among the enclave people, since it is difficult for them to prove their enclave-status if wrongly convicted of illegal infiltration. In case of apprehension, they are either 'pushed back' forcefully into their parent state or imprisoned. Being pushed back forcefully into their own state creates yet another hazard for these enclave dwellers since they have set up their own life and livelihood in the enclaves over the years. 'Once we are forcefully pushed back to Bangladesh, it is almost impossible to come back to the enclave, and especially in the current situation of the fences',[88] says a Bangladeshi enclave resident in India.

While, on the one hand, the restriction of movement between the enclaves and the parent state is a problem, being forcefully pushed back into their states is no solution either. The idea of 'being forcefully pushed back' into their own states forms an interesting but complex narrative in the context of the enclaves. It is, in fact, quite easy for the neighbours to create an issue out of any kind of movement by the enclave population. 'All they have to do is report to the BSF that we are illegal Bangladeshi infiltrators, and we will immediately be sent to the jail. Earlier it was a three-month term for such convictions. Currently it has been extended to two years and two months. There are plans for further extension, for up to three years'.[89] The hassles that the 'push-back' policy of the border guards create for the enclave people indicates that the more important issue for the latter is their integration into the host states as officially recognised citizens rather than access to their parent state.[90] Such issues form a platform for the citizenship demands of the enclave people. Push-backs are not unique to enclave residents but are a common occurrence along the West Bengal-Bangladesh border, where civilians are forcefully 'pushed back', either into their own state or into the neighbouring state by the border guards, where the victims of push-backs are stranded between legalities pertaining to citizenship of India and Bangladesh.[91]

Lack of suffrage rights

The lack of voting rights of the enclave people prevents them from voicing their problems in either the local *Panchayats*/Unions or to the political parties. 'Our plight never comes up as an agenda with the leaders even during elections. The leaders invest their energy only towards their voters, in the Indian villages around. We are not entitled to vote, so no one cares to talk about us',[92] laments Bimal, resident of a Bangladeshi enclave in India.

Livelihood

Livelihood opportunities for the enclave dwellers are few, other than agricultural practices. The Partition played havoc with them by separating them from their agricultural fields. Plots of land were scattered not just on either side of the border but also on the same side between the enclaves and their surroundings. The lives of these people deteriorated, as Rabbani puts it aptly, 'from peasant to sharecropper, tenant to landless and sharecropper to non-cropper'.[93] With the population of the enclaves soaring rapidly in the absence of any government administered Family Planning Programmes,[94] earning a living with the limited availability of resources has been the main crisis of the enclave inhabitants. The economic blockade that the enclaves have been forced into left their people with little option but illegal transactions with their neighbours.

Working as labourers elsewhere in the state or even abroad, which has become a usual occurrence all along the border, is a risky proposition for the enclave population because of the lack of documents. This makes them doubly vulnerable to false allegations of infiltration.[95] 'We do not have any industries in the enclaves, not even such cottage-industries as *beedi*-making. We are unable to work as labourers in India, since we do not have a union card, unlike the Indian labourers. While they (Indian labourers) can come into the *Chhit* to work as labourers, we cannot do the same outside the *Chhit*', complains Iqbal, resident of a Bangladeshi enclave in India.[96] Experiences of travelling outside the enclaves as labourers have not always been good. The threat of persecution has kept most of the enclave people away from such livelihood opportunities.[97]

The BRAC[98] credit programme offers loans to some of the residents of the Indian enclaves in Bangladesh for supporting their personal economic initiatives or to help meet their harvest shortcomings. Yet the absence of official documents remains a constant impediment with only those residents who obtained membership to BRAC before 1993 being eligible for such credit assistances. With the introduction of the Voter Identity Card in India in 1993, the ambiguous identity of the enclave residents became all the more prominent, making their stateless position visible and rendering them ineligible for assistance from Bangladeshi organisations. A large number of the enclave people are, thus, deprived of the BRAC credit assistance programmes due to the lack of an official identity (Voter Identity Card).[99]

Scarcity of food is an inevitable outcome of the lack of livelihood opportunities and the restriction on movements for the enclave-dwellers. A growing population adds to the crisis. The productivity of the available agricultural lands remains low due to the lack of access to advanced technology by the farmers within the enclaves, including restrictions on using shallow pumps and buying livestock. The restricted amount of economic transactions adds to the crisis.

Attitude of the border guards towards the enclave people

The attitude of the border guards towards the enclave residents is unfavourable. 'Madhya Mashaldanga is about 2.3 kilometres from the border, while Dakshin

108 *Spatial disparities*

Mashaldanga (in Bangladesh) is about 1 kilometre from the border. In between these two territories, there is Indian territory where BSF is posted. If only we did not have that stretch of the territory in between, we could easily travel to Bangladesh. But BSF does not allow us to traverse that path at any cost',[100] says a resident of a Bangladeshi enclave in India.

The border guards take advantage of the undocumented status of the enclave-dwellers. Even if instances of murder or abuse by miscreants from neighbouring areas occur within the enclaves, the border guards or the police do not take them up because of the 'foreign territory' status of the enclaves. 'We ourselves solve such cases, since police would not take up these cases',[101] complains Hafizul, a resident of an Indian enclave in Bangladesh.

This encourages both physical and verbal assaults on the enclave-dwellers by neighbouring villagers. Complaints such as 'we cannot speak with as much vigour as the neighbouring Bangladeshis',[102] speaks amply of the sense of crisis that these enclave-dwellers go through.

The border guards' attitude towards the enclave-dwellers is either one of ignorance or of abusive aggressiveness. Akbar Alam narrates how the border guards used to take the enclave-dwellers away for no reason at all or for minor reasons and beat them up brutally or imprison them for months. 'These days, the situation is a bit better, though things have not changed too radically',[103] he says.

That things have not changed radically is proved by what Md. Iqbal Ali Sheikh says. As enclave-dwellers, there are restrictions on their movement as well as on the amount of agricultural goods or food items that they can carry. 'If the amount exceeds a bit, the border guards make us do menial work such as cleaning garbage or even human excrement or else simply put us behind bars for months together',[104] says Iqbal Ali.

The male-enclave dwellers are also made to work as corvee labourers by the border guards for constructing and/or maintaining the border fences. 'If we do not agree to do it, they threaten us. Undocumented as we are, we always have the fear of being apprehended by the border guards and so, are bound to comply with these kind of demands', says Iqbal Ali.[105] The border guards often have roads built through the enclaves for their own convenience, which the enclave people are prohibited from using.[106] Interestingly, this is another example of illegal border-crossings by official actors.[107] Traversing the enclaves makes a border guard as illegal a trespasser as an enclave resident moving out of his/her enclave.

Platform for miscreants

The theft of cattle, crops and poultry is a regular occurrence inside the enclaves. 'Theft occurs in the light of the day. We try our best to dissuade them from stealing our stuff, but to no avail. If we persist, then they threaten us, just because we are enclave people',[108] says an enclave resident.

'People from the neighbouring areas behave very badly with us. If we talk back, they become violent, use swear words, might even put our homes on fire or might forcefully take away our cattle',[109] is how Md. Anisur sums up the basic crisis of the enclave population.

The enclave inhabitants are often jeopardised by the police, border guards and neighbours for events in which they have no involvement whatsoever.[110] Incidents of rape, molestation, theft and murder inside the enclaves, mostly perpetrated by miscreants from the surrounding non-enclave areas,[111] go unrecorded and, hence, unpunished. A resident of an Indian enclave in Bangladesh narrates an incident that happened in 2010:

> Some Bangladeshi miscreants attempted burglary inside the Indian enclave, when some of them were held by the enclave dwellers and beaten up. As revenge, the rest of their gang members put fire to 160 of our huts in the enclaves the next day. It has been a year now and there has been no substantial aid coming from either India or Bangladesh other than a few tarpaulins and clothes. We have not been able to rebuild our houses and still live in make-shift enclosures made from tin sheets.[112]

Haven for smugglers

Cattle smugglers often use the enclaves as transits for smuggled cattle. However, the enclave inhabitants rarely engage in such practices themselves for fear of being doubly jeopardised. 'They take their cattle through the *Chhits*, but we are not involved in these practices because, as it is, we are perpetually threatened by the fear of persecution',[113] says Bimal Burman, an enclave resident.

Their territorial crisis prevents them from inviting any further chances of being harassed. Complains Md. Anisur:

> We do have smuggling activities inside the *Chhits*, but we do not have anyone to report these. If we try approaching the *Pradhan*, he says it is our fault. The *Chhit* inhabitants are rarely involved in these activities themselves because we know we do not have any resort if we land up in trouble. We have no other option but to let others carry on such activities using the *Chhit* as a transit because there is no one who will come to our rescue if we are attacked by the smugglers. The BSF never comes to the *Chhits* to enquire about our needs.[114]

The smugglers store their smuggled items in the enclaves, using them as transit points before arranging for the final smuggling across the border. 'Again it is we who are victimised in such instances, and never the smugglers actually involved',[115] says Ziauddin, resident of a Bangladeshi enclave.

The enclaves are havens for illegal or banned cultivation like that of *ganja* (hemp). As part of a larger drug network, cultivators are provided with seeds and fertilisers by the smugglers' syndicates for cultivating *ganja*,[116] though they are often not aware of the network they are part of or of the ban on such cultivation. The border officials or the police cannot prevent this from happening due to restrictions on entering the enclaves.[117]

110 *Spatial disparities*

While the sense of being disowned is clear in responses such as, 'we live in perpetual fear. We do not have an identity – nor do we have a local *Panchayat-Pradhan* or a State',[118] a sense of confinement is also evident in responses such as, 'we feel as if we are living in a jail'.[119] The complex territorial status of the enclaves has clearly resulted in a complex perception of belonging and/or exclusion amongst its inhabitants. This narrative of belonging is corroborated by the fact that in the case of those enclave dwellers who are convicted for a crime, the final discharge from the jail is often delayed even after the completion of their terms. 'Where will they release us? To which country? Bangladesh does not accept us as its citizens',[120] says Bimal, resident of a Bangladeshi enclave. It is after much deliberation that they are returned back to their enclaves.

Counter-enclaves

The condition of the counter-enclaves makes that of the enclaves even more visible. A counter-enclave is a piece of land belonging to the host state but surrounded by enclaves. Nazirhat II Gram Panchayat is a counter-enclave and an Indian territory surrounded by the Bangladeshi enclave of Madhya Mashaldanga on the Indian side of the border. Residents of Nazirhat II are Indian citizens but need to travel through the Bangladeshi enclaves in order to get to the Indian territories for schools, hospitals, their livelihood, shops, etc. In spite of its unique territorial position, its inhabitants insist that access to basic facilities has not been a problem, as all the people in this enclave have Indian documents proving their citizenship status like ration cards, voter cards, etc.[121]

Despite the basic similarity with the enclaves, in terms of being enclaved within enclaves, the counter-enclaves still enjoy access to schools, hospitals, markets, etc. unlike the enclaves with no access to any such facilities. Though the counter-enclave residents need to travel across enclaves to reach these facilities, which makes them infiltrators for the time when they are on enclave lands, they still lead a better life than the enclave residents only because of their official citizenship status.

Residents of counter-enclaves maintain a lukewarm cordiality with their enclave neighbours, since they need to access the enclave lands to reach hospitals, schools, markets, etc. They even attend each other's festivals to maintain this cordiality,[122] says Saraswati, a resident of Nazirhat II counter-enclave. Simply by virtue of being located on the 'right side' of the border, the inhabitants of counter-enclaves enjoy a better life than those inhabiting the enclaves on the 'wrong side', despite the similarity in their spatial uniqueness. The role of the border becomes undeniably visible in such narratives.

Local administration

Many of the enclaves have formed their own administrative councils, *Chhitmahal Nagarik Samiti* (Enclave Citizens' Committee),[123] which are small administrative bodies and extensions of the larger committee formed of enclave residents of both India and Bangladesh to demand for citizenship rights. Intra-enclave disputes of

Spatial disparities 111

any kind are, most often, mediated by such councils, in the absence of any legal or administrative machinery of the state within the enclaves. 'The *Chhits* have their own councils. We select one of our senior members as the head of the council. There is no formal election as such. The entire process is performed verbally', informs Bimal Burman.[124] The choice of the word 'citizen' as part of the name of the administrative councils bears the irony of the situation of the enclave residents – a people who have been fighting for a citizenship status for more than 65 years.

Usually the councils have one chairman and nine members. The area of the enclave council is divided into wards (usually three but depending on the size of the enclave), each being represented by three members. The larger enclaves might hold an informal election for forming their councils, where local leaders from neighbouring areas might be invited by the enclave-dwellers to supervise the election process. Only the male enclave inhabitants are allowed to vote, keeping the gendered nature of the system intact amidst such deprivation and destitution. The smaller enclaves stick to simpler selection methods.[125]

These councils do not simply have their own heads and members, but also *chowkidars* (village police)[126] and *kerani* (clerks). 'The enclave residents collect a fund from amongst themselves, which is paid as an honorarium to these people for their service.'[127] 'We ourselves try to discipline those enclave inhabitants who create nuisance within the enclaves, though the number of such offenders is very few. In the absence of any legal system, who would want to create a problem anyway?',[128] adds Md. Kamal Hussein, an enclave resident.

The literal translation of the term used by the enclave residents to describe the nature of the local governance (*shamajik bichar*)[129] is 'social justice' – a form, as explained by the people themselves, characterised by the absence of a state-recognised judicial institution and existence of a social institution. It is formed and obeyed by the enclave residents. The term *shamajik bichar* might be interpreted as social administration or social arbitration, but the literal translation – social justice – in fact, stresses the abysmal state of justice – social, political and economic, in the enclaves. This explains the negative undertone of the enclave residents when using this term, and is made clear in responses such as: 'In the absence of a proper legal institution, the miscreants can operate without fear. They know that possibilities of a severe punishment are rare here. Social justice (*shamajik bichar*) is the *most* that we can expect'.[130]

The nature of economic transaction (including land transactions) between the enclave people or between them and their neighbours is also called *shamajik kenabecha*[131] or social transaction by them, given the unofficial nature of the process.[132]

Religious institutions like temples or mosques play important roles as places where arbitrations and transactions take place in enclaves. An enclave resident adds that the demand for citizenship for both the Hindus and Muslim residents of the enclaves is equally strong, irrespective of the host state.[133] This aspect points towards the complex pattern of identification with regard to religion that the enclave people are part of.

It is the state of statelessness that binds them together more than religion, just as a 'bordered status' binds the border inhabitants together more than their social,

112   *Spatial disparities*

political or economic identities. A sense of being wronged by fate, as echoed by many of the border inhabitants ('it is a sin to be born at the border')[134] rings large in the responses of the enclave residents as well: 'We feel ashamed to say that we are born as enclave people',[135] says Hafizul, an enclave resident.

A 'state of exception'

The vulnerable existence of the enclave residents in the context of the absence of state machineries within the enclaves evokes the idea of the 'bare life' of the *homo sacer*[136] – a man who may be killed and yet not sacrificed. The pretexts posed by the states, especially India, with regard to the imminent loss of territory and prospective citizens that the enclave exchange would entail make the evocation stronger. The states would rather let the enclaves be havens for lawlessness and its residents perish than have them given away to the other states as officially recognised citizens.[137] The inclusion of the enclaves in the juridical framework of the states is, ironically, in the form of their exclusion, and this is what thrusts them into a 'state of exception'[138] – a state of 'being outside, and yet belonging'.[139] 'The rule applies to the exception in no longer applying, in withdrawing from it'[140] is what aptly describes the legal state of the enclaves. It is this state of exception that has become the rule[141] in the enclaves.

The creation of a 'fairly formal legal system of their own',[142] in the form of enclave councils and land registration procedures, testifies to the role that *necessity* plays in the creation of the state of exception. That 'necessity has no law' is indeed testified by the situation of the enclaves. The adage can be interpreted in two ways. One is that necessity does not recognise any law. The second is that necessity creates its own law.[143] The enclaves are a study in both. On the one hand, the necessities of the principles of sovereignty and the citizenship issues of India and Bangladesh fail to recognise any law within the enclaves. On the other, the enclave people create their own socio-legal councils meting out basic juridical services out of sheer necessity.

An understanding of the citizenship questions of the enclave people highlights the dilemma between inclusion and membership – incapacity of inclusion into the whole of which it is a member[144] (being detached from the parent state) and failure to become a member of the whole in which it is already included[145] (exclusion from the host state). As sovereign powers, the states decide the trajectory of its people and its territory, pushing them into a 'bare life' – in terms of pushing the lives to extreme vulnerability.[146]

The impression of a vulnerable 'bare life' rings clear in the response of Karim Baksh, an enclave resident, when he says: 'We lead a life like animals here. Even the animals are tracked and recorded by the government, but not us'.[147] Responses of the enclave residents show that years of deprivation have driven them to thoughts of violent agitations lest their demand for citizenship is not met. 'We are trying to co-operate with the government by wanting to be part of the state',[148] says Suren Burman, adding that the delay in the decision-making process of the governments of India and Bangladesh simply reflects the ignorance of the leaders

Spatial disparities 113

concerned, who perceive the enclave crisis merely as a bilateral affair, instead of trying to understand the reality of survival of its people.[149]

The irony is that both India and Bangladesh are party to the International Covenant on Civil and Political Rights (ICCPR)[150] and the International Covenant on Economic, Social and Cultural Rights (ICESCR)[151] under the auspices of the Universal Declaration of Human Rights.[152] The condition of the enclave people makes a complete farce of such declarations and covenants by depriving them of all those rights which these declarations intend to ensure. In fact, their condition poses a serious challenge to the progress of various development goals, including the MDGs,[153] such as access to safe drinking water, sanitation, health service, etc.,[154] besides depriving them of the NREGA[155] work opportunities, primary education, *Anganwadi*[156] and such other facilities provided by the host state. Though this applies to the entire stretch of the border between India and Bangladesh, and several other backward areas in India, the geographical specificity of the enclaves makes the situation worse by not just preventing the existing initiatives from reaching the people, but also by preventing the situation of the enclaves from being officially documented.

Demand for citizenship

The demand for citizenship status of the host states where the enclaves are geographically situated has been a natural culmination of the trajectory of the enclaves. Such demands make perfect sense when seen in the light of the history of most of these inhabitants, as well as, their dependence on their neighbours. 'We have always been living here, right through generation. Naturally we want to be Indian citizens',[157] says a resident of a Bangladeshi enclave in India. Concern for the next generation is the prime factor when it comes to the demand for citizenship status. 'We are approaching old age. At least our children can have a proper future',[158] says Fatema Bibi, an enclave resident.

Apart from the ruins of the pillars marking the border between the host states' territories and the enclaves (the pillars are absent in most of the places), no other distinguishable mark of difference can be pointed out between the two. The similarity in profile of the people of the neighbouring villages and the enclaves renders it impossible for an outsider to distinguish an enclave from non-enclave territory, unless pointed out. It is solely the citizenship issue which keeps the enclave people from leading an unhindered life like their neighbours.

Life at the border has its own share of complexities, including restrictions on movement. The location of the enclave residents makes them doubly jeopardised. Official recognition as citizens of the state will, at least, reduce some of the vulnerabilities associated with living along the border. 'We want to be Indian citizens, and nobody here has a different view on this',[159] is how Md. Iqbal, resident of a Bangladeshi enclave in India, voices the unanimity of the demand, with others supporting him in his claim.[160]

An official citizenship status would also mean that the enclave residents could avail of passports, with which they could legally visit their relatives on the other

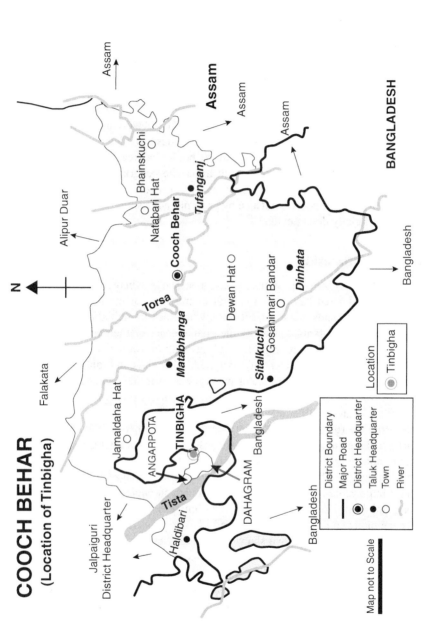

Map 3.2 Location of *Tinbigha*. Cooch Behar. Redrawn map. Source: Cooch Behar District Map, Govt. of India.

Spatial disparities   115

side of the border, without fear of being persecuted. 'Ever since the fencing, we have not been able to visit our relatives on the other side. We do not even have the required documents for passport',[161] complains Md. Kamal Hussein. The prospect of the exchange of enclaves has, in fact, already increased the prices of the enclave lands,[162] in contrast to their falling prices a few years ago.

An interesting observation during the interviews was that the responses of some of the interviewees, mostly constituting women who had married into the enclaves, reflected a confused perception of citizenship – an outcome, perhaps, of a cognitive dissonance.[163] Respondents belonging to the post-Partition generations (those who were born into the enclaves) as well as women married into these enclaves often lacked a clear perception of the history of the formation of the enclaves, or a clear mental map of their unique geographical position. Their initiation into the movement for citizenship has been externally imposed by their families/husbands. Their responses regarding the demand reflect this imposition. Rebecca Khatun, a resident of an Indian enclave in Bangladesh, spontaneously replied that she wanted to 'go to India', on being asked about her choice of citizenship. After a condemnatory look from her husband, she quickly rectified herself saying, 'No, sorry, I mean I want to remain as a part of Bangladesh'.[164]Such confusion in responses were not too rare.

Eleven-year-old Sabina Akhtar, daughter of the chairman of an Indian enclave in Bangladesh, on being asked about her idea of the citizenship issue, highlighted the hazards faced by the enclave people due to the lack of an officially recognised status. Her reply (which sounded more like a prepared speech than an impromptu response) covered everything from the lack of educational facilities in the enclaves and the deprivation of children vis-à-vis the Bangladeshi children in their neighbouring villages, to how, in spite of having equal potential, the enclave children were notable to fulfil their dreams of pursuing a career. She clearly pointed out how her dream of becoming a doctor might be shattered if they were not given Bangladeshi citizenship.[165] That this performance of enlightening me on the enclave crisis was rehearsed was clearly visible, with no time wasted in constructing sentences in sequence. It is not hard to realise that such responses from the current generation of the youth and the women married into the enclaves are externally imposed, and hence either lack confidence or spontaneity. They are also indicative of the complex and often confused pattern of perception about issues like citizenship, belonging, inclusion and exclusion over generations of people undergoing the perils of the Partition and its aftermath.

The *Tinbigha* trajectory

The citizenship issue has a starkly different dimension in the case of Dahagram and Angarpota – the two Bangladeshi enclaves in India, with access to Bangladesh mainland across the border by the *Tinbigha* Corridor, as mentioned earlier.[166] Following its inauguration in June 1992, the corridor was initially opened for the residents of Dahagram at every alternate hour in the day, between 6AM and 6PM. From 2001 onwards, the corridor began operation continuously between 6AM

116 *Spatial disparities*

and 6PM each day. Agitation by the enclave residents was followed by an agreement between the Prime Ministers of India and Bangladesh – Manmohan Singh and Sheikh Hasina, on 19 October 2011,[167] which provided for 24-hours operation of the corridor. It is manned by the BSF[168] since it is an Indian territory.

A 24-hour connection with the mainland has been a boon for Dahagram, not just in terms of access to administrative and legal institutions, basic facilities and markets of Bangladesh, but of having obtained Bangladeshi citizenship as well. 'The situation here is much better now, after the corridor has been opened for the whole day. We can bring bricks, cement, sand, etc. for constructing our homes here. My husband works as a van driver plying passengers between Bangladesh and here. We are doing fine as Bangladeshi citizens',[169] says Jarina Begum of the

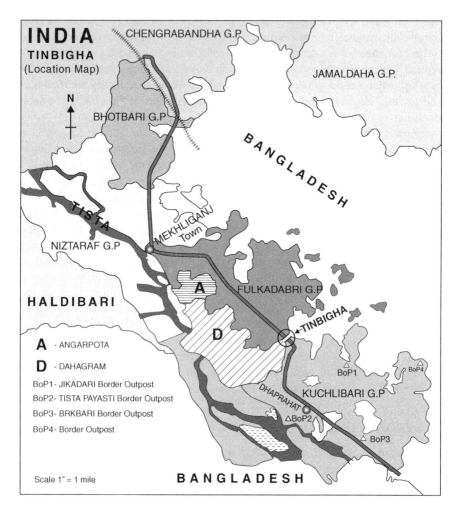

Map 3.3 Location map of *Tinbigha*. Redrawn map. Source: Cooch Behar District Map, Govt. of India.

Angarpota enclave. Old-age stipends, provided by the Dahagram Union Parishad, have improved the lives of the aged people of Dahagram as well.[170]

In the pre-corridor period, the situation of these enclave residents was no different from that of the other enclaves. This explains why many of the enclave residents had their education in and initial business transactions with their neighbouring Indian villages.[171] All this has changed for the current generation, who now has access to hospitals, schools and markets right inside their enclaves, funded and constructed by the Bangladesh government. 'We now get a good price for our crops, cattle and land',[172] informs a visibly satisfied Akbar, resident of Angarpota. Relief from the wrongdoings of miscreants and the border guards,[173] as well as the official documentation of land transactions, have been some of the major reasons for the residents of Dahagram to rejoice. Plans for constructing bridges over the *Tinbigha* for the enclave residents are also on the agenda of India and Bangladesh.[174]

As 'recognised' Bangladeshi citizens, these people emphasise their affluence, and hence, their wish to 'remain' a part of Bangladesh. In fact, they term their movement to 'remain a part of Bangladesh' as an attempt to 'free Dahagram from India'.[175] A resident of Dahagram explains the movement in the following way:

> We want to remain a part of Bangladesh. We want Dahagram to be free from them. But they (Indians who have been affected by the *Tinbigha* Corridor) want to seize Dahagram as their own territory. They have also been complaining about the privileges which we have been provided following the opening of the Corridor. They try their best to hamper the facilities like electricity or free movement. Our forefathers have fought for a free Bangladesh. Why would we want to be a part of India now?[176]

These responses come as a stark contrast to the sort of responses regarding citizenship of the inhabitants of the other enclaves.

Dahagram being territorially closer to the Bangladesh mainland has had a different trajectory from the other enclaves right from the beginning of the enclave question in 1947. It has been 'more important as an idea of territory "saved" from the clutches of a "spatially greedy" Indian state, than as a material geographic reality',[177] as Jason Cons rightly puts it. In fact, this status of Dahagram was recognised by the state of Bangladesh when the Zia government[178] issued sixteen 'Civil Guns' to Dahagram in 1977 to be used for defence – signalling an effort to secure Dahagram-Angarpota as part of its national territory.[179] The fact that 'the guns are spoken of almost reverentially'[180] by the residents as 'symbols of belonging'[181] indicates the difference between the narratives of Dahagram and the rest of the enclaves.

Enumerating the residents of Dahagram through a census conducted by Bangladesh in 1981 was yet another attempt to officially claim Dahagram as part of Bangladesh.[182] These narratives portray the residents of Dahagram as 'rights-bearing' citizens[183] of Bangladesh, in contrast to the stateless condition of the residents of the rest of the enclaves.

Claims over territories in the context of the *Tinbigha* Corridor still persist, with the West Bengal government deciding to construct a community centre and rest

Figure 3.2 Hospital in Dahagram, 2011.

house in the *Tinbigha* corridor, despite objections from the BGB and in violation of the international border law on the construction of permanent establishments on the 150-yard stretch from the zero point.[184] The BGB has made its objections clear on this decision of West Bengal and has decided to prevent the construction if West Bengal goes ahead with its plans.[185]

Territoriality becomes decisive in the production of these different versions of narratives. While *territorial detachment* decides the responses of the inhabitants of the rest of the enclaves, *territorial attachment* shapes the ideas of belonging among the residents of Dahagram. Narratives of belonging coincide with those of the idea of the nation in such spontaneous responses, redefining notions of spatiality, citizenship and liberty in the process.[186] In fact, narratives from Dahagram add another dimension to the concepts of proxy citizenship. While the movement for 'freeing' Dahagram from the clutches of India positioned its Muslim residents 'as stoic sufferers holding their land in the name of a Muslim Bengali state',[187] the Hindus of Dahagram actively campaigned 'to demonstrate that Dahagram's residents "desired" to be part of India'.[188]

Claim, counter claim and issues of control over the *Tinbigha* Corridor have, in recent times, taken a performative turn, with the residents of Dahagram-Angorpota as well as Mekhligunj and the local administrative officials demanding that the routine regime of flag hoisting and marching by the BSF and the BGB be made more spectacular, like the Wagah Border performance every evening.[189] The retreat ceremony at the Wagah border is a show of state power and control, performed as a spectacle, aiming to convey the omnipresence of the states at their borders to the civilian audiences as well as a reminder to the border forces on both sides. Calling for a similar ceremonial performance at the *Tinbigha* Corridor[190] has similar implications for India and Bangladesh, especially at one of the most sensitive and

Spatial disparities 119

Figure 3.3 Tinbigha Corridor leading to mainland Bangladesh, 2011.

disputed territories at the border. The complicated territorial and political situation of *Tinbigha* Corridor explains why the call for such a spectacular show of strength has been demanded in this particular place rather than any other border post between India and Bangladesh.

Organised movements

Initiatives of organising the people of the enclaves have been a difficult task, given the scattered nature of the geographical location of the enclaves, as well as restrictions on their activities and movements. However, a *Chhitmahal Nagorik Committee* (Committee of Enclave People) was formed by some individuals of the Indian enclaves in Bangladesh in a public meeting on 26 January 1972, following the birth of Bangladesh in 1971. The main purpose of the committee was to lodge complaints with government institutions regarding the question of human rights as provided for in the bulletin of the meeting.[191] Other committees were also formed by the migrants, however small in number, from the Indian enclaves to the Indian mainland, who took initiatives to mediate between the enclave residents and the government of India. Yet such initiatives failed to garner any support from either the government officials or the political parties.[192] The deteriorating condition of the enclave people despite the presence of the committees stands proof of this neglect.

120 *Spatial disparities*

After some initial efforts at organising a protest movement in demand for citizenship of the enclave residents, the Bharat-Bangladesh Enclaves Exchange Coordination Committee (BBEECC) was, finally, formed in 1994 by Dipak Sengupta (Dinhata, Cooch Behar district of West Bengal). His son, Diptiman Sengupta, started leading the movement and the committee from October 2009. The committee consisted of enclave residents from both Indian and Bangladeshi enclaves. Ever since its inception, the BBEECC has been actively pursuing the enclave issue, submitting several memorandums and survey reports to various governmental departments, besides organising regular meetings and demonstrations in favour of the implementation of the Indira-Mujib Treaty. In 2000, the committee met with the Indian Home Minister, Lalkrishna Advani, discussing possible solutions to the problem. So far, the committee has handed over six letters to the current Chief Minister of West Bengal (and the Leader of the Opposition in West Bengal State Assembly before 2011), Mamata Banerjee, requesting the rapid execution of the exchange programme,[193] as well as attending to the citizenship issues of some of the enclave residents, especially the children.[194] Inactivity on the part of leaders and government officials forced the members of the committee to organise a hunger strike in March 2012 at Dinhata led by the senior enclave residents. The focus of the demonstration was to draw the attention of the administrative officials and the media towards the enclave question. Unfortunately, the demonstration, in spite of disquieting governmental officials for a while, failed to produce any concrete action towards the fulfilment of the enclave exchange agreement.[195] In fact, as a way of making their case for incorporation stronger, the enclave residents started observing and celebrating the national events of the host state, like Republic Day, over the last few years.[196]

The efforts of the committee gradually started seeing positive results, attracting the attention of the media and the larger civil society.[197] Unnecessary harassment of the enclave residents by the police and border guards also reduced. 'In the last couple of years, incidents of false convictions against enclave residents have reduced due to the on-going movement',[198] says Md. Iqbal Ali from a Bangladeshi enclave in India.

Surveys of the enclaves were done in 2012, enumerating the population and specifying their other geographical details.[199] Bilateral initiatives for the implementation of the exchange have been renewed from 2011, although debates regarding them had never completely ceased in the intervening years. Considerations over the loss of land by India, as was being debated by political parties,[200] as well as issues of citizenship and migration, kept delaying the process. Debates over the loss of land and potential citizens have done the rounds in the Indian political scenario, which delayed the presentation of the exchange bill in the Parliament for a long time.[201]

In a meeting between Salman Khurshid, India's Minister of External Affairs, and Bangladesh's Minister of Foreign Affairs, Dipu Moni, in Dhaka (Bangladesh's capital) in February 2013,[202] the urgency of taking a final call on the enclave question was recognised by both states, besides other unresolved land issues along the border between India and Bangladesh. The signing of MOUs[203] regarding the border agreement (including the exchange of enclaves) and the exchange of maps showing the demarcation of borders between India and Bangladesh were certainly positive steps ahead.[204] Bangladesh's Prime Minister, Sheikh Hasina's visit to Delhi in September 2013 gave the issue the necessary impetus.[205] The bill, in the meantime, made its way to the Parliament.[206] Bangladesh, all along, kept its pressure alive on India for the passing of the bill, since it was primarily the government of West Bengal that was apprehensive about the exchange given its problems with loss of land and population.[207] The enclave residents under the leadership of the BBEECC kept its movement active through public litigation cases regarding fundamental rights and security questions.[208]

Exchange

The enclave question and the civil society movement regarding their exchange saw a tangible outcome on 1 August 2015, when India and Bangladesh exchanged 162 enclaves between themselves. This meant that the enclave residents could now choose between the citizenship of the host country where the enclaves are geographically located (i.e. residents of Bangladeshi enclaves in India could have Indian citizenship and vice versa) or move to the country of which the enclaves are administrative parts (residents of Bangladeshi enclaves in India could move to Bangladesh and be Bangladeshi citizens). During the time of exchange, there were an estimated 53,000 enclave residents who acquired citizenship status of either state. Of the 51 Bangladeshi enclaves in India, covering an area of 7110 acres, 14,863 residents took up Indian citizenship. On the other side of the border, 37,532 residents of the 111 Indian enclaves in Bangladesh, covering 17,161 acres, took Bangladeshi citizenship. Another 989 residents of Indian enclaves in Bangladesh wished to resettle to India, though, eventually 920 of them resettled by 30 November, and the remaining 61 changed their minds and stayed back in Bangladesh.[209]

At a tangible level, the exchange of enclaves has been a long overdue solution to a complex territorial, administrative and human rights crisis caused by Partition. While the first provision for exchange following the Nehru-Noon Pact of 1958 and its final execution in 2015 took some 57 years, the enclave question, in the intervening years, had always made its presence felt in India-Bangladesh bilateral affairs. The exchange of enclaves resolved the issue by officially recognising its residents as citizens of the states to which they chose to belong. The exchange also made the enclave situation a national question of formal granting of citizenship documents to the enclave residents and settling/rehabilitating the residents for sustainable livelihood options. Development of the enclaves, in terms of economy, housing, health and education came under the purview of the national (India and Bangladesh) and to an extent provincial (West Bengal) governments. The question remained: how did the exchange actually help the enclave residents, apart from giving them formal access to citizenship? The condition of the enclaves following the exchange amply answers the question.

The leader of BBEECC, Diptiman Sengupta's change of political affiliation from Forward Bloc to BJP turned the enclave issue into an ego clash between two

122 *Spatial disparities*

warring political factions. The central government in India led by BJP washed its hands of the enclave question immediately after the exchange was done and restricted its responsibilities to merely allocating funds for the rehabilitation and development of the residents. The West Bengal government led by Trinomool Congress (TMC) was expected to see to its implementation. The government of India sanctioned Rs. 1005.99 crore on 2 December 2015 for rehabilitation and upgradation of infrastructure, aimed largely towards the returnees from Indian enclaves in Bangladesh. The sanction was made for a period of five years to the West Bengal government from 2015–16 to 2019–20.[210]

The matter boiled down to each government holding the other responsible, keeping the enclave residents in that very uncertain condition that they were fighting to overcome for the last six decades.

More than half of the enclave residents in India are yet to receive their ration cards with which to access subsidised rations. They still need to buy daily amenities and household items at the steep market price and are, thus, unable to access basic food supplies under the food security provision of the government.[211] Even the lists made on the basis of surveys among the residents regarding their choice of citizenship were flawed, having missed several names. The residents who did not find their way to the lists are still caught in the limbo – broken families and separated relatives living on Indian and Bangladeshi enclaves on both sides of the border.[212] Health or education facilities are yet to come and death following unavailability of access to hospitals, as has been the trajectory of the enclaves so far, still plagues the residents.[213] The battle for recognition has, now, given way to the battle, often violent, for rehabilitation and infrastructural development of the enclaves.[214] The crisis of still having to carry fake identities looms large among enclave dwellers, despite the exchange. Students admitted to schools with fake identities of fathers in the pre-exchange period are yet to get their original identities and family names back – the process, often, being hampered by procedural complications.[215]

The fact that the enclave narratives are not just outcomes of state-building but also evolve within the hegemonic structure of statehood, much like the border narratives discussed in the preceding chapter, is highlighted by two significant aspects: the movements of the enclave people demanding citizenship, resulting in the recent debates between the enclave residents and the West Bengal government, and the creation of semi-formal legal bodies within the enclaves modelled on the *Panchayats*/Unions in the neighbouring villages of the host state.

The enclave narratives are not limited to their efforts for accommodating themselves within the state structure but, in fact, have a direct effect on one of the more important pillars of statehood in a democratic state, i.e. the elections. The effect is not simply in terms of the conflicting views of political parties regarding the political question of enclave exchange,[216] but also on the results of elections. In the recent *Panchayat* elections in West Bengal (July 2013), the areas surrounding the Bangladesh enclaves in the Cooch Behar district of West Bengal unanimously voted against the Mamata Banerjee-headed Trinomool Congress (TMC) for her failure to execute the exchange of the enclaves with Bangladesh.[217] The enclave

Spatial disparities 123

exchange issue, by virtue of being a national issue, has to be executed between the central governments of India and Bangladesh. But as the host of the Bangladeshi enclaves, West Bengal plays a very important role in the process of ratification of the treaties and the final execution of the process of exchange. The failure of the TMC to make any progress in the enclave issue affected the people's decision in the *Panchayat* elections, where the Indian villages surrounding the Bangladeshi enclaves made their dissatisfaction known by voting out TMC, despite the latter's victory in most of the other districts of West Bengal. The enclave question affects not just the enclave people themselves but those in the surrounding areas, through various legal and illegal interactions (including fake identities, access to local markets and access to basic needs as well as miscreant activities). The results of the *Panchayat*elections are a reflection of this overwhelming effect that the enclaves have on the neighbouring people, as well as a re-emphasis of the fact that enclave narratives, too, express themselves within the framework of statehood.

These narratives also, in a way, contest and redefine the idea of the enclaves as a space of exception. Even within the structure of power of the state (including the power to exclude), the enclave narratives create their own unique ways of negotiating their bare life. Interactions with neighbours and the effect on the electoral decisions of the very state that excludes them are ways of contesting and questioning the sovereign power of the state. In being a space of exception through the exclusionary practices of the state, the enclaves share a similar fate with the *Chars* and *Ghoj* areas along the West Bengal-Bangladesh border.

The enclaves also attain a subalternity through their questioning of the role of the state as the container, as do the other border narratives along the West Bengal-Bangladesh border. The extension of enclave houses into neighbouring areas, neighbouring areas being affected by accidents in the enclaves like fire, people from neighbouring areas owning land inside the enclaves and the similar profile of the people (culture, language, customs) are some of the more visible examples of the subversive nature of the enclave narratives. In spite of such similarities in nature, the non-enclave border narratives of the West Bengal-Bangladesh border become more visible than the enclave narratives in state discourses and public debates because they directly question the sovereign power of the state at its international borders. The enclaves, on the other hand, being 'contained' within the larger territorial jurisdiction of the states, fail to hit at the roots of the vulnerability of state hegemony. Despite questioning the role of the state as the container (through border-crossings between enclaves and their non-enclave surroundings), they fail to threaten the states' sovereignty in ways that the international border does, although they are a result of the creation of the border in the first place.

The India-Bangladesh enclaves have travelled a full circle. From being thrust into statelessness by the imperatives of state-building to leading a bare life, from hoping to be incorporated into the states to an organised movement for the realisation of their demand for citizenship, the narratives of the enclaves reveal the enclave peoples' attempt to 'give to the empirical form of a population the moral attributes of a community' (Chatterjee, 2004).The journey has, in the process, not just seen the creation of a unique identity of the enclave people but has made them

124 *Spatial disparities*

an integral part of the larger community of border people as well. The perception of themselves as 'enclave people' stands as an indication of this attribute.

The complex patterns of interactions along the West Bengal-Bangladesh border amongst the border people, including the civilians, border guards and other administrative bodies, combine differing and often conflicting views on the questions of territorial imperatives, citizenship, nationality, religion, caste, gender and economy. The enclaves add yet another dimension to it. The fact that territorial imperatives and border issues have gained significance like never before despite debates in favour of a borderless world and the unhindered flow of commodities and cultural trends, is strongly emphasised by the India-Bangladesh enclave narratives.

The India-Bangladesh border enclaves are geographically unique, ethno-culturally rooted in history and politically vulnerable. Narratives produced in them are not just absent elsewhere in the non-border non-enclave areas of India and Bangladesh, but are absent or seen in very different forms in the other enclaves of the world. They show how territoriality and identity can be intertwined in very complex ways. They feed into the larger array of border narratives and the framework of border consciousness, where we see the interplay between spatiality and cultural identity in various different forms, some of which I have tried to highlight in this book. The India-Bangladesh enclave narratives, through their geographical specificity and cultural/political uniqueness, provide examples of 'miniature societies attempting to survive in the interstices of the modern world state system'.[218] In fact, till their recent exchange and consequent formal inclusion into the state system, the enclaves were prototypes of what van Schendel calls 'zomia'[219] and which Scott explores in-depth – a region 'whose peoples have not yet been fully incorporated into nation-states'.[220]

Chars **and** *Ghoj*

Apart from the enclaves, there are other unique land formations, like *Chars* and *Ghoj*, seen in lower river basins and riverine areas along the West Bengal-Bangladesh border. They are what have been aptly called 'environmental borderlands' by Lahiri-Dutt and Samanta, in not just being located at peripheries of the mainland but also for being the 'grey area of legitimacy'.[221] *Chars*, *Ghoj* and enclaves are political units but which also cut across fixed socio-political categories. Hence they become what Scott describes as ungovernable borderlands or 'nonstate spaces',[222] characterised by an anarchism in terms of existing beyond state control.

Chars are island-like silt depositions in the lower parts of river basins. They are characteristically impermanent in nature. They come into being due to silt deposition but are frequently eroded away by the river too. Use of the *Chars*, be it in terms of settling, livelihood practices or even as transit for humans and goods, has to be done keeping this impermanence in consideration. The residents of the *Chars* are called *choruas* in the local parlance and their lives are as uncertain and, thus, nomadic as the impermanent nature of the *Chars* would drive them into.[223]

Spatial disparities 125

The *Chars* of the Gangetic basin, some of which later became border land-masses following the Partition, began to be populated during the latter half of the 1900s, when refugees began pouring in across the border. The ones who ended up in the *Chars* were mostly peasants, unlike the first wave of refugees to West Bengal, who were almost necessarily the professionals, without direct attachment to the soil. But the peasants were the last to migrate because of their dependence on agricultural land. By the time the peasants migrated to West Bengal, cities and the surrounding areas were already populated, making it difficult for the peasant communities to settle there. The *Chars*, still then unpopulated, were the remaining resort for settlement, like the islands of Sundarbans, which were mostly populated by the later peasant migrants from East Bengal.[224] Thus, residing in the *Chars* has never been the first option for the *choruas* – most of whom were either late migrants forced to settle down in the *Chars* or were rendered stateless while in transit from Bangladesh to India. It was the agricultural skill of the Bangladeshi migrants that made the *Chars* habitable and also turned them into agricultural lands.[225] But the impermanence of the landmasses themselves does not change the stateless nature of the *choruas*. This has also been beneficial to illegal settlers, or those involved in illegal cross-border trading. The invisibility provided by *Char*-life has given them safe shelters and livelihood opportunities, outside the vigilant eyes of the state. Bangladeshi migrants who came later did so with support from their kin and/or neighbours who had settled earlier in the *Chars*. This explains the presence of entire villages constituting of Bangladeshi migrants, legal and illegal, in many of the *Chars* along the West Bengal-Bangladesh border. In fact the *Chars* act, in a way, as an entry point to 'official' citizen status for those who wish to move ahead from statelessness and be recognised as citizens. The 'informal chain of local political leaders, panchayat members, and community development block officials' provide these illegal *Char*-settlers with 'valid' documents they require to claim citizenship status, like voter identity cards or ration cards.[226] In this, the *Chars* also become part of the border culture of being the transition zones between illegality and legality.

The stateless status of the *Char* residents complicates their relation with the mainland people as well. Coupled with that is the suspicion of the mainlanders regarding the *choruas* in terms of fear of theft and/or loot of resources like grain, vegetables, cattle from the mainland due to the lack of the same in the *Chars*. But the *Chars* are also, for those mainlanders involved in illegal trading, a haven for stocking of contraband items to be smuggled across the border, away from the vigilant eyes of the border forces.

In their excellent study of the Damodar *Chars*, Lahiri-Dutt and Samanta have identified certain factors which make *Char* inhabitation difficult, like the 'convo-luted legalistic language of the land documents, the difficulty of proving owner-ship of *Char* lands by its residents and acquiring such documents, continuation of rent payment for a lost land/eroded *Char*, difficulty in accessing the land docu-ment officials and finally establishing rights over resurfacing *Chars*'.[227] Vanish-ing and resurfacing of *Chars* are a usual phenomenon, keeping its residents in a constant state of flux. The matter is made all the more complicated when the

126 *Spatial disparities*

Chars are located in a riverine border, like Jalangi in Murshidabad (West Bengal) where a *Char* might erode from the Indian side and resurface on the Bangladesh side of the river and vice versa, driving the residents into more acute statelessness. As Lahiri-Dutt and Samanta rightly point out, physical possession of lands in the case of a *Char* is of utmost importance unlike other land possessions, because land documents do not help much in matters of such shifting landmasses.[228] The pattas provided by the respective state governments to the refugee migrants are often rendered useless when a *Char* merges with the mainland or when a *Char* ceases to exist due to erosion or changing river course.[229] The fact that in Bengal a *Char* attains a recognised status only after it exists for twenty years makes things even more complicated. Not all *Chars* fit into the definition of 'land' required to be recognised officially. Most of them lack the permanence, infrastructure, sanitation or connectivity to be able to enter the officio-legal recognition of a habitable/inhabited landmass.[230] Thus, physical possession of the landmass is of utmost importance and, hence, conflict over claim and counter-claim of existing and newly-emerging *Chars* is a regular affair.[231]

Char-life creates a milieu akin to borderland consciousness but which is also, in a way, unique. It is almost a subculture within the larger rubric of 'border culture', characterised by uncertainty, vulnerability as well as a desperation to survive. No wonder the *Char*-dwellers of Bengal are called 'some of the most desperate people in the country'.[232] *Char* life, anywhere in the world, has its own issues. And location of such *Chars* across state borders adds to the difficulty of living and earning in these landmasses – the *Chars* along the riverine borders between West Bengal and Bangladesh being apt examples. As 'fracture'[233] or 'shatter' zones of the states,[234] brought about by Partition and state-making processes at large, enclaves and *Chars* along the West Bengal-Bangladesh border question the all-pervasive omnipresence of the state machinery at the state margins, where the materiality of the state's sovereign power is at its most tangible version. It is not simply the relation between these fracture zones and the respective states which is at stake in the enclaves, *Chars* or other such 'non-state' regions, but also the subject-status of its inhabitants,[235] as the citizenship issues of their residents would clearly indicate. The geographical peripheries of the state act as a litmus test for the identities of its residents – putting their loyalty to question every day. The complex geopolitical crisis of such landmasses as enclaves and *Chars* (and *Ghoj*, as the following part would suggest), adds to the anxiety of the inhabitants.

A *Ghoj*[236] is yet another example of a landmass which, though part of a state, negotiates the uncertainty of exclusion or statelessness in their daily lives. The hastily drawn border between India and Bangladesh has resulted in a number of *Ghoj* lands which have been incorporated into one of the states, though they geographically intrude into the neighbouring territory and are surrounded by the neighbouring territory on its three sides. They are connected to their parent state by a narrow stretch of land, creating a chicken's neck formation. They are also affected by the changing course of the river like the *Chars*. 'These territories are havens for the smugglers who get the Indian women to bring certain items from the Indian side, collect all the smuggled items in these territories and then smuggle the items into the other areas of Bangladesh',[237] says Pradip, a resident of an Indian *Ghoj*. *Ghoj* and *Chars* are affected by the changing courses of the rivers. While agriculture remains the preferred occupation of the *Char* and *Ghoj* residents, the uncertainty of the effect of the river on the landmass forces them to resort to other options, like agricultural labourers in others' fields or labourers in other *Chars* or even the mainland, if one can manage to. Livestock farming and fishing are the other available options for the *choruas* and, in fact, have increasingly become an equal engager as agriculture, or even a replacement in some cases. The impermanent nature of the land on which they live is compensated by the permanence of the water they are surrounded by. This explains their growing dependence on water-driven occupations, like fishing. But even the changing course of a river followed by drying up of a part of it or the construction of dams in the upper basin areas affect their water-dependent livelihood options. This pushes them not just into destitution and dependence on the neighbouring state for resources, but also to resorting to illegal means of earning a living. 'Earlier we would depend on fishing in the Ichhamati river which used to flow along the *Ghoj*. Ever since this part of the Ichhamati has dried up (followed by a change in its course), we have become completely dependent on the Bangladeshis for our food, daily necessities and even education. We have no other resource left other than smuggling',[238] says a resident of an Indian *Ghoj* surrounded by Bangladeshi territory on its three sides.

In a densely populated region like Bengal, including West Bengal and Bangladesh, the relationship of the people with the land has always been important,

Figure 3.4 India's border fence through which the land indicated above (*Ghoj*) passes, 2012.

128   *Spatial disparities*

in terms of optimum use of land and its resources. The relation becomes all the more complex when it comes to borderlands, because the significance and sensitivity of the use of land and resources takes a new turn. Appropriation and use of land and resources along the borderlands of the states often questions the states' role as the sovereign power and challenges the integrity of the states at spaces where the states are most vulnerable territorially, culturally and politically – its borderlands.[239] Likewise, the livelihoods practiced in these vulnerable territories like enclaves, *Chars* or *Ghoj* 'create new forms of economic citizenship that are beyond the state'.[240]

Notes

1 Sills, D.L. (Ed.). (1968) *International Encyclopedia of the Social Sciences*, Volume 5. p. 61.
2 Hanks, P. (Ed.). (1971) *Encyclopedic World Dictionary*. p. 58.
3 Rabbani, Md. G. (2005–2006) Stateless in South Asia: Living in Bangladesh-India Enclaves. *Theoretical Perspectives: A Journal of Social Sciences and Arts*. 12 & 13. p. 1.
4 Robinson, G.W.S. (1959) Exclaves. *Annals of the Association of American Geographers*. 49. pp. 283–295.
5 Rabbani, 2005–2006, p. 2.
6 Ibid.
7 Between 2011 and 2012 when I was conducting my field studies in the India-Bangladesh enclaves, the exchange had not taken place. The civil society movement for the exchange of enclaves between the two states was in full swing. When I came back to rework on my doctoral dissertation later in 2016, the exchange had already taken place, whereby Indian enclaves in Bangladesh officially became a part of Bangladesh and vice versa. The exchange process and the current scenario have, thus, been included at the end of the previously existing chapter from the dissertation.
8 Discussed in the Introduction.
9 Chatterji, J. (1999) The Fashioning of a Frontier: The Radcliffe Line and Bengal's Border Landscpae, 1947–52. *Modern Asian Studies*. 33(1). pp. 185–242.
10 Cooch Behar Merger Agreement. (1949). Available from: http://coochbehar.nic.in/htmfiles/royal_history2.html.
11 Rabbani, 2005–2006, pp. 3–9.
12 Ibid. p. 33.
13 Van Schendel, W. (February 2002) Stateless in South Asia: The Making of the India-Bangladesh Enclaves. *The Journal of Asian Studies*. 61(1). p. 122.
14 In 1947, there were 130 Indian enclaves and 95 Pakistani enclaves, which were reduced to 123 Indian and 74 Pakistani enclaves by 1965 through boundary agreements. Further reduction in their numbers to the current figure of 111 Indian enclaves and 51 Bangladeshi enclaves, however, has not been very clearly spelt out. Van Schendel, 2002, p. 118.
15 Chakrabarty, C. (8 January 2013) Nei desher baromashya. *Ei Samay*. [Online] Available from: www.epaper.eisamay.com/epapermain.aspx?queryed=9&eddate=01/08/2013. [Last accessed: 15 August 2013].
16 Van Schendel, 2002, p. 124.
17 Rabbani, 2005–2006, p. 29.
18 Efforts are still on by the Bangladesh government for the return of Enemy Property to the Hindus who had left behind their property in East Pakistan after partition. Afraad, K. (5 November 2009) Dakhal kora Hindu sampatti ferate ek dhap egolo Bangladesh. *Ananda Bazar Patrika*. [Online] Available from: www.anandabazar.com/archive/1091105/5bdesh1.htm. [Last accessed: 17 September 2013].

Spatial disparities 129

19 The Foreigner's Act 1946. Available from: http://mha.nic.in/pdfs/The%20Foreigners %20Act,%201946.pdf; Interview with Phulmoni, resident of a Bangladeshi enclave in India (Bakhalir *Chhit* of Kurigram district of Bangladesh in Cooch Behar district of West Bengal, 16 March 2012).
20 Discussed in Chapter 3.
21 Interview with Phulmoni, resident of a Bangladeshi enclave in India (Bakhalir *Chhit* of Kurigram district of Bangladesh in Cooch Behar district of West Bengal, 16 March 2012).
22 Interview with Md. Iqbal Ali Sheikh, resident of a Bangladeshi enclave in India (Purba Bakhalir Chhara *Chhit* of Kurigram district of Bangladesh in Cooch Behar district of West Bengal, 16 March 2012).
23 Acquired Territories (Merger) Act 1960. Available from: www.constitution.org/cons/ india/shed01.htm#FIRST SCHEDULE.
24 *Tin* is both the Bengali and Hindi word for the number 3. A *bigha* is a unit of measurement of area of a land, commonly used in Nepal, Bangladesh and a few states in India, including West Bengal. The size of a *bigha* varies considerably from place to place. In West Bengal as well as Bangladesh (both of which were part of the undivided province of Bengal before the partition of 1947), the *bigha* was standardised under British colonial rule at 1600 square yards or 0.3306 acre, which is often interpreted as being 1/3 acre. *Tinbigha* means 3 *bighas*, i.e. a corridor measuring 3 *bighas* or 1 acre approximately.
25 H.M. Ershad became the Chief Martial Law Administrator in 1982, following a bloodless coup on 24 March 1982. He finally took over as President of Bangladesh on 11 December 1983 by replacing A.F.M. Ahsanuddin Chowdhury and held the post continuously till 1990.
26 (Article in Press) Cons, J. (2012) Narrating Boundaries: Framing and Contesting Suffering, Community, and Belonging in Enclaves Along the India-Bangladesh Border. *Political Geography*. p. 1–10. Available from: http://dx.doi.org/10.1016/j.polgeo.2012.06.004; Tinbigha: Agreements and Verdicts. Available from: http://coochbehar.nic.in/htmfiles/ tinbigha_contd.html. [Accessed: 10 August 2013].
27 Quoted in Roy, K. (Ed.). (2013) *Uttarbanger Shimanta*. Kolkata: D.C. Book Agency. p. 59.
28 Van Schendel, 2002, p. 124.
29 Ibid.
30 Ibid.
31 Ibid. p. 125.
32 Catudal, H.M. (1979) *The Exclave problem of Western Europe*. Tuscaloosa: University of Alabama Press; Chatterji, J. (1999) The Fashioning of a Frontier: The Radcliffe Line and Bengal's Border Landscape. *Modern Asian Studies*. 33. pp. 185–242; Karan, P.P. (1966) The India-Pakistan Enclave Problem. *The Professional Geographer*. 18. pp. 23–25; Kaur, N. (2002) The Nowhere People. *Frontline*. 19; Robinson, G.W.S. (1959) Exclaves. *Annals of the Association of American Geographers*. 49. pp. 283–295; Vinokurov, E. (2007) *A Theory of Enclaves*. Lantham, MD: Lexington Books; Whyte, B. (2002) *Waiting for the Esquimo: An Historical and Documentary Study of the Cooch Behar Enclaves of India and Bangladesh*. Melbourne: University of Melbourne Press; Rabbani, Md. G. (2005–2006) Stateless in South Asia: Living in Bangladesh-India Enclaves. *Theoretical Perspectives: A Journal of Social Sciences and Arts*. 12 & 13. Dhaka: Centre for Alternatives.
33 Van Schendel, W. (February 2002) Stateless in South Asia: The Making of the India-Bangladesh Enclaves. *The Journal of Asian Studies*. 61(1). pp. 115–147; (Article in Press) Cons, J. (2012) Narrating Boundaries: Framing and Contesting Suffering, Community, and Belonging in Enclaves along the India-Bangladesh Border. *Political Geography*. pp. 1–10; Cons, J. (2012) Histories of Belonging(s): Narrating Territory, Possession, and Dispossession at the India-Bangladesh Border. *Modern Asian*

130 *Spatial disparities*

Studies. 46(3). pp. 527–558; Jones, R. (2009) Sovereignty and Statelessness in the Border Enclaves of India and Bangladesh. *Political Geography.* 28(6). pp. 373–381; Jones, R. (2010) The Border Enclaves of India and Bangladesh: The Forgotten Lands. In Diener, A. and Hagen, J. (Eds.) *Borderlines and Borderlands: Political Oddities at the Edge of the Nation-State.* New York: Rowman Littlefield; Shewly, H.J. (2013) Abandoned Spaces and Bare Life in the Enclaves of the India-Bangladesh Border. *Political Geography.* 32. pp. 23–31.

34 'জন্ম সার্টিফিকেট, পোলিও কার্ড কিছু নেই. আমরা শুধু মানুষ নামে পরিচিত।' Interview with Md. Anisur, resident of a Bangladeshi enclave in India (Madhya Mashaldanga *Chhit* of Kurigram district of Bangladesh in Cooch Behar district of West Bengal, 15 March 2012).

35 Van Schendel, 2002, p. 129.

36 Interview with Nirendranath Burman, deputy-head of *Panchayat* of Kalmati village, Dinhata (Cooch Behar district of West Bengal, 16 March 2012).

37 Interview with Kamal Debnath, resident of a Bangladeshi enclave in India (Shibprasad Mustafi *Chhit* of Kurigram district of Bangladesh in Cooch Behar district of West Bengal, 17 March 2012).

38 Interview with Md. Iqbal Ali, resident of a Bangladeshi enclave in India (Madhya Mashaldanga *Chhit* of Kurigram district of Bangladesh in Cooch Behar district of West Bengal, 15 March 2012).

39 Interview with Hafizul, resident of an Indian enclave in Bangladesh (Dahala-Khagrabari *Chhit* of Cooch Behar district of West Bengal in Panchagarh district of Bangladesh, 5 October 2011).

40 Interview with Md. Karim Baksh, resident of a Bangladeshi enclave in India (Karala *Chhit* of Kurigram district of Bangladesh in Cooch Behar district of West Bengal, 17 March 2012); Staff Reporter. (10 June 2010) Pares her prastab. *Ananda Bazar Patrika.* [Online] Available from: www.anandabazar.com/10uttar4.htm. [Last accessed: 15 August 2013].

41 Interview with Kamal Debnath, resident of a Bangladeshi enclave in India (Shibprasad Mustafi *Chhit* of Kurigram district of Bangladesh in Cooch Behar district of West Bengal, 17 March 2012).

42 Van Schendel, 2002, p. 135.

43 Interview with Md. Iqbal Ali, resident of a Bangladeshi enclave in India (Madhya Mashaldanga *Chhit* of Kurigram district of Bangladesh in Cooch Behar district of West Bengal, 15 March 2012).

44 Rabbani, 2005–2006, p. 42.

45 Van Schendel, 2002, p. 129.

46 Ibid.

47 Rabbani, 2005–2006, pp. 37–38.

48 Below Poverty Line (BPL) is an economic benchmark and poverty threshold used by the government of India to indicate economic disadvantage, and to identify individuals and households in need of government assistance and aid. It is determined using various parameters which vary from state to state and within states. The present criteria are based on a survey conducted in 2002. Internationally, an income of less than $1.25 per day per head of purchasing power parity is defined as extreme poverty. Criteria are different for rural and urban areas. In its Tenth Five-Year Plan (2002–2007) survey, BPL for rural areas was based on the degree of deprivation in respect of thirteen parameters, with scores from 0–4: landholding, type of house, clothing, food security, sanitation, consumer durables, literacy status, labour force, means of livelihood, status of children, type of indebtedness, reasons for migrations, etc.

49 'ভারতীয় রা এখানে চাষ করে নিয়ে যায়. আমরা না পাই কর, না পাই আশ্বাস. ভারতে ওরা হয়ত বি পি এল. এদিকে ছিটে চাষ করে-ছিটে তো কর দিতে হয় না. সুতরাং পুরোই মুনাফা. ভারতে তো ওদের নামে কোনো জমি নেই, তাই বি পি এল. এখানে চাষ করে. আমরা কিছু বললে হুমকি দেয়. এই বিষয় ভারত সরকার কিছু করে না।' (Indians cultivate their lands here. We cannot do anything about it. They do not own any land in India, and

Spatial disparities 131

are so in the BPL list. Here they do not have to pay any tax. So for them, it is only profit. If we complain, they threaten us.) Interview with Md. Kamal Hussein, resident of a Bangladeshi enclave in India (Karala *Chhit* of Kurigram district of Bangladesh in Cooch Behar district of West Bengal, 17 March 2012).

50 Quoted in Rabbani, 2005–2006, p. 52.

51 1 bigha = 0.3306 acre

52 Interview with Kamal Debnath, resident of a Bangladeshi enclave in India (Shibprasad Mustafi *Chhit* of Kurigram district of Bangladesh in Cooch Behar district of West Bengal, 17 March 2012).

53 Rabbani, 2005–2006, p. 38.

54 Interview with Bimal Burman, resident of a Bangladeshi enclave in India (Bakhalir Chhara *Chhit* of Kurigram district of Bangladesh in Cooch Behar district of West Bengal, 15 March 2012).

55 Van Schendel, 2002, p. 129.

56 Rabbani, 2005–2006, p. 62.

57 Interview with Md. Iqbal Ali, resident of a Bangladeshi enclave in India (Madhya Mashaldanga *Chhit* of Kurigram district of Bangladesh in Cooch Behar district of West Bengal, 15 March 2012); Staff Reporter. (19 June 2013) Mathabhanga lagoya Bangladesher 3 chhitmahaley cholchhe Charam arajakata. *Ganashakti.* [Online] Available from: http:// ganashakti.com/bengali/news_details.php?newsid=26339. [Last accessed: 15 August 2013].

58 Interview with Bhabani Burman, resident of a Bangladeshi enclave in India (Bakhalir Chhara *Chhit* of Kurigram district of Bangladesh in Cooch Behar district of West Bengal, 15 March 2012).

59 Interview with Md. Iqbal Ali, resident of a Bangladeshi enclave in India (Madhya Mashaldanga *Chhit* of Kurigram district of Bangladesh in Cooch Behar district of West Bengal, 15 March 2012).

60 Interview with Fatema Bibi, resident of a Bangladeshi enclave in India (Madhya Mashaldanga *Chhit* of Kurigram district of Bangladesh in Cooch Behar district of West Bengal, 15 March 2012).

61 Interview with Karim Baksh, resident of a Bangladeshi enclave in India (Karala *Chhit* of Kurigram district of Bangladesh in Cooch Behar district of West Bengal, 17 March 2012).

62 Interview with Saif Ali, resident of a Bangladeshi enclave in India (Karala *Chhit* of Kurigram district of Bangladesh in Cooch Behar district of West Bengal, 17 March 2012).

63 Rabbani, 2005–2006, pp. 42–43.

64 Interview with Fatema Bibi, resident of a Bangladeshi enclave in India (Madhya Mashaldanga *Chhit* of Kurigram district of Bangladesh in Cooch Behar district of West Bengal, 15 March 2012).

65 Interview with Dalim Bibi, resident of a Bangladeshi enclave in India (Batrigach *Chhit* of Lalmonirhat district of Bangladesh in Cooch Behar district of West Bengal, 18 March 2012).

66 Interview with Fatema Bibi, resident of a Bangladeshi enclave in India (Madhya Mashaldanga *Chhit* of Kurigram district of Bangladesh in Cooch Behar district of West Bengal, 15 March 2012).

67 Interview with Bhabani Burman and Bimal Burman, residents of a Bangladeshi enclave in India (Bakhalir Chhara *Chhit* of Kurigram district of Bangladesh in Cooch Behar district of West Bengal, 15 March 2012).

68 Interview with Rebecca Khatun, resident of an Indian enclave in Bangladesh (Dahala-Khagrabari *Chhit* of Cooch Behar district of West Bengal in Panchagarh district of Bangladesh, 5 October 2011).

69 Interview with Md. Riazul Islam, resident of an Indian enclave in Bangladesh (Bewladanga *Chhit* of Cooch Behar district of West Bengal in Panchagarh district of Bangladesh, 5 October 2011).

132 *Spatial disparities*

70 Interview with Shahid Haq, resident of a Bangladeshi enclave in India (Dahagram *Chhit* of Lalmonirhat district of Bangladesh in Cooch Behar district of West Bengal, 6 October 2011).

71 Interview with Fatema Bibi, resident of a Bangladeshi enclave in India (Madhya Mashaldanga *Chhit* of Kurigram district of Bangladesh in Cooch Behar district of West Bengal, 15 March 2012).

72 Cons, 2012, p. 546.

73 Saha, A. (14 February 2013) Premer taney chhitmahalei samsar petechhen Arzu. *Ananda Bazar Patrika*. [Online] Available from: www.anandabazar.com/archive/1130214/14uttar3.html. [Last accessed: 15 August 2013].

74 Interview with Md. Iqbal Ali, resident of a Bangladeshi enclave in India (Madhya Mashaldanga *Chhit* of Kurigram district of Bangladesh in Cooch Behar district of West Bengal, 15 March 2012).

75 Interview with Fatema Bibi, resident of a Bangladeshi enclave in India (Madhya Mashaldanga *Chhit* of Kurigram district of Bangladesh in Cooch Behar district of West Bengal, 15 March 2012).

76 Ibid.

77 Van Schendel, 2002, p. 127.

78 Ibid.

79 Ibid.

80 Ibid. p. 128.

81 Ibid. p. 132.

82 Ibid. p. 131.

83 Chattopadhyay, A. (3 May 2012) Punarbashaner daye nijerai nichhen mariya chhit-mahalbashi. *Ananda Bazar Patrika*. [Online] Available from: www.anandabazar.com/archive/1120503/3bdesh2.html. [Last accessed: 15 August 2013].

84 Interview with Nirendranath Burman, deputy-head of Kalmati village *Panchayat*, Dinhata (Cooch Behar district of Bangladesh adjacent to Bakhalir Chhara *Chhit* of Kurigram district of Bangladesh, 16 March 2012).

85 Ibid.

86 Interview with Md. Ziauddin Miah, resident of a Bangladeshi enclave in India (Kismat Batrigach *Chhit* of Lalmonirhat district of Bangladesh in Cooch Behar district of West Bengal, 18 March 2012).

87 Interview with Suren Burman, resident of a Bangladeshi enclave in India (Shibprasad Mustafi *Chhit* of Kurigram district of Bangladesh in Cooch Behar district of West Bengal, 17 March 2012).

88 Interview with Saif Ali, resident of a Bangladeshi enclave in India (Karala *Chhit* of Kurigram district of Bangladesh in Cooch Behar district of West Bengal, 17 March 2012).

89 Interview with Md. Anisur, resident of a Bangladeshi enclave in India (Madhya Mashal-danga *Chhit* of Kurigram district of Bangladesh in Cooch Behar district of West Bengal, 15 March 2012).

90 Staff Reporter. (27 August 2013) Bangladesher push-back, durbhogey chhitmahaler jubok. *Ei Samay*. [Online]. Available from: http://eisamay.indiatimes.com/state/bangladeshs-pushback-chitmahals-youth-is-in-trouble/articleshow/22089807.cms. [Last accessed: 9 September 2013].

91 Roy, R. (29 April 2012) Kajolrekha swopno dekhen, uthoney ghurchhey ariful. *Ananda Bazar Patrika*. [Online] Available from: www.anandabazar.com/archive/1120429/29mur1.html. [Last accessed: 17 September 2013]; Sayed, S. and Bhattacharya, S. (30 April 2012) Chhele ke ebar schooley bhorti korben Kajolrekha. *Ananda Bazar Patrika*. [Online] Available from: www.anandabazar.com/30mur2.html. [Last accessed: 17 September 2013].

92 Interview with Bimal Burman, resident of a Bangladeshi enclave in India (Bakhalir Chhara *Chhit* of Kurigram district of Bangladesh in Cooch Behar district of West Bengal, 15 March 2012); Ray, R. (2 September 2013) Chhitmahal binimoye netara

Spatial disparities 133

udashin: voter bajarey er daam nei, tai? *Ei Samay*. [Online] Available from: www. epaper.eisamay.com/Details.aspx?id=6126&boxid=4021265. [Last accessed: 9 September 2013].

93 Rabbani, 2005–2006, p. 34.

94 Ibid. p. 30.

95 Interview with Md. Iqbal Ali, resident of a Bangladeshi enclave in India (Madhya Mashaldanga *Chhit* of Kurigram district of Bangladesh in Cooch Behar district of West Bengal, 15 March 2012).

96 Ibid.

97 Interview with Bimal Burman, resident of a Bangladeshi enclave in India (Bakhalir Chhara *Chhit* of Kurigram district of Bangladesh in Cooch Behar district of West Bengal, 15 March 2012).

98 The BRAC (Bangladesh Rehabilitation Assistance Committee) is a private commercial bank in Bangladesh, with its headquarters in Dhaka. The bank is partially owned by BRAC, the largest non-government organisation in the world, and the International Finance Corporation, the private sector arm of The World Bank Group and ShoreCap International.

99 Interview with Md. Ghulam, BRAC officer in an Indian enclave in Bangladesh (Dahala-Khagrabari *Chhit* of Cooch Behar district of West Bengal in Panchagarh district of Bangladesh, 5 October 2011).

100 'মধ্য মশাল দাঙ্গা থেকে বর্ডার ২.৩০ কি মি. দক্ষিণ মশাল দাঙ্গা থেকে হাফ কি এক কি মি দুরে, দুদিকে বাংলাদেশের মধ্যে ৮০ হাত ইন্ডিয়ার রাস্তা. ওটা না থাকলেই আমরা বাংলাদেশে যাতায়াত করতে পারতাম. ওখানেই দিঘলদারি বি এস এফ ক্যাম্প. ওখান দিয়ে যাতায়াত করা একেবারেই নিষেধ।' Interview with Md. Iqbal Ali, resident of a Bangladeshi enclave in India (Madhya Mashaldanga *Chhit* of Kurigram district of Bangladesh in Cooch Behar district of West Bengal, 15 March 2012).

101 Interview with Hafizul, resident of an Indian enclave in Bangladesh (Dahala-Khagrabari *Chhit* of Cooch Behar district of West Bengal in Panchagarh district of Bangladesh, 5 October 2011).

102 'আশেপাশের বাংলাদেশের বাসিন্দা দের মত দাপটে কথা বলতে পারি না।' Interview with Momin Rezzak, resident of an Indian enclave in Bangladesh (Kajaldighi *Chhit* of Cooch Behar district of West Bengal in Panchagarh district of Bangladesh, 5 October 2011).

103 Interview with Akbar Alam, resident of a Bangladeshi enclave in India (Angarpota *Chhit* of Lalmonirhat district of Bangladesh in Cooch Behar district of West Bengal, 6 October 2011).

104 Interview with Md. Iqbal Ali Sheikh, resident of a Bangladeshi enclave in India (Purba Bakhalir Chhara *Chhit* of Kurigram district of Bangladesh in Cooch Behar district of West Bengal, 16 March 2012).

105 Ibid.

106 Interview with Suren Burman, resident of a Bangladeshi enclave in India (Shibprasad Mustafi *Chhit* of Kurigram district of Bangladesh in Cooch Behar district of West Bengal, 17 March 2012).

107 The previous example was that of the BSF crossing the border to take stock of communal violence on the Bangladesh side – discussed in Chapter 1.

108 Interview with Md. Iqbal Ali Sheikh, resident of a Bangladeshi enclave in India (Purba Bakhalir Chhara *Chhit* of Kurigram district of Bangladesh in Cooch Behar district of West Bengal, 16 March 2012).

109 'ছিটমহলের সমস্যা- বাইরের লোক মারধর করে, গালিগালাজ করে, জবাব দিলে মারপিট করে, আগুন ধরিয়ে দেয়, গরু লুট করে নিয়ে যায়।' Interview with Md. Anisur, resident of a Bangladeshi enclave in India (Madhya Mashaldanga *Chhit* of Kurigram district of Bangladesh in Cooch Behar district of West Bengal, 15 March 2012).

110 Ibid.

111 Interview with Md. Riazul Islam, resident of an Indian enclave in Bangladesh (Bewladanga *Chhit* of Cooch Behar district of West Bengal in Panchagarh district of Bangladesh, 5 October 2011).

134 *Spatial disparities*

112 Ibid.

113 Interview with Bimal Burman, resident of a Bangladeshi enclave in India (Bakhalir Chhara *Chhit* of Kurigram district of Bangladesh in Cooch Behar district of West Bengal, 15 March 2012).

114 Interview with Md. Anisur, resident of a Bangladeshi enclave in India (Madhya Mashaldanga *Chhit* of Kurigram district of Bangladesh in Cooch Behar district of West Bengal, 15 March 2012).

115 Interview with Md. Ziauddin Miah, resident of a Bangladeshi enclave in India (Kismat Batrigach *Chhit* of Lalmonirhat district of Bangladesh in Cooch Behar district of West Bengal, 18 March 2012).

116 Rabbani, 2005–2006, p. 56.

117 Karmakar, K. (8 June 2005) Indian Enclaves in 2 Districts Safe Havens for Criminals, Large Scale Hemp Cultivation in Enclaves in Dinajpur, Panchagarh. *The Daily Star.* [Online] Available from: http://archive.thedailystar.net/2005/06/08/d50608070178. htm. [Last accessed: 12 August 2013].

118 'এমনিতেই আমরা ভয় থাকি, কোনো পরিচয় নেই, প্রধান বা রাষ্ট্র কিছু নেই।' Interview with Md. Anisur, resident of a Bangladeshi enclave in India (Madhya Mashaldanga *Chhit* of Kurigram district of Bangladesh in Cooch Behar district of West Bengal, 15 March 2012).

119 Interview with Md. Iqbal Ali, resident of a Bangladeshi enclave in India (Madhya Mashaldanga *Chhit* of Kurigram district of Bangladesh in Cooch Behar district of West Bengal, 15 March 2012).

120 'অনেক সময় শাস্তির মেয়াদ শেষ হলেও ছাড়ে না. কোথায় ছাড়বে? কোন দেশে. বাংলাদেশ কে বলে তোমাদের লোক. বাংলাদেশ নেই না।' (Many a times they do not release the convicts even after the completion of their terms. Where will they release us? To which country? Bangladesh does not accept us as its citizens.) Interview with Bimal Burman, resident of a Bangladeshi enclave in India (Bakhalir Chhara *Chhit* of Kurigram district of Bangladesh in Cooch Behar district of West Bengal, 15 March 2012).

121 Interview with Saraswati Das, resident of an Indian counter-enclave within a Bangladeshi enclave in India (Nazirhat village of Cooch Behar district of West Bengal in Madhya Mashaldanga *Chhit* of Kurigram district of Bangladesh, 15 March 2012).

122 Ibid.

123 Van Schendel, 2002, p. 133.

124 Interview with Bimal Burman, resident of a Bangladeshi enclave in India (Bakhalir Chhara *Chhit* of Kurigram district of Bangladesh in Cooch Behar district of West Bengal, 15 March 2012).

125 Rabbani, 2005–2006, p. 55.

126 Interview with Md. Riazul Islam, resident of an Indian enclave in Bangladesh (Bewladanga *Chhit* of Cooch Behar district of West Bengal in Panchagarh district of Bangladesh, 5 October 2011).

127 Interview with Momin Rezzak, resident of an Indian enclave in Bangladesh (Kajaldighi *Chhit* of Cooch Behar district of West Bengal in Panchagarh district of Bangladesh, 5 October 2011).

128 Interview with Md. Kamal Hussein, resident of a Bangladeshi enclave in India (Karala *Chhit* of Kurigram district of Bangladesh in Cooch Behar district of West Bengal, 17 March 2012).

129 'এখানে টাকা টা সমস্যা নয়. সব চেয়ে বড় সমস্যা হলো নাগরিকত্বের. থানা, পুলিশ কিছু নেই. সামাজিক বিচার আছে, মসজিদ-এ বিচার হয়।' (The biggest problem here is of citizenship. We do not have police, *thanas.* We have social arbitration/justice. The trials take place at mosques.) Interview with Iqbal Hussein, resident of an Indian enclave in Bangladesh (Dahala-Khagrabari *Chhit* of Cooch Behar district of West Bengal in Panchagarh district of Bangladesh, 5 October 2011).

130 Interview with Iqbal Hussein, resident of an Indian enclave in Bangladesh (Dahala-Khagrabari *Chhit* of Cooch Behar district of West Bengal in Panchagarh district of Bangladesh, 5 October 2011). (The use of italics is my own and is meant to hint

at the limits of such social arbitration as expressed in the tone of speech of the narrator.)

131 'জমি কেনা বেচা হয় কিন্তু নিজেদের নিজেদের মধ্যে. কোনো দলিল নেই. সামাজিক কেনাবেচা।' (We have land transactions between ourselves without any official document. It's just social transaction.) Interview with Iqbal Hussein, resident of an Indian enclave in Bangladesh (Dahala-Khagrabari *Chhit* of Cooch Behar district of West Bengal in Panchagarh district of Bangladesh, 5 October 2011).

132 Ibid.

133 Interview with Hafizul, resident of an Indian enclave in Bangladesh (Dahala-Khagrabari *Chhit* of Cooch Behar district of West Bengal in Panchagarh district of Bangladesh, 5 October 2011).

134 Interview with Hare Krishna Mondol, resident of Char Meghna (Nadia district of West Bengal, 21 October 2011).

135 'জন্ম পরিচয় দিতেও লজ্জা করে, যে আমাদের ছিট-এ জন্ম।' Interview with Hafizul, resident of an Indian enclave in Bangladesh (Dahala-Khagrabari *Chhit* of Cooch Behar district of West Bengal in Panchagarh district of Bangladesh, 5 October 2011).

136 Agamben, G. (1995) *Homo Sacer: Sovereign Power and Bare Life* (trs. Daniel Heller-Roazen). Stanford, CA: Stanford University Press.

137 Ray, R. (2 September 2013) Chhitmahal binimoy netara udashin: voter bajarey er daam nei, tai? *Ei Samay*. [Online] Available from: www.epaper.eisamay.com/Details. aspx?id=6126&boxid=4021265. [Last accessed: 9 September 2013].

138 Agamben, 1995, p. 8.

139 Agamben, G. (2005) *State of Exception* (trs. Kevin Attell). Chicago, London: University of Chicago Press. p. 35.

140 Agamben, 1995, p. 18.

141 Benjamin, W. (2003) On the Concept of History (trs. Harry Zohn). In Eiland, H. and Jennings, W. (Eds.). *Walter Benjamin: Selected Writings, Vol. 4, 1938–1940*. Cambridge: Harvard University Press, Belknap Press.

142 Van Schendel, 2002, p. 129.

143 Agamben, 2005, p. 24.

144 Agamben, 1995, p. 25.

145 Ibid.

146 Ibid. p. 88; Clad, J.C. (1994) Slowing the Wave. *Foreign Affairs*. 95. pp. 139–150.

147 'পশুর মত বাস করি. তাও তাদের সরকার লক্ষ্য রাখে. আমাদের রাখে না।' Interview with Karim Baksh, resident of a Bangladeshi enclave in India (Karala *Chhit* of Kurigram district of Bangladesh in Cooch Behar district of West Bengal, 17 March 2012).

148 Interview with Suren Burman, resident of a Bangladeshi enclave in India (Shibprasad Mustafi *Chhit* of Kurigram district of Bangladesh in Cooch Behar district of West Bengal, 17 March 2012).

149 Ibid.

150 The International Covenant on Civil and Political Rights (ICCPR) is a multilateral treaty adopted by the United Nations General Assembly on 16 December 1966, and in force from 23 March 1976. It commits its parties to respect the civil and political rights of individuals, including the right to life, freedom of religion, freedom of speech, freedom of assembly, electoral rights and rights to due process and a fair trial. As of March 2012, the Covenant had 74 signatories and 167 parties, India and Bangladesh being two of them. India became a party to ICCPR on 10 April 1979, while Bangladesh became a party on 6 September 2000.

151 The International Covenant on Economic, Social and Cultural Rights (ICESCR) is a multilateral treaty adopted by the United Nations General Assembly on 16 December 1966, and in force from 3 January 1976. It commits its parties to work towards the granting of economic, social and cultural rights (ESCR) to individuals, including labour rights and the right to health, the right to education and the right to an adequate standard of living. As of October 2012, the Covenant had 160 parties. A further seven countries, including

136 *Spatial disparities*

the United States of America, had signed but not yet ratified the Covenant. India became a party to ICESCR on 10 April 1979, while Bangladesh became a party on 5 October 1998.

152 The Universal Declaration of Human Rights (UDHR) is a declaration adopted by the United Nations General Assembly on 10 December 1948 at Palais de Chaillot, Paris. It consists of 30 articles, which have been elaborated in subsequent international treaties, regional human rights instruments, national constitutions and laws. The International Bill of Human Rights consists of the Universal Declaration of Human Rights, the International Covenant on Economic, Social and Cultural Rights, and the International Covenant on Civil and Political Rights and its two Optional Protocols.

153 The Millennium Development Goals (MDGs) are eight international development goals that were officially established following the Millennium Summit of the United Nations in 2000, following the adoption of the United Nations Millennium Declaration. All 193 United Nations member states and at least 23 international organisations have agreed to achieve these goals by the year 2015. The goals are: 1) Eradicating extreme poverty and hunger, 2) Achieving universal primary education, 3) Promoting gender equality and empowering women, 4) Reducing child mortality rates, 5) Improving maternal health, 6) Combating HIV/AIDS, malaria, and other diseases, 7) Ensuring environmental sustainability, and 8) Developing a global partnership for development.

154 Rabbani, 2005–2006, p. 41.

155 National Rural Employment Guarantee Act (discussed in Chapter 1).

156 *Anganwadi*, literally meaning 'courtyard shelter', was started by the Indian government in 1975 as part of the Integrated Child Development Services programme to combat hunger and malnutrition in children. *Anganwadi* centres also generally provide basic health care facilities in the villages. More than 13,00,000 *Anganwadi* and mini-*Anganwadi* centres are operational throughout India at present, providing supplementary nutrition, non-formal pre-school education, nutrition and health education, immunization, health check-up and referral services.

157 'আমাদের বাপ ঠাকুরদারা এখানেই থেকেছে, আমরাও এখানেই থেকেছি বরাবর. আমরা ভারতের নাগরিকই হতে চাই।' Interview with Md. Iqbal Ali, resident of a Bangladeshi enclave in India (Madhya Mashaldanga *Chhit* of Kurigram district of Bangladesh in Cooch Behar district of West Bengal, 15 March 2012).

158 Interview with Fatema Bibi, resident of a Bangladeshi enclave in India (Madhya Mashaldanga *Chhit* of Kurigram district of Bangladesh in Cooch Behar district of West Bengal, 15 March 2012).

159 'আমরা ভারতের নাগরিক হতে চাই. এবিষয়ে এখানে কেউ দ্বিমত নয়।' Interview with Md. Iqbal Ali, resident of a Bangladeshi enclave in India (Madhya Mashaldanga *Chhit* of Kurigram district of Bangladesh in Cooch Behar district of West Bengal, 15 March 2012).

160 Interview with Hafizul, resident of an Indian enclave in Bangladesh (Dahala-Khagrabari *Chhit* of Cooch Behar district of West Bengal in Panchagarh district of Bangladesh, 5 October 2011).

161 Interview with Md. Kamal Hussein, resident of a Bangladeshi enclave in India (Karala *Chhit* of Kurigram district of Bangladesh in Cooch Behar district of West Bengal, 17 March 2012).

162 Staff Reporter. (24 January 2011) Banchanar asanka bashinda der: Chhitmahal gulitey jomi-r dor ratarati dosh gun. *Ananda Bazar Patrika.* [Online] Available from: www. anandabazar.com/24bdesh01.htm. [Last accessed: 15 August 2013].

163 Festinger, L. (1962) *A Theory of Cognitive Dissonance.* Stanford, CA: Stanford University Press.

164 Interview with Rebecca Khatun, resident of an Indian enclave in Bangladesh (Dahala-Khagrabari *Chhit* of Cooch Behar district of West Bengal in Panchagarh district of Bangladesh, 5 October 2011).

165 Interview with Sabina Akhtar, resident of an Indian enclave in Bangladesh (Bewladanga *Chhit* of Cooch Behar district of West Bengal in Panchagarh district of Bangladesh, 5 October 2011).

Spatial disparities 137

166 Both the Nehru-Noon Agreement (1958) and the Indira-Mujib Accord (1974) provided for the *Tinbigha* Corridor, although its construction had to wait till 1992.
167 A protocol was signed between India and Bangladesh on 8 September 2011 to keep the Corridor open for 24 hours, which was followed by the finalisation of the protocol on 19 October 2011.
168 Cons, 2012, p. 537.
169 Interview with Jarina Begum, resident of a Bangladeshi enclave in India (Angarpota *Chhit* of Lalmonirhat district of Bangladesh in Cooch Behar district of West Bengal, 6 October 2011).
170 Ibid.
171 Interview with Akbar Alam, resident of a Bangladeshi enclave in India (Angarpota *Chhit* of Lalmonirhat district of Bangladesh in Cooch Behar district of West Bengal, 6 October 2011).
172 Ibid.
173 Ibid.; Cons, 2012, p. 537.
174 Ghosh, P. (30 May 2010) Delhi-Dhaka joutha udyog: simante noya manchitra toiri hobe, Tinbighaye uralpool- o. *Ananda Bazar Patrika*. [Online] Available from: www. anandabazar.com/archive/1100530/30desh1.htm. [Last accessed: 15 August 2013].
175 Interview with Akbar Alam, resident of a Bangladeshi enclave in India (Angarpota *Chhit* of Lalmonirhat district of Bangladesh in Cooch Behar district of West Bengal, 6 October 2011); Staff Reporter. (8 September 2011) Dahagram Celebrates While Other Enclaves Unhappy. *The Daily Star*. [Online] Available from: http://archive.thedailys tar.net/newDesign/news-details.php?nid=201609. [Last accessed: 13 August 2013].
176 Interview with Shahid Haq, resident of a Bangladeshi enclave in India (Dahagram *Chhit* of Lalmonirhat district of Bangladesh in Cooch Behar district of West Bengal, 6 October 2011).
177 Cons, 2012, p. 531.
178 Zia-ur Rahman was the seventh president of Bangladesh, from 1977 to 1981.
179 Cons, 2012, p. 547.
180 Ibid.
181 Ibid.
182 Ibid. p. 549.
183 Ibid. p. 550.
184 Explained in the Introduction.
185 District Correspondent. (17 April 2013) Violation of Boundary Law: India to Build Rest House in Border. *Banglanews24.com*. [Online] Available from: www.bangla news24.com/English/detailsnews.php?nssl=784b2f7298d4084fb327911e3bbec42a&n ttl=1704201368025. [Last accessed: 2 September 2013].
186 Cons, 2012, p. 545.
187 Ibid.
188 Ibid. p. 555.
189 The Wagah Border between India's Amritsar and Pakistan's Lahore witnesses a border ceremony at the border gate, two hours before sunset every day. The retreat ceremony is conducted by Pakistan Rangers and India's Border Security Force. Over the years the Wagah ceremony has become a major tourist attraction, bringing tourists from both sides of the border to the gallery seats at the site, made for the purpose.
190 Saha, A. (21 February 2017). Wagah'r moto hok Tinbigha. *Ananda Bazar Patrika*. [Online] Available from: www.anandabazar.com/district/uttarbanga/government-is-not-taking-any-initiative-to-make-tin-bigha-corridor-a-tourist-place-1.567788. [Last Accessed: 25 June 2017].
191 Rabbani, 2005–2006, p. 53.
192 Ibid. pp. 53–54.
193 Chakrabarty, C. (8 January 2013) Nei desher baromashya. *Ei Samay*. [Online] Available from: www.epaper.eisamay.com/Details.aspx?id=1954&boxid=23413515. [Last accessed: 13 August 2013].

138 *Spatial disparities*

194 Staff Reporter. (4 April 2010) Sishu-r nagarikatwa pete mukkhamantrir kachhe committee. *Ananda Bazar Patrika*. [Online] Available from: www.anandabazar.com/4uttar7.htm. [Last accessed: 15 August 2013].

195 Interview with Diptiman Sengupta (original name), Secretary of BBEECC, Dinhata (Cooch Behar district of West Bengal, 19 March 2012).

196 Staff Reporter. (26 January 2011) Prajatantra Divas udjapan niye tatparata tungey. *Ananda Bazar Patrika*. [Online] Available from: www.anandabazar.com/26uttar4.htm. [Last accessed: 15 August 2013].

197 Kolkata Bureau (8 September 2012) Kolkata Viswavidyalaye chhitmahal niye goltable. *Banglanews24.com*. [Online] Available from: www.banglanews24.com/detailsnews.php?nssl=8f98db3e1b0af0f45e1dfb508695da0f&nttl=08092012137455. [Last accessed: 15 August 2013].

198 Interview with Md. Iqbal Ali, resident of a Bangladeshi enclave in India (Madhya Mashaldanga *Chhit* of Kurigram district of Bangladesh in Cooch Behar district of West Bengal, 15 March 2012).

199 Bhattashali, A. (20 April 2012) Chhitmahaley nagarikatwa niye shamikhsha. *BBC Bangla*. [Online] Available from: www.bbc.co.uk/bengali/news/2012/04/120420_mb_eclave_nationality.shtml. [Last accessed: 15 August 2013].

200 Staff Reporter. (9 December 2012) Bangladesher shongey shal shimanta chukti niye BJP-r dwarastha Kendra. *Ananda Bazar Patrika*. [Online] Available from: www.anandabazar.com/archive/1121209/9desh3.html. [Last accessed: 15 August 2013].

201 Disagreement over the territorial issue of the enclaves between the political parties has prevented the exchange bill from being passed in the Houses of Parliament in India. Parashar, S. (26 July 2013) Dipu Moni to Seek BJP Support for India-Bangladesh Land Agreement. *The Times of India*. [Online] Available from: http://articles.timesofindia.indiatimes.com/2013-07-26/india/40814572_1_land-boundary-agreement-constitution-amendment-bill-enclaves. [Last accessed: 13 August 2013]; Staff Correspondent. (27 January 2012) No Enclave Exchange: Mamata Now Opposing Land Boundary Deal with Dhaka. *The Daily Star*. [Online] Available from: http://archive.thedailystar.net/newDesign/news-details.php?nid=220097. [Last accessed: 15 August 2013].

202 Ghoshal, J. (17 February 2013) Shoujanya: Dhaka-e Mamatar dhal holen Khurshid. *Ananda Bazar Patrika*. [Online] Available from: www.anandabazar.com/archive/1130217/17bdesh2.html. [Last accessed: 13 August 2013].

203 Memorandum of Understanding.

204 Staff Reporter. (17 February 2013) Chhitmahal jot chharatey shohomot. *Ebela*. [Online] Available from: www.ebela.in/details/4781-14492378.html. [Last accessed: 13 August 2013].

205 Ghoshal, J. and Afrad, K. (18 February 2013) Delhi safar-e Hasina, Tista chuktir jot katchhe. *Ananda Bazar Patrika*. [Online] Available from: www.anandabazar.com/archive/1130218/18bdesh1.html. [Last accessed: 13 August 2013].

206 Gupta, S. (26 March 2013) Consensus Emerging on Statute Change Bill. *The Hindu*. [Online] Available from: www.thehindu.com/news/national/consensus-emerging-on-statute-change-bill/article4551808.ece. [Last accessed: 13 August 2013].

207 Staff Reporter. (23 July 2013) Sthal shimanta chukti dhruto rupayaney chap dichhe Dhaka. *Ananda Bazar Patrika*. [Online] Available from: www.anandabazar.com/archive/1130723/23bdesh4.html. [Last accessed: 15 August 2013]; Staff Reporter. (20 August 2013) Mamatar apottitey pesh holo na sthal shimanto bill. *Ananda Bazar Patrika*. [Online] Available from: www.anandabazar.com/20desh3.html. [Last accessed: 3 September 2013].

208 Staff Reporter. (27 August 2013) Nagorikatwer dabitey high court-e 162 chhitmahal. *Ei Samay*. [Online] Available from: http://eisamay.indiatimes.com/state/demand-for-citizenship-chitmahal-in-HC/articleshow/22089895.cms. [Last accessed: 3 September 2013]; Chakrabarty, C. (29 August 2013) Nirapatta debey ke, proshno tuley

Spatial disparities 139

andoloney chhitmahal. *Ei Samay*. [Online] Available from: www.epaper.eisamay. com/Details.aspx?id=6025&boxid=154125890. [Last accessed: 3 September 2013].

209 Ministry of External Affairs, Exchange of Enclaves between India and Bangladesh, (Press Release, 20 November 2015), cited in Shewly, H.J. (9 March 2016). India and Bangladesh Swap Territory, Citizens in Landmark Enclave Exchange. *Migration Policy Institute*. (Online Journal) Available from: www.migrationpolicy.org/article/ india-and-bangladesh-swap-territory-citizens-landmark-enclave-exchange.

210 Staff Reporter. (15 March 2017). India Bangladesh Land Boundary Agreement (LBA). *Business Standard*. [Online] Available from: www.business-standard.com/ article/government-press-release/india-bangladesh-land-boundary-agreement-lba-117031500616_1.html. [Last accessed: 19 June 2017].

211 Staff Reporter. (30 January 2017). Chora daamey kerosene ration-i shabek chhit-e. *Ananda Bazar Patrika*. [Online] Available from: www.anandabazar.com/district/uttarbanga/ no-ration-card-enclave-residents-forced-to-buy-kerosene-at-high-price-1.556184. [Last accessed: 19 June 2017].

212 Staff Reporter. (14 February 2017). Kantatarer dupashei roye giyechhen swami stri. *Ananda Bazar Patrika*. [Online] Available from: www.anandabazar.com/district/ uttarbanga/border-splitted-the-two-humans-being-the-husband-and-wife-1.564069#. [Last accessed: 19 June 2017].

213 Ghosh, N. (4 June 2017). Bridhhar mrityu, bitorko shabek chhitey. *Ananda Bazar Patrika*. [Online] Available from: www.anandabazar.com/district/uttarbanga/controversy-over-death-of-an-elderly-lady-1.622990?ref=uttarbanga-new-stry. [Last accessed: 19 June 2017].

214 Staff Reporter. (17 June 2017). Chhitbashider opor lathi. *Ananda Bazar Patrika*. [Online] Available from: www.anandabazar.com/district/uttarbanga/complaint-against-police-for-lathiCharge-on-chitmahal-people-1.629496?ref=uttarbanga-new-stry. [Last accessed: 19 June 2017].

215 Ghosh, N. (8 September 2017) Firiye din babar naam, dabi. *Ananda Bazar Patrika*. [Online] Available from: www.anandabazar.com/district/uttarbanga/return-my-father-s-identity-a-student-from-chitmahal-shouts-1.671174?ref=uttarbanga-new-stry. [Last accessed: 8 September 2017].

216 Staff Reporter. (3 December 2009) Chhitmahal niye samsad-e Nripen. *Ananda Bazar Patrika*. [Online] Available from: www.anandabazar.com/archive/1091203/3uttar4. htm. [Last accessed 15 August 2013].

217 Das, R. (30 July 2013) Chhitmahaler issue-te Trinomool ke lal card dekhalen voter-ra. *Samakal*. [Online] Available from: www.samakal.net/print_edition/details.php? news=17&view=archiev&y=2013&m=07&d=30&action=main&menu_type=& option=single&news_id=359419&pub_no=1484&type. [Last accessed: 14 August 2013].

218 Van Schendel, 2002, p. 126.

219 Van Schendel, W. (2002). Geographies of Knowing, Geographies of Ignorance: Jumping Scale in Southeast Asia. *Environment and Planning D: Society and Space*. 20. pp. 647–668.

220 Scott, J. (2009). *The Art of Not Being Governed: An Anarchist History of Upland Southeast Asia*. New Delhi: Orient Blackswan. p. ix; Scott describes the non-state or extra-state status of zomia as an act of 'deliberate statelessness'. In this, the enclave situation is more similar to Agamben's idea of the 'state of exception' where the exclusion of the people from the state system is brought about by the states themselves, rather than the people. In fact, the people make every effort to 'be included' in the state-making process. But the similarity between the enclaves and the idea of zomia lies in their being an extra-state territory beyond the control regime of the states, and often posing a challenge to the same.

221 Lahiri-Dutt, K. and Samanta, G. (2013). *Dancing with the River: People and Life on the Chars of South Asia*. New Haven, London: Yale University Press. p. 17.

140 *Spatial disparities*

222 Scott, 2009, p. 13.
223 Lahiri-Dutt and Samanta, 2013, p. ix
224 The migrants to the *Chars* were also mostly of the lower castes, due to their historical association with agricultural professions. The caste factor of late migrants settling in the islands of West Bengal will be discussed in-depth in the next chapter.
225 Lahiri-Dutt and Samanta, 2013, p. 99.
226 Ibid. p. 142
227 Ibid. p. 38.
228 Ibid. p. 39.
229 Ibid. p. 114.
230 Ibid. p. 50.
231 Ibid. p. 101.
232 Ibid. p. 40.
233 Scott, 2010, p. 242.
234 Ibid. p. 326
235 Ibid. p. 330.
236 A *Ghoj* is a piece of land which intrudes into the territory of the neighbouring state and is attached to the parent state by a thin strip of land.
237 'চোরাচালানকারী দের আখড়া. মালগুলো এনে এখানে জড়ো করে. বাংলাদেশী রা ইন্ডিয়ান মহিলাদের দিয়ে ওগুলো আনায়. তারপর ওখান থেকে চালান দেয়. ওরা পুরোপুরি বাংলাদেশী দের ওপর নির্ভরশীল হয়ে পড়েছে- বাজার, খাওয়ার, শিক্ষা সব কিছুর জন্য।' Interview with Pradip, resident of an Indian *Ghoj* 'tero ghor' protruding into Putkhali village, Benapole (Jessore district of Bangladesh, 16 February 2012).
238 Ibid.
239 We shall look at this in some more detail in the next chapter on the relation between borderland spaces and identity politics in the context of caste, religion, etc.
240 Lahiri-Dutt and Samanta, 2013, p. 199.

4 Ethno-cultural concerns

Appropriation of marginal spaces

Introduction

Spatial marginality of a people affects ways in which their identities take shape. The previous chapters looked at how the border as a spatial category affects economic identities and territorial imperatives of a people. This chapter aims to understand how socio-cultural identities of a people, like caste, religion, ethnicity, are likewise affected and, often, decided by their spatial category of being a *border people*.

Following the partition of Bengal in 1947, there began a mass exodus of refugees between the newly-created states of East Pakistan and West Bengal.[1] The initial wave of Hindu refugees who came from East Pakistan to West Bengal was essentially the urban population, a majority of whom were professionals. Most of them settled in and around Calcutta and its suburbs with the help of their friends, relatives, caste members and other influential social networks.[2] The exodus continued well into the 1960s, after which there was a break till 1971,[3] when a new wave of refugees migrated into West Bengal from the newly-formed state of Bangladesh.[4] Beginning from the 1950s and especially in the 1970s, the majority of the refugees constituted agricultural communities, unlike the initial phase of urban, mostly middle-class migrants. Because of their dependence on the land that they worked on, the agricultural communities were, understandably, the last ones to leave their lands and migrate to West Bengal.[5]

Most of these migrants settled along the border between West Bengal and Bangladesh for two reasons. Firstly, the cities and suburbs had already been full with the newly settled migrants, who found work in the various academic, technical and professional institutions available in these areas,[6] resulting in a scarcity of non-agricultural liveable land. Secondly, the agricultural skills of the peasant migrants could hardly be put to use in these urban and semi-urban areas which lacked cultivable land. The border areas were, and still are, majorly rural areas with vast stretches of cultivated lands. So settling away from urban areas, including border villages, was an obvious decision for these peasant migrants.

Most of these later migrants belonged to the *Namasudra*[7] caste – one of the castes in the social hierarchy and specific to Bengal both in terms of their history and nomenclature. The major concentration of the *Namasudra* settlement in the

142 *Ethno-cultural concerns*

Bengal province in the pre-Partition period was in and around the areas of Khulna, Jessore, Faridpur, Dacca (now Dhaka), Mymensingh and Bakargunj in the eastern side of the province followed by 24 Parganas, Midnapore, Burdwan, Nadia, Pabna, Rajshahi and Rangpur in the middle parts of Bengal. Among these, the *Namasudras* from Jessore, Khulna, Pabna, Rajshahi and Rangpur (which underwent Partition) migrated to West Bengal on the Indian side of the border after the Partition in 1947. They migrated in phases beginning in 1947 till about 1965 and even later, though the number reduced in the later phases. Most of the *Namasudras* crossed the border and settled along the border areas along the length of the Bengal border.[8] This explains the concentration of a *Namasudra* population in the border districts of 24 Parganas, Nadia, Murshidabad and Dinajpur in West Bengal. Caste identities of the majority of the people whom I interviewed as well as those of the border population in general (indicated by census reports) along the West Bengal-Bangladesh border areas reveal their *Namasudra* and/or scheduled status – verifying the logic of later phases of migration of *Namasudra* and other lower castes.

The West Bengal-Bangladesh border, as the geographical marker of the sovereignty of the states of India and Bangladesh, has been witness to intense patrolling, fencing and surveillance mechanisms. The profile of the border people, their lives and livelihood practices and their movement have been a cause of concern for the states. India has been particularly concerned with the issue of migrant people settling along the border, especially because migrants coming into West Bengal after 1964 are liable to be labelled as illegal ones, unlike those before the stipulated deadline who were given an official refugee status.[9] Thus, migrants settling along the border after 1964 have perturbed the state ever since. In the interaction which followed between the illegal migrants and the state, caste has been seen to play an implicit, yet decisive part, whereby caste identities of the migrants have decided the kind of treatment they would have from the states, including the border guards and government institutions. The political leaders, the bureaucrats and the legislative bodies have been seen to take the caste factor, other than the religious identities, into consideration while deciding on their agendas with regard to illegal migrants.

This chapter looks at two narratives where the ethno-religious and caste identities of migrants, settled along the West Bengal-Bangladesh border, have played vital roles in the nature of negotiation between them and the state. It also looks at certain aspects of interaction between the border guards and border civilians, and between the border civilians themselves, where ethno-religious and caste identities have had a role to play, albeit latently.

The Marichjhapi massacre of 1979

The event

Following the formation of Bangladesh in 1971 and the military coup of 1975, West Bengal saw the renewed influx of refugees from Bangladesh, of which most were of *Namasudra* caste. The Congress government of West Bengal[10] was unwilling

Ethno-cultural concerns 143

to accommodate them within West Bengal. Apart from being small in number, these refugees lacked family and caste connections of the previous middle-class refugees, as a result of which they had to depend solely on the government for their survival. On claims of unavailability of vacant lands in West Bengal, the government adopted the policy of settling the *Namasudra* refugees to other provinces within India. Another vital reason for these policies was to weaken the strength of the *Namasudra* movement, which had its roots in the eastern parts of Bengal during the late nineteenth century.[11] The scattering of these refugees would not only dismember the *Namasudra* community but also ensure the prevention of the rise of the *Namasudras* in the tri-caste[12] hierarchy of West Bengal's electoral politics.[13] Thus, these refugees were forced to settle in semi-arid, rocky, inhospitable lands called Dandakaranya in the neighbouring regions of West Bengal,[14] with little or no infrastructural support from the government. Their agricultural skills were of little use in the forestareas of Dandakaranya. A hostile land coupled with quarrels with the local tribal population made life and livelihood difficult for the refugees.[15] Besides, they were culturally, physically and emotionally removed from the environment that they had left behind in Bangladesh.[16]

When, after independence in 1947, the Congress party formed the government in independent India, as well as the provincial government in West Bengal, Left Front – an alliance of Left parties, constituted the opposition in West Bengal assembly. During the first phase of refugee influx from East Pakistan into West Bengal in 1947-48, the Left Front, as the party-in-opposition, acted as the mouthpiece for the refugees in their fight for squatter colonies in West Bengal against the Congress government in power, thus creating a strong electoral base among the refugees in the post-Partition days of 1947.[17] The second wave of refugees in 1975[18] furthered the possibility of an increase in the Left Front's electoral base. The Left Front leaders took up their cause and demanded that the Congress government settle them within their 'native Bengal'[19] rather than have them settled away from Bengal, on lands where other communities, mostly tribal, had previous rights of use, and where these refugees were not entitled to affirmative action programmes since their castes were not recognised as scheduled castes in the provinces. The Left Front opposition played on these grievances to obtain a political base among these *Namasudra* refugees.[20] Left leaders evoked utopic ideas of a 'return to homeland' that the refugees cherished and lured them to settle in West Bengal,[21] especially in one of the islands in Sundarbans[22] called Marichjhapi.

The Left-backed United Central Refugee Council (UCRC)[23] together with the Udbastu Unnayanshil Samity (UUS)[24] convinced the refugees of a prosperous life and access to unlimited resources on their resettlement on the island. The refugees sold the last of their belongings to make arrangements for their journey back to their 'own' land.

By the time the refugees embarked upon their journey to Marichjhapi in around 1977, Bengal had seen one of the most decisive political changes in the post-Partition phase – the Left Front's victory in the state assembly election of West Bengal in 1977. Having come to power in West Bengal, the disposition of the Left Front leaders towards the refugees took a drastic turn. Refugee resettlement

144　*Ethno-cultural concerns*

policies began to be reviewed. As the Left Front now constituted the government, the refugees now became a liability for them and the politics of resettlement changed nature and, hence, form. The enormity of the responsibility of resettling refugees dawned on the Left Front government. This was a burden that it was not ready to shoulder.

The Left Front government, thus, reversed its policy of refugee resettlement within Bengal and adopted the policy of preventing the refugees from reaching Marichjhapi and resettling there. To that end, government forces attempted to stop the refugees on their way to the island. The position of the *Namasudra* refugees was legally in an arguable state because of the government's decision to consider refugees after 1964 as illegal. This made the Left Front government in West Bengal less obligated to the refugees than to their already-existing refugee voters in West Bengal, who had a prior demand on the state's limited resources.[25] The same Left Front which had backed the refugees' cause for return to West Bengal from Dandakaranya now considered the refugees as 'intrusions' on state resources. The government made use of police forces at the station and at posts which the refugees crossed on their way to the island in order to stop them from reaching Marichjhapi.[26]

Some of the refugees, nevertheless, managed to escape police resistance at the various stations and posts, and reached Marichjhapi in phases throughout the year of 1978. By this time, the resistance of the Left Front against refugee resettlement in West Bengal was in full swing. The leaders of the Left Front who were in the forefront in calling the refugees back to West Bengal from Dandakaranya were members of smaller allies of the Left Front, namely the Revolutionary Socialist Party (RSP) and hence, lacked command over the framing of refugee resettlement policies. The Communist Party of India (Marxist) [CPI(M)], as the dominant ally, was at the helm of affairs. It was the CPI(M)'s decision to reverse the refugee resettlement policies of West Bengal and, accordingly, not let any more refugees into West Bengal. Thus, the smaller allies of the Left Front despite their best efforts could not do much for the refugees. The refugees, thus, began resettling on the island all by themselves with an efficacy that is hard to come by in the history of refugee resettlement in India. The *Namasudras*, over years of constantly encountering the hostile marshy and forest tracts of East Bengal, had emerged as a formidable peasant community.[27] Their resettlement efforts at Marichjhapi were a reflection of their evolution as an agrarian community. Over the following year, by their own efforts, they established a viable fishing industry, salt pans, a health centre and schools – all without a trace of government support[28] and despite the unfavourable environment of the island. The island, inundated with saline water, was unfit for large-scale agriculture. That the refugees, at times, had to survive on begging has been testified by the villagers of the neighbouring islands.[29]

In order to dislodge the refugees from Marichjhapi, an economic blockade was started by the West Bengal government in and around the island in January 1979, together with the promulgation of the Forest Preservation Act in order to isolate the refugees economically, cutting off their access to food, water and other basic requirements. The ones who swam to the nearby island to get help were massacred by police forces.[30] When the economic blockade failed to budge the refugees, a violent eviction policy was adopted through the blatant use of firearms between 14 May and 16 May 1979,[31] resulting in the massacre of several refugees. Most of what the refugees had, so far, built on the island was razed to the ground. People were killed and their bodies thrown into the rivers. This made the exact count of the number of deaths impossible since there was no human settlement downstream to observe the number of bodies.[32] 'Hired' gangs were made to assist the police.[33] Of the approximately 14,000 families who had started on this fateful journey from Dandakaranya to Marichjhapi in West Bengal, about 10,000 returned back to their previous settlement at Dandakaranya in a state of complete destitution. Many others found themselves in shanties and railway tracks in and around Calcutta and other parts of West Bengal.[34] Most among the remaining families were massacred in their fight against the state, though there was a complete denial by the state of any massacre having occurred at all.

Official records fail to throw light on the magnitude of the massacre.[35] But the way the state machinery came down heavily upon the refugees cannot be termed anything less than a massacre, the economic blockade itself having caused a huge amount of harm to the refugees' lives and livelihoods. Press coverage or any other intervention on the part of the civil society were successfully prevented[36] despite Marichjhapi not being too far away from Kolkata, the headquarters of West Bengal. The CPI(M) congratulated its participant members on their successful operation at Marichjhapi and made their refugee policy reversal explicit by stating that 'there was no possibility of giving shelter to these large number of refugees under any circumstances in the State'.[37] The whole episode was pushed to the backseat where it remained largely unheard and unknown for more than two decades.

Official explanation

The Forest Act[38] was officially cited by the government in defence of its policy of forced eviction of refugees from the island. In order to make the refugee resettlement at Marichjhapi look like an illegal intrusion, the West Bengal government also cited the then-on-going Tiger Project campaign and declared Marichjhapi a part of the Reserve Forest area. Chief Minister Jyoti Basu declared that the occupation of Marichjhapi was an illegal encroachment on Reserve Forest Land and on the World Wildlife Fund-sponsored Tiger Project. He declared that further attempts by the refugees to settle on the island would force the government to take 'strong action'.[39] Accordingly, on 27 January 1979, the government prohibited any movement into and out of Marichjhapi under the Forest Act and promulgated Section 144 of the Indian Criminal Penal Code, making it illegal for five or more persons to gather on the island at any given time[40] – that eventually turned into a full-fledged economic blockade, depriving the refugees any access to resources.[41] The West Bengal government claimed that the refugees were 'in unauthorised occupation of Marichjhapi which is part of the Sundarbans Government Reserve Forest violating, thereby, the Forest Act'.[42]

146   *Ethno-cultural concerns*

No national political party was ready to take up the cause of the refugees since the *Namasudras* hardly implied a powerful ally in national politics, despite their history of struggle and resistance in the nationalist politics of India before 1947. Though the Scheduled Tribes and Castes Commission of the government of India was obligated to support the refugees' cause, it did not intervene publicly in the matter.[43] The restrictions imposed on the press by the government of West Bengal made it difficult for the former to publish whatever little news they could gather about the massacre.[44] The economic blockade resulted in a large number of victims of starvation and disease on the island between January and May 1979, even before the start of direct police action in May 1979.[45]

Ironically, neither the World Wildlife Fund (WWF) nor any of the other environmental non-governmental organisations made any declaration in support of the government's claim of Marichjhapi being a part of the Reserve Forest area, nor was there any official lobbying on the part of any non-state organisation for the government to undertake such eviction policies.[46] Even after news of the massacre became public, the scale of the evicted population, estimated at 600,000, was found to be unrealistic for the NGOs to provide relief.[47] With no aid coming from the Central government as well, the Left Front government in West Bengal found the forceful eviction of the refugees a far more effective policy than the cumbersome process of finding vacant lands in other parts of the state and rehabilitating them.

The government made use of the on-going Tiger Project, which had international support and WWF backing. Dr Karan Singh, Chairman of the Project Tiger steering committee, was widely quoted in support of the urgency of the project. Organisations wanting to highlight the human cost of such projects were wrongly interpreted as being insensitive to ecological concerns. WWF literature which blamed the poor for being the 'most direct threat to wildlife and wildlands'[48] was widely quoted by the West Bengal government as well. True, there were reports of the refugees cutting trees and selling them to middlemen from surrounding islands. Some of the refugees themselves were quoted as having done the same. The profiteers of this timber business, though, were the leaders who had brought the refugees to the island. Yet these acts, instead of being seen as desperate attempts by the refugees to survive, were seen as intended encroachment. Organisational imperatives necessitated downplaying and ignoring the human cost paid by the poor people for environmental preservation. Loss of lives was accepted as a necessary price to pay for conservation. The refugees tried to draw attention to their own efforts at resettlement without harming the natural resources by citing examples of the twelve settlements that they had, in the meantime, built for themselves, including laid-out roads, drainage channels to prevent water-logging, a school, a dispensary, smithies, a pottery, cigarette workshops, a bakery, several fisheries, boat-building yards, numerous boats, market places and a dyke system to hold back the tide.[49]

The eviction of people ready to risk death, even if unarmed, has always been a difficult task for the state. Such strength and determination, which would, in many instances, be considered heroic, was now seen as 'anti-state, subversive, and environmentally unfriendly'.[50] In spite of not being directly associated with

Ethno-cultural concerns 147

the eviction, eco-tourism-promoting bodies acted as incentives for these governmental policies. The prospect of developing Marichjhapi as a profitable tourist destination was prioritised over refugee resettlement. The government took efforts to project itself as environmentally sensitive. It could reap future profits as long as the massacre could effectively be prevented from being exposed.[51] The refugees, being falsely portrayed as environmentally unfriendly, failed to garner either aid or support for their cause.

The conflict between environmental preservation and people's rights has been, for a long time, at the heart of the trade-offs between human rights and ecological preservation. The laws which secure the Indian state's ownership and control over its forests have always been fraught with an uneasy truce with people's involvement in forest resources. During the latter part of the twentieth century, people's participation in forest conservation was being encouraged, at one level, while an opposing force was also at play. In the draft bills of the Forest Laws from around the late 1970s, 'technologies of control' were being strengthened rather than the scope for 'people's participation'.[52] The misuse of the law in Marichjhapi was another case of this strengthening of control. First, the refugees were lured by the government to leave Dandakaranya and settle on the island. Then, on their arrival, the government announced that the Tiger Project in Sundarbans was under threat from their resettlement on the island. Laws, put to misuse, not just massacred thousands of refugees, but also succeeded in covering up the incident behind the larger concerns of the preservation of natural resources.

Left Front, in its long tenure in West Bengal, has often found favour with its people for providing 'good governance'.[53] Such applause for governance can only be possible as long as events like Marichjhapi do not come to the forefront. Debates on these massacres are especially important in places like India where judicial institutions are often languid, if not non-functional. Even after the Marichjhapi incident, the government officials of West Bengal, including the Chief Minister, not just made frequent trips to other parts of the world without being questioned about the massacre, but the Left Front also held the West Bengal government for the next 34 years. The incident did not find any mention in academic publications till about the 1990s, more than a decade and a half after the incident. All that was ever debated in the academic circuit was a misleading representation of the incident. As one of the cadres of CPI(M) later rued in an interview: 'After all, when in opposition during the mid-70s, we were the ones who cried hoarse for refugee resettlement at Marichjhapi. Unfortunately, everything changed once we came to power'.[54]

This had always been the case, as rightly put by the All Bengal Namasudra Association to the Simon Commission in 1929, much before the Marichjhapi massacre: 'It has been seen in more than one case that British members of the Indian Civil Service, on account of their living in this country for a long time, and by coming into contact with only a section of the people, are mentally captured by the ideas of those few people who are in the position of social aristocrats'.[55] This statement holds true for not just the case of the *Namasudras* in Bengal but for the state of subaltern representations in India, especially in the late colonial and

148   *Ethno-cultural concerns*

post-colonial era which, ironically, saw a hue and cry about the representation of the subalterns in Indian historiography.

Caste/class/ethnicity/religion: the complex web

The presence of castes and sub-castes within the larger frames of class categorisations has always been an integral part of the Indian social structure. The show of resistance by the *Namasudras*, one of the many Untouchable castes in India, in Marichjhapi highlights one of the strongest yet unpronounced reasons behind the massacre.

Though of a similar ethnic background (Hindu and Bengali), the refugees who came to Marichjhapi were the ones belonging to the most lowly-held castes of the Hindu Bengali society, the *Namasudras*. Their agrarian base coupled with their caste identities made their efforts at resettlement on the island a matter of serious discomfort for the state. Not only were they contesting the state's role as the sole decider and provider, they were also doing it as a community belonging to the lowest rung of the social ladder. Their resettlement efforts were not simply reversing the state-subject equation; they were challenging the elite-subaltern equation as well. For the Indian state, *cultural outcastes* have always posed a bigger threat than *cultural outsiders*. The West Bengal government was no different. If 'the essence of sovereignty remains in the power to exclude',[56] then the Marichjhapi massacre surely was sovereignty in its most powerful form. The massacre was a re-emphasis of the hard reality that the identities of the subjects are never meant to overshadow those allocated to them by the state.

The issues of ethnicity (Bengali) and religion (Hinduism) also played important roles in the Marichjhapi narrative. When the state announced an economic blockade on the island, there were a few radical groups based in mainland West Bengal who came forward in support of the refugees. However, their motives were related to the creation of an ethnic homeland rather than resettlement of the refugees. Their involvement, therefore, ruined the last hopes for the refugees since it made the government all the more apprehensive about their agenda.

Radical groups known as *Amra Bangali* (We are Bengalis) and *Nikhil Banga Nagarik Sangha* (All Bengal Citizens Group) supported the refugees with an aim to create a *Bangalistan* or *Bangabhumi* – land for the Bengalis. Their goal was the creation of a Bengali territory constituting West Bengal, Tripura, parts of Assam, Meghalaya, Bihar, Jharkhand, Orissa, the Andamans, Nepal and Myanmar, and the whole of 'Swadhin Bangladesh'[57] (Free Bangladesh) at the site of the border between West Bengal and Bangladesh. This land, according to these groups, would be strictly for the ethnic Hindu-Bengalis, as opposed to the Muslim-Bengalis of Bangladesh. These groups, according to intelligence reports, were opposed to the idea of certain Hindu-dominated parts of undivided Bengal being made part of Bangladesh as a result of the Partition. Their creation of a Hindu-Bengali territory would be their answer to the hasty partition of Bengal in 1947.[58] Volunteers from these organisations helped the refugees by distributing copies of route maps from Calcutta to Marichjhapi and a rough sketch of the island even before the exodus started in full swing around 1978. Their demand for a 'Hindu homeland' including parts of Bengal and Bangladesh was corroborated by several demonstrations, which they staged in front of the office of the Bangladesh Deputy High Commission in Kolkata.[59] These groups also formed their own armed wings called *Bangasena* (Bengal Army), volunteers of which were active members of the resistance movement formed by the refugees. Their active involvement in the incident was corroborated later by one of their own volunteers, presently living in the outskirts of Calcutta, to a newspaper.[60] These agendas of a free Bengali homeland based on ethnicity had their roots in one of the factions of the Bengal Provincial Muslim League before Partition, when 'Huseyn Shaheed Suhrawardy and Abul Hashim had co-authored a proposal for a united and sovereign Bengal, independent of both India and Pakistan'.[61] Such reflections stand testimony to the fact that the Partition was, indeed, a continuous process which expressed itself in various forms years after the boundary line was drawn.

The involvement of such radical groups with demands of a Hindu-Bengali home-land further added to the complication of the identity politics of which the refugees were already victims. The refugees were already being made to pay the price for belonging to the *Namasudra* community despite being ethnically similar to the majority population of West Bengal – a factor which, in fact, they were trying to highlight in their defence. But the radicalisation of their Bengali identity through the involvement of the radical Bengali groups made their position susceptible to state repression. The refugees were torn between the politics of identities which were thrust upon them and in which they hardly had a choice.

Territorial implication

The border between West Bengal and Bangladesh has always been witness to the overlapping of socio-cultural identities. The premise for the creation of the borders could, in the first place, never accommodate the dynamics of identities which underscored the process. With the passage of time, these identities manifested themselves in far more complex ways than the states were ready for. The Liberation War of 1971 in East Pakistan, resulting in the creation of Bangladesh, redefined the bordering process in subtle yet intense ways. Increasingly, religion as the basis for separation between the two states lost ground, with a mix of religious communities inhabiting both sides of the border. Moreover, the fact that ethnicity and language ('Bengali' or 'Bangla') were the main bases for the formation of Bangladesh further complicated the process of reinforcing the border. With people of identical ethnic backgrounds, identical languages and shared social and cultural histories on both sides of the border, the physical reinforcement and materiality of the state's presence at the border gained prime significance.

For the refugees, settling in Marichjhapi was symbolic of their return to their homeland that they had left behind in Bangladesh, not simply because of the similarity in topographical features but also, and perhaps more importantly, because of the close proximity of Marichjhapi to Bangladesh, across the border. Certainly, Dandakaranya did not evoke such nostalgia. The location of Marichjhapi near the

150 *Ethno-cultural concerns*

West Bengal-Bangladesh border, therefore, was a significant cause for the refugees wanting to resettle there instead of Dandakaranya.

For the state, having control over the island was not simply about appropriating a space within its bounded territorial limits. It was about controlling the very 'limit' that defined the state. Borders, as symbols of the state's unquestionable sovereign control, are also the spaces where the states are most vulnerable. Use or appropriation of the border spaces are, understandably, reminders for the states of the success of their control regimes. This is what made Marichjhapi, as a border island strategically important and its consequent appropriation by a group of *Namasudra* refugees, a cause of serious threat to the government of West Bengal.

The *Matua* trajectory

The second narrative brings us to recent years, i.e. 2009, the place being Thakurnagar in Bongaon in the North 24 Parganas district of West Bengal and located very close to the Petrapole-Benapole border Land Port (LP) between the North 24 Parganas district of West Bengal and the Jessore district of Bangladesh. The event we are looking at here is that of *Baruni Mela* – a week-long fair organised by the *Matua* community (primarily consisting of *Namasudra* refugees from Bangladesh). The fair, newspaper reports said, was graced by the presence of political figures (MLAs, MPs, as well as candidates for forthcoming elections) paying homage to *Barama* – the religious leader of the 50-million strong *Matua* community in India, at the *Matua* headquarters at Thakurnagar. More than 10 million *Matuas* live in West Bengal alone, indicating a 10-million strong vote-bank for any party in West Bengal who succeeds in gaining their support.

Two aspects are similar in the narratives of the Marichjhapi massacre and the *Matua* trajectory, so far expressed through the incident of the *Baruni mela* alone. One is the nature of the people involved, i.e. *Namasudras*, on the one hand, and the state (represented through political figures), on the other. The second is the nature of location of the two incidents, i.e. the West Bengal-Bangladesh border. What has changed, perhaps, in the years following the Marichjhapi massacre (between 1979 and 2009) is the nature of negotiation between outcastes and the state. Studying the change in the pattern of negotiation between the people living (or attempting to live) along the border, and the state, helps in our understanding of spatial narratives created by the reality of the border and the evolution of a *border consciousness*.

Organised ideology

Matuas have their origin in Harichand Thakur who, in the mid-nineteenth century, propounded certain ideas in the Oraikandi village of Faridpur district in then undivided Bengal. Born into a *Vaishnava Namasudra* family (the original surname being *Biswas*),[62] Harichand's ideas spoke essentially in favour of the downtrodden, so-called lower castes of the Bengali society. The *Namasudras* were largely influenced by the *Bhakti* movement of the fifteenth century, which emerged as a

Ethno-cultural concerns 151

deviant stream of philosophy within the *Vaishnava* cult.[63] A section of the followers of the *Vaishnava* cult believed in the upliftment of the downtrodden sections of society and, thus, professed an all-inclusive ideological practice. These sects from within the *Vaishnavas* appealed to the low-caste population in India, including the *Namasudras*. The 'non-formal, equalitarian rural variant'[64] of the *Vaishnava* ideology became popular within the *Namasudra* community and it is from such an ideological background that the founder of the *Matua* sect, Harichand Thakur, came. The influence of the deviant *Bhakti* sects on the *Matua* ideology did not simply give an anti-hierarchy stance to their ideology, but also initiated an alternative 'discourse of dignity'[65] and tried to create an 'autonomous social space' where this discourse could be asserted.[66] The rise of the *Matuas*, as an essentially *Namasudra* community, to a position of power in the electoral politics of West Bengal is reflective of the creation of such a space. In fact, the very nomenclature *Matua* bears signs of an anti-hegemonic stance. The elite Hindu population would ridicule the followers of Harichand's ideology as *motto* or people drunk with their own spiritual outpourings (*matoyara*). This was a way devised by the upper caste Hindus as well as respectable *Vaishnavas* to distance themselves from the followers of this sect. Harichand used this very ridicule in strengthening the solidarity of the sect and named it *Matua* – a word absent in the elite lexicon.[67] The flag of the *Matuas* (red body with white borders) is symbolic of their philosophy of combining spiritual devotion (*bhakti*) with material action (*karma*). 'The dictum of *Hate kam mukhe nam* (doing worldly duties while chanting His holy name), as Harichand defined it, became the guiding principle of the *Matua* philosophy of life',[68] creating the foundation for the later association of the *Matuas* with the electoral politics of Bengal.

The *Matuas* were organised into a sect by Harichand's son, Guruchand Thakur, born in 1846. Guruchand 'formalised the doctrine of the sect to suit better the needs of an emerging lower caste peasant community'.[69] He made his objectives clear when he explained that the reason for lack of respect for the *Namasudras*, in spite of the numerical strength of the community, was their lack of power, and that 'it was power alone which could command respect'.[70] The *Namasudras*, as described earlier in the chapter, were essentially an agricultural community, tied to the land economy in Bengal. The trajectories of most of the *Namasudras* of Bengal are similar in that they were the last ones to leave their lands in East Pakistan after Partition and, hence, the last ones to arrive in West Bengal as refugees, unlike the elite Hindu professionals. The *Matuas* settled in Thakurnagar off Bongaon in the North 24 Parganas district in West Bengal. Like Marichjhapi, Bongaon is a border municipality and at a distance of seventeen kilometres (fifteen minutes' drive) from Gaighata that houses the headquarters of the *Matuas*. The *Matuas*, like the rest of the *Namasudra* community, migrated to West Bengal in phases, right from 1948 (following the Partition) till about 1978 (following the formation of Bangladesh and renewed communal violence). Over the years, the *Matua* community in Thakurnagar has become stronger in number with the coming of new migrant *Namasudras* from Bangladesh. Over 90% of the *Matuas* in West Bengal are, thus, refugees and migrants from East Pakistan/Bangladesh.[71]

152   *Ethno-cultural concerns*

The trajectory of promises of a better life and living to these *Matuas* by the political leadership of the time, especially the Left Front, is also similar to that of the *Namasudra* communities who were lured by the Left Front to come and settle in Marichjhapi. The ones who came immediately after the Partition till about 1963 attained official refugee status. But the ones who came to West Bengal after 1964 were officially labelled 'illegal migrants', since the then-Congress government in power declared that migrants who came after 1964 would be eligible for government relief and rehabilitation aids only if they settled outside West Bengal in other regions of India.[72] The peasants, who migrated still later, post-1971, following the Bangladesh Liberation War, were labelled as illegal by every definition.[73] Still, a large number of migrants who migrated after 1964 and well after 1971 preferred to settle in West Bengal, mostly in rural areas, associating themselves with the kind of work that they were doing all their life, i.e. agriculture. The *Matuas* were no exception. Yet the treatment meted out to these two sets of *Namasudra* communities (in Marichjhapi and in Thakurnagar) by the ruling Left Front varied distinctly, despite the similarities in the territorial specificity of the two locations.

This difference can be traced to the time of migration as well as socio-religious issues, apart from the way in which these two communities negotiated their subaltern status. Both were initially seen as potential vote-banks by the Left Front leaders. But while the *Namasudras* at Marichjhapi failed to hold on to that negotiating power, the *Matua Namasudras* at Thakurnagar successfully organised themselves into a community who could make or break any political party's career. The sheer number of *Matuas* also became decisive. A 10-million vote-bank will bring any political leader of any stature to their doorstep. And so it did. Moreover, Marichjhapi, located in the far southern part of the West Bengal-Bangladesh border in the inaccessible mangroves of the Sundarbans, proved to be a wiser location for atrocities – away from the glare and knowledge of the urban crowd of Kolkata. Thakurnagar in Bongaon is a more strategically located point along the border, with Petrapole in close proximity. News of any kind of atrocities, especially physical, would easily find its way into the newspapers.

Though the *Matuas* did traditionally vote for the Left Front, their grievances against the party simultaneously grew. The issue of unfulfilled promises of infrastructural development in the region coupled with the grievance of being labelled as 'infiltrators' in public parlance, with the encouragement of the West Bengal government, gradually built a strong resistance within the *Matuas* against the Left Front.[74] The turning point was brought about by the then party in opposition (and now the party in power) in West Bengal, the Trinomool Congress (TMC). The TMC, headed by Mamata Banerjee, was quick to realise the potential of both the location of the concentration of the *Matuas* (i.e. the border area) as well as the numerical strength of the community as far as electoral politics in West Bengal was concerned.[75]

Beginning with charitable grants towards the *Matua* community in the form of donations and land grants, to becoming a member of the *Matua* organisation (*Matua Mahasangha*) herself – Mamata left no stone unturned to ensure complete support from the *Matua* voters.[76] What is interesting, and this is where their narrative differs from the *Namasudras* of Marichjhapi, is how the *Matua Nama-sudras* negotiated their position and rose to power. Religious conceptualisation of the *Matua* sect played a very important role in this negotiation.

Overlapping of 'being' and 'becoming'

Historically, the trajectories of the *Namasudras* have shown an overlapping of 'being' (*jati* or caste) and 'becoming' (*varna* or rank – the Hindu hierarchical structure based mainly on profession) – concepts which are otherwise sharply separated from one another in the Hindu ideology. While *jati*, in Hindu philosophy, is considered a real social group,[77] which one can only be born into, *varna* is a conceptual scheme,[78] based largely on a common profession and 'a common social language'.[79] *Varna* is flexible in nature and one could gain or lose *varna* status. The overlapping of these two concepts in the narratives of caste identities of the lower castes in India shows how these concepts of 'being' and 'becoming' have been 'selectively appropriated'[80] by these castes 'to improve their own position'[81] within the social set-up.

Ethno-religious factor

The *Matuas*, though essentially a caste-based community, organised and projected themselves as a religious sect – as the followers of Harichand and Guruchand Thakur. Manjulkrishna, the vice-president of the *Sangha*, puts it more clearly: 'It is a religion as we have a prophet in Guru Harichand, my great-great-grandfather, whose teachings we follow. But it's more of a movement that seeks to uplift the downtrodden and tells you what an ideal family life should be'.[82] The *Matuas* constructed an 'ideological community'[83] that would submerge the inchoate class distinctions within the group and set it against its Other,[84] i.e. the hegemonic presence of the elite Hindus in the politics of West Bengal. The moment a religious label is tagged onto a community, especially in India, its relation with the state becomes a sensitive issue. Thus, the *Matuas* used religion as a weapon in their negotiation with the state, unlike the *Namasudras* at Marichjhapi whose religious factor could not be used to draw sympathy. In fact, the involvement of radical ethno-religious groups in the Marichjhapi incident worsened their cause. The fact that the religious index has been an importance stance used by the *Matuas* to defend their cause, including the betterment of their community and cross-border ties, becomes clear during the *Matua Mela* (fair) at Thakurnagar[85] where exhibitions on Hindu Samhati (Hindu Unity) are put up in the fairgrounds where thousands of *Matuas* gather.[86] The *Matua* community can, apparently, identify with the cause of the exhibition: that of spreading awareness about the atrocities on Hindus by the Islamic fundamentalists in Bangladesh because they have themselves been subject to the same, especially in the massive Hindu exodus of the years 1947–48, 1951, 1964, 1971 and 1992 from erstwhile East Pakistan and, later, Bangladesh into West Bengal. 'As a matter of fact, in the anti-Hindu pogrom in Bangladesh in 2001, many of the victims were actually across-the-border relatives and extended

154   *Ethno-cultural concerns*

family members of the *Matuas* of West Bengal',[87] says one of the organisers of the exhibition. The visibly increasing influence of organisations like Hindu Samhati hints at the larger agenda of incorporating the so-called lower orders, like the *Matuas*, into the larger Hindu fold with an aim to strengthen the Hindu vote-bank, especially in areas where political parties like the RSS or the BJP are yet to make a strong impact, like Bengal. With the increasing political importance of the *Matuas* as a community, the *Matua Mela* is also growing in stature and participation. Matuas join the festivities in Thakurnagar travelling all the way from not just various parts of India but from Bangladesh as well. The *Matua Mela* has turned into a thriving economy, with a diverse mix of household items, foods, clothing and tools for agricultural use on offer for the visitors.[88] The gathering also has its negative side in being the hub for illegal and smuggled items – many of them procured from the other side of the border.[89]

Legal implication

The time of migration of the *Matua* refugees also favoured their cause. The first influx of these *Namasudra Matuas* as refugees from East Pakistan was in 1948, when Pramatharanjan Thakur, the grandson of Guruchand Thakur, migrated to West Bengal, bought forest lands from a local *zamindar* (landlord) of Gaighata, christened the place as 'Thakurnagar', built a small house and started living there from the 13 March 1949.[90] The *Matuas*, thereafter, came in phases and gathered mostly at Thakurnagar, under the auspices of Pramatharanjan's descendants, apart from other districts in West Bengal such as Howrah, South 24 Parganas, Nadia, Cooch Behar, Malda, North Dinajpur and South Dinajpur. Of the eight districts which host the *Matuas*, seven are border districts of West Bengal (except Howrah) – a factor that makes the strategic location of the *Matuas* all the more prominent. Their initial migration in 1948 ensured their official 'refugee' status, though with the lapse of time, later migrants came to be labelled 'infiltrators'. But by the time the issue of illegal migration found ground in electoral agendas in West Bengal, the *Matuas* had already organised themselves into a sect. The *Namasudras* at Marichjhapi came at a time (1977–78) when migration from Bangladesh into West Bengal had already been officially declared as 'illegal', which tagged the *Namasudras* as an unwanted intrusion from the very beginning. They could not claim to have any official refugee status, unlike the *Matuas* who could trace their initial migration to an officially recognised migration. The Left Front's misguided political stance of supporting the *Namasudras*' cause of settling within West Bengal resulted in the massacre at Marichjhapi. The claim over land was stronger for the *Matuas* since that held by the Thakur family had been 'bought' by their ancestor, Pramatharanjan, from the then local *zamindar*, unlike the *Namasudras* at Marichjhapi who did not have any official claim over the space (the island of Marichjhapi) that they had appropriated.

Political implication

The *Matua Mahasangha* as an organisation is very well-structured with details of all its members across the country recorded and tracked. Binapani Devi or

Barama, as she is known amongst followers, is the wife of Pramatharanjan Thakur, the grandson of Guruchand who took the initiative to settle the *Matuas* in Thakurnagar and organise them into a strong community. Ninety-six-year old *Barama* is the chief advisor to the *Sangha* and has the last word in any matter involving the *Matuas*, while her two sons hold important administrative positions in the *Sangha*. The TMC realised that obtaining *Barama*'s support could decide the support base from the *Matuas*. Therefore, *Matua* fairs, the construction of temples and gatherings were officiated under the banner of the political party.[91]

The Thakurnagar railway station is currently being developed as a 'model' one. A stadium and a railway hospital are among the other things promised. The foundation for a college has already been laid. Mamata, despite not being a *Matua* herself, took membership of the *Sangha* and eventually was made its 'Chief Patron',[92] an honour conferred on her by none other than *Barama* herself. Not that the Left Front did not try to make amends for their faults in dealing with the *Namasudra* community. Left Front leaders have visited *Barama*, promised land grants for building research institutes dedicated to the *Matuas* and announced awards in the name of Harichand and Guruchand Thakur, the first recipient being *Barama*'s elder son Kapilkrishna Thakur. All this was after the Left Front realised the importance of the *Matua* voters in the preceding Panchayat and Lok Sabha elections (2008 and 2009, respectively), where the *Matua* votes turned against them and in favour of the TMC, resulting in a major loss of the vote-bank for the Front. But the Left Front lost in the last round of the game of wooing *Matua* support when *Barama*'s younger son, Manjulkrishna Thakur, was chosen as the TMC's candidate from the Gaighata constituency of the Bongaon subdivision (which constitutes Thakurnagar) and eventually succeeded in the Assembly Elections (2011), when he was elected as the Minister to the Legislative Assembly (MLA) from his constituency. This made him a *Namasudra* MLA from a border constituency – a major departure from the narrative of the Marichjhapi *Namasudras*. This, though, is not too unusual as far as the connection between the Thakur family and the politics of Bengal is concerned. Manjulkrishna's father, Pramatharanjan, was also an MLA in the West Bengal Assembly in 1962, and later a Congress MP from Nabadwip (in Nadia district, West Bengal) in 1967.[93] This was the reason cited by the Congress leaders who visited *Barama* in May 2012 to enquire about her well-being. When questions of political intentions were raised, the Congress leaders were quick to suggest that this was a courtesy visit to the wife of the late Pramatharanjan Thakur, a Congress MP, and was not driven by political intentions – the irony being that it took some 45 years for them to decide on the importance of a courtesy visit to the *Matua* head. Efforts have not been in vain for the TMC, as the results of the *Panchayat* elections in July 2013 suggest.[94] The effort put in by all political parties to extend influence over the *Matua* community continues, and reaches apex around elections. The BJP is leaving no stone unturned to bring the *Matuas* under a pan-Indian political discourse through a visible incorporation into the Ambedkarite Dalit movement.[95]

In fact, the spectre of the Marichjhapi massacre, too, keeps haunting the current political scenario in West Bengal, where the TMC often uses the incident against the Left Front as an electoral agenda. The survivors and witnesses of

156 *Ethno-cultural concerns*

the Marichjhapi incident also recall the massacre, not just as memories but also through memorials held for those killed on the actual day.[96] Such occurrences indicate that negotiations between the low-caste refugees and/or infiltrators and the state machinery at the borders are an on-going process, which evolve and mature together with the evolution of the border.

Territorial implication

What makes Manjulkrishna's stance as a political figure different from that of his father is the issue of infiltration and citizenship. What needs to be seen is whether this rise to power of a downtrodden caste actually makes a difference to the (il)legality of their citizenship status. It is here that the specificity of the concentration of the *Matuas* at the border becomes important. Illegal migration from Bangladesh to West Bengal still continues unabated. A majority of migrants, still, settle around the border areas, apart from those who settle in the cities, away from the borders.[97] In fact, there are existences of whole villages constituted of illegal Bangladeshi migrants, who have obtained official documents (ration and voter cards) required to prove themselves as legal residents of West Bengal. 'Most of them are Hindus, primarily SC-s and ST-s',[98] says Riazul.

A whole range of livelihoods have emerged, which depend on the existence of the border, including those related to illegal border-crossing.[99] The major portions of those who cross the border belong to the lower rungs of the society, including the *Namasudras* – which, in the process, include refugee *Matuas*.[100] The Left Front 'simply overlooked the serious problem of continuous migration or infiltration; but began to recognise those people in a sort of clandestine manner by providing the migrants with ration cards at least in some areas'.[101] While this surely increased the vote-bank of the Left Front, the issue of infiltration was not effectively solved.

The issue of citizenship has now been tied up with the *Matuas* in a decisive way, since this is an issue that the political parties are not comfortable addressing while the *Matuas* are a community that they cannot afford to ignore. Even Mamata, with her political stance of successfully bringing the *Matuas* into the political fold of West Bengal, remains tight-lipped about the sect's main grievance: that of the deportation of thousands of its members from West Bengal as alleged infiltrators.[102] While one of the *Matua* heads fulfils the responsibilities of an important political figure in regional politics, the ways of negotiation of cross-border infiltration and citizenship issues by the rest of the community make for an interesting study, especially with Manjulkrishna ensuring 'a meaningful change to the lives of the downtrodden and the refugees'.[103] The narrative of these *Namasudras*, both in the cases of Marichjhapi and the *Matuas*, is a result of the convergence of their spatial and social identities, as they negotiate between the identities of being infiltrators/illegal migrants and a low-caste community. Such a convergence results in a political narrative, made unique by the specificity of its location at the border.

Ethno-cultural concerns   157

Anti-hegemonic aspects in the history of the Namasudras

Tendencies of accommodating myths and notions related to higher castes into their own ideology have been integral to the discourse of identity formation of the *Namasudras*. If attempts to trace their genealogy to a Brahmin origin (as has sometimes been done by the *Matuas*)[104] has been one side of this tendency, then entering the realm of electoral politics has been the other. Electoral politics in Bengal has been, almost exclusively, the forte of the elite Hindu castes (Brahmin, Kshatriya, Vaishya), as mentioned earlier. Entering the realm of politics in Bengal has been the *Namasudras*' way of 'appropriating symbols of authority and divesting them of their symbolic significance'.[105] The appropriation of political space and divesting it of its elitist exclusivity has been their way of negotiating with the hegemonic order. In fact, it was this anti-hegemonic stance that saw the non-participation of the *Namasudras* in the nationalist movements in India in the early twentieth century, since these were led by high caste Hindu gentry.[106]

A study of the history of the *Namasudras* demonstrates that 'the different constituents of the community had been seeking in different ways to reorientate the relations of power in indigenous society'.[107] This meant that from the very beginning, different streams of negotiation were devised by the community. 'While the *Namasudra* elites desired a share of new economic opportunities and political power, as it was gradually devolved in institutional politics through successive constitutional reforms, the peasantry cared more for community honour and liberation from economic oppression and social discrimination',[108] the common grudge being against the elite Hindu gentry of Bengal. The elite *Namasudras* aimed to secure a place for themselves 'within the wider community, i.e. the nation' (and this was being made possible by 'the constitutional reform of 1935 which compelled all the other nationalist parties to recognise their position');[109] the peasant community having lost their leadership looked for alternative alignments. This pushed their movement into being appropriated by other political streams from 1940s onwards.[110] If the history of the *Matuas* reflects the first strand of the *Namasudra* narrative, the events at Marichjhapi are reflective of the second, i.e. the (mis)appropriation of their movement. The *Namasudra* movement took shape in 1872 in the form of the first organised social protest of the *Namasudras* against their social status in Bakargunj-Faridapur (then parts of united Bengal) and reached its high point during the *Swadeshi* period[111] (1905–11). Thereafter, the movement thinned down upon entering constitutional politics in the 1930s. While a part of the community remained faithful to B. R. Ambedkar's Scheduled Caste Federation,[112] others either joined the Congress, the Hindu Mahasabha against the Muslims,[113] or the Bengal Provincial Kisan Sabha.[114] The Partition dealt the final blow to the movement, dividing the community geographically. Henceforth, their 'caste' identity started overlapping with other relationships[115] – social, political and territorial. In fact, the continued support of the *Namasudra* elites for the Left Front despite the Marichjhapi massacre testifies to the varying aspirations within the community, where the peasant class (the majority of the *Namasudras*

158 *Ethno-cultural concerns*

at Marichjhapi being of peasant origin) failed to garner the support of the elite *Namasudras* – political aspirations being the most evident cause. While the territorial specificity of the *Namasudra* settlement in the case of Marichjhapi went against their cause, this was precisely what the *Matuas* took advantage of. Both events stand proof of the intertwining of caste discourses with spatial narratives, with or without success.

It has often been the aim of the dominant socio-political machinery of the state to appropriate or suppress subversive movements which might pose a challenge to the hegemonic order. The Partition and its consequent migration trends made it difficult for the state to appropriate the *Namasudra* movement because of the coupling of the aspect of social marginality with that of territorial marginality. The new identity of being a border people that these *Namasudra* migrants now acquired made it difficult for the hegemonic orders to either completely appropriate or trivialise their presence. The starkness of the difference of 'dealing with' the *Namasudra* presence in the border areas between the two major events discussed above, i.e. the Marichjhapi massacre and the politics of the *Matuas*, reflects the dilemma, gradual process of realisation and consequent modification of the policies of the state with regard to its negotiation with the community.

Caste narratives elsewhere along the West Bengal-Bangladesh border

Caste profile

The border area between West Bengal and Bangladesh abounds in instances of the convergence of social identities with territorial marginalities. While the Marichjhapi event in the Sundarbans and the concentration of *Matuas* in the North 24 Parganas of West Bengal provide the best examples of such a convergence, the whole length of this border is, in fact, marked by the same feature. Migration from East Pakistan and, later, Bangladesh of agricultural communities, mostly *Namasudras*, into India (West Bengal being the most affected for being a border province) ensured *Namasudra* settlements, even if not as community-based concentrations, along the length of the West Bengal-Bangladesh border. *Namasudras* constitute a large part of that civilian population, especially on the West Bengal side of the border, who negotiate the border and its various apparatuses. The interviewees (without conscious selection) mostly belong to the scheduled or otherwise non-Brahmin castes and scheduled tribes of India. Interestingly, the Muslim respondents often have similar surnames to the Hindu castes,[116] on both sides of the border. These bear hints of their origin (as being one of the castes in undivided Bengal and India, at large), though they may have converted to Islam during the expansion of the religion, mostly under extreme conditions of socio-economic misery brought about by their status of a low-caste within the Hindu religious fold. Narratives of the elite Hindu migrants preferring to settle in the flourishing cities and towns in West Bengal and the agriculture-dependent communities such

Ethno-cultural concerns 159

as the Scheduled Castes (SC)/Scheduled Tribes (ST)/Other Backward Classes (OBC) settling, almost by economic compulsion, in the rural areas, including the borders, holds true not just for Marichjhapi or the *Matuas*, but along the whole length of the border.

Most of the *Namasudras* and Hindu SC/STs living along the border are engaged in agricultural jobs.[117] They are often concentrated in an area with a majority of the people of a neighbourhood sharing the same caste, represented by their surnames, for example, *Mahato, Bagdi, Mondol, Biswas, Burman, Pal, Haldar*, etc. Dinhata in the Cooch Behar district of West Bengal is an example. Many of the villages under the Dinhata subdivision are caste-based where the predominance of one or the other castes prevails. *Mahato, Bagdi, Mondol, Biswas* and *Burman* are some of the surnames which one frequently comes across, creating such neighbourhoods as *Burman-para*(neighbourhood), *Mondol-para, Bagdi-para*, etc. Nirendranath Burman explains: 'In this village, everybody is *Burman* like Santosh Burman, Kshitish Burman, Khogen Burman, Babu Burman, Ramesh Burman. On that side of the village, the *Malakars* live, who work as gardeners'.[118]

Oraon (one of the scheduled tribes) villages are also seen in Purba Bakhalir Chhara Enclave (Bangladeshi Enclave in India), consisting mostly of Partition migrants from Rangpur district (Bangladesh). The Bangladesh Liberation War of 1971 triggered an exodus of migration of people belonging to various Hindu castes, and understandably, most of them related to agricultural jobs, into West Bengal, adding to the population of the various castes along the border. 'After the Bangladesh War, a lot of Hindus have migrated to this place, like the *Pals* and the *Haldars*', says Kuddus Rahman of Jalangi (West Bengal).[119]

Some of the villages in these border areas are found to be inhabited by the Hindu *Mahishya* caste[120] – that has its origin as a cultivator caste. Some of them have later opted for skilled labour. Villages consisting primarily of people belonging to the *Mahishya* caste are frequently found in the border districts of West Bengal. 'This is predominantly a *Mahishya* village, with a few Brahmin and SC/ST families', says Jasimuddin Mondol,[121] reiterating a common response among many of the border villages visited during my field visits. 'There are hardly any SC/ST families here. Most of these people are Hindu *Mahishya*', says a respondent from yet another border village in Nadia district.[122] Similar responses confirming the existence of predominantly scheduled caste/tribe villages are also common along many of the border villages along the West Bengal-Bangladesh border. 'In general the number of Hindus is more here. There are mostly SC/ST families here. In fact, STs are the largest in number', says Dayamay Datta of Teipur, Nadia district.[123] A respondent in Goga (Bangladesh) is more specific in mentioning the population profile when he says, 'There are some Hindus in Goga. Besides that, there are the *Bagdi, Kumor, Kamar*' (scheduled castes).[124] Goga is a village on the Bangladesh side of the border and shares its border with Gaighata (West Bengal), the headquarters of the *Namasudra Matuas*. This response indicates the similarity between the profile of the communities (*Namasudras*) on both sides of the West Bengal-Bangladesh border and explains the cross-border ties between them.

160 *Ethno-cultural concerns*

Some of the respondents of the border villages narrate how they, as a caste-community, were brought by the British administrators from other parts of India and settled in the area that they presently inhabit – that eventually became the border area after the Partition. Prasanta Mondol narrates how his ancestors had been brought over from Nagpur in Bihar to Char Meghna (which they currently inhabit) as labourers in indigo plantations during the second half of the seventeenth century. 'Initially, it was just 2 or 3 families, which later increased to a whole village', he says.[125]

The concentration of various scheduled castes and tribes in the areas which now form part of the border between West Bengal and Bangladesh can be largely traced back to colonial administration, like the instance above, where tribal populations often known for their capacity for hard work as well as for their tradition of agricultural engagements were used by British administrators (including indigo planters) as cheap labour in their plantations. While most of the plantations were concentrated in the area which is now the border (districts like Nadia, Murshidabad and 24 Parganas still have ruins of the indigo warehouses beside the rivers which pass through them), cheap labour, mostly from tribals or low-castes (*Namasudras* in many cases) was sourced from the tribal belts of Bengal, Bihar, Orissa and Madhya Pradesh. These labourers settled in these areas, initially as bonded labourers and, eventually, post-1947, as cultivators and agricultural labourers, thus constituting a large portion of what became the 'border population'. Hare Krishna Mondol confirms the migration narrative when he narrates how

> the British had brought these tribals from Midnapore and the Chhota Nagpur area in Bihar to Char Meghna as labourers in indigo plantations. A Guru by the name of Jadu Pandit from Bihar had once visited this place and confirmed that these tribes were originally a barber caste (*Napit*) and had been forcefully made to engage in agricultural jobs by the British. The Guru also added that they were not as lowly a caste as they eventually ended up being, which made other higher castes look down upon them.[126]

Livelihood

The livelihoods of these castes and tribes are still categorised in certain ways. As Md. Tafikul Islam says:

> There are indigenous population (scheduled castes and tribes) here. Their relation with the other non-tribal population is cordial. These scheduled castes and tribes are mostly engaged as labourers in brick-kilns or other small-scale manufacturing businesses, or work as van-drivers or agricultural labourers. There is a *Das*-locality here and the community mostly works as labourers in brick-kilns and in jute fields, or is engaged as labourers in sand dredging.[127]

Information like the above also suggests that these so-called low-castes rarely 'own' land. Land ownership in Hindu society has mostly been held by the elite

Ethno-cultural concerns 161

castes. The lower castes and, over the years, the indigenous population (including the tribes), have been engaged in these lands as labourers. Though some of these castes have gradually prospered and also own land, eventually, it is still the Hindu upper castes who maintain monopoly. The lower the position of the caste in the social ladder, the rarer is their possibility of owning land. Minu Bagdi confirms the trend when she says, 'this is a tribal village and our main occupation is agriculture. Most of us are agricultural labourers and there are very few landowners'.[128] Apart from informing me that the SC/STs are primarily engaged as agricultural labourers or as labourers in factories, Ranjit also added that the SC/STs hardly own any land and mainly work as agricultural labourers. In fact, 'the largest numbers of labourers are sourced from these (SC/ST) communities', he says.[129] Md. Riyaz Mondol confirmed this response when he said that 'the main occupation of the SC/ST is to be engaged as agricultural labourers. They rarely own land'.[130]

In terms of illegal livelihood practices, it is, again, the *Namasudra* refugees along the West Bengal-Bangladesh border who are the most vulnerable. The connections, though not spelt out, are nevertheless clear. Since the caste profile of the migrants settled along this border is predominantly *Namasudra* and tribal, responses like 'most of the smugglers originate from the refugees who have settled near the border',[131] indicate an unstated yet clear association between the migrant *Namasudra* refugees and illegal cross-border practices. 'The main reason why the refugees take to illegal practices is to make money as fast as possible. They have left the last bit of their possessions in Bangladesh and, so, are in urgent need of money. While labour-work fetches them about Rs. 150 a day, smuggling fetches them about Rs. 300. So smuggling is a better and faster way of earning for these refugees',[132] says a BSF border guard. These responses are clear indications of the vulnerability of the border people with regard to any sort of tags imposed by the state – the *Namasudra* community constituting the major portion of the former.

Festivities

The border areas witness festivals which are exclusive to the various indigenous castes and tribes, apart from the usual Hindu religious festivities, such as *Durga Puja, Kali Puja*,[133] etc. *Sarai* is one such festival of the indigenous tribal population (*Adivasi*) held during each full-moon, where a clay idol of a certain deity is made for the purpose of the ritual and the tribal population sings and dances in praise of the deity.[134]

Minu Bagdi informs us that the relation between the tribal population and the *Bangalis*('Bengalis' – implying the higher Hindu castes) is cordial. 'The *Bangalis* come to our *parab* (festivity) but not during the actual *puja* (ritual). They come to our homes and eat from our hands' is how the cordiality is defined by Minu, a woman farmer belonging to one of the scheduled castes at Mathurapur village of Hili, the border Land Port between West Bengal and Bangladesh.[135]

Hare Krishna Mondol also explains another such festivity in a village dominated by the *Mahatos, Mondols* and *Sardars*: 'They speak *shadri* dialect, practice

162 *Ethno-cultural concerns*

sarna religion and worship the branch of *Pakor* tree. They consume *Hariya* (a locally-brewed alcohol) in every festivity, slaughter poultry and goat during *Goyal* puja'.[136] These people have their origin in Bihar's Chota Nagpur region from where they were brought to Char Meghna by the British planters as labourers in indigo plantations, says Hare Krishna.[137]

Rupali Mahato talks of *Hari Naam Jogya* – a three-day festival of chanting the praises of the deity, which is a yearly ritual observed by the scheduled castes concentrated in a village in Char Meghna.[138] Or as Binoy Pramanik of Teipur, Nadia district, says, 'The SCs observe the *Manasa* Puja here'.[139]

The *Tusu* festival in Char Meghna is yet another example of such a tribal festival. It is a month-long celebration by women belonging mostly to the *Kudumi* tribe, who gather every evening over a month at a particular place in the village and sing verses dedicated to a girl named *Tusu*. Myth has it that a girl named *Tusu*, belonging to a *Kudumi* tribe in Mayurbhanj (present day Jharkhand district in India and a neighbouring province of West Bengal), was abducted by Muslim invaders sometime in the eighteenth century. The *Kudumis* along with the *Santhals* (another tribe) protested against the incident and placed it before the *Nawab* of Bengal. The *Nawab* punished the abductors and returned *Tusu* to her family and tribe. Though *Tusu*, unable to bear the shame of being abducted, ended her life, the spirit of protest has ever since been celebrated by the tribal people through the *Tusu* festival, where hymns dedicated to *Tusu* and her struggle for dignity are sung for a month.[140] Such customs indicate the spirit of resistance among the indigenous people. Apart from confirming the migration paradigm of the tribes from other parts of India to what is now the border area, the *Tusu* festival is also indicative of a tradition of resistance posed by these indigenous populations against elite domination. Be it the *Namasudra* movement against the Hindu elites, the Marichjhapi narrative or the *Matua* narrative vis-à-vis the dominant political structure in West Bengal, challenging the hierarchy has always been their means of making themselves heard.

In many of these border villages, festivals and rituals of the tribal population are the major festivals, if not the only ones. This has largely to do with the high expenditure of the Hindu festivals like *Durga* or *Kali Puja*, unlike tribal festivities which depend more on physical participation (singing, dancing, chanting hymns). Responses confirming the predominance of tribal festivities and the rarity of Hindu festivals have been recorded in many of the border villages. 'In this village, the number of *Adivasis* is more and it is the *Adivasis* who have most of the big festivities', says Nikhil Bagdi.[141]

The issue of the collection of funds required for organising Hindu festivals like *Durga Puja* is common in many of these villages, indicating the numerical weakness of the Hindu higher castes in these predominantly tribal border villages. The few Hindu families find it difficult to gather the required funds for organising such festivals. 'We do organise *Durga Puja*, but not everyone readily gives funds. So we have to organise it on a small scale', laments Parbati Mohanto.[142] In fact, Rupali Mahato, while narrating the *Hari Naam Jogya* ritual, also adds that it is the only major festival held in that area since the Hindus are unable to organise *Durga Puja* due to lack of funds. 'At best they (Hindus) organise *Lakshmi Puja*[143] on a small scale, without a *pandal*,[144] with the limited funds that they are able to collect sometimes',[145] she says.

In the context of festivities along the West Bengal-Bangladesh border, a religious aspect is also noticeable in the interaction between the border civilians and the border guards, apart from the religious aspect of caste-based interactions between the civilians themselves discussed so far. Almost all the BSF camps on the West Bengal border have small temples/shrines of either *Kali* or *Shiva*.[146] Over the years, this has become a usual occurrence in the BSF camps of the West Bengal border. Religious festivals are often celebrated in these small temples within the BSF camps with much grandeur where, in some cases, the civilians are allowed to participate (in terms of distribution of *Prasad*[147] to locals, participation in the rituals, etc.). At one level, this seems a good platform for bonding initiatives on the part of the border guards. At the same time, the religious allusion is more than overwhelming. As it is, religious symbols, in any form, should be avoided in any official establishment, which includes the defence forces and, thus, the BSF. Moreover, a large portion of the border civilians along the West Bengal-Bangladesh border is Muslim. The threat of persecution that the civilians consistently deal with is further accentuated by the strong presence of the religious overtone amongst the majority of the BSF forces. Muslim religious festivals like *Eid* are celebrated mostly by the locals, and rarely, if ever, by BSF initiatives. The few Muslim officials within the BSF battalions observe their rituals by themselves (for example, observing the *Namaaz*), but rarely are Muslim religious festivals organised by camp officials on a scale like Hindu festivals such as *Kali Puja*.

Religion does not evoke sweet memories for the people of undivided Bengal who saw the worst form of religious fanaticism during the creation of this border. Ever since the Partition, religion has been a sensitive issue with the people of both India as well as Bangladesh. The complex nature of the mixed religious population on either side of the border has made the situation all the more complicated. The overwhelming presence of a religious undertone in the camps of the border guards adds to the complexity. In some border areas, such religious festivals in the camps are the only initiatives taken by the border guards to involve the locals, as Kuddus Rahman points out: 'The BSF does not otherwise talk to us or enquire about our well-being. The only programme that they organise is the *Kali Puja* inside the camp and no other cultural programmes. They enjoy the *Puja* by themselves and do not encourage the entry of local people',[148] which Nikhil phrases as 'their (BSF's) personal *Puja*'.[149] Or as Binoy Pramanik points out more clearly, 'apart from the Independence Day celebration in the areas, the only other programme that the BSF organise is the *Kali Puja* within the camp premises. They ask the Hindu community of the area to participate in the *Puja*'.[150] A complex web of patriotism and religious affiliation is, thus, at play in the relations between the border civilians and the border guards along the West Bengal-Bangladesh border.

Recognition of caste status

Many of the people belonging to scheduled castes and tribes in a number of areas on the border are yet to receive the formal document/certificate from the government

164 *Ethno-cultural concerns*

of India confirming their caste/tribe status. Complaints regarding the negligence of the government towards these people as reasons behind their marginal existences at the border have been common in the responses. The officials responsible for pursuing the official procedures for the certificates to be formally passed and handed over to the people keep delaying the process. Complains Sabitri Mahato:

> Most of us here are ST. We are the indigenous people of this place. But most of us do not have the certificates because one or the other official, who are supposed to sign the papers, is unavailable. If the MLA signs, the BDO (Block Development Officer) delays; if the BDO does it, the *Panchayat Pradhan* does not. This means that we, in Karimpur, are yet to receive our certificates, while the rest of Nadia have got theirs. The certificate would have helped our cause.[151]

Hare Krishna Mondol is more vehement about this issue when he talks of a movement that has been initiated for pursuing the cause of the issue of certificates to the people of Char Meghna, almost all of whom belong to the scheduled tribes: 'The whole population of this village is ST but are yet to receive their certificates. There is an on-going movement regarding this issue. Everyone else in the other parts of the district has got their certificates except for this *Char*'.[152] In spite of having the required proof of their caste/tribe identity (documents issued by the British administrators or even local *zamindars* to their ancestors with regard to their service as labourers), these indigenous people are unable to get an official recognition of their caste/tribe status from the government of India.

Bijoy Mondol assumes that political complexities are the reasons for this situation where co-ordination between the officials responsible for the processing of these certificates is driven by political compulsions. 'We, still, have not been able to get our certificates, in spite of having all the documents. I have visited the Writer's Building (the administrative office in Kolkata from where the West Bengal government functions) many times, but the SDO (Sub-Divisional Officer) is not co-operating. Now that there has been a change in the ruling party, chances have only reduced', says a visibly-anxious Bijoy.[153]

Narendranath Ghosh, the MLA from Karimpur, in an effort to explain the situation, points to the confusion in some of the circumstances where the tribes complain of negligence:

> The complaint that official negligence is responsible for delay in issuing the certificates is not entirely true. There is a confusion regarding their caste and tribe status. Sometimes they may apply for a ST certificate while, in reality, they may be SC. There are debates regarding this issue. Judging their status merely from their surnames is not enough. Though their festivities and rituals indicate their tribal status, but the official process requires more verification.[154]

This delay in providing the certificates to these people is somewhat of a conscious negligence on the part of the government and has largely to do with the

Ethno-cultural concerns   165

issue of illegal infiltration. The issue of illegal migrants crossing the borders from Bangladesh into West Bengal has an impact on the decisions of the officials when it comes to recognition of any kind of identity of the people living along the West Bengal-Bangladesh border. Ways of dealing with this crisis vary circumstantially. Whether it is the violence against the low-castes in Marichjhapi, or the attempt to make use of a politically empowered low-caste organisation (*Matuas*) or whether it is the dilemma and delay in recognising the caste/tribe status of a community, the discomfort of the state regarding the border people has always been manifest in the various interactions between them. If violence and delay in recognition is one part of the trajectory, then issuing fraudulent voter and ration cards to illegal migrants for electoral purposes is another integral part.[155] The tightrope walk between legality and illegality, between being a rightful citizen and an illegal infiltrator, therefore, becomes part of the survival trajectories of the people along the West Bengal-Bangladesh border.

Conclusion

Along the length of the West Bengal-Bangladesh border, the presence of low-castes and tribes among the border civilians is too visible to be denied. Not surprisingly, it is these border civilians who face the vulnerabilities associated with living in the border areas – being labelled as 'infiltrators' is an example. The exercise of the sovereign power of the state at the border is manifested through the border guards, fences and surveillance mechanisms. It is the border civilians who negotiate the reality of the state's presence every day. While this is one aspect of the border narrative, using the border for a better living is another equally undeniable aspect. Various patterns of negotiation between the border civilians and the state have, thus, evolved where the socio-political and ethno-religious identities of the people have been modified and redefined to suit their survival needs. The same people who are at the receiving end of the wielding of the state's power are also the ones who make use of their social and territorial marginality. The narratives of the border people along the West Bengal-Bangladesh border make a very pertinent study with reference to this claim. And more so, because it is on this border(ed) space that the border people trade caste and ethno-religious identities simultaneously.

The history of the *Namasudra* movement in Bengal testifies to an interesting feature of this community – that of demonstrating features of caste and ethno-religious consciousness at the same time. Even when the *Namasudras* were striving to create a caste identity for themselves with regard to empowering themselves in the field of electoral politics (non-participation in the nationalist movements being their chosen form of resistance), they were also seen to participate, with much vigour, in class-based movements like the *Tebhaga* movement, under the Communist-dominated Kisan Sabha leadership and the religion-based movements of the Hindu Mahasabha, in and around 1946–47.[156] The shift from caste-based alliances to class and religious affiliations, or rather the simultaneous negotiation between caste, class and religious identities of the lower caste communities,

166 *Ethno-cultural concerns*

is what is still manifested along the West Bengal-Bangladesh border. The clash between ethno-religious sensibilities and border realities is an obvious outcome.[157]

The interaction between the state and its marginal inhabitants has never been easy. The social, religious, gendered or geographical marginality of a people brings it into conflict with statist agendas of appropriation, either through non-recognition of their citizenship status (SC/STs of border villages and enclave residents are examples) or through a forceful appropriation of their identities. The borders, as a state's territorial delimitation, are spaces where the sovereign power of the state is the most visibly realised and embodied in the border guards, fences and surveillance mechanisms. Therefore, the activities, movements and perceptions of the border people become issues of concern to the state. The identities of the border civilians become decisive in the tactics and policies adopted by the state in securing and sanctifying its borders. Ethno-religious and caste identities are some of the aspects which become integral to the narrative of negotiation between the border civilians and the states concerned. The West Bengal-Bangladesh border is an important study in the understanding of the nature of such negotiations.

The creation of the West Bengal-Bangladesh border has had a direct effect on the profile of the border people along it. As a natural culmination of the partition and refugee movement, the *Namasudras* have become the predominant caste along the border. As outcastes, they not just represent the border space but also redefine and re-appropriate it. The Marichjhapi incident, the *Matua* trajectory and the predominance of *Namasudras* in the livelihood practices and festivities along the border are examples of such representation and re-appropriation.

The ethno-religious aspects of the identities of the border people have, since Partition, been integral to border narratives, albeit in different intensities, forms and contexts. Religion as a basis for Partition had an immediate effect on the partitioned people in terms of their movements across the border to settle in states of their choice. Gradually, the overwhelming reality of surviving the border united the people living along it, across religion or other socio-economic identities. Yet ethno-religious issues and narratives were not completely lost, as is evident from various border narratives. Be it the radicalisation of an event (the involvement of Hindu Bengali radical groups in the Marichjhapi event), be it through empowering a caste-based sect into a political force (the projection of *Matuas* as a religious sect), or be it the nature of festivities along the border (the predominance of tribal festivities over Hindu religious festivals; the presence of Hindu shrines in the camps of the border guards), ethno-religious narratives have existed all along, albeit in a latent form, in the creation of border narratives along the West Bengal-Bangladesh border.

The uniqueness of the West Bengal-Bangladesh border lies in its uniqueness of concentration of *Namasudra* castes along its entire length and on both its sides. On the Bangladesh side, the aspect of lower caste fails to become visible because of the religious factor, in spite of a major portion of the Bangladeshi border civilians sharing a similar caste (mostly *Namasudra*) with their counterparts across the border. On the Bangladesh border, religious identity takes over caste identity. But on the West Bengal side, caste identities are an unpronounced but overwhelming

Ethno-cultural concerns 167

presence in the profile of the people. This also explains the pattern of responses from the interviewees in terms of religious or caste identities on the West Bengal border. In instances where Hindu villages are surrounded by Muslim villages on the West Bengal border, the presence of caste identities within them is overshadowed by the religious aspect of their existence. 'We are surrounded by a Muslim village'[158] is the kind of usual response in such cases. At other times, when two or more predominantly Hindu villages exist side by side, issues of castes appear in the responses (*Das para*, *Mondol para*, *Bagdi para*, etc.).[159] Thus, religious and caste identities decide the creation of the 'Other' for the border people.

Caste and ethno-religious aspects in the negotiation between a state and its people are not unique to the West Bengal border and, in fact, are a widespread occurrence in other parts of India and Bangladesh. Yet the uniqueness of caste and ethno-religious questions along the West Bengal-Bangladesh border are manifested in the effect that this border has on such narratives. It is the reality of the border that moulds and reshapes certain aspects of these narratives to make them spatially unique, by tying them to the specificity of the border milieu. The Marichjhapi event, including the involvement of radical ethno-religious groups, the political empowerment of the *Matuas* using their spatial identity and cross-border ties, and the overwhelming presence of *Namasudra* culture and involvement in the border milieu, are indications of such unique border narratives along the West Bengal-Bangladesh border.

The caste and ethno-religious profile of the people on both sides of this border also make the narrative unique when compared to the other Indian or Bangladeshi borders. A mix of religious communities, similar ethnic composition, language and culture on both sides of the border not just make this border unique but also, in many ways, weaken the purpose of its existence – as a line of separation and containment. The links, movements and exchange patterns across the border are largely based on such caste and ethno-religious links and are, perhaps, what contests the unquestionable sovereign power that the states of India and Bangladesh attempt to wield along it.

Caste and ethno-religious narratives of the West Bengal-Bangladesh border are some of the better examples of the conflict between the conceived and perceived notions of the border people and the state regarding the border space. Creation of the *thirdspace*[160] finds resonance in caste and ethno-religious narratives – as voices of the 'subaltern counter-publics',[161] and offers a logic 'which goes against the convention of rational either/or choices'.[162] The simultaneous presence of caste and ethno-religious aspects in the border narratives are indications of that logic. The 'hot margins' of this *thirdspace*, as exhibited by the dynamics of the caste factor along the border, exhibit a solidarity – whether it is forced by the urgency of the situation (Marichjhapi) or organised as a sectarian force (*Matuas*). The sense of solidarity is as pronounced in the responses of the other border inhabitants across caste, even if they themselves are unaware of this unorganised solidarity. Solidarity over a spatial question and in the practice of subalternity 'becomes the fundamental language of political action against hegemonic languages'.[163] The Marichjhapi event, the *Matuas* or the caste-based livelihood practices and

168 *Ethno-cultural concerns*

festivities along the border are such subaltern practices in being alternative ways of gaining access to resources otherwise denied by the state.

Caste and ethno-religious subaltern narratives, like the ones discussed above, also indicate 'an accommodation with the structure of domination',[164] much like the livelihood practices and enclave narratives along this border.[165] The narratives are not directly intended towards a refusal or denial of the framework of the state but rather towards accommodating their own survival needs within the dominant structures. The striving for recognition as citizens by the Marichjhapi refugees, the engaging in electoral politics of the state by the *Matuas* or the striving to survive within the structures of the state machinery at the borders are indications of such accommodations. What, nevertheless, makes these narratives unique are the ways the civilians re-interpret and redefine the space of the borderland to suit their survival needs. In the process, alternative ideas and techniques of gaining access to resources are reproduced by the border civilians.

Years of production of such subaltern narratives along the border crystallise into a pattern of consciousness among the people living and surviving the border every day – a consciousness that has been termed here as a *border consciousness*. A spatial feature is what constitutes this border consciousness, where the reality of the border is recurrent in all the activities, perceptions and negotiations between the border people themselves, and between the border people and the border guards on both sides of the border, although in varying forms.

The border inhabitant 'is a figure of enormous potential, as her multiplicity allows a new kind of consciousness to emerge'[166] – a consciousness that 'moves beyond the binary relationships and dichotomies that characterise traditional modes of thought'.[167] The Marichjhapi refugees, the *Matuas* and the various other lower castes trading their border(ed)-status – whether as passive victims or as active perpetrators – subvert the predominant statist definitions of such binaries as centre-periphery, us-them or legal-illegal.

Border consciousness as a form of subaltern consciousness is also characterised by a 'common sense',[168] constituted of two, often contradictory, types of consciousness – the one which has been imbibed from the past and the other which is the real 'lived' circumstance.[169] This is what makes subaltern consciousness 'an ambiguous, contradictory and multiform concept'[170] – features which also characterise the border consciousness. The imbibed history of culture (including caste and ethno-religious identities) clashes with the lived realities of nation-building (creation of the border) and drives the people to absorb 'new ideas, new techniques, new ways of living, which constantly modifies and enriches common sense by adapting to new conditions of life and work'.[171] Caste and ethno-religious narratives along the West Bengal-Bangladesh border discussed so far are the manifestations of such adaptations.

The Marichjhapi narratives, *Matua* narratives or the concentration of caste-based villages and livelihoods along this border are also examples of micro-level spatial consciousness in themselves, where the concentration of a specific community over a space and the appropriation of the space by the community can be said to have crystallised into a unique spatial psyche or consciousness – manifested

Ethno-cultural concerns 169

through diverse social, political, economic and religious narratives. Yet the spatial uniqueness of the West Bengal-Bangladesh border has engulfed this micro-level spatial consciousness into its fold and has modified the smaller narratives into the larger framework of border consciousness – a spatial consciousness characterised by the overwhelming presence of the border.

This chapter provides yet another building block towards the construction of the thesis that aims to study the evolution of border consciousness manifested through the various strands of border narratives. The chapter analyses how caste and ethno-religious narratives converge at the border to produce the complex fabric of border consciousness and, thus, contributes towards the understanding of the border psyche along the West Bengal-Bangladesh border.

Notes

1 For a detailed understanding of the refugee exodus across the newly-created border between West and East Bengal (and, later, Bangladesh), see Chatterji, J. (1994) *Bengal Divided: Hindu Communalism and Partition, 1932–1947*. Cambridge: Cambridge University Press; Chatterji, J. (2007) *The Spoils of Partition: Bengal and India-1947–1967*. Cambridge: Cambridge University Press; Fraser, B. (2006) *Bengal Partition Stories: An Unclosed Chapter*. (trs. Sheila Sen Gupta). London: Anthem; Samaddar, R. (1999) *The Marginal Nation: Transborder Migration from Bangladesh to West Bengal*. New Delhi: Sage; Van Schendel, W. (2005) *The Bengal Borderland: Beyond State and Nation in South Asia*. London: Anthem; Roy, H (2012). *Partitioned Lives: Migrants, Refugees, Citizens in India and Pakistan, 1947–1965*. New Delhi: Oxford University Press.

2 Chakrabarti, P.K. (1990) *The Marginal Men: The Refugees and the Left Political Syndrome in West Bengal*. Kalyani, West Bengal: Lumiere Books; Bose, N.K. (1968) *Calcutta: A Social Survey*. Bombay: Lakshmi Publishing House.

3 The Bangladesh Liberation War (1971) resulted in the birth of Bangladesh through the re-naming of erstwhile East Pakistan. The war was followed by a military coup by Zia-ur-Rahman resulting in the death of Mujibur Rahman (1975). This incident gave rise to widespread riots that made the survival of the existing Hindus in Bangladesh, mostly belonging to the agricultural class, all the more difficult.

4 Islam, S.S. (1984) The State in Bangladesh under Zia (1975–81). *Asian Survey*. 24(5). pp. 556–573.

5 Bose, P.K. (Ed.). (2000) *Refugees in West Bengal*. Calcutta: Calcutta Research Group.

6 Bose, 1968.

7 The caste system in India had its roots in the *varna* system of the Hindu scriptures, where people were assigned their castes in accordance with their jobs or professions. Gradually, the caste system became a hereditary structure from a purely profession-based classification. Those people who were involved mostly in menial occupations were considered the most lowly-held in the caste hierarchy. With the passage of time and the increasing orthodoxy of higher castes, the caste system became rigid and the lowest castes began to be considered as 'Untouchables', whom the higher castes were careful not to come in contact with. The Untouchables constituted a number of lowly-held sub-castes, the *Namasudras* being one of them. The *Namasudras* were largely a hard-working agrarian community known for their agricultural and artisan skills. They were one of the biggest communities in Bengal, mostly concentrated in the eastern side of undivided Bengal (later Bangladesh) with a long tradition of fighting caste-Hindu domination and voicing their concern against various ignominies of the caste system. The migrant population from Bangladesh to West Bengal,

170 *Ethno-cultural concerns*

   post-partition, consisted of a large section of the *Namasudra* population. Their migration continued, actively, till the late twentieth century.

8 Interview with Dayamay Dutta, a refugee from Kushtia in Bangladesh residing in Teipur (Nadia district of West Bengal, 24 October 2011).

9 Van Schendel, W. (2005) *The Bengal Borderland: Beyond State and Nation in South Asia*. London: Anthem.

10 In 1972, Congress party formed the provincial government in West Bengal with Siddhartha Sankar Roy as the Chief Minister. Congress also formed the central government in India during this time with Indira Gandhi as the Prime Minister.

11 Bandyopadhyay, S. (1997) *Caste, Protest and Identity in Colonial India: The Namasudras of Bengal, 1872–1947*. Surrey: Curzon Press.

12 The three castes which were considered to belong to the uppermost rungs of the Hindu caste hierarchy were the *Brahmins* (priests), *Kshatriyas* (warriors) and *Vaishyas* (merchants). The *Sudras* (the *Namasudras* being a sub-caste within the larger *Sudra* caste) were considered to be the lowest. Though in the Vedic ages, these caste categorisations depended on the kind of jobs that the people associated themselves with, the hierarchy later became hereditary and, hence, rigid. The *Brahmin-Kshatriya-Vaishya*, thus, became the elite tri-caste in the caste hierarchy.

13 Mallick, R. (February 1999) Refugee Resettlement in Forest Reserves: West Bengal Policy Reversal and the Marichjhapi Massacre. *The Journal of Asian Studies*. 58(1). p. 105.

14 The region known as Dandakaranya comprised parts of Orissa and present-day Chhattisgarh.

15 Khanna, S.N. (29 June 1978) Dandakaranya Refugees Refuse to Budge. *The Overseas Hindustan Times*.

16 Pal, M. (Ed.). (2011). *Nijer Kothaye Marichjhapi*. Kolkata: Gangchil.

17 Chakrabarti, 1990, p. 19.

18 A second wave of refugee influx from Bangladesh to West Bengal in 1975 was brought about by the worsening political situation following the assassination of Sheikh Mujib-ur Rahman, the then Prime Minister of Bangladesh.

19 The refugees were 'Bengali' in their ethnic origin. People of both West Bengal and Bangladesh were of the same ethnic background, that of 'Bengali'. The partition was done only on the basis of religion, with West Bengal becoming a Hindu-majority province and Bangladesh a Muslim-majority state.

20 Mallick, 1999, p. 106.

21 Ram Chatterjee of the Revolutionary Socialist Party (RSP), an ally of the Left Front, went to Dandakaranya and asked the refugees to come and resettle in Marichjhapi with the assistance of the Left Front.

22 Sundarbans is a delta formed by the Hugli River off the Bay of Bengal and houses the world's largest single block of tidal halophytic mangrove forests. It is home to the Royal Bengal Tiger and several other rare marine and land animal species. It consists of hundreds of islands, separated by narrow creeks and canals. The total area of the Sundarbans, including the water, forest, islands and inhabited cultivated lands, is 40,000 square kilometres, of which more than two-thirds is in Bangladesh (since the creation of the West Bengal-Bangladesh border). The rest belongs to West Bengal, of which the land area is about 9,630 square kilometres. Marichjhapi is one of the islands in the Sundarbans on the West Bengal side of the border.

23 The United Central Refugee Council (UCRC) was the council formed within the Left Front specifically for handling refugee resettlement and rehabilitation programmes.

24 Udbastu Unnayanshil Samity (UUS) was the association formed by the refugees led by leaders chosen from amongst themselves.

25 Chatterjee, N. (1992) *Midnight's Unwanted Children: East Bengali Refugees and the Politics of Rehabilitation*. Ph.D. dissertation (Unpublished). Brown University, cited in Mallick, 1999, p. 107.

26 Ibid.
27 Bandyopadhyay, 1997,p. 28.
28 Mehta, P., Pandey, L.N. and Visharat, M. (1979) 'Report on Marichjhapi Affairs'. April 18, mimeographed. Mehta, Pandey and Visharat were Members of Parliament appointed by Prime Minister Morarji Desai, despite the objections of the West Bengal government, to visit and investigate Marichjhapi prior to the eviction. As quoted in Mallick, 1999, p. 107.
29 Mallick, 1999, p. 108.
30 Ibid. p. 109.
31 Source: Interview with Indian Administrative (IAS) Secretary of the West Bengal Government, in Mallick, 1999, p. 110.
32 Ibid. p. 114.
33 Ibid.
34 Ibid.
35 The exact number of deaths could never be counted due to the nature of the massacre. Different accounts put it anywhere between 50 and over 1,000, though the official toll was two. Bhattacharya, S. (25 April 2011) Ghost of Marichjhapi Returns to Haunt. *Hindustan Times*. [Online] Available from: www.hindustantimes.com/specials/Cover age/Assembly-Elections-2011/Ghost-of-Marichjhapi-returns-to-haunt/Assembly Elections2011-DontMiss/SP-Article10–689463.aspx. [Last accessed: 7 August 2013].
36 Chatterjee, 1992, p. 312.
37 Communist Party of India (Marxist). (1982) *Rajnaitik-Sangathanik Report* (Political-Organisational Report) adopted at West Bengal State Conference 14th Plenary Session. Calcutta: West Bengal State Committee, from Mallick, 1999, p. 111.
38 Sections 20–27 of Chapter II (Reserve Forest), The Indian Forest Act, 1927, Ministry of Law, Government of India.
39 Chatterjee, 1992, pp. 298–299.
40 Mallick, 1999, p. 110.
41 Ibid.
42 Refugee Relief and Rehabilitation Department, West Bengal Government. (1979). 'Problems of Refugees from Dandakaranya to West Bengal.' Letter from Deputy Secretary to Zonal Director, Ministry of Home Affairs, Government of India. No. 3223-Rehab/DNK-6/79, from Mallick, 1999, p. 107.
43 Sikdar, R.K. (1982) Marichjhapi Massacre. *The Oppressed Indian*. 4(4). pp. 21–23.
44 Mallick, 1999, p. 108.
45 Biswas, A. (1982). Why Dandakaranya a Failure, Why Mass Exodus, Where Solution? *The Oppressed Indian*. 4(4). pp. 18–20.
46 Mallick, 1999, p. 115; Map of Sundarbans showing Marichjhapi: https://commons. wikimedia.org/wiki/File:Sunderbans_map.png.
47 Fernandes, W., Das, J.C. and Rao, S. (1989) Displacement and Rehabilitation: An estimate of Extent and Prospects. In Fernandes, W. and Ganguly Thukral, E. (Eds.). *Development, Displacement and Rehabilitation*. Delhi: Indian Social Institute. p. 78.
48 Chatterjee, P. and Finger, M. (1994) *The Earth Brokers*. London: Routledge. p. 70.
49 Ibid. pp. 340–341.
50 Mallick, 1999, p. 118.
51 Montgomery, Sy. (1995). *Spell of the Tiger*. Boston: Houghton Mifflin. pp. 27–28.
52 Pathak, A. (2002) *Law, Strategies, Ideologies: Legislating Forests in Colonial India*. New Delhi: Oxford University Press. p. 115.
53 Kohli, A. (1996) Can the Periphery Control the Centre? Indian Politics at the Crossroads. *The Washington Quarterly*. 19(4). p. 121.
54 Bhattacharya, 25 April 2011.
55 Simon Commission. (1929) *Indian Statutory Commission: Selections from Memoranda and Oral Evidence by Non-Officials (Part II)*. Reprinted 1988. Delhi: Swati Publications.

172 *Ethno-cultural concerns*

56 Clad, J.C. (1994) Slowing the Wave. *Foreign Affairs*. 95. pp. 139–150.
57 Ray, A. (24 May 2010) *Mystery of Marichjhapi*. [Online] Available from: http://marichjhapi-mystery.blogspot.co.uk/. [Last accessed: 5 August 2013].
58 Ray, A. (17 May 2010) Bullets and Hunger. *The Times of India*.
59 Ibid.
60 Ibid.
61 Chatterji, J. (February 1999) The Fashioning of a Frontier: The Radcliffe Line and Bengal's Border Landscape, 1947–52. *Modern Asian Studies*. 33(1). p. 197; in the 1970s, involvement of Bengali historians, academics, barristers, spiritual leaders was proof of the favour that Nikhil Banga Nagarik Sangha found among a group of influential Bengalis, who identified with the group's ideological and political vision.
62 Bandyopadhyay, 1997, p. 36.
63 The *Bhakti* movement is a Hindu religious movement in which the main spiritual practice is loving devotion among the *Shaivite* and *Vaishnava* saints. The *Bhakti* movement, having originated in the southern part of India in the fourteenth century, swept through central and northern India till about the seventeenth century. Over the years, it gradually became associated with a group of teachers or *sants,* who taught that caste, religion or ritual should not come in the way of unadulterated love for god. Though *Shaivites* (worshippers of lord *Shiva*) practiced *Bhaktism* as well, it was the *Vaishnava* (worshippers of lord *Vishnu*) stream of *Bhaktism* that gained an immense following across India.
64 Bandyopadhyay, 1997, p. 31.
65 Scott, J.C. (1989) Everyday Forms of Resistance. In Colburn, F.D. (Ed.). *Everyday Forms of Peasant Resistance*. New York: M.E. Sharpe. p. 26.
66 Bandyopadhyay, 1997, p. 33.
67 Ibid. p. 37.
68 Ibid. p. 42.
69 Ibid. p. 37.
70 Haldar, M. *Sri Sri Guruchand Charit* (1943), as quoted in Bandyopadhyay, 1997, p. 50.
71 Hindu Samhati. (12 April 2008) *Hindu Samhati's Exhibition: Thakurnagar, West Bengal*. [Online] Available from: http://hindusamhati.blogspot.co.uk/2008/04/hindu-samhati-exhbition-thakurnagar.html. [Accessed: 6 August 2013].
72 This is why the *Namasudra* refugees were forced to settle in Dandakaranya outside West Bengal.
73 Van Schendel, 2005, p. 212
74 Mazumdar, J. (20 March 2010) Matua Millions for Mamata. *Open Magazine*. [Online] Available from: www.openthemagazine.com/article/nation/matua-millions-for-mamata. [Last accessed: 6 August 2013].
75 Ibid.
76 Jacob, S. (28 April 2011) Political Parties Woo Matua Community. *Business Standard*. [Online] Available from: www.business-standard.com/article/economy-policy/political-parties-woo-matua-community-111042800083_1.html. [Last accessed: 6 August 2013]; Dasgupta, P. (13 November 2010) Caste Not a Poll Factor in Bengal: But Matuas Could Swing It for Didi. *Tehelka*. [Online] Available from: http://archive.tehelka.com/story_main47.asp?filename=Ne131110Caste_not.asp. [Last accessed: 6 August 2013].
77 Beteille, A. (1992). *Society and Politics in India: Essays in a Comparative Perspective*. Delhi: Oxford University Press.
78 Ibid.
79 Srinivas, M.N. (1991) Varna and Caste. In Gupta, D. (Ed.). *Social Stratification*. Delhi, Oxford: Oxford University Press. p. 33.
80 Bandyopadhyay, 1997, p. 45.
81 Ibid.

Ethno-cultural concerns   173

82 Dasgupta, 13 November 2010, *Tehelka*.
83 Freitag, S B. (1989) *Collective Action and Community: Public Arenas and the Emergence of Communalism in North India*. Berkeley, Oxford: University of California Press.
84 Bandyopadhyay, 1997, p. 6.
85 Maitra, S. (26 March 2017). Elakar ghore ghoreo dhalao khawadawa. *Ananda Bazar Patrika*. [Online] Available from: www.anandabazar.com/district/dhaksinbanga/ north-south-24-paraganas/motua-people-celebrated-their-festival-1.586439?ref=north-south-24-paraganas-ft-stry. [Last accessed: 17 July 2017]; Maitra, S. (27 March 2017). Punyo-snaner abege bhashlen Matua bhoktora. *Ananda Bazar Patrika*. [Online] Available from: www.anandabazar.com/district/dhaksinbanga/north-south-24-paraganas/ matua-mela-at-thakurnagar-1.587043?ref=north-south-24-paraganas-new-stry. [Last accessed: 17 July 2017].
86 Hindu Samhati, 12 April 2008.
87 Ibid.
88 Maitra, S. (28 March 2017). Kenabechaye khushi dokani. *Ananda Bazar Patrika*. [Online] Available from: www.anandabazar.com/district/dhaksinbanga/north-south-24-paraganas/motua-people-is-celebrating-their-festival-1.587564?ref=north-south-24-paraganas-new-stry. [Last accessed: 17 July 2017].
89 Staff Reporter (24 March 2017). Matua mela-e nirapottar kotha bhebe atok hochhe be-ayini mod. *Ananda Bazar Patrika*. [Online] Available from: www.anandabazar.com/ district/dhaksinbanga/north-south-24-paraganas/hooch-been-detained-for-the-security-in-motua-fair-1.585353?ref=north-south-24-paraganas-new-stry. [Last accessed: 17 July 2017].
90 Dasgupta, 13 November 2010, *Tehelka*.
91 Basu, S.P. (5 November 2009) Matua O Mamata: Sangha ebawng dawler tanaporen. *Ananda Bazar Patrika*. [Online] Available from: www.anandabazar.com/archive/ 1091105/5edit3.htm. [Last accessed: 6 August 2013].
92 Maitra, S. (15 March 2010) Mamata Matuader Chief Patron. *Ananda Bazar Patrika*. [Online] Available from: www.anandabazar.com/15pgn1.htm. [Last accessed: 6 August 2013].
93 Dasgupta, 13 November 2010, *Tehelka*.
94 West Bengal State Election Commission. Available from: www.wbsec.gov.in/.
95 Maitra, S. (8 September 2017) Matua der tanar cheshta BJP'r. *Ananda Bazar Patrika*. [Online] Available from: www.anandabazar.com/district/dhaksinbanga/north-south-24-paraganas/bjp-is-trying-to-atract-the-matua-community-1.671202?ref=north-south-24-paraganas-new-stry. [Last accessed: 8 September 2017].
96 Bhattacharya, 25 April 2011, *Hindustan Times*; Bhadra, K. (1 February 2013) Wound still raw for Marichjhapi survivors. *The Times of India*. [Online] Available from: http://articles.timesofindia.indiatimes.com/2013-02-01/kolkata/36683701_1_survi vors-boat-narayan. [Last accessed: 7 August 2013].
97 Paul, S. (14 January 2011) Illegal immigration: East Bengal in West Bengal. *India Today.in*. [Online] Available from: http://indiatoday.intoday.in/story/east+bengal+in+ west+bengal/1/126587.html. [Last accessed: 6 August 2013].
98 Interview with Riazul Mondol, resident and teacher in a primary school at Balurghat (South Dinajpur district of West Bengal, 24 January 2012).
99 Discussed in Chapter 1.
100 Interview with a BSF official at Shikarpur BSF camp (Nadia district of West Bengal, 21 October 2011).
101 Bandyopadhyay, S. (27 March—2 April 2011) Who Are the Matuas? *Frontier: The Citizenship Issue*. 43(37).
102 Dasgupta, 13 November 2010, *Tehelka*.
103 Bose, R. (31 March 2011) Why the Matuas Matter. *The Hindu*. [Online] Available from: www.thehindu.com/news/national/why-the-matuas-matter/article1585641.ece. [Last accessed: 6 August 2013].

174 *Ethno-cultural concerns*

104 Bandyopadhyay, 1997, p. 48.
105 Ibid. p. 49.
106 Ibid. p. 51.
107 Ibid. p. 8.
108 Ibid.
109 Ibid. p. 9.
110 Ibid.
111 Swadeshi Movement (1905–1911) was part of the Indian Independence movement and was an economic strategy against the British based on the principle of *swadeshi* or self-sufficiency. It involved boycotting British products, on the one hand, and developing domestic products and production processes, on the other. It was started following the announcement by Lord Curzon to partition Bengal in 1905. The decision of partition was annulled in 1911 following the movement.
112 Bhimrao Ramji Ambedkar (1891–1956) was an Indian jurist, politician, historian and economist. As independent India's first law minister, he was the principal architect of the Constitution of India. A Dalit himself, he campaigned against social discrimination and inspired the Dalit (Untouchables) movement in India.
113 The Akhil Bharatiya Hindu Mahasabha (All India Hindu Assembly) was a right-wing Hindu nationalist political party in India, founded in 1914 in Amritsar, following the All India Hindu Conference in 1910 in Allahabad. Pandit Madan Mohan Malaviya and Lala Lajpat Rai were among its most prominent leaders. The Mahasabha had tried hard to woo the Scheduled castes, including the *Namasudras*, into its fold. The concentration of the *Namasudras* in the Jessore and Faridpur districts of Bengal was, in fact, the prime reason for the Mahasabha's demand for inclusion of these two districts into West Bengal during partition.
114 The Akhil Bharatiya Kisan Sabha (All India Farmers' Assembly) was the peasants' front of the undivided Communist Party of India (CPI), formed in 1929 to mobilise peasant grievances against the atrocities of *zamindars*, resulting in the peasants' movement in India. The Bengal Provincial Kisan Sabha was the provincial branch of the All India Sabha and was led by the Communist Party.
115 Bandyopadhyay, 1997, pp. 9–10.
116 The surnames indicate the caste status of Hindus since the caste structure has its origin in profession-related hierarchies, as mentioned earlier.
117 Discussed in Chapter 1.
118 Interview with Nirendranath Burman, resident and Deputy *Panchayat*-head at Kalmati village, Dinhata (Cooch Behar district of West Bengal, 16 March 2012).
119 Interview with Kuddus Rahman, resident and chairman of local committee of a political party at Jaykrishnapur village, Jalangi (Murshidabad district of West Bengal, 22 October 2011).
120 The *Mahishya* caste is said to have its origin from the union of a Kshatriya father and a *Vaishya* mother. Initially, they were considered similar to the *Kaibartta* caste and were catagorised as *Jele Kaibartta* (fishermen) and *Hele Kaibartta* (farmer). Gradually, the movement for a separate caste status amongst the *Mahishyas* gained momentum till they were given a separate caste status in the 1921 Census of India. The fact that the *Mahishyas* were the largest Hindu caste in Bengal favoured their cause.
121 'এটা মহেশ্যা-প্রধান গ্রাম. কিছু ব্রাহ্মন আছে. ২-১ ঘর এস সি/এস টি হবে।' Interview with Jasimuddin Mondol, resident and farmer at Mathurapur village (Nadia district of West Bengal, 22 October 2011).
122 Interview with Imtiaz Mondol, resident and farmer at Mathurapur village (Nadia district of West Bengal, 22 October 2011).
123 Interview with Dayamay Dutta, resident and teacher at Teipur (Nadia district of West Bengal, 24 October 2011).
124 Interview with Imran, resident at Goga village, Sharsha (Jessore district of Bangladesh, 15 February 2012).

Ethno-cultural concerns 175

125 'ঠাকুরদার মুখে শুনেছি আমাদের বাড়ি নাকি আসলে ছিল বিহার এর নাগপুর. ওখান থেকে ব্রিটিশ রা আমাদের নীল চাষ করতে এখানে এনেছিল. তখন ২/৪ ঘর এসেছিল. তার থেকে এতটা হয়েছে।' (I have heard from my grandfather that we are originally from Nagpur region of Bihar. The British had brought us here as labourers in indigo plantations. Initially, it was just 2/3 families, which later increased to a whole village.) Interview with Prasanta Mondol, resident and farmer at Char Meghna (Nadia district of West Bengal, 21 October 2011).

126 Interview with Hare Krishna Mondol, resident and member of *Panchayat* at Char Meghna (Nadia district of West Bengal, 21 October 2011).

127 'আদিবাসী সম্প্রদায় আছে, কম. তাদের সাথে বাকিদের সম্পর্ক ভালো. ভাটায়ে কাজ করে, ভ্যান চালায়ে, ব্যবসা করে. দাসেদের পারা আছে, তারা মূলত মুটের কাজ করে. আর বালি কাটার কাজ করে।' Interview with Md. Tafikul Islam, resident and farmer at Panitor village, Basirhat (North 24 Parganas district of West Bengal, 17 January 2012).

128 Interview with Minu Bagdi, resident and farmer at Mathurapur village (South Dinajpur district of West Bengal, 24 January 2012).

129 'এস সি/এস টি বেশি. লেবার, কৃষি করে. নিজেদের জমি কম তাদের. মূলত লেবার খাটে. লেবার এর বেশিরভাগ ওই কমিউনিটি থেকেই আসে।' Interview with Ranjit, resident and head of *Panchayat* at Jamalpur village (South Dinajpur district of West Bengal, 24 January 2012).

130 'এস সি/এস টি আছে অল্প. এদের পেশা কৃষি, লেবার. লেবার বেশি, জমির মালিক কম।' (The main occupation of the SC/ST communities is cultivation, labourer. In fact the largest numbers of labourers are sourced from these (SC/ST) communities.) Interview with Md. Riyaz Mondol, resident and farmer at Dahapara village (South Dinajpur district of West Bengal, 25 January 2012).

131 Interview with a BSF official at Shikarpur BSF camp (Nadia district of West Bengal, 21 October 2011).

132 Ibid.

133 *Kali Puja* is one of the more prominent religious festivals of the Hindus of India, and especially the Bengali Hindus of Bengal (West Bengal and Bangladesh), celebrated in praise of the deity *Kali*.

134 Interview with Nikhil Bagdi, resident and agricultural labourer at Mathurapur village (South Dinajpur district of West Bengal, 24 January 2012).

135 'বাঙালি দের সাথে এমনিতে কোনো অসুবিধা হয় না. আমাদের পরবে বাঙালি-রা আসে খেতে, পূজোর সময় আসে না. আমাদের বাড়িতে আসে, হাতে খায়।' Interview with Minu Bagdi, resident and agricultural labourer at Mathurapur village (South Dinajpur district of West Bengal, 24 January 2012).

136 Interview with Hare Krishna Mondol, resident and member of *Panchayat* at Char Meghna (Nadia district of West Bengal, 21 October 2011).

137 Ibid.

138 Interview with Rupali Mahato, resident of Char Meghna (Nadia district of West Bengal, 21 October 2011).

139 Interview with Binoy Pramanik, resident and farmer at Teipur (Nadia district of West Bengal, 24 October 2011).

140 Mohanta, B.K. (2011) Tusu Festival of the Kudumis of Northern Orissa: Origin and Causes. *Journal of Sociology and Social Anthropology*. 2(1). pp. 23–29.

141 Interview with Nikhil Bagdi, resident and agricultural labourer at Mathurapur village (South Dinajpur district of West Bengal, 24 January 2012).

142 Interview with Parbati Mohanto, resident of Ghunapara-Dhumron village (South Dinajpur district of West Bengal, 25 January 2012).

143 *Lakshmi Puja* is another prominent religious festival of the Hindus in India celebrated in praise of the deity *Lakshmi*, goddess of wealth.

144 *Pandal* is the temporary wooden shelter generally built for housing idols in big Hindu religious festivals.

145 Interview with Rupali Mahato, resident of Char Meghna (Nadia district of West Bengal, 21 October 2011).

146 Both *Kali* and *Shiva* are very prominent Hindu deities.

147 *Prasad* is the offerings distributed among the devotees after the ritual is over.

176 Ethno-cultural concerns

148 'বি এস এফ আমাদের সাথে এমনিতে কথা বলে না, খোঁজ নেয়না, কোনো অনুষ্ঠান করে না, আর ক্যাম্প এর ভেতর কালী পূজা হয়, নিজেরাই আনন্দ করে, সিভিল লোক ভেতরে যায় না।' Interview with Kuddus Rahman, resident and chairman of local committee of a political party at Jaykrishnapur village, Jalangi (Murshidabad district of West Bengal, 22 October 2011).

149 'ক্যাম্প এ কালী পূজা হয়, ওদের পার্সোনাল পূজো।' (Kali puja is held inside the camp. It is their personal puja.) Interview with Nikhil Bagdi, resident and agricultural labourer at Mathurapur village (South Dinajpur district of West Bengal, 24 January 2012).

150 'স্বাধীনতা দিবস এর দিন অনুষ্ঠান করে, আর ওদের ক্যাম্প এর কালী পুজো তে গ্রামের হিন্দু সম্প্রদায় কে বলে তোমরা এস, ঠাকুরের জন্য গান বাজনা কর।' Interview with Binoy Pramanik, resident and farmer at Teipur (Nadia district of West Bengal, 24 October 2011).

151 'এখানে মূলত এস টি, আমরা এখানকার আদি বাসিন্দা, সবার সার্টিফিকেট নেই, কারণ কারোর না কারোর সই পাওয়া যাচ্ছে না, এম এল এ দিচ্ছে তো বি ডি ও দিচ্ছে না, সে দিচ্ছে তো প্রধান দিচ্ছে না, নদীয়া তে তাই সার্টিফিকেট দেওয়া বন্ধ আছে, করিমপুর এর এদিকে, বাকি নদিয়া হয়ে গেছে, সার্টিফিকেট টা পেলে আরেকটু সুবিধা হত।' Interview with Sabitri Mahato, resident and ICDS (Integrated Child Development Services) volunteer at Char Meghna (Nadia district of West Bengal, 21 October 2011).

152 Interview with Hare Krishna Mondol, resident and member of Panchayat at Char Meghna (Nadia district of West Bengal, 21 October 2011).

153 Interview with Bijoy Mondol, resident and member of Panchayat at Shikarpur (Nadia district of West Bengal, 21 October 2011).

154 Interview with Narendranath Ghosh, resident and MLA from Karimpur Constituency (Nadia district of West Bengal, 24 October 2011).

155 Paul, S. (14 January 2011) Illegal immigration: East Bengal in West Bengal. India Today.in. [Online] Available from: http://indiatoday.intoday.in/story/east+bengal+in+west+bengal/1/126587.html. [Last accessed: 6 August 2013].

156 Bandyopadhyay, 1997, p. 243.

157 Clashes between Muslim border civilians and BSF over issues of accessing burial grounds outside the fence are a usual occurrence along the West Bengal-Bangladesh border – a result of border mechanisms disrupting age-old customs. Staff Reporter (10 October 2009) Gorosthaney jetey badha, uttejona. Ananda Bazar Patrika. [Online] Available from: www.anandabazar.com/archive/1091010/10uttar2.htm. [Last accessed: 17 September 2013].

158 Interview with Saraswati Das, resident of Nazirhat village, Dinhata (Cooch Behar district of West Bengal, 15 March 2012).

159 Interview with Nirendranath Burman, resident and Deputy-head of Panchayat of Kalmati village (Cooch Behar district of West Bengal, 16 March 2012).

160 Soja, E. (1996) Thirdspace. Cambridge, MA: Blackwell.

161 Fraser, N. (1990) Rethinking the Public Sphere: A Contribution to the Critique of Actually Existing Democracy. Social Text. 25/26. p. 67.

162 Young, R.J.M. (1995) Colonial Desire: Hybridity in Theory, Culture, and Race. New York: Routledge. p. 26.

163 Lionnet, F. (1989) The Politics and Aesthetics of Metissage. In Autobiographical Voices: Race, Gender, Self-Portraiture. Ithaca, London: Cornell University Press. p. 6.

164 Scott, 1989, p. 21.

165 Discussed in Chapters 1 and 2.

166 Feghali, Z. (2011) Re-articulating the New Mestiza. Journal of International Women's Studies Special Issue. 12(2). p. 61.

167 Ibid.

168 Discussed in Chapter 1.

169 Gramsci, A. (1971) Selections from the Prison Notebooks (trs. Quintin Hoare and Geoffrey Nowell Smith). London: Lawrence and Wishart. pp. 325–343.

170 Ibid. p. 243.

171 Guha, R. (Ed.). (1989) Subaltern Studies VI: Writings on South Asian history and society. Delhi: Oxford University Press. p. 173.

5 Gendered practices
Perpetrators, victims, accomplices

Introduction

This chapter will highlight certain gendered practices and forms of interaction between the civilian border people themselves and between them and the border guards across the West Bengal-Bangladesh border. The interaction between the male, female and other gendered categories of civilians, and the largely male border guards, throws light on certain gendered aspects, which are both physical and socio-cultural in nature. These gendered narratives attain a unique nature in the backdrop of their spatial specificity of being border narratives. Some of these practices have been discussed in previous chapters in other contexts, as gendered aspects of livelihood, territorial imperatives or ethno-religious narratives. This shows that most forms of social and political interactions between the state and its subjects are gendered – implicitly or explicitly. Having a separate chapter on these gendered practices might, in that case, seem to be superfluous – given that many of these narratives have been discussed in previous chapters. But the very fact that gender concerns are intertwined in the previous narratives and are integral to the everyday practices across the border demands our attention.

Borderlands between two states are the space where the presence of the latter's sovereign power is most strongly felt. Border fences, border guards and various surveillance mechanisms deployed by the respective states are the visible manifestations of this power machinery.[1] Negotiating the physical presence of the state is integral to the everyday lives of the border dwellers. Interaction with the border guards constitutes part of that negotiation, as has been discussed at length in the previous chapters. A nuanced understanding of these interactions reveals a narrative which is not just a sovereign-subject discourse, but is heavily gendered in its disposition. The nature and form of interaction largely depends on the gender positions of the people involved, i.e. the largely male border guards, on the one hand, and the civilians – male, female, transgender – on the other. The spatial specificity of the borderland adds to the discourse and provides a framework for understanding gendered practices within the larger discourse of power structures best revealed across the border lines of states.

The studies on gendered practices along this border, so far, have primarily focussed on either sexual abuse of female civilians by male border guards and/or

178 *Gendered practices*

physical abuse of male civilians by male border guards in the context of human rights concerns.[2] While these studies do, in fact, bring out the more blatant features of gender relations on this border, they overlook the finer nuances of such relations. The condition of women at this border is no different from most other backward areas in India, especially some of the more isolated rural areas.[3] What makes their lives doubly jeopardised is their bordered existence.

Education

The literacy rates of the districts of West Bengal suggest that some of the lowest, as per the Census of India 2011, have been recorded in the border districts,[4] though the overall literacy rates among Indian women has seen a rise in the last decade.[5] The 2001 census reveals that the literacy rate among rural women in West Bengal, 53.16%, is much below that of rural men (73.13%), urban women (75.74%) and urban men (86.13%).[6] The border areas of West Bengal constitute a substantial part of these rural areas, apart from the non-border rural ones, and, thus, contribute towards the general backwardness in literacy rates, especially those of women.[7]

Various border regulations laid down by the government of India, including restrictions on movement near the fence, use of the border road by the civilians especially in times of emergency, use of the fence gates and restrictions on the gathering of more than five persons at a time near the fence after 5PM, coupled with a sense of insecurity brought about by the sensitised ambience of the border, has had a direct effect on the literacy rate of people living along the border. Women are doubly affected – for being border inhabitants and for being women.[8]

Anxiety over the safety of girls associated with travelling along the border areas on their way to educational institutions is an obstacle to education. The lack of higher educational institutions near the border implies that those wanting to pursue higher education have to travel to the nearest towns or cities (the average distance being anything between 12 to 13 kilometres[9] and 24 to 25 kilometres[10]) for this purpose. The decreasing rate of education in the higher schools and colleges in the border areas, compared to that of primary education,[11] explains how travelling distances in the border areas pose a threat to the people. For the women living in the border areas, the anxiety is doubled, given the chances of physical/ sexual abuse by other male civilians and/or border guards.[12] This explains why most of the girls in these areas are married off right after school and instances of girls pursuing higher education are negligible.[13]

The condition of male education in the border areas seems comparatively better, given the higher number of male border residents travelling to higher education institutions at distant places.[14] But the persistent fear of persecution looms large among the male border civilians in response to my questions regarding travelling to distant places for education. Moreover, the lack of employment opportunities, on the one hand, and the lure of fast income through cross-border illegal practices, on the other, act as disincentives to education for many of the boys in the border areas.[15]

Gendered practices   179

The recurrent concern among both the male and female respondents regarding restrictions on movement in the border areas clearly indicates the negative impact of the border on their education and the literacy scenario at large.

Marriage

The usual age of marriage for girls in the border villages is between 13 or 14[16] (which is below the legal age[17]) and 18 or 19.[18] Anxiety over abuse by border guards is one of the main reasons why girls are married off, preferably to non-border areas, at this young age.[19]

Moreover, girls are not allowed to travel to far-off places by themselves to earn a living, except when they are victims of trafficking. Parents prefer them marrying off to places, preferably away from the border areas, rather than keeping a non-earning family member at home. The demand for dowry[20] by the groom's family from the bride's parents increases automatically if the groom is a resident of a non-border city. Thus, it is often not possible for parents/guardians of girls living in the border areas to marry them away from the border into cities or towns because of the amount of dowry demanded. Family members often resort to spending their entire savings to marry off daughters to cities and towns away from the border areas.[21]

The concern over marriage is no less for the male civilians living along the border, for they often find it difficult to obtain brides from non-border areas to marry into border areas.[22] Affluence and assurance of observation of all marriage rights do not necessarily help them obtain brides due to their marginal location.[23] Incidents of prospective brides rejecting marriage proposals on realising the difficulties of border lives are not rare,[24] nor are incidents of guests attending marriages in border areas being harassed by border guards.[25]

The West Bengal-Bangladesh border used to be a porous one where civilians on either side could move uninhibitedly before the border fences were constructed (from 1986 onwards).[26] In fact, marriages across the borders, though illegal because of citizenship differences and visa requirements, were common occurrences before the fencing.[27] Sometimes even the border guards would know of these events but would hardly ever interfere, as long as they did not pose security risks. These marriages would have been merely inter-village events before the border was created in 1947.

Such age-old practices die hard, even if international borders emerge abruptly for political reasons. Generations take time to realise the unfeasibility of the age-old practice of inter-village marriage in the context of the sensitivity of the border zone. Likewise, the reality of the border between West Bengal and Bangladesh, made visible by the fences, gradually seeped into the lives of the border residents. Eventually, inter-village marriages reduced in number, given the risk associated with cross-border movements across the fences, till they *almost* ceased to exist.[28]

Experiences of organising the marriage ceremonies of the civilians of the Indian *Ghoj* shed light on the complications which the fencing has created. The

180   *Gendered practices*

residents of Daulatpur *Ghoj*[29] narrate their experiences of organising marriage ceremonies. Most of the girls from this Indian pocket are married to Bangladeshi villages around it. The official complications associated with marrying these Indian girls into Indian villages across the fence lead them to establish matrimonial ties with their Bangladeshi neighbours to whom they have easier access and pre-existing acquaintances.[30] If a marriage has to be organised across the fence, the BSF officials must be informed beforehand, who in turn inform senior officials. Information is gathered about the groom's and bride's family. Only if they are satisfied do they allow one family to travel across the fence into the *Ghoj*.[31] Indians from the *Ghoj*, married into neighbouring Bangladeshi villages, have to face the hassles of obtaining Bangladeshi citizenship – which is often illegally procured, to bypass the complicated legal procedure of cross-border marriages.[32]

The very definition of a cross-border marriage has changed after the construction of the fence. While the difficulties of border life keep away prospective brides from marrying into border areas, instances of wanting to marry a border resident for the prospect of affluence brought about by cross-border smuggling are also there. Bijon, a journalist in Jessore (Bangladesh), talks about how marriages with border residents, nowadays, are almost always driven by concerns over cross-border practices.[33]

Affluence brought about by such practices is manifest in the large decorative houses near the border areas – owners of which are the locally-known faces involved in cross-border smuggling.[34] It is these men who are prospective grooms for many families. This is especially true of the Land Port of the Petrapole-Benapole border between the Jessore district in Bangladesh and the North 24 Parganas of West Bengal – a border that thrives as much on smuggling networks as it does on legal trading. 'The fact that the groom is a resident of Benapole itself increases his prospect in the marriage market', says Bijon with a wry smile.[35]

The issue of dowry is closely related to the reality of the border. The custom of giving dowry to the groom's family by the bride's is often reversed in case of grooms belonging to border areas. It is often the groom who has to give a certain amount of dowry as a settlement to bring a bride into his family. This, as the responses of the male interviewees suggest, is often a cause for embarrassment for the groom and his family. While affordability of large sums of dowry is the concern for brides living in border areas (paying extra sums to be married into non-border families), that of the grooms has to do more with reversal of customs resulting in embarrassment.[36] The fact that the groom 'fails to' find himself a bride 'even after earning a handsome living' is a matter of serious concern for the men.[37] 'The very word "border" evokes a Bangladesh-like feeling and indicates a distanced existence from the Indian mainland', is how Bilal, a prospective groom, phrases it.[38] Some of the male respondents choose to stay with their in-laws (a custom observed by the brides after their marriage in most parts of India) in non-border areas even at the risk of it being labelled 'unmanly' behaviour, since their wives cannot be made to stay in the border villages.[39] Finding better livelihood opportunities is also cited as a reason for this step.[40]

Migration and trafficking

The partition of Bengal in 1947 was marked by a refugee exodus across the West Bengal-Bangladesh border. Thousands of refugees, both men and women, migrated from one side to the other of the newly-formed West Bengal-East Pakistan (later Bangladesh) border. The gender-specific harassment of refugees by border guards has, since, been integral to the evolution of the West Bengal-Bangladesh border.[41] What started with the Partition and the consequent creation of this border continues unabated and, in fact, in new forms, all along its length even after six decades of the Partition.

The reasons for migration have changed over the years. While political turmoil leading to life-threatening situations was the main factor for migration till the mid-1970s, economic prospects became the decisive factor in the 80s and 90s owing to neoliberal reforms and expansion of job markets, especially in India.[42] Communal tensions have resurfaced as an important factor in recent times as a result of fundamentalist forces and misguided nationalistic ideologies in both India and Bangladesh. Reasons driving migrants to move across the border keep evolving. What does not change, though, is the treatment meted out to women migrants.[43] While firing and/or imprisonment is the usual way of controlling male border crossers,[44] sexual abuse makes for an important method of control besides physical violence, when it comes to female crossers.[45]

The physical abuse of male border crossers has lately been seen to attain a gendered nature as well. A number of incidents of forced nudity followed by abusive attacks on their sexual organs by the border guards have been reported in recent years[46] – a trend rarely seen even five years before.

Trafficking, mostly of women and children, has accompanied the formation of the border and has increased manifold in the last few decades.[47] Over the years, trafficking has become rampant all along the border region.[48] It has evolved into one of those economies which thrive on the existence of borders and which have largely contributed to India's entry into the watch-list of countries around the world involved in human trafficking,[49] with West Bengal becoming the region in India with the highest number of intra and inter-state trafficking.[50] In most cases of trafficking, women are duped or coerced into this trade. Male domination coupled with endemic poverty and land alienation results in the large-scale destabilisation and displacement of women in this region. A direct result is an increase in the trafficking of women across the borders.[51]

Trafficking across this border is almost always a one-way flow, i.e. from Bangladesh to India,[52] owing to a bigger market and better profits that Indian trafficking business ensures. Women from the Indian side of the border are mostly trafficked internally, i.e. to other provinces of India. While the international flow of trafficking from India is mostly to the Middle East,[53] and rarely to Bangladesh,

182 *Gendered practices*

women from the border areas (and also from some of the more interior parts) of Bangladesh are almost always trafficked to India, both as an entry point to other international destinations of the trade as well as for trafficking within India.[54]

Trafficking, being a less risky and more profitable business than drug smuggling, has increased alarmingly every year, giving birth to an organised network of traffickers, both at the national and international levels. The network is spreading at great speed, and the border areas between West Bengal and Bangladesh are the most important platforms for this network.[55] The involvement of some of the public representatives and border guards has provided a safe haven for traffickers along this border.[56]

The pimps or *dalals* (in local parlance) allure the women into prospects of jobs, luxurious lives and often good marriages, following which they are 'trafficked at a convenient period with the help and assistance of a section of dishonest members of law-enforcing agencies and border guards'.[57]

Ironically, it is often a woman who locates the target in the village and initiates the process of trafficking – including making acquaintance with the target, obtaining her confidence, putting forward future prospects of better living/better marriage and leading her on to the next level of the trafficking network. In most case studies, the person to have led the victim into the trafficking network has been a woman or a few women, posing as a friend/group of friends. For example, Anima, aged 17 years, was led into a network functioning around the Hili border (between South Dinajpur in West Bengal and Dinajpur in Bangladesh) in December 2011 by a woman who called herself Rina (aged around mid-40s, as guessed by Anima). Rina came to the Mathurapur village in Hili (she was not a local resident of Hili) and after having decided on her target, established friendly relations with Anima. One day, when Anima's parents (who work as agricultural labourers) were away at work, Rina led Anima to the local railway station from where they travelled to Delhi in India. While in Delhi, Anima was kept in a house with several other girls, mostly older than her, and made to perform domestic work. They were often beaten up for their mistakes. After some days, each of them, including Anima, were sent off to other houses to be employed as domestic helps. Fortunately, Anima did not have to undergo sexual abuse in this case. On the basis of the complaint that her parents had lodged with the police, Anima was rescued and brought back to her home by organisations working against trafficking in Hili.[58]

Nilufer Rahman, a lawyer with the Dinajpur District Court in Bangladesh, narrated the case of a woman who was taken to the Khanpur border area in Dinajpur (Bangladesh), by a man and was made to establish acquaintance over the phone with another man on the Indian side of the border. She was kept in one of the houses in that area, near the border, while the pimp was arranging for her to cross over to the other side at an opportune moment. However, the lady of the house where she had been kept suspected the plan and informed the police, who then arrested the girl as well as the Bangladeshi pimp. The Indian counterpart could not, however, be apprehended.[59]

Yet another woman, aged 35, was trafficked from a village in Dinajpur (Bangladesh) all the way to Rajasthan (western India). The pimp who took her to the

Gendered practices 183

Bangladesh border was a woman, who claimed to have come from Rajasthan to sell clothing accessories. Her Indian counterpart received her at the border and led her to Rajasthan. Even after her rescue and return to her village in Bangladesh, the woman found it difficult to undo her training in the Rajasthani language and customs, which she had acquired during her stay in Rajasthan. She took some time to revive her language (Bengali) and lifestyle after her return.[60] The fear of being trafficked by women pimps is such that incidents of false allegation based on mere suspicion leading to violent abuse and death of an innocent (and in a recent case, that of a mentally-challenged) woman have also been seen in recent times.[61]

In a number of cases, the pimps are locally-known faces and well acquainted with the border guards. In many cases, they are seen to establish family relations with local people to give credibility to their presence in the area, and/or set up a seemingly-legal business like a travel agency to be able to set up a network for trafficking.[62] Securing the border guards' involvement and co-operation helps in their operation. When co-operation does not come through, then the change in duty shifts of a batch of guards is often utilised by the pimps to cross the border.[63]

The festival of *Durga Puja* is a time when certain points along the West Bengal-Bangladesh border are opened for the civilians to meet at the border or even cross over to the Indian side to attend the festival and then go back. The Hili border at Dinajpur (Bangladesh) is one such site. The details of people crossing over for the festivities are often not properly recorded by the border guards, given the immense rush that these occasions create. Such occasions, as Ms. Nilufer Rahman points out, are opportune moments for traffickers.[64]

Disabled children are mostly trafficked for organ trafficking or for begging, or even for the sex trade. A huge number of the trafficked Bangladeshi children are serving terms in Indian custody. These children are mostly deceived into this network by a person promising to take them for a day out. They are mostly kidnapped from their schools, especially in border areas like Hili and Jaypurhat, which act as easy transit points for traffickers.[65] Ms. Rahman narrated a case where a group of children had been taken to Rangpur, a Bangladeshi district bordering West Bengal, to be trafficked. The children somehow became suspicious of the pimp's motive and started crying. The pimp, for fear of being suspected by the other passengers on the bus, disappeared, leaving the children behind. The driver of the bus took the children to Raniganj from where they were rescued. Some sections of borders are ill-reputed for child trafficking, like the Hili border, which supplies children to the various shipping docks and other places to be used as child labourers and sex workers.[66] In some cases, they are used as sex workers by the border guards themselves, and the children are often physically abused for disobeying the commands of the latter.[67]

Reasons ranging from poverty to preference for a son (thus selling the daughter to a trafficker for a few thousand rupees), displacement due to natural calamities, consumerism (desire for luxury items), unemployment, availability of cheap and bonded labour, false adoption, fraud, coercion, kidnapping and deceitful marriages are some of the more common ones for trafficking.[68] Both men and women are trafficked to be used as camel jockeys (mainly boys), for pornography, organ

184 *Gendered practices*

trade, sex tourism, begging and drug trafficking, and as domestic child servants and for work in sex parlours and liquor bars,[69] apart from the most usual reason of forced prostitution. In the case of women victims, physical vulnerability in the form of sexual abuse often becomes the prime concern, whereas being involved with a drug network or being duped into organ trade is usually a bigger threat for male victims of trafficking. Deceitful marriages,[70] domestic violence and dire poverty make women more vulnerable to trafficking.[71]

Some of the points along the West Bengal-Bangladesh border have developed as safe and convenient transit points for trafficking, namely the border between South 24 Parganas (West Bengal) and Jessore (Bangladesh), South Dinajpur (West Bengal) and Dinajpur (Bangladesh), and Jalpaiguri (West Bengal) and Panchagarh (Bangladesh).[72] The routes in these border areas used as transits for trafficking are locally known as *ghats* (ports). The existence of busy markets and towns is the reason why some places, like the ones mentioned above, become important trafficking sites. The pimps hand over the victim to the next level in the network (i.e. the pimp's counterpart on the other side of the border) as soon as they get hold of the target. One pimp does not hold on to the victim for too long for fear of being traced. Towns or markets near the border ensure a busy mobile crowd where the movement of the pimp and the victim can safely remain untraced.

The direct relation between trafficking and prostitution is not difficult to establish, given the flourishing of brothels along this West Bengal-Bangladesh border.[73] In a red-light area in Changrabandha, one of the important border points along this border, more than 60% of the sex workers were traced to be from Bangladesh.[74] About 20% of the inmates in Indian brothels at any given point of time come from Bangladesh and Nepal.[75] The actual number is much higher, since not all trafficking cases are reported. The *Bangladesh Manabadhikar Samannya Parishad*, a human rights organisation in Bangladesh, reported, in 2000, that there were 30,000 Bangladeshi women who made up a chunk of the total number of sex workers in Kolkata, and that 10,000 child sex workers of Bangladeshi origin were found in various brothels in Mumbai and Goa in India.[76] One of the reports by *Sanlaap*[77] – a developmental organisation in West Bengal working in the field of violence against women and children, revealed two very important things. One was that women prostitutes migrate from one red light area to another; and two, that 90% of the red light areas that these women identified as having worked in are located along the Bangladesh border. In Dinbazaar, yet another red light area in West Bengal bordering Bangladesh, many sex workers had mothers coming from Bangladesh.[78] This also suggests the viciousness of the circle of prostitution. These women mostly ended up in these red light areas after being duped or coerced by pimps who survive on cross-border trafficking. Illiteracy increased their vulnerability, while for some, their mothers' entry into these areas automatically pushed them into it, due to the social stigma and discrimination that accompanies prostitution.

The rise in prostitution along the border is also indicative of the general scenario of deprivation in the border regions, in terms of the lack of opportunities for education and livelihood, and this affects women the most. While the male population in this region moves to cities and towns or even abroad in search of a livelihood, the women fall prey to or are forced into prostitution. The added disadvantage for these women prostitutes in the border region is that they are caught between the police, on the one hand, and criminals, on the other. Being located near the border, they are often forced to give shelter to criminals and smugglers who cross the borders illegally and take refuge in the brothels. The police not just harass these women in the process of looking for these criminals, but also demand unpaid sex from them.[79] The involvement of the border guards and the police in trafficking is widely-known in this region, though it rarely is reported.[80] A large number of sex workers, domestic helps and labourers from Bangladesh are found working in India and elsewhere, illegally, in spite of the existence of regular outposts of border guards. Abuse, both physical and emotional, often goes unaddressed for their lack of access to legal aid as well as a general lack of awareness regarding their options.[81]

The 'foreign' tag for the women who end up in prostitution after having crossed the border illegally makes them doubly vulnerable since they are left out of whatever little help or rescue and rehabilitation work is done by the NGOs or from state initiatives and programmes because of being foreign nationals. All these women are made to cross the borders without proper papers or proofs of citizenship. They end up being stateless, without recourse to any legal resort.[82]

A large number of cases go unrecorded simply because the victims' families do not encourage filing a case with the police or it does not fall under the legal definition of trafficking. As long as any sort of physical abuse has not been proven, cases of trafficking are difficult to prove even if the reason for them has clearly been sex trade or forced domestic services. This means that hundreds of women and children are trafficked every year without officially being recognised as such.[83]

Even after being rescued, acceptance into the family and society becomes difficult for the victims.[84] Trafficked victims are re-victimised upon their return by way of social stigma and are often forced to end their lives.[85] Rupali Mahato,[86] while discussing stigmatisation of trafficked women, talked about a festival that is celebrated by women mostly belonging to the Kudumi tribe, who gather every evening over a month at a particular place in the village and sing praises for a girl named Tusu.[87] The mythological story that she narrated was related to the kidnapping of a girl and her return to her society.[88] The story was narrated as a reference to the fact that social stigmatisation has accompanied elopement and abduction from time immemorial and continues to do so even today – the stigma attached to trafficking being an example.

Ms Rahman, who is also associated with the government-run trafficking cell in Dinajpur (Bangladesh), explained how the prospect of earning quick money and obtaining luxury items in the form of gifts from customers also act as factors, besides the fear of stigmatisation, for victims not wanting to be rescued.[89] Remittances to families happen to be bigger prospects for these victims than being able to return to family life.[90]

Diseases like HIV/AIDS form an integral part of the vicious circle of underdevelopment, poverty, trafficking and prostitution in the border areas. Such

186 *Gendered practices*

diseases follow the same path as the trafficked women and men. Illegal migrant men and women are often the carriers of HIV/AIDS across the border. Ironically, the border guards form a significant proportion of those infected with HIV/AIDS – an indication of not just their visits to the local border brothels,[91] but also of their awareness of and involvement in the whole process of trafficking.

Some organisations, both government as well as non-government, run shelter homes for trafficked women and children,[92] though most of these NGOs operate from Dhaka (the capital of Bangladesh) instead of the border areas.[93] The rescued women and children who are not accepted back into family life are supported by these organisations until they find themselves a suitable and legal job or till they decide to marry.[94]

Advocate Dilwar Hussein, Public Prosecutor in the Dinajpur High Court, gives more importance to the lack of manpower in the border camps as reason for such widespread trafficking incidents[95] rather than the nexus between the traffickers and the border guards. The number of police officers serving a judicial area, he says, is also far less than the situation demands.[96] On an average, about 20 cases of trafficking are reported every month.[97] Infrastructural gaps coupled with the BGB's involvement in the trafficking practice act as obstacles for the NGOs, as well as for some of the government-run organisations that are struggling to stop cross-border trafficking practices. He emphasises more on the involvement of the BSF in the trafficking network, rather than the BGB. The BSF, he reminds me, has a better communication system and surveillance mechanism than the BGB.[98] Thus, the involvement of the BSF in trafficking practices is amply clear, given that cross-border movement across the fence and along the border road should ideally be easier for the BSF to track.[99]

Though trafficking is rampant in every part of India and Bangladesh, as reports suggest, the West Bengal-Bangladesh border still remains significant to the understanding of gendered border practices in this context. The fact that most of the trafficked victims found in India originate in Bangladesh and that issues of state sovereignty (in terms of the failure to prevent such trades) and citizenship are involved in cross-border trafficking makes the West Bengal-Bangladesh border specifically significant.

Lands outside the border fence

The border fencing[100] affects women and men border residents in different ways. The attitude of the BSF towards civilians who cross the fence is also often driven by gendered concerns.

The daily chore of presenting identity cards at the gates which open to the fenced-out farmlands has been discussed in previous chapters. The condition is even more miserable for those whose homes have been fenced out. Presenting voter cards at the gates for travelling to educational institutions, hospitals or the families of relatives and friends constitute their daily routine.[101] For the farmers, this is a long process where the BSF cross-checks the identity cards with the persons using them as well as the tools and cattle which the farmers carry for farming.[102] There are scheduled times for the BSF to open the gates.[103] The process often delays the farmers' work and becomes a serious concern in the summer months, as they prefer tilling their lands in the early hours of the morning to escape the afternoon heat.[104] But the fencing regulations often force them to begin and continue their work till the late hours of the day. Farmers falling prey to heat strokes and dehydration are not uncommon.[105]

In the case of women, the concerns are different and restrictions more stringent. In most of the border posts, they are rarely allowed to go to the other side of the fence. Though there are no official rules regarding this, it is the BSF officials who devise such unofficial rules. The reason they cite is women's safety. They fear that if these women are let outside the fence, then there is a possibility of them being harassed by the Bangladeshis.[106] As Bangladesh does not have fencing along its border with India, there is a gap between India's fence and the Bangladesh territorial jurisdiction, known as the No-Man's Land. And since there are no border guards posted at the 'zero point' for either of the states, it means that the Bangladeshi people can actually move right up to India's fencing. The BSF fears that once outside the fencing, the women (as well as the men) are outside its direct jurisdiction and, hence, prone to harassment by the Bangladeshis.[107] 'Women do not go to the other side of the fence. They do not work there. Hence, they do not need to go. We try to make them feel secure', states a BSF official at one of the border camps.[108] Most of the civilian men also agree on the point of security hazards when it comes to the question of women moving beyond the fence.[109] Some also raise questions of the vulnerability of women in terms of falling prey to smuggling practices once outside the fence. The lack of women BSF constables makes it easier for women to smuggle items, points out one of the former heads of a village *Panchayat* in a border village.[110] However, for women who work hard to earn a living in these impoverished border areas, this unwritten rule often poses a major problem. They complain of being prohibited by the BSF from taking food across the fence to the male members of their families working in the fenced-out farmlands.[111]

Sabitri Mahato of Char Meghna complains: 'They would not let me go to the other side because I am a woman, whereas they let the men go'.[112] She owns two *bighas*[113] of land outside the fence, which she, along with her husband and two children, depend on for their living. The BSF does not let her go to the field along with her husband, which, she emphasises, is quite a problem for people like them (farmers) because 'here, women work as much as men do. How else would they earn a living?'[114]

The situation is all the more difficult for those women who either do not have a male member at home or have male members who are incapable of farming (due to physical disabilities or medical conditions). These restrictions on women's movements across the fence act as reminders of their incapability to fend for themselves in the absence of a male member in the family. The border, especially the fence, thus contributes towards the maintenance of gendered hierarchies.

188 *Gendered practices*

The BSF also prohibits young male members (below 18 years of age) of families to take food to the fenced-out farmlands because they often do not possess identity cards.[115] Sabitri, at the time of the interview, was considering leasing out her fenced-out land to a Bangladeshi farmer. In that way, she could at least earn, though illegally, from the produce of her land.[116] In fact, this is something that many of the Indian farmers who happen to have their land outside the fence consider as an option, despite knowing the illegal nature of the practice.[117] Instead of going through the ordeal of getting past the fence every day, having to show one's card at the outpost and working under such restrictions, many of the farmers feel that leasing out the land might be a better option. They, of course, risk either losing their lands or having it become a political issue between the two states, leading to more stringent rules for border residents.

The theft of crops by Bangladeshi miscreants from the fenced-out lands is another important reason why farmers with such lands complain and even consider an illegal leasing out.[118] Imtiaz Mondol complains of the BSF's inactivity in helping the civilians prevent such thefts: 'The BSF claims that since the fields from where the crops are stolen are outside the fence, they are outside the jurisdictional area of the BSF'.[119] Officially, the land till the actual borderline or the 'zero point' is Indian territory. The BSF, as India's border security force, has legal powers of surveillance and necessary action till the 'zero point', including the lands outside the fence. But the fence, as the responses and daily chores of the civilians suggest, has redefined binaries such as inside-outside for both the civilians as well as the border guards.

Complaints about the BSF not wanting to help the farmers or residents outside the fence are common.[120] Dayamay Dutta, while confirming these complaints, is also careful to point out that the BSF might not always be in a position to help, given its rigorous duty timings.[121] Such responses are indicative of a sense of fear among the local residents regarding the BSF. Interestingly, the act of fencing itself poses no problem for the civilians. It is just the way the border guards manage the gates which is of concern to them.[122]

Physical and verbal abuse

Incidents of physical abuse, including the killing of civilians by border guards, have become characteristic of the West Bengal-Bangladesh border. It is replete with such occurrences.[123] Reports of firing by border guards, mostly the BSF, do not fail to make their presence felt in the newspapers of both West Bengal and Bangladesh, though the official records of the BSF show lower numbers.[124] Suspected smugglers and intruders are brutally beaten up and, in many cases, shot dead. Civilians often fall victims to cross-border firing between the BSF and the BGB,[125] as also in cases of protesting against the BSF's involvement in smuggling.[126] Extreme measures such as 'shoot to kill' have had their genesis in the 1952 Prevention of Smuggling Ordinance promulgated by East Pakistan to curb cross-border smuggling practices which followed the creation of the Bengal border in 1947 and the beginning of the document regime in 1952.[127]

Gendered practices   189

Complaints about bad behaviour and verbal abuse by the border guards are not uncommon among the border people.[128] 'Treating like dogs' is the kind of phrase used by some of the civilians for describing the nature of behaviour meted out to them by the BSF.[129] Border restrictions regarding use of the border road by civilians also invite abuse from the BSF.[130] 'Unnecessary abuse' has, over the years become a part of the border peoples' narratives, who negotiate the fence and the border guards every day.[131] Complaints to police regarding these abuses rarely bear fruit and are, often, met with threats and further abuses.[132]

Often the border guards shoot a person and leave his body near the fence[133] or hang him in the camp[134] – an act of cautioning others about the extent of power held by them. Examples of false cases filed against civilians by the border guards are not rare. Rashid Haq narrates how one of the BSF constables, in order to fight allegations of his involvement in smuggling practices, shot a smuggler with whom he was involved at other times as an accomplice. This act was justified on grounds of self-defence by him.[135]

One border resident, Saiful, whose legs had already been damaged by a polio attack, was wrongly nabbed by the BSF when they found him roaming near the fence and they beat him up after tying his hands with a handcuff and his legs with a rope.[136]

Yet another person, wrongly arrested by the BSF after being brutally beaten, was about to be shot when one officer showed pity and left him to die near the riverine border. Unable to move, he was stuck in the riverine mud for hours till one of the BSF officers tied a pumped-up air pillow round his neck and threw him into the river. The tide brought him back to the Bangladesh side of the river, where he belonged.[137] Physical and verbal assaults of innocent locals of all social and economic standing – from farmers to teachers, to doctors, anybody for that matter, are integral to living near the West Bengal-Bangladesh border, laments Gourab Sarkar.[138]

One way of torturing cross-border cattle smugglers by the BSF, especially the ones who use the river to smuggle cattle,[139] is of attacking the smuggler while still in the river with the BSF's own patrol boat. The smugglers are hit by the speed-boat till they are badly injured and are forced to surrender.[140] Incidents such as these are often, though not necessarily, preceded by a clash over the bribe money that the border guards demand from the smugglers.[141]

While citing such responses is not to be seen as an attempt to generalise the essentially violent or dishonest nature of the border guards, it is, nevertheless, worth noticing the recurrence of words such as 'dishonest' and 'brutal' in the description of the border guards by the civilians who negotiate the guards everyday – legally or for illegal purposes.

Such incidents of violence are very common in riverine borders, since violation of the borderline by the civilians, especially fishermen, is easier here. Fishermen often mistakenly cross the 'imaginary' borderline in the river and fall prey to brutalities by the border guards.[142]

Children as young as 10–12 years are also not spared from the violence. Zakir Sharif, aged 11, has been a victim of BSF brutalities. In an incident where the BSF had been chasing a group of smugglers, Zakir happened to come across a BSF

190 *Gendered practices*

border guard involved in the chase, quite by chance. While the smugglers escaped, Zakir bore the brunt of the BSF guard's wrath. His pleas of innocence were met with abusive language. It was the collective plea of the local people which saved Zakir's life on that fateful day. An innocent child bore the brunt of the BSF's frustration for its failure to deal with the real culprits.[143] There are incidents of children spending significant parts of their lives in jail for being wrongly accused by the border guards of taking part in suspicious activities near the border.[144]

By far the most brutal incident (and a widely reported one) has been that of a 15-year-old girl, Felani Khatun, of the Kurigram border area, Bangladesh. She and her father, Nurul Islam, used to work as a domestic help and a labourer, respectively, in India. Having her marriage fixed for 8 January 2011, Felani and her father were crossing the border fence from the Indian (West Bengal) side on the morning of 7 January 2011 to return to their home in Kurigram, Bangladesh. While Nurul Islam successfully crossed the border with the help of a ladder that he had arranged for crossing the fence, Felani's dress (*kameez*) got entangled in the barbed wire of the fence. She screamed out in fear, hearing which the BSF constables on duty came there and fired at Felani from point-blank range. Felani, shot and hanging from the fence, pleaded for water but to no avail since none of the witnesses working near the border area dared to help her out of fear of the BSF. She bled to death and remained hanging in the same way for nearly five hours before her body was finally taken away by BSF constables and handed over to the BGB the next day.[145]

Most of the incidents of violence on women by border guards pertain to cases of border-crossing for smuggling or other purposes.[146] In the context of violence, it is mostly the women involved in petty smuggling on a day-to-day basis who face the *lathi*[147] and sometimes the gun. One of the BGB officials in a BGB camp at the Hili border confesses to the use of the *lathi* as a way of disciplining the women involved in smuggling.[148] He also adds that most of these women smugglers are also sex workers in these border regions and survive on smuggling and/ or prostitution for a living.[149]

Illegal border crossers also include those who cross the border for availing of medical services. A number of people from Bangladesh, mostly poor and lacking access or resources for valid documents, cross the border for medical purposes. They are an easy catch for the pimps who earn their living by helping them to cross the borders illegally.[150] Incidents of brutalities by the border guards on their being apprehended are, thus, common occurrences among the illegal border crossers. Incidents of rape and abuse of women crossers (even if accompanied by men) indicate the violent nature of the treatment of illegal practices by the BSF.

On one occasion, a woman accompanying her husband across the border was raped by the BSF and her husband killed for protesting against the act.[151] On another occasion, a woman suspect was strip-searched by the BSF and raped in the presence of her family. Her complaints went unheard.[152] Punishments, if any, for the border guards for such violent actions amount, at best, to a suspension followed by a transfer to a different posting, although promises of 'strict actions' are made by higher officials.[153] The trial of the concerned BSF officials in the Felani

Khatun case serves as an example of the weakness in the legal system for punishing accused border guards. Even though the alleged BSF official, Amiyo Ghosh, was tried in the Felani case under Section 304 of the Indian Penal Code (unintentional killing) and Section 146 of the BSF Act,[154] he was acquitted because of the lack of required witnesses who could have proved the accusation. Human Rights organisations slammed the verdict as a sham and Felani's father vowed to take the case to the international court of justice. The accused was acquitted in a retrial, leaving all hopes of justice dashed to the ground.[155] The verdict also highlights the weakness of state-devised border laws in bringing justice to the border dwellers. These laws often fail to address the gap between statist definitions of justice and the realities of border lives. Continuation of physical violence across the border shows the failure of legal institutions and jurisprudence to address the immediate concerns and everyday negotiations of the border dwellers. Between 2010 and 2015, atleast 236 Bangladeshis have been, reportedly, killed by the BSF according to the Bangladesh Human Rights organisation Ain o Salish Kendra.[156]

Border residents clearly state that both women and men are equally abused by the BSF.[157] Minu Bagdi agrees that the BSF abuse border civilians irrespective of their gender,[158] though local representatives of political parties and the heads of the local village *Panchayats* in the border areas often try to establish the decreasing trend in violence,[159] as an attempt to cover up their own failure in addressing the issue.

Sexual intonation in the treatment of women civilians by border guards

If the physical and verbal abuse of men and women is a common occurrence in the border areas, so are occurrences of border guards demanding sexual favours from women civilians along the West Bengal-Bangladesh border. Some women gather the courage to defy the offer. Some are forced to give in, either for fear of persecution or because such favours ensure the smooth operation of cross-border smuggling practices.[160] Male civilians are often helpless in these instances of indecent offers made by the border guards to their women, for fear of harassment by border guards.[161] But the women civilians are not always, necessarily, victims of such circumstances. If coercive sexual favours from border guards are a reality, so are instances of women offering sexual favours to border guards in return for co-operation in smuggling.[162] While cash bribes are the usual trajectory for male smugglers, sexual favours are often an option chosen by the female smugglers for ensuring co-operation from the border guards. However, women border residents belonging to professions not directly related to the border also do not escape sexual harassment by the border guards.[163]

Women respondents involved in cross-border smuggling practices speak of the 'lenient' or 'sympathetic' attitude of the border guards towards such practices, which is indicative of the gendered nature of interaction between the latter and some women border civilians.[164] The relation between the border guards and these women is more personal in nature, including sexual or even culinary favour (asking the women to cook food for them since the food that they are given in camps

192 *Gendered practices*

is not as good),[165] and is as integral to understanding gendered border narratives as are violent negotiations. Sympathy hardly finds a place in negotiations between the male civilians and the male border guards.

Pradhans as patriarchs

A visible feature in the border villages is the role of the heads and members of local village governments, i.e. the *Panchayats* in West Bengal and the Union *Parishad* in Bangladesh, as mediators between the civilians and the border guards. The *Panchayat*/Union *Parishad* heads (*Pradhans*), mostly male, communicate with the border guards on behalf of the civilians living along the border. The *Panchayats* and Union *Parishads* do have elected female members in the council body,[166] but the *Pradhans*/Chairmen are, still, mostly male. And this is a feature common to almost all the village-level local governments in India and Bangladesh. It is these heads who act as mediators between the civilians and the border guards.

The heads are the paternal figures in a village, which is evident from the way the villagers express their reverence as well as their dependence on them. Md. Rashidul Haq admits that the border guards do not encourage direct interaction with the civilians and prefer to interact only with the *Pradhans*.[167] The *Pradhans* are aware of their roles as local patriarchs and, in fact, take pride in it.[168]

The *Pradhan*'s ability to understand the paraphernalia associated with administration, his ability to convey the issues clearly and his ability to understand the limitations of the border guards are posed as reasons by the border guards themselves when explaining their preference for interacting with the *Pradhans*.[169]

But the role of the *Pradhans* as mediators and local patriarchs is limited by the stronger patriarchal position of the border guards. The influence of the *Pradhans* on the border guards is not just non-binding but also largely dependent on the individual attitude of the border guard concerned. Complaints from some of the *Pradhans* regarding the arrogant attitude of the border guards towards them[170] throw light on the relation between the two categories of local patriarchs in the border areas – the *Pradhans* and the border guards.

Unstated patriarchy

The kind of forced reverence that border guards expect from the civilians indicates the idea of the strong patriarchal position that they imagine themselves to be in. The unstated rule of giving right of way to the vehicles of the border guards and dismounting from one's own vehicles when a vehicle of the border guards passes by indicates the existence of such forced reverence. Fear of persecution and abuse forces the civilians to abide by these unstated rules.[171] 'Why (*should we comply with these rules*)? Are they kings?' asks an angry Sabitri Mahato, after explaining how such rules have evolved in the border areas, especially after the construction of the fence and the border roads.[172]

Responses like 'go and complain to your father' are common among the border guards in cases of complaints from civilians over such unauthorised but stringent

Gendered practices 193

rules.[173] Examples of similar responses from border guards like, 'is this your father's road?' are also narrated by other civilians.[174]

The free use of the civilians' resources without payment[175] is an integral part of the patriarchal undercurrent that runs below the formal and legally sanctioned protector-subject relation between the border guards and the civilians. The local police stations avoid taking complaints from the civilians, citing jurisdictional formalities as the reason.[176]

Interestingly, even the police and other administrative bodies accept the role of the border guards as the patriarchs in the West Bengal-Bangladesh border areas, as an Officer-in-Charge (OC) at the Murutia Police Station in Nadia district (West Bengal) admits. 'Locals depend more on the BSF than the administration because the BSF is an armed force', he says. When asked why the police, despite being an armed force like the BSF, fails to gain the faith of the locals, he quickly admits that, 'BSF knows better how to handle the border'.[177]

These responses hint towards a clear prioritisation of the BSF at the West Bengal-Bangladesh border over the regular police mechanisms.[178] In the context of border control, the regular police mechanisms are marginalised. The patriarchal nature of the state in the context of the borderland is, thus, not limited to a theoretical construct[179] but manifests itself in real visible forms – embodied in the border guards.[180]

Other forms of gendered border narratives

A unique form of gendered border narrative can be witnessed in some parts of the West Bengal-Bangladesh border where a large number of transgenders or *hijras* are seen to be actively involved in illegal cross-border activities.[181] They involve themselves mostly in smuggling drugs across the border. The Hili border between West Bengal's South Dinajpur district and Bangladesh's Dinajpur district is a case in point.

Fearlessly squatting along the railway tracks running along the Bangladesh border, mostly in an intoxicated state and in very close proximity to the camps of the border guards, they talk about their involvement in cross-border smuggling practices. They also mention how their unique gendered status helps them in their work. The fact that they are transgenders saves them from the physical abuse perpetrated by the border guards on the other 'normal male and female' smugglers. The fact that they are 'neither male nor female' helps them in their work.[182]

Contradictory factors like 'dislike' and 'sympathy' come up spontaneously in the narratives of the *hijras* when it comes to explaining why the border guards do not want to mingle with them or even stop them from dealing in illegal activities.[183] Sheena, a *hijra* working in the Hili border area, points to the sheer dislike that the border guards have for the emasculated status of the *hijras*,[184] while Rajib, another *hijra* working in the Hili border area, explains that the border guards are actually sympathetic towards the *hijras* since they lack social support in terms of family and friends. 'They spare us on humanitarian grounds', he quips.[185] This

194 *Gendered practices*

explains why more than 200 *hijras* are involved in cross-border smuggling practices in the Hili port alone.[186]

Such contradictory versions of 'dislike' and 'sympathy' are further verified through the responses of the border guards regarding the widespread involvement of the *hijras* in illegal activities. The question of dignity is clear in responses like 'it does not look good if we interact with *hijras*, which is why we generally avoid arresting them. Moreover, their families do not accept them. If we stop them from doing these, how will they survive?'[187] Even the sincerest efforts from the border guards to highlight the humanitarian aspect of the matter fail to hide the disrespectful pity in their tone of speech.

The earning of *hijras* has, over the years, become profitable, especially in and around the Hili border area. Instances of men choosing to undergo medical procedures to 'become' *hijras* or even 'disguising themselves as one, have increased at an alarming rate.[188] The lives and livelihood practices of the *hijras* on the West Bengal-Bangladesh border cannot be overlooked if one has to understand gendered border practices – practices which show how gendered identities evolve into a spatial narrative on the margins of the state.

Women border guards

The border guards, on both sides of the border, are essentially a male force. The first female recruits of BGB happened as recently as 2016;[189] the BSF had, so far, a few women constables in non-combat roles like searching women smugglers and infiltrators.[190] The first batch of women to be recruited in combat roles passed out on 28 July 2012 and moved on to their training phases.[191] The first combat woman officer in BSF was recruited in March 2017.[192] Women under and up to the age of 25 may be recruited as direct-entry officers in the rank of Assistant Commandants (ACs), and are eligible to lead their troops along the Pakistan and Bangladesh border.[193]

A male Company Commander of a BSF camp in Nadia (West Bengal) is simultaneously hopeful and apprehensive about the decision to recruit women officers. He says that while they will strengthen the force by their presence, the infrastructural hazards would also be a serious concern,[194] referring to the lack of basic facilities and privacy required for them.

I met two of the six women constables in one of the BSF camps in Murshidabad (West Bengal). They informed me that all six of them are from West Bengal and are Bengali-speakers,[195] unlike the male BSF recruits, most of whom come from other parts of India, far away from their postings on the West Bengal border, and are Hindi-speakers. The main job of the female border guards is to frisk the women border crossers, crossing for any purpose.[196] Ironically, women smugglers, some of the witnesses confirm, find it easier to 'deal' with women constables posted at the fence gates rather than male constables, since the former are 'easier to convince' in the matter of letting them cross the border.[197] During a recent field visit in July 2017, I noticed an interesting behavioural pattern among the women BSF constables posted along the border camps. Answering questions posed by border guards regarding my whereabouts, especially as an outsider moving about in border areas, has been a part of my field visits all along. But the attitude and behaviour of the border guards, so far, has not been unnecessarily rude, despite having heard about the same from the local civilians. The ways of the border guards, with me, might have been stern at times, but not impolite per se. During a recent field visit, I noticed that the attitude and body language of the women border guards (of whom there have been increasing number of recruits in recent years) were visibly discourteous. The women constables were unnecessarily insolent in their routine queries about my name, work, research, etc. – that distinctly stood opposed to the comparatively more courteous interactions which their male counterparts had with me. The ill-manners were such that I was, often, forced to protest against such impoliteness. That this has been a growing behavioural pattern among the women BSF constables was also corroborated by the civilians. 'What rude language these women guards use!', says a local border resident at Char Meghna in Nadia district.[198] I wondered whether such visible performance of sternness had to do with the attempt to reverse the general image of the women guards as complicit, easily convincible and approachable in matters of 'controlling' the border, and as such, not fit to 'man' a strategically sensitive space such as the borderland. Questions of whether such performances by the women border guards were part of the process to fit into the overtly patriarchal structure of the state embodied in the border guards along the state's borders became part of my research in understanding the creation of a border consciousness.

Restriction on the use of lethal weapons by border guards

In an effort to reduce violence along its borders, the government of India decided to arm the BSF with non-lethal weapons in 2009, following requests from the BGB to prevent the killings of Bangladeshis by the BSF on the India-Bangladesh border.[199] The need to abide by the internationally-recognised Rules of Engagement (RoE) that call for maintaining peace at the border 'at any cost' has been the focus of the meetings between the BSF and BGB over the issue of the use of weapons.[200] While the effort at maintaining peace at the borders is a laudable one, responses from the BSF Commanding Officers in the border outposts bring out the undercurrents of such decisions.

The BSF, under this regulation, is to use pump-action guns with rubber bullets in the first-fire and challenge-fire rounds. Firing from regular guns would be the next step, though ensuring the 'sanctity and security of the Indian border would be the first (priority) in any case'.[201]

However, the decision has encouraged more illegal activities across the West Bengal-Bangladesh border. 'The smugglers used to be more afraid of BSF earlier, but now they are less so', says a Company Commander of a BSF camp at Shikarpur in Nadia (West Bengal).[202] Attacks on the BSF by smugglers and other miscreants have increased following the decision[203] – a fact corroborated by the BSF officials themselves.[204] This is, indeed, an irony that plays out all along the length

196 *Gendered practices*

of the border, where the 'armed' border guards evoke a sense of security and threat, simultaneously. This dilemma is amply expressed in the responses of the border civilians where, on the one hand, they speak of the violent attributes of the border guards with regard to the use of weapons and, on the other, of their diminishing power with regard to 'protecting' the civilians in the context of their use of non-lethal weapons. These ambiguous narratives of protection and violation of human rights are integral to the narratives and consciousness of the border people, including the border guards themselves.

Rupali Mahato admits that there has been an increasing sense of insecurity among the border civilians following the decision. It is the threat of firing from the BSF that keeps the miscreants away, and 'this policy is creating a lot of problems'[205] by making the smugglers more emboldened.[206] Not just the smugglers but the civilians wronged by the border guards also sometimes resort to the physical abuse of the guards, as an act of resistance to years of abuse by them.[207]

The possession of weapons and the nature of weapons, in the case of the border guards, produce two parallel strands of narratives on the West Bengal-Bangladesh border. The power to use weapons gives the border guards a chance to exercise patriarchal dominance along the border. It also brings in the issue of the violation of human rights with regard to the abuse of border crossers, and especially those involved in some sort of illegal activity. The restriction on the use of lethal weapons, on the other hand, has a derogatory effect on the border guards' sense of dominance over the civilians. It also brings in the issue of the loss of security for civilians, especially those who are not directly associated with border-crossing. The powerful patriarchal presence of the border guards is, interestingly, misused by miscreants in threatening or even robbing civilian households. Miscreants 'dressed as BSF' have been reported to have made their way into civilians' houses and robbed them.[208] Narratives of patriarchal dominance and symbolic emasculation become integrally linked to the border narratives with reference to gendered interactions between the border guards and the civilians. Plans for observing the joint ceremony of 'lowering of the flags' by the BSF and the BGB in Petrapole-Benapole border (as is currently held between BSF and Pakistan Rangers[209] in Wagah on the India-Pakistan border) can be seen as efforts to restore the powerful patriarchal image of the border guards along the West Bengal-Bangladesh border.[210] Another usual response by the BSF on the issue of use of weapons has to do with their experiences at the Kashmir border between India and Pakistan. A common response has been:

> It is easier to control the border in Kashmir because there are no restrictions on firing. We can easily fire at someone moving around near the border. Posting at the Bengal border is a matter of misfortune for us. We often let go the poor locals on grounds of poverty and lack of livelihood options. But they are often the first ones to say that we have allowed them to smuggle. Moreover, here we are helpless when it comes to dealing with miscreants because of this restriction on the use of lethal weapons. Here the smugglers test and tease our masculinity (*mardangi ko lalkarta hai*).[211]

Mixed reaction of the civilians towards the border guards

An interesting mix of responses from the civilians regarding the border guards makes it difficult to label these interactions as purely those of domination or subjugation. Two categories of civilians are seen to be favourable towards the border guards. The first category is those who have not been directly victimised by the BSF but whose lives and livelihood, nevertheless, depend largely on the efficient patrolling of the border by the border guards.[212] 'The attitude of the BSF is generally good. They are only bad with bad people (indicating smugglers)', says Subodh, an employee at a currency-exchange counter at the Petrapole border, North 24 Parganas (West Bengal). People like him feel that it is the efficient border management of the border guards that makes honest ways of life and livelihoods possible along the West Bengal-Bangladesh border.[213]

The second category is of those involved, directly or indirectly, in cross-border illegal activities and is largely dependent on the co-operation of the border guards. They, too, feel that the co-operation of the border guards ensures the smooth running of their businesses and livelihoods.[214]

Unfavourable responses regarding the border guards come from those civilians who pursue honest means of livelihood, like farming, but have to deal with the BSF daily[215] and from those associated with professions not directly related to the border, like teachers, doctors, tailors and labourers.[216] This category of people is probably the worst sufferers in terms of being the victims of violent dominance by the border guards, as well as of the nexus of illegality functioning along the border, without being party to it.

While the nature of interaction between the BSF and the civilians on the West Bengal side of the border highlights complex narratives of patriarchal domination, co-operation and resistance, that between the BGB and the civilians on the Bangladesh side of the border reveals some more unique features of control and co-operation.

Relations between Bangladeshi border civilians and the BGB: language as a decisive factor

The nature of interaction between the BGB and the Bangladeshi border civilians is symbolic of a pattern of co-operation and complicity that is not seen on the West Bengal side of the border. Vicious forms of hostility and violence are rarely seen on the Bangladesh border, unlike its West Bengal counterpart.

The BGB is as much a representative of the sovereign power of the state in the Bangladesh border areas as is the BSF on the West Bengal side. But the attitude of the BGB officials patrolling the Bangladesh border is visibly protective, even lenient, towards the Bangladeshi border civilians. More like a guardian, the BGB uses warnings and, at best, admonitions while dealing with civilians involved in unlawful activities. Instances of direct physical abuse or even the use of abusive language are rare.[217]

198   *Gendered practices*

This is not to suggest that unlawful activities are any less on the Bangladesh side of the border. Cross-border activities clearly indicate the involvement of 'both' sides in their operation. Nor is physical abuse completely absent here. Residents of Hili narrate how the BGB, though only in rare cases, beats up those caught smuggling drugs or other items across the border. 'How much more would they tolerate?' wonders Jumaira – indicating the BGB's general tendency towards being tolerant and lenient, and reverting to violent means only when situations go out of control.[218]

Language plays a very important role on both sides in the relation between the border guards and the civilians. Most officers of the BSF originate from other parts of India and are mostly Hindi-speakers, while the native and the most widely-spoken language of West Bengal (including its border areas) is *Bangla* (Bengali). This results in an obvious communication gap between the Hindi-speaking border guards and the *Bangla*-speaking local civilians.[219] Civilians on the West Bengal border rarely, if at all, speak or even understand Hindi, while few BSF officials are able to learn *Bangla* during their posting periods on the West Bengal border. The BSF finds it difficult to identify with the local language and culture of the *Bangla*-speaking civilians and, thus, resort to abusive language.[220]

There are a few *Bangla*-speaking BSF officers along the West Bengal border. But complaints about them from civilians are, ironically, even more than of the Hindi-speaking officers. These officers avoid using *Bangla* while interacting with civilians.[221] This seems to be a common occurrence on the West Bengal border and can only be explained by the attempt of the BSF to carefully maintain a distance between itself and the civilians.[222]

Sabitri Mahato explains that, often, the Hindi-speaking BSF constables are still easy to interact with (in whatever broken Hindi the locals can manage to speak), compared to the *Bangla*-speaking BSF constables. Preventing the civilians from taking advantage of the language affinity is the reason why the *Bangla*-speaking BSF officers tend not to use *Bangla*. '*Bangla*-speaking BSF officers do not use *Bangla*, they use Hindi, so that we do not ask for any help', explains Nirendranath Burman.[223] Such complaints indicate the fear among the *Bangla*-speaking BSF officers of being seen as biased towards 'their own people'.

Interestingly, these very *Bangla*-speaking BSF officers, who converse in Hindi at other times, resort to *Bangla* while negotiating with smugglers.[224] Thus, the use and/abuse of language is driven by circumstances and interests.

Complaints by women civilians often involve the issue of sexual insinuation in the use of language by the BSF. Hatred for the Bengali-people and the *Bangla* language is cited as a reason for the mistreatment of women border civilians.[225] On the other hand, narratives of the BSF in the form of poetry reveal its reverence for Hindi as a mother tongue – as being symbolic of love for the motherland and human empowerment in general.[226] In the current scenario of a saffronisation of the state by the current government, use of Hindi as the *lingua franca* gains all the more significance at the border areas, where the ominous triad of nationalism, patriotism and fundamentalism wreak havoc. The celebration of Hindi Divas, Nagar Rajbhasha Karyannayan Samity's gatherings[227] – all feed into the state's homogenisation programme along its borders along linguistic-cultural lines.

Gendered practices 199

The need to recruit more co-operative *Bangla*-speaking BSF officers on the West Bengal border is felt by civilians across genders and professions. Narendranath Ghosh feels that having *Bangla*-speaking BSF officers on the West Bengal border would help the civilians to better convey their problems to the border guards.[228] Issues of miscommunication over language have failed to gain the required support of the Indian government, though the erstwhile Left Front government in West Bengal had placed this issue before the central government.[229]

Though the BSF officers deny that language differences are an important issue,[230] the responses of the civilians clearly reveal the nature of miscommunication that language creates in their interaction with the border guards. It also re-emphasises the fact that while language plays an important role in preserving cross-border links between the people of West Bengal and Bangladesh, it creates a cultural difference between the West Bengal border civilians and the BSF. This acts as a very important factor when it comes to the issue of how border narratives along the West Bengal-Bangladesh border question the role of the concerned states not simply as the political containers but as the cultural containers as well. The futility of the Bengal border in terms of becoming a cultural partition is questioned in a number of ways, language being the most pertinent one.

The BGB, on the other hand, can comfortably communicate with the Bangladeshi border civilians by virtue of sharing a common language, i.e. *Bangla*. Language plays an important role in bridging the gap between the BGB and the Bangladeshi civilians. Sharing a common language, interestingly, prevents frequent instances of the use of abusive speech by the BGB.[231] Civilians on the West Bengal border are often heard speaking favourably of the BGB rather than of the BSF. 'The public would rather take BGB as a friend and consider the BSF as their enemy', says Nirendranath Burman of Kalmati village in Cooch Behar (West Bengal),[232] questioning, albeit unconsciously, the role of the state as a container.

The use of *Bangla* by civilians on both sides of the West Bengal-Bangladesh border poses an obvious challenge to the border guards, especially the Hindi-speaking ones, in terms of the difficulty in distinguishing a Bangladeshi from an Indian.[233] This has forced the Indian government to consider introducing *Bangla* lessons for the BSF in order to 'improve relations with the locals'.[234] The plan to recruit *Bangla*-speaking local civilians from border areas into the BSF service is yet another step towards resolving the issue of the communication gap.[235]

Responses from some of the BGB constables on the general violent attitudes of the BSF throw light on some more factors which, the BGB officers feel, contribute towards the unfavourable relation between the BSF and the civilians. While the communication gap is a major factor, alcohol consumption[236] and staying away from their families for too long are other factors that contribute towards the general violent nature of the BSF.[237] BGB officials, the majority of whom are Muslims by religion,[238] consider alcohol consumption within the BSF (a large majority of who are non-Muslims) a reason for its abusive mentality. Some of the civilians on the West Bengal border agree to the fact that alcohol consumption is often a reason behind BSF's abusive attitude.[239] Talks about the BSF's military failure on the Indo-Pakistan and Indo-China border followed by the BSF's

200 *Gendered practices*

recourse to violence on the Bangladesh border are common among the Bangladeshi border civilians and the BGB.[240] Such responses indicate the BGB's ideas about the BSF's misguided patriarchal domination. Alcohol consumption (leading to an unstable emotional condition) and the lack of family life (resulting in a social and emotional vacuum) coupled with the failure to exercise domination in other borders are reasons for the BSF's misuse of power along the West Bengal-Bangladesh border, feels the BGB.[241] Higher BSF officials also consider alcohol consumption among the constables as a reason for their misuse of power and the miserable conditions that the BSF constables find themselves in.[242] Efforts at awareness campaigns against alcohol consumption are common in the BSF journals.[243]

Increasing suicidal tendencies among the BSF supports such views.[244] A social and emotional vacuum, coupled with the imposition of restraints on the use of power, have, recently, increased the number of suicide cases in the BSF.[245] Such tendencies also highlight the fact that the border guards are as much under the strain of surviving border life as are the border civilians.

The BGB also has its own narrative of the possession and eventual loss of patriarchal power. While the decision on using non-lethal weapons resulted in narratives of the loss of power for the BSF, the mutiny in the Bangladeshi border forces serves as the BGB's own narrative of loss of power.[246] 'The BGB has become somewhat weak after the mutiny. It has almost become like children, who live at the mercy of others (indicating both the Bangladesh state and the BSF). Gradually, though, it is regaining its old vigour',[247] says a BGB official. He also points out how restrictions on firing back at the BSF, following the mutiny, have dampened the BGB spirits.[248]

For the BGB, the idea of wielding power pertains more to the nature of its interaction with the BSF rather than its own border civilians.[249] For the BSF, the wielding of power relates more to disciplining its own border civilians rather than its interactions with the BGB.[250] This also explains the difference in opinion among the civilians about the border forces on the West Bengal and the Bangladesh border.

Bonding attempts

Unfavourable responses towards the BSF from the border civilians on the West Bengal border explains the recent attempts made by the BSF to improve communication with the local people on the border. Cultural events, sports events and educational programmes in some of the border villages along the West Bengal border are a direct result of such efforts.[251] Civic Action Programmes organised by the BSF, including medical check-ups, computer training, canteen facilities, sports, debates, blood donation camps, BSF Foundation Day celebrations, 'Hindi Divas' celebrations[252] and tourist visits are also part of its efforts in this regard.[253] Border guards also make use of festivals like *Durga Puja*, *Kali Puja* and *Eid*, to create a platform for interaction between the border people of both sides – when civilians and border guards from the other side are invited, good wishes and

Gendered practices 201

sweets exchanged and fireworks and cultural programmes enjoyed together.[254] Friendly matches between the BSF and the BGB constitute yet another way of creating platforms for bonding between the border guards and the civilians on both sides,[255] as do BSF-BGB Joint Exercises across the border, including 'Sundarban Maitri' (March 2016)[256] and UNDOC Indo-Bangladesh Border Strengthening Workshop On Countering Human Trafficking and Smuggling of Migrants (April 2016).[257] Some of the poems composed by BSF guards hint towards bonding initiatives by hinting at the pride in being 'offered a soldier's hand'.[258]

One of the aims of the educational programmes organised by the BSF is to increase awareness among the civilians, especially students in school, about the role of the BSF as the protector and patriarchal figure of the border areas.[259] Attempts to introduce Hindi language courses in local primary schools by the BSF have, nevertheless, not seen much success.[260] Recruiting local youths in unofficial posts in the BSF camps have also been on the rise as a means to involve local civilians in the 'running' of the border as well as to have them as mediators between the guards and the civilians.

These bonding efforts have not necessarily been popular with all the BSF officers posted along this border.[261] During some of the cultural events organised by the BSF, especially during religious festivals, there have been attempts of illegal border-crossings and smuggling by the border people, as pointed out by the BSF officials themselves.[262] 'We have to control them. During these festivals, the civilians, in a frenzy to meet their relatives on the other side of the border, often cut across the fences. They are illiterate and, hence, difficult to control', says a BSF officer in BRC'pur BSF camp in Nadia (West Bengal).[263] The equation of illiteracy with emotional instability and the *need to control* clearly indicates the control regime at work across the border. On a number of occasions, planned border fairs have been called off by border guards[264] or have been held under strict surveillance.[265] The suspicious nature of the BSF is also clearly revealed in its journals, where one of the challenges of the BSF border guards has been pointed out as 'being suspicious of the people'.[266] The persistence of the threat factor in the bonding attempts is clearly spelt out when even by the drinking water kiosks arranged by the BSF officers during festivals, the identity cards of the civilians are asked to be presented.[267] The uncertainty of such cross-border interactions during festivals leaves the border civilians unhappy since many of them wait for such occasions to meet their relatives from the other side of the border – the only remaining link to a past that they have left behind.[268]

Celebration of Mother Language Day on the 21st of February every year has become one of the most significant celebrations across the border, with a number of cultural programmes being held in border areas. Bangladesh's celebration of the triumphant recognition of *Bangla* as the national language is shared by West Bengal, on the other side of the border, with its celebration of *Bangla* as the mother tongue of its Bengali populace and as a language signifying an identification with the larger *Bangla*-speaking population of a once-united Bengal.[269] The Language Day celebrations along the border areas constitute cultural festivities on both side but rarely involve any cross-border movement of people. Hence,

202 *Gendered practices*

the border guards are more open to the idea of celebrating this event unlike other religious festivals which often involve people crossing the border to participate in the festivities on the other side – inviting suspicion and increased surveillance from the border guards.

Conclusion

One of the significant characteristics of the West Bengal-Bangladesh border is the fact that its entire length is densely populated, unlike the borders that India shares with either Pakistan or China.[270] Numerous villages, including farmlands, rivers and lakes, characterise the border. Thus, controlling this border implies controlling not just natural boundaries or deploying armed forces but, more importantly, controlling people. The nature of governance that has been established by India and Bangladesh along this border in the last six decades reveals two levels of operation – the totalising or *en masse*[271] control of the border civilians, and negotiations with individual persons[272] depending on the context and situation. *En masse* control over the border is manifested in various surveillance mechanisms, patrolling by the border guards and even the bonding attempts by the BSF. But it is the pattern of individual control that sheds light on the complexity of governance mechanisms. The gendered forms of violence between the male civilians and the male border guards (including both the use of weapons on one another, as well as the sexual abuse of suspected smugglers by the border guards), the interaction between the male border guards and the *hijras* and the sexual insinuation in the various interactions between the male border guards and the female civilians – are symbolic of such individual patterns of control. While *en masse* control mechanisms reveal the more generally known forms of gendered practices along the border, the individual patterns point towards the least recognised but no less significant gendered border narratives. That 'border maps are also body maps'[273] and that cartographic exigencies leave their imprint on the people they effect are borne out by the various gendered narratives witnessed across the Bengal border.

The study of interactions between the border guards and the civilians on the West Bengal-Bangladesh border in existing literature has, so far, highlighted the state as the oppressor, the border civilians as the victims and the border area as merely a periphery where all sorts of marginalisation and victimisation occur. The interaction between the women civilians and male border guards has been the only index for the study of gendered narratives along this border. This chapter shows that there are many more complex strands of narratives beneath such linear narratives of perpetrator-victim discourses. It also shows that gendered border narratives on the West Bengal-Bangladesh border are not limited to male perpetrator-female victim binaries but play out in all sorts of gendered combinations across varied levels of social standing. The variation in the gendered aspect in the relation between the male border guards and the male civilians on both sides of the border, between the male border guards and *hijras*, between the male border guards and female civilians on the West Bengal border, between the male border guards on both sides of the border and the role of women pimps in women's

Gendered practices 203

trafficking – reveal the complex web of gendered relations operating along this border, apart from confirming some of the more generally studied aspects of the border in question, like the general condition of women civilians along it and the overarching performance of masculine patriarchy by the border guards towards both male and female civilians. Gender narratives are not unique to borderlands. They are witnessed in varying forms and nature in non-border areas as well. But the specificity of a borderland moulds gendered narratives in a way so as to give them a spatial dimension.

In the process of the creation of such spatially-driven gendered narratives, the border people redefine the space itself. While the states produce a certain version of their borderlands (as spaces of separation from the neighbour, as containers of their own civilians and as the space for the exercise of unquestionable sovereign control), the border people, including the civilians and the border guards, reproduce the space through questioning and redefining the state's version. The borderland, as a meeting place for both *perceived and conceived*[274] spaces, turns itself into a *thirdspace*[275] of lived reality and a platform for 'common sense' to crystallise into a spatial consciousness, binding both the civilians and the border guards as embodiments of the state, in a common spatial identity of a 'border people'.

Notes

1 Donnan, H. and Wilson, T.M. (1999) *Borders: Frontiers of Identity, Nation and State*. Oxford: Berg.
2 Samaddar, R. (1999) *The Marginal Nation: Transborder Migration from Bangladesh to West Bengal*. Thousand Oaks, London: Sage; Chatterji, J. (1999) The Fashioning of a Frontier: The Radcliffe Line and Bengal's Border Landscape, 1947–52. *Modern Asian Studies*. 33(1). pp. 185–242; Van Schendel, W. (2005) *The Bengal Borderland: Beyond State and Nation in South Asia*. London: Anthem; Jones, R. (2012) Spaces of Refusal: Rethinking Sovereign Power and Resistance at the Border. *Annals of the Association of American Geographers*. 102(3). pp. 685–699; Banerjee, P. (2010) *Borders, Histories, Existences: Gender and Beyond*. New Delhi: Sage; Banerjee, P. and Basu Ray Chaudhury, A. (Eds.). (2011) *Women in Indian Borderlands*. New Delhi: Sage; Newspaper reports on border violence as well as reports by human rights organisations such as Odhikar (www.odhikar.org) and Human Rights Watch (www.hrw.org) focus on the abuse of male border civilians by the border guards as acts of human rights violation in general, rather than as cases of gendered abuse.
3 Chakrapani, C. and Kumar, S.V. (Eds.). (1994) *Changing Status and Role of Women in Indian Society*. New Delhi: M.D. Publications; Rath, N. (1996) *Women in Rural Society: A Quest for Development*. New Delhi: M.D. Publications; Verma, S.B. (2005) *Status of Women in Modern India*. New Delhi: Deep & Deep.
4 Census of India 2011, Ministry of Home Affairs, Government of India.
5 In terms of women's education, West Bengal ranks 19th compared to male education, where it ranks 22nd, among all the 35 States and Union Territories in India, though a comparison of the percentage of literacy for males and females in West Bengal points to a higher percentage of literate males (82.67) as compared to females (71.16) on a national basis. While this indicates a slightly better condition of female literacy in West Bengal compared to male literacy, it also points to the general lack of literacy among women in India at large. Census of India, 2011. Government of

204 *Gendered practices*

India. Available from: www.censusindia.gov.in/2011-prov-results/data_files/india/Final_PPT_2011_chapter6.pdf7 p. 111.

6 Census of India, 2001. [Online] Available from: www.wbhealth.gov.in/old/statistics/LiteracyRate.htm. [Accessed: 20 July 2013].

7 The literacy rate of West Bengal is 77.8% as per Census of India 2011 of which the literacy rates for the border districts (in descending order) of West Bengal are the following: North 24 Parganas-84.95, Darjeeling-79.92, S. 24 Parganas-78.57, Nadia-75.58, Cooch Behar-75.49, South Dinajpur-73.86, Jalpaiguri-73.79, Murshidabad-67.53, Malda-62.71 and North Dinajpur-60.13. Census of India, 2011. Available from: http://censusindia.gov.in/2011-prov-results/prov_data_products_wb.html.

8 Banerjee and Basu Ray Chaudhury, 2011, p. 35.

9 Interview with Md. Tafikul Islam, resident of Panitor border, Basirhat (North 24 Parganas district of West Bengal, 17 January 2012).

10 Interview with Riazul Mondol, resident of Balurghat (South Dinajpur district of West Bengal, 24 January 2012).

11 In Jamalpur, on the Hili border, the rate of education in primary schools is 60% while that in higher schools is 20%. Interview with Ranjit, resident of Jamalpur, Hili (South Dinajpur district of West Bengal, 24 January 2012).

12 My experience of field studies along the border districts of West Bengal and Bangladesh has also been indicative of the general sense of insecurity among the border people and specific sense of insecurity among women. A woman travelling around interviewing people in the border areas, unaccompanied by male family members, has warranted often unwanted curiosity and warnings from both the civilians and the border guards. The risk of 'travelling around in the border areas and that, too, as a woman' has been conveyed to me numerous times in the course of my field studies.

13 Interview with Parbati Mohanto, resident of Dhumron village (South Dinajpur district of West Bengal, 25 January 2012).

14 Interview with Animesh, resident of Bindol village (North Dinajpur district of West Bengal, 26 January 2012).

15 Interview with Parbati Mohanto, resident of Dhumron village (South Dinajpur district of West Bengal, 25 January 2012).

16 Interview with Minu Bagdi, resident of Mathurapur village (South Dinajpur district of West Bengal, 24 January 2012)

17 The legal age for marriage in India is 18 for females and 21 for males. In 2012, the High Court declared that Muslim women could marry at 15. Additionally, the report declared that, 'In spite of these legal provisions, child marriage is still widely practiced and a marriage solemnized in contravention of these provisions is not void even under the new PCMA, 1929, the Hindu Marriage Act, 1955 and also under the Muslim Law'. Source: http://lawcommissionofindia.nic.in/reports/report205.pdf.

18 Interview with Riazul Mondol, resident of Balurghat (South Dinajpur district of West Bengal, 24 January 2012).

19 Interview with Parbati Mohanto, resident of Dhumron village (South Dinajpur district of West Bengal, 25 January 2012).

20 Payment of dowry is now prohibited under the 1961 Dowry Prohibition Act in Indian civil law and, subsequently, by Sections 304B and 498a of the Indian Penal Code (IPC). Despite anti-dowry laws in India, it is still a common illegal practice.

21 Interview with Sabitri Mahato, resident of Char Meghna (Nadia district of West Bengal, 21 October 2011)

22 Interview with Gokul, resident of Kalmati village (Cooch Behar district of West Bengal, 16 March 2012).

23 Though girls who are comfortable with their husband's involvement in illegal livelihood practices do marry into the border areas, the general scenario is bleak.

Gendered practices 205

24 Interview with Gokul, resident of Kalmati village (Cooch Behar district of West Bengal, 16 March 2012).

25 A bus carrying a bride's family and relatives was stopped at a BSF check-post on its way to a border village in Nadia (West Bengal), where it had to remain for the night, and was allowed entry into the village and, subsequently, to the groom's house only the next morning. Interview with Prasanta Mondol, resident of Char Meghna (Nadia district of West Bengal, 21 October 2011).

26 Interview with Sabitri Mahato, resident of Char Meghna (Nadia district of West Bengal, 21 October 2011); fencing details – discussed in the Introduction; for further details of sanctioned and completed border fences, see http://mha.nic.in/pdfs/BM_MAN-IN-BANG(E).pdf.

27 Interview with Bikram, resident of Lakshmidari village, Bhomra (Satkhira district of Bangladesh, 12 February 2012).

28 Interview with Bikram, resident of Lakshmidari village, Bhomra (Satkhira district of Bangladesh, 12 February 2012); italics my own, to highlight the fact that cross-border marriages have not *completely* ceased to exist. They still occur, though illegally.

29 Belonging to North 24 Parganas district of West Bengal but surrounded on three sides by the Jessore district of Bangladesh.

30 With no border guards' outposts between this Indian *Ghoj* and the surrounding Bangladeshi territory, movement between the *Ghoj* and Bangladesh is easier than accessing the Indian mainland due to the BSF outpost at its entrance.

31 Interview with Asha, resident of Daulatpur village belonging to North 24 Parganas of West Bengal and located in Chougachha, Jessore district of Bangladesh (16 February 2012). I accessed the *Ghoj* from the Bangladesh side of the border, having travelled through the Jessore district to reach this Indian pocket. This means I crossed the border without much fuss from Bangladesh to an Indian village inside the *Ghoj*. I was driven from the Jessore town through the surrounding areas of the *Ghoj* and we parked our car outside the *Ghoj*. I walked inside the *Ghoj*, interviewed its residents and was also shown the geographical specificities of the *Ghoj* by them. The Indian territory (of which the *Ghoj* was a part) could be seen across the farmland, at the entry to which was a BSF outpost. Starting from the outpost, a narrow stretch of land extended towards the *Ghoj* till it widened to become the *Ghoj* surrounded by Bangladeshi territory (creating a chicken's neck formation). But there was no BSF or BGB outpost on the other side of the *Ghoj* where it was surrounded by Bangladeshi territory, which made it possible for me to enter it from the Bangladesh side without any obstacle. The *Ghoj* extended into the Bangladeshi territory in such a way that a single courtyard was divided into the Bangladeshi territory, on one side, and the Indian territory, on the other. The two sets of huts facing each other belonged to two different states.

32 Interview with Asha, resident of Daulatpur village belonging to North 24 Parganas of West Bengal (Chougachha, Jessore district of Bangladesh, 16 February 2012).

33 Interview with Bijon, resident and journalist with a Bengali daily in the Jessore town (Jessore district of Bangladesh, 16 February 2012).

34 Interview with Ujjal Ghosh, resident of Bongaon (North 24 Parganas district of West Bengal, 20 September 2011); Interview with Bijon, journalist with a Bengali daily in Jessore town (Jessore district of Bangladesh, 16 February 2012).

35 Interview with Bijon, journalist with a Bengali daily in Jessore town (Jessore district of Bangladesh, 16 February 2012).

36 Interview with Hare Krishna Mondol, resident of Char Meghna (Nadia district of West Bengal, 21 October 2011).

37 Hossain, A. (19 May 2010) Brides Wanted: Across the Fence. *The Telegraph.* [Online] Available from: www.telegraphindia.com/archives/archive.html. [Last accessed: 11 September 2013].

206 *Gendered practices*

38 Interview with Bilal, resident of Basirhat (North 24 Parganas district of West Bengal, 17 January 2012).

39 In the Indian culture and marriage custom, it is considered 'unmanly' and shameful for men to stay with their in-laws after marriage, other than visits of a few days.

40 Interview with Md. Kamal Hussein, resident of a Bangladeshi Enclave in India (Cooch Behar district of West Bengal, 17 March 2012); the lack of employment opportunities in the border areas have been discussed in Chapter 1.

41 Menon, R. and Bhasin, K. (1998) *Borders and Boundaries: Women in India's Partition.* New Delhi: Kali for Women; Butalia, U. (1998) *The Other Side of Silence: Voices from the Partition of India.* New Delhi, London: Penguin; Fraser, B. (2006) *Bengal Partition Stories: An Unclosed Chapter* (trs. Sheila Sen Gupta). London: Anthem.

42 Samaddar, 1999, p. 61.

43 Banerjee and Basu Ray Chaudhury, 2011, p. 31.

44 Reports by *Odhikar* and Human Rights Watch, as well as newspaper reports from both West Bengal and Bangladesh, throw light on incidents of firing by border guards on border crossers, the majority of whom are male crossers.

45 Banerjee and Basu Ray Chaudhury, 2011, p. 35.

46 Staff Reporter. (19 January 2012) Pacharkari ke nogno korey prohar, oshontushto mukhyamantri. *Ananda Bazar Patrika.* [Online] Available from: www.anandabazar.com/ archive/1120119/19mur1.html. [Last accessed: 11 September 2013]; Chowdhury, P. (20 January 2012) Marer chhobi procharey Pak haat-e dekchhe Naya Dilli. *Ananda Bazar Patrika.* [Online] Available from: www.anandabazar.com/archive/1120120/20mur1. html. [Last accessed: 22 July 2013].

47 Hameed, S., Hlatshwayo, S., Tanner, E., Türker, M. and Yang, J. (2010) *Human Trafficking in India: Dynamics, Current Efforts, and Intervention Opportunities for the Asia Foundation.* Stanford: Stanford University Press.

48 Banerjee and Basu Ray Chaudhury, 2011, p. 31.

49 Ibid.

50 Staff Reporter. (1 April 2017) Manush pacharey Pashchim Banga shirshei, tekka ditey parchhe na kono rajya. *Ananda Bazar Patrika.* [Online] Available from: www. anandabazar.com/state/west-bengal-is-in-the-top-position-in-human-trafficking-1.589984?ref=hm-new-stry. [Last accessed: 5 August 2017].

51 Banerjee and Basu Ray Chaudhury, 2011, p. 31.

52 This trend also helps us to understand the nature and flow of certain commodities (women are commoditised in the process of trafficking) across the West Bengal-Bangladesh border, discussed in Chapter 1.

53 *Anti-Trafficking Programs and Promoting Human Rights: A Grassroots Initiative* (2002). Sponsored by Royal Danish Embassy. Jessore: Rights Jessore.

54 According to reports gathered by one of the biggest human rights organisations in Bangladesh, Rights Jessore, about 7,00,000 to 20,00,000 women and children are being trafficked (mainly to India and also to Pakistan and Middle East) every year – a trade involving 10 to 12 billion Bangladesh Taka (BDT). *Anti-Trafficking Programs,* 2002, p. 18.

55 Rai, U. (May 2011) Trafficking Is Big Business along the Indo-Bangladesh Border. *Infochange.* [Online] Available from: http://infochangeindia.org/livelihoods/features/ trafficking-is-big-business-along-the-indo-bangladesh-border.html. [Last accessed: 22 July 2013].

56 *Anti-Trafficking Programs,* 2002, p. 19.

57 Ibid.

58 Interview with Minu Bagdi, resident of Mathurapur village, Hili (South Dinajpur district of West Bengal, 24 January 2012).

59 Interview with Nilufer Rahman (actual name), lawyer in Dinajpur District Court (Dinajpur district of Bangladesh, 7 October 2011).

60 Ibid.

Gendered practices 207

61 Hajra, B. (28 June 2017). Pachar shondehe mardhore mrityu. *Ananda Bazar Patrika.* [Online] Available from: www.anandabazar.com/district/nodia-murshidabbad/mentally-challenged-lady-beaten-to-death-by-public-1.634688?ref=nodia-murshidabbad-new-stry. [Last accessed: 18 July 2017].

62 Haldar, S. (5 February 2017). E to moder jamai go. *Ananda Bazar Patrika.* [Online] Available from: www.anandabazar.com/district/nodia-murshidabbad/fraud-man-arrested-at-hanskhali-1.559252#. [Last accessed: 18 July 2017].

63 Interview with Nilufer Rahman (actual name), lawyer in Dinajpur District Court (Dinajpur district of Bangladesh, 7 October 2011).

64 Ibid.

65 Interview with Advocate Dilwar Hussein (original name), Public Prosecutor in Dinajpur High Court (Dinajpur district of Bangladesh, 7 October 2011).

66 Interview with Binoy Krishna Mullick (original name), General Secretary of Rights Jessore (Jessore district of Bangladesh, 8 February 2012).

67 Interview with Nilufer Rahman (original name), lawyer in Dinajpur District Court (Dinajpur district of Bangladesh, 7 October 2011).

68 *Anti-Trafficking Programs,*2002, p. 22.

69 Ibid.

70 Ibid

71 Interview with Advocate Dilwar Hussein (original name), Public Prosecutor in Dinajpur High Court (Dinajpur district of Bangladesh, 7 October 2011).

72 *Annual Report 2009.* Jessore: Rights Jessore, p. 15.

73 Banerjee and Basu Ray Chaudhury, 2011, p. 33.

74 Banerjee, P., Basu Ray Chaudhury, A. and Bhaduri, A. (2010) *Bengal-Bangladesh Border and Women.* Policies and Practices, No. 36. Kolkata: Mahanirban Calcutta Research Group. p. 20.

75 *Anti-Trafficking Programs,* 2002, p. 18.

76 Ibid.

77 *Project: Linkage, A Situational Analysis on Trafficking and Prostitution in Dinbazaar (Jalpaiguri) and Changrabandha (Cooch Behar).* A Sanlaap Initiative Report, supported by Gana Unnayan Parshad and Human Development Centre. p. 18. Quoted in Banerjee, Basu Ray Chaudhury and Bhaduri, 2010, p. 20.

78 *Anti-Trafficking Programs,* 2002, p. 20.

79 Banerjee, Basu Ray Chaudhury and Bhaduri, 2010, p. 52.

80 Tanya, a girl charged and convicted under the Foreigner's Registration Act 1946, and serving a jail term at a correctional Home for Women in Kolkata, indicated the involvement of border guards – both BSF and BGB – in the process of trafficking. She narrated how the *dalal* (pimp),who frequently took her and her family from Bangladesh to Mumbai (India) to work as domestic helps, used to negotiate with the border guards while crossing the border, to ensure that none of the guards stopped them from doing the same. Banerjee, Basu Ray Chaudhury and Bhaduri, 2010, p. 52.

81 News of abuse of domestic helps of Bangladeshi origin in various cities in India in recent times point towards this inhuman tendency of employers who depend on the illegal migrants from Bangladesh for domestic services despite being aware of their illegal status in India but turn a blind eye or even accuse them of being illegal infiltrators when events of physical/sexual abuse occur.

82 The Ministry of Home Affairs in India has provisions for keeping cases of trafficking of foreign nationals out of the provision of the Foreigner's Act, though the process of having to prove that the movement from Bangladesh to India was involuntary happens to be difficult for trafficked persons. Moreover, the process involves documentary, forensic and material evidence on the part of the trafficked victim to prove her/himself as a victim. Ministry of Home Affairs, Government of India. Available from: http://mha.nic.in/pdfs/AmdmntAdvForeign-030512.pdf.

208 *Gendered practices*

83 Interview with Binoy Krishna Mallick (original name), General Secretary of Rights Jessore (Jessore district of Bangladesh, 8 February 2012).

84 Interview with Nilufer Rahman (original name), lawyer in Dinajpur District Court (Dinajpur district of Bangladesh, 7 October 2011).

85 Interview with Subir Biswas, volunteer in a NGO in Tiyor (South Dinajpur district of West Bengal, 25 January 2012).

86 Interview with Rupali Mahato, resident of Char Meghna (Nadia district of West Bengal, 21 October 2011).

87 Discussed in Chapter 3.

88 Interview with Rupali Mahato, resident of Char Meghna (Nadia district of West Bengal, 21 October 2011).

89 Interview with Nilufer Rahman (original name), lawyer in Dinajpur District Court (Dinajpur district of Bangladesh, 7 October 2011).

90 Interview with Binoy Krishna Mullick (original name), General Secretary of Rights Jessore (Jessore district of Bangladesh, 8 February 2012).

91 Banerjee, Basu Ray Chaudhury and Bhaduri, 2010, p. 50.

92 Interview with Nilufer Rahman (original name), lawyer in Dinajpur District Court (Dinajpur district of Bangladesh, 7 October 2011).

93 Interview with Advocate Dilwar Hussein (original name), Public Prosecutor in Dinajpur High Court (Dinajpur district of Bangladesh, 7 October 2011).

94 Interview with Nilufer Rahman (original name), lawyer in Dinajpur District Court (Dinajpur district of Bangladesh, 7 October 2011).

95 BGB camps are located every five to six kilometres, while there are five to six patrols in duty at the border at any given time. This is a negligible number given the vast stretch of border that Bangladesh shares with India. Discussed in the section 'Border guards' in the Introduction.

96 The police stations have anything between 20 to 30 police officers, including constables and Officers-in-Charge, for about 20,00,000 people, which is the approximate number of people that each police station serves. Interview with Advocate Dilwar Hussein (original name), Public Prosecutor in Dinajpur High Court (Dinajpur district of Bangladesh, 7 October 2011).

97 Ibid.

98 The BSF has built a ring road along its borders with Bangladesh and uses advanced technologies for surveillance. There are BSF camps every two kilometres along the border road and at least ten to twelve constables on duty at any given time.

99 Interview with Advocate Dilwar Hussein (original name), Public Prosecutor in Dinajpur High Court (Dinajpur district of Bangladesh, 7 October 2011).

100 Discussed in the Introduction.

101 Interview with Hare Krishna Mondol, resident of Char Meghna (Nadia district of West Bengal, 21 October 2011).

102 Interview with Md. Rashid Haq, farmer and resident of Ramnagar village (Murshidabad district of West Bengal, 9 November 2011).

103 Interview with Jasimuddin Mondol, resident of Mathurapur (Nadia district of West Bengal, 22 October 2011).

104 Interview with Kuddus Rahman, resident of Jaykrishna village, Jalangi (Murshidabad district of West Bengal, 22 October 2011).

105 Interview with Animesh, resident of Bindol (North Dinajpur district of West Bengal, 26 January 2012).

106 Interview with a BSF official in BRC-pur BSF camp (Nadia district of West Bengal, 22 October 2011).

107 Ibid.

108 'মহিলা-রা যায় না, ওরা তো আর ওদিকে কাজ করে না, তাই যাওয়ার দরকার পড়ে না. আমরা চেষ্টা করি ওদের সিকিওর ফিল করানোর।' Interview with a BSF official in BRC-pur BSF camp (Nadia district of West Bengal, 22 October 2011).

Gendered practices 209

109 Interview with Dhiman Biswas and Prasanta Mondol, residents of Mathurapur and Char Meghna, respectively (Nadia district of West Bengal, 22 October 2011 and 21 October 2011).

110 Interview with Banchharam Mondol, ex-*Pradhan* of Mathurapur village *Panchayat* (Nadia district of West Bengal, 22 October 2011).

111 Interview with Sabitri Mahato, resident of Char Meghna (Nadia district of West Bengal, 21 October 2011).

112 'আমি মেয়ে বলে ওদিকে যেতে দেয় না. ছেলেদের যেতে দেয়।' Interview with Sabitri Mahato, resident of Char Meghna (Nadia district of West Bengal, 21 October 2011).

113 A *bigha* is standardised at 1,600 square yards or 0.3306 acres, which is often interpreted as being 1/3 acre.

114 'আমাদের এখানে মেয়েরা পুরুষ দের মতই খাটে. না খাটলে খাবে কি?' Interview with Sabitri Mahato, resident of Char Meghna (Nadia district of West Bengal, 21 October 2011).

115 Interview with a BSF official at Asharidoho BSF camp (Murshidabad district of West Bengal, 9 November 2011); younger members of the family or women members taking lunch for the farm workers is a very common and widespread rural practice in agrarian communities in rural South Asia.

116 Interview with Sabitri Mahato, resident of Char Meghna (Nadia district of West Bengal, 21 October 2011).

117 Ibid.

118 Interview with Banchharam Mondol, resident of Mathurapur (Nadia district of West Bengal, 22 October 2011).

119 Interview with Imtiaz Mondol, resident of Mathurapur (Nadia district of West Bengal, 22 October 2011).

120 Interview with Hirak Kanti Munshi, resident of Mathurapur (South Dinajpur district of West Bengal, 24 January 2012).

121 Interview with Dayamay Dutta, resident of Teipur (Nadia district of West Bengal, 24 October 2011).

122 Interview with Kuddus Rahman, resident of Jalangi (Murshidabad district of West Bengal, 22 October 2011).

123 More than 35 cases of violence by the BSF in the form of firing or brutal attacks have been reported in a single Bengali daily, *Ananda Bazar Patrika*, between October 2009 and February 2013. Other newspapers carry reports as well but *Ananda Bazar Patrika*, as the leading Bengali daily, has been chosen to highlight the frequency of such incidents. Reports of *Odhikar* and the Human Rights Watch also highlight the situation of violence perpetrated by the border guards along the West Bengal-Bangladesh border.

124 BSF recorded 32 casualties in 2010 alone. Tiwary, D. (1 December 2012) Legalize Cattle Smuggling on Bangladesh Border: BSF Chief. *The Times of India*. [Online] Available from: http://articles.timesofindia.indiatimes.com/2012-12-01/india/35530471_1_bsf-men-bangladesh-border-indo-bangla-border. [Last accessed: 23 July 2013]. An idea about the actual numbers might be guessed from the reports of human rights organisations.

125 Interview with Hare Krishna Mondol, resident of Char Meghna (Nadia district of West Bengal, 21 October 2011).

126 Staff Reporter. (19 February 2017). Mardhore abhijukto BSF jawan. *Ananda Bazar Patrika*. [Online] Available from: www.anandabazar.com/district/dhaksinbanga/north-south-24-paraganas/bsf-jawaan-being-accused-of-beating-a-man-1.566736. [Last accessed: 18 July 2017].

127 Roy, H. (2012). *Partitioned Lives: Migrants, Refugees, Citizens in India and Pakistan, 1947–1965*. New Delhi: Oxford University Press. p. 69.

128 Staff Reporter. (23 February 2017) Grambashi-BSF sangharsha Tufangunj-e, gulibidhho ek jubak. *Ananda Bazar Patrika*. [Online] Available from: www.anandabazar.com/district/uttarbanga/clash-between-villagers-and-bsf-in-tufanganj-1.568819#. [Last accessed: 18 July 2017]; Staff Reporter. (28 March 2017) BSF-Grambashi

210 *Gendered practices*

sangharshe jakham shaat. *Ananda Bazar Patrika*. [Online] Available from: www. anandabazar.com/district/uttarbanga/7-injured-in-clashes-between-villagers-and-bsf-in-jalpaiguri-1.587598?ref=uttarbanga-new-stry. [Last accessed: 18 July 2017].

129 'আগে তো কুত্তা মনে করত সাধারণ লোককে. এখন সেটা একটু কম।' (Earlier they used to treat us like dogs. Now the tendencies to do so have decreased a bit.) Interview with Ranjit, resident of Jamalpur village (South Dinajpur district of West Bengal, 24 January 2012).

130 Interview with Md. Rashid Haq, resident of Ramnagar (Murshidabad district of West Bengal, 9 November 2011).

131 Interview with Nikhil Bagdi, resident of Mathurapur (South Dinajpur district of West Bengal, 24 January 2012).

132 (7 August 2012). India: Threatened with Violence for Reporting Torture to Police. *Asian Human Rights Commission*. Available from: www.humanrights.asia/news/urgent-appeals/AHRC-UAU-026-2012. [Last accessed: 17 September 2013].

133 Interview with Subodh Majumdar, resident of Bongaon (North 24 Parganas, 20 September 2011).

134 Staff Reporter. (25 March 2010) BSF camp e Bangladeshi r deho. *Ananda Bazar Patrika*. [Online] Available from: www.anandabazar.com/archive/1100325/25uttar5. htm. [Last accessed: 17 September 2013].

135 Interview with Rashid Haq, resident of Ramnagar (Murshidabad district of West Bengal, 9 November 2011).

136 Interviewwith Bibek, resident of Debhata (Satkhira district of Bangladesh, 12 February 2012).

137 Ibid.

138 Interview with Gourab Sarkar, resident of Hili (South Dinajpur district of West Bengal, 25 January 2012).

139 Discussed in Chapter 1.

140 Interview with Bibek, resident of Debhata (Satkhira district of Bangladesh, 12 February 2012).

141 Ibid.

142 Interview with Asha, resident at Chaugachha (Jessore district of Bangladesh, 16 February 2012).

143 Interview with Pranabesh, resident of Ramnagar (Murshidabad district of West Bengal, 9 November 2011).

144 Interview with Jahan, resident of Koya village, Jivannagar (Chuadanga district of Bangladesh, 11 February 2012).

145 (2011) Teenage girl, Felani, killed by the BSF firing at Anantapur border under Kurigram district. *Fact-finding report*. Dhaka: Odhikar; The trial of the convicted BSF official in the Felani Khatun case had been conducted on 20 August 2013 by the General Security Court of Sonari Camp of the BSF Cooch Behar Sector, as per the promise made by the Indian government to Bangladesh regarding justice for the Felani case. Staff Reporter. (21 August 2013) Felani hotyar bichar shuru BSF camp'e. *Ananda Bazar Patrika*. [Online] Available from: www.anandabazar.com/archive/1130821/21uttar3.html. [Last accessed: 30 August 2013].

146 Interview with Nikhil Bagdi, a resident of Mathurapur village (South Dinajpur district of West Bengal, 24 January 2012).

147 A *lathi* is a hard wooden stick used by the border guards to ward off infiltrators, smugglers and any person that they might be suspicious of.

148 'গার্ড দের মার খায়ে, বাড়ি খায়ে।' (The guards often use *lathis* to control the women.) Interview with a BGB official at Hili BGB camp (Dinajpur district of Bangladesh, 8 October 2011).

149 Ibid.

150 Interview with Ratan, resident of Debhata village (Satkhira district of Bangladesh, 12 February 2012).

151 Ibid.

Gendered practices 211

152 Ibid.; Staff Reporter. (8 March 2003) Migrant Rape Charge on Border Troops. *The Telegraph*. [Online] Available from: www.telegraphindia.com/archives/archive.html. [Last accessed: 11 September 2013].

153 PTI. (19 January 2012) B'desh Demands Immediate Action against BSF Personnel. *IBN Live*. [Online] Available from: http://ibnlive.in.com/generalnewsfeed/news/bdesh-demands-immediate-action-against-sf-personnel/952929.html. [Last accessed: 23 July 2013].

154 BSF Act and Rules. (March 2004) Available from: http://bsf.nic.in/doc/bsfActRules.pdf. p. 156.

155 Islam, M.S. (8 September 2013) Felani Verdict a Big Disappointment. *The Financial Express*. [Online] Available from: www.thefinancialexpress-bd.com/index.php?ref=Mj BfMDlfMDhfMTNfMV85Ml8xODI1OTg=. [Last accessed: 11 September 2013]; Staff Reporter. (7 January 2016) Felani Killing: Justice Denied, Border Killings Continue. *The Daily Star*. [Online] Available from: www.thedailystar.net/country/felani-killing-justice-denied-border-killings-continue-198391. [Last Accessed: 5 August 2017].

156 Staff Reporter, 7 January 2016, *The Daily Star*.

157 Interview with Amol, resident of Kodalkati (Murshidabad district of West Bengal, 11 November 2011).

158 Interview with Minu Bagdi, resident of Mathurapur village (South Dinajpur district of West Bengal, 24 January 2012).

159 Interview with Hirak Kanti Munshi, secretary of the local committee of a political party in Balurghat (South Dinajpur district of West Bengal, 24 January 2012).

160 Interview with Minu Bagdi, resident of Mathurapur village (South Dinajpur district of West Bengal, 24 January 2012).

161 'বি এস এফ অনেক সময় মহিলাদের দিকে খারাপ ভাবে তাকায়ে. কিন্তু আমরা সাধারণ মানুষ আর কি বলব? মার খেয়ে যাব হয়ত।' (The BSF often eye the women in a degrading manner. But as common people, what can we do? Probably we will be beaten if we try to protest.) Interview with Nikhil Bagdi, resident of Mathurapur village (South Dinajpur district of West Bengal, 24 January 2012).

162 Interview with Parbati Mohanto, resident of Ghunapara-Dhumron village (South Dinajpur district of West Bengal, 25 January 2012).

163 Interview with Gourab Sarkar, resident of Hili border (South Dinajpur district of West Bengal, 25 January 2012).

164 Discussed at length in Chapter 1; interview with Parbati Mohanto, resident of Ghunapara-Dhumron village (South Dinajpur district of West Bengal, 25 January 2012); Van Schendel, 2005, p. 372.

165 Interview with Parbati Mohanto, resident of Ghunapara-Dhumron village (South Dinajpur district of West Bengal, 25 January 2012); discussed in Chapter 1.

166 Banerjee, Basu Ray Chaudhury and Bhaduri, 2010, p. 51.

167 'আমাদের সাথে কথা বলার চেষ্টা করেনা. মেম্বার প্রধান ছাড়া আমাদের সাথে কথা বলেনা।' (The BSF do not talk to us. They only talk to the members or *Pradhans*.) Interview with Md. Rashidul Haq, resident of Lalgola (Murshidabad district of West Bengal, 9 November 2011).

168 'আমি যখন মেম্বার ছিলাম, তখন কোনো সমস্যা হলে বি এস এফ এর বড় কর্তা-দের সাথে আলোচনা করতাম. কোনটার সমাধান হত, কোনটা হত না. মেম্বার দের কথা তাও শোনে বি এস এফ-রা।' (When I was a member of the *Panchayat*, I would talk to the senior officers of the BSF in case of any problem. Some of the problems would be solved, some not. The BSF still pays heed to members but not general civilians.) Interview with Banchharam Mondol, ex-*Pradhan* of *Panchayat* at Mathurapur village (Nadia district of West Bengal, 22 October 2011).

169 Interview with the Company Commander of BRC-pur BSF camp (Nadia district of West Bengal, 22 October 2011).

170 'তারা তখন প্রধান দের কাছে আসে. আমরা হয়ত ওদের নিয়ে ক্যাম্প এ গেলাম, তখন হয়ত সেন্ট্রি বলল সাহেব এখন খেয়ে দেয়ে ঘুমাচ্ছে, বিকেলে ফেরত যেতে. বিকেলে ফেরত গিয়ে দেখলাম সাহেব হয়ত বেরিয়ে গেছেন. এভাবে আমাদের বার বার যাওয়া সমস্যা, কাজটাও পিছিয়ে যায়।' (The common people come to the *Pradhans* with their problems. We take them to the BSF camp. It often happens that the sentry tells us that

212 *Gendered practices*

the Commander is resting at the moment and asks us to go back in the evening. When we go back to the camp in the evening, we see that the Commander is out on some work. We have to go back another day. This way, the work gets delayed.) Interview with Nirendranath Burman, deputy-*Pradhan* of Kalmati village *Panchayat* (Cooch Behar district of West Bengal, 16 March 2012).

171 Interview with Nirendranath Burman, Deputy-*Pradhan* of Kalmati village *Panchayat*, Dinhata (Cooch Behar district of West Bengal, 16 March 2012).

172 Interview with Sabitri Mahato, resident of Char Meghna (Nadia district of West Bengal, 21 October 2011).

173 'যা, তোর বাপ কে বল।' Interview with Balaram Mahato, resident of Char Meghna (Nadia district of West Bengal, 21 October 2011).

174 'তোর বাবার রাস্তা?' Interview with Pranabesh, resident of Ramnagar (Murshidabad district of West Bengal, 9 November 2011).

175 Ibid.

176 Ibid.; for issues like hassles over fence crossing or use of the border road, the negotiation between the civilian and the border guards does not need to be reported to the local police stations. But in case of the arrest or apprehension of a border crosser, i.e. in cases where the seized goods need to be reported and auctioned or where arrested persons need to be imprisoned and tried, the matter needs to be reported to the police. The border guards do not possess legal power to imprison a person, though this lack is often misused by them through physical abuse and violence.

177 'বি এস এফ-রা জানে বর্ডার কি করে হ্যান্ডেল করে।' Interview with Biplab Ganguly (original name), Officer-in-Charge of Murutia Police Station (Nadia district of West Bengal, 22 October 2011).

178 West Bengal Police is one of the two police forces of West Bengal, the other being Kolkata Police (whose jurisdiction is specifically the metropolitan city of Kolkata). The Director General of Police heads the West Bengal police and reports to the Home (Police) Department of the Government of India. The jurisdiction of the West Bengal Police includes the eighteen revenue districts of the state (excluding the metropolitan city of Kolkata), as per the Police Act of 1861.The border districts of West Bengal are covered by the two zones of the West Bengal Police – the North Bengal Zone (consisting of Jalpaiguri, Darjeeling, Cooch Behar, North Dinajpur, South Dinajpur and Malda) and the South Bengal Zone (consisting of Nadia, Murshidabad, North 24 Parganas and South 24 Parganas). The police stations are responsible for the prevention and detection of crime, maintenance of public order, enforcing law, making security arrangements for government functionaries, legislative bodies, local self-government and public figures.

179 Banerjee, P. (2010) *Borders, Histories, Existences: Gender and Beyond*. New Delhi: Sage; Banerjee, P. and Basu Ray Chaudhury, A. (Eds.). (2011) *Women in Indian Borderlands*. New Delhi: Sage; Mayer, T. (Ed.). (2000) *Gender Ironies of Nationalism: Sexing the Nation*. New York: Routledge; Jerome, R. (Ed.). (2001) *Conceptions of Postwar German Masculinity*. Albany: State University of New York Press; Nandy, A. (1983) *The Intimate Enemy: Loss and Recovery of Self under Colonialism*. New Delhi: Oxford University Press; Kaplan, C., Alarcon, N. and Moallem, M. (Eds.). (1999) *Between Woman and Nation: Nationalisms, Transnational Feminisms, and the State*. Durham, NC: Duke University Press; Reeser, T.W. (2010) *Masculinities in Theory: An Introduction*. Malden, MA: Wiley-Blackwell.

180 Some of the poems composed by border guards also point towards a patriarchal aspect through the projection of the BSF as the chief protector of the borders and the all-in-all figures with regard to the service of the nation. A poem named 'Seema Suraksha Bal Mein "G" Duty' (Duty of G in BSF) by P.C. Patnayak, Field G Team, BSF, Area Headquarters, Jalpaiguri, is an example. *Uttar Vang Prahari Samachar Patrika*. (December 2012). 4(14).

Gendered practices 213

181 Interview with Bijon, journalist with a Bengali daily in Jessore town (Jessore district of Bangladesh, 16 February 2012); Discussed in Chapter 1.

182 'মহিলা বা পুরুষ না হওয়াটাই সুবিধার. হিজরা হওয়ার কারণে বি এস এফ/বি জি বি ছেড়ে দেয়।' (Not belonging to either of the sexes helps. The BSF and BGB spare us because we are *hijras*.) Interview with Sheena Akhtar, *hijra* and resident of Hili (Dinajpur district of Bangladesh, 8 October 2011).

183 Ibid.

184 Ibid.

185 'হিজরা হওয়ার কারণে বি এস এফ/বি জি বি ছেড়ে দেয়. মানবিক কারণে. বলে, "ফ্যামিলি দেখে না, খাবে কি?"' (The BSF and BGB spares us because we are *hijras*. They spare us on humanitarian grounds, saying "their family does not look after them, how will they survive?" ') Interview with Rajib, *hijra* and resident of Hili (Dinajpur district of Bangladesh, 8 October 2011).

186 Interview with Rajib, *hijra* and resident of Hili (Dinajpur district of Bangladesh, 8 October 2011).

187 'আমরা হিজরেদের সাধারণত ধরি না. ভালো দেখায়ে না. তাছাড়া ওদের তো কেউ দেখার নেই. এটা বন্ধ করলে খাবে কি?' Interview with a BGB official at Hili checkpost (Dinajpur district of Bangladesh, 8 October 2011).

188 'এরকম হয় যে ছেলেরা অপারেশন করিয়ে হিজরা হয়, বা হিজরা সাজে যাতে গার্ড-রা না ধরে।' (Often men undergo operation to become *hijras*, or dress-up as *hijras* to escape the border guards.) Interview with Bijon, journalist with a Bengali daily in Jessore town (Jessore district of Bangladesh, 16 February 2012).

189 Benapole Correspondent. (1 August 2016). First Female Members of Border Guards Bangladesh Report to Work. *Bdnews24.com*. [Online] Available from: http://bdnews24.com/bangladesh/2016/08/01/first-female-members-of-border-guard-bangladesh-report-to-work. [Last accessed: 6 August 2017].

190 Staff Reporter. (30 November 2009) *The Telegraph*. [Online] Available from: www.telegraphindia.com/1091130/jsp/bengal/story_11802257.html. [Last accessed: 11 September 2013]; Banerjee, Basu Ray Chaudhury and Bhaduri, 2010, p. 47.

191 IANS. (November 2012) BSF Women Closer to Creating History. *Deccan Herald*. [Online] Available from: www.deccanherald.com/content/15920/bsf-women-closer-creating-history.html. [Last accessed: 24 July 2013].

192 Staff Reporter. (26 March 2017). BSF Gets First Woman Combat Officer after 51 Years. *Hindustan Times*. [Online] Available from: www.hindustantimes.com/india-news/bsf-gets-first-woman-field-officer/story-L9seWIYMqv4rt5wR9CMvJP.html. [Last accessed: 6 August 2017].

193 PTI. (8 July 2013) Women Officers to Be Inducted for First Time in BSF. *Zeenews.com*. [Online] Available from: http://zeenews.india.com/news/nation/women-officers-to-be-inducted-for-first-time-in-bsf_860549.html. [Last accessed: 24 July 2013].

194 Interview with a BSF official at Shikarpur BSF camp (Nadia district of West Bengal, 21 October 2011).

195 Interview with Ganga Ghosh and Bimala Haldar, BSF guards at Lalgola (Murshidabad district of West Bengal, 11 November 2011).

196 Ibid.

197 Interview with Riazul Mondol, resident of Balurghat (South Dinajpur district of West Bengal, 24 January 2012).

198 Interview with a local resident at Char Meghna (Nadia district of West Bengal, 20 July 2016).

199 PTI. (22 May 2011) BSF to Use 'Non-Lethal' Weapons Along Indo-Bangla Border. *Zeenews.com*. [Online] Available from: http://zeenews.india.com/news/delhi/bsf-to-use-non-lethal-weapons-along-indo-bangla-border_707946.html. [Last accessed: 24 July 2013].

200 Ibid.

201 Ibid.

214 *Gendered practices*

202 'আগে এরা বি এস এফ-কে বেশি ভয় পেত. এখন কম।' Interview with a BSF official at Shikarpur (Nadia district of West Bengal, 21 October 2011).

203 'এমনকি বাংলাদেশীরা বি এস এফ কে মেরেছে, তাও বি এস এফ গুলি করেনি।' (Even the Bangladeshi miscreants have attacked the BSF and the BSF has not retaliated back.) Interview with Apurba Kumar Biswas, resident of Petrapole border area, Bongaon (North 24 Parganas district of West Bengal, 20 September 2011).

204 Tiwary, 1 December 2012, *The Times of India*.

205 Interview with Rupali Mahato, resident of Char Meghna (Nadia district of West Bengal, 21 October 2011).

206 Tiwary, 1 December 2012, *The Times of India*.

207 Interview with Kuddus Rahman, resident of Jaykrishnapur village, Jalangi (Murshidabad district of West Bengal, 22 October 2011).

208 Staff Reporter. (29 October 2009) BSF r poshake dakati shimanter gram e. *Ananda Bazar Patrika*. [Online] Available from: www.anandabazar.com/archive/1091029/29south7. htm. [Last accessed: 17 September 2013].

209 Pakistan Rangers is part of the Paramilitary Forces of Pakistan and is under the direct control of the Ministry of the Interior of the Pakistan Government. One of their main duties is to maintain law and order on Pakistan borders, apart from maintaining security in war zones and assisting the police.

210 Staff Reporter. (13 March 2011) Wagah r kuchkawaj ebar Petrapole eo. *Ananda Bazar Patrika*. [Online] Available from: www.anandabazar.com/archive/1110313/13desh3. htm. [Last accessed: 17 September 2013].

211 Interview with a BSF constable at Dahakhola BOP (Nadia district of West Bengal, 20 July 2016).

212 Interview with Subodh Majumdar, resident of Petrapole, Bongaon (North 24 Parganas district of West Bengal, 20 September 2011).

213 Ibid.

214 Interview with Parbati Mahato, resident of Ghunapara-Dhumron village (South Dinajpur district of West Bengal, 25 January 2012).

215 Interview with Balaram Mahato, resident of Char Meghna (Nadia district of West Bengal, 21 October 2011).

216 Interview with Gourab Sarkar, resident of Hili (South Dinajpur district of West Bengal, 25 January 2012). Also, interview with Minu Bagdi, resident of Mathurapur (South Dinajpur district of West Bengal, 24 January 2012).

217 Interview with Md. Ismail, resident of Matila village (Jhenaidah district of Bangladesh, 11 February 2012).

218 'বি জি বি ধরলে মারে৷ কত সহ্য করবে?' (Sometimes the BGB beats up the smugglers. How much more would they tolerate?) Interview with Jumaira, resident of Hili (Dinajpur district of Bangladesh, 9 October 2011).

219 Though Hindi is the national language of India, it is not the common language for the entire state's population. Every province in India has its own local language, subclassified into hundreds of more localised dialects. For West Bengal, the most common language (and of the official ones) is *Bangla*, with its many dialects across various parts of West Bengal. In this matter, West Bengal shares the same language with Bangladesh, where *Bangla* is the official language of the whole state and is the one common language that almost the entire population speaks, though with local variations in dialects.

220 Interview with Rashid Hussein, resident of Lalgola (Murshidabad district of West Bengal, 8 November 2011).

221 Interview with Apurba Kumar Biswas, resident of Petrapole, Bongaon (North 24 Parganas district of West Bengal, 20 September 2011).

222 'বাঙালি বি এস এফ-রা বাংলা বলে না।' (The *Bangla*-speaking BSF do not use Bangla.) Interview with Balaram Mahato, resident of Char Meghna (Nadia district of West Bengal, 21 October 2011).

Gendered practices 215

223 'বাঙালি বি এস এফ-রা বাংলা বলতে চায় না, হিন্দী বলে, পাছে আবার কেউ হেল্প চায়ে।' (The *Bangla*-speaking BSF do not use Bangla. They use Hindi, to prevent any local from asking for help from them.) Interview with Nirendranath Burman, resident of Dinhata (Cooch Behar district of West Bengal, 16 March 2012).

224 'বাঙালি বি এস এফ-রা আমাদের সাথে বাংলায়ে কথা বলে না. হিন্দী বলে. কিন্তু দু নম্বরী কাজ করার সময় দরকারে ঠিকই বাংলা বলে।' (The *Bangla*-speaking BSFs do not speak to us in *Bangla*. They use Hindi. But when it comes to their involvement in any illegal activity, they do revert to *Bangla* if the situation demands so.) Interview with Hirak Kanti Munshi, resident of Balurghat (South Dinajpur district of West Bengal, 24 January 2012).

225 Banerjee, Basu Ray Chaudhury and Bhaduri, 2010, p. 43.

226 The poem named 'Nari Shakti' composed by Arun Kumar, Commander, South Bengal Frontier, is an example. *Bagher Garjan*. (October–December 2012). 26.

227 *Uttar Vang Prahari Samachar Patrika*. (July–December 2013).

228 Interview with Narendranath Ghosh, resident of Karimpur (Nadia district of West Bengal, 24 October 2011).

229 Interview with Rashid Hossein, resident of Lalgola (Murshidabad district of West Bengal, 8 November 2011).

230 Interview with a BSF official at Shikarpur BSF camp (Nadia district of West Bengal, 21 October 2011).

231 'একজন বাঙালি আরেকজন বাঙালির সাথে কেন খারাপ ব্যবহার করবে?' (Why would a Bengali behave badly with another Bengali?) Interview with Lata, resident of Nepar Mor village, Maheshpur (Jhenaidah district of Bangladesh, 11 February 2012).

232 'পাবলিক বরং বি জি বি কে বন্ধু মনে করতে পারে, বি এস এফ কে শত্রু ভাববে।' Interview with Nirendranath Burman, resident of Kalmati village, Dinhata (Cooch Behar district of West Bengal, 16 March 2012).

233 Interview with a BSF official at Asharidoho BSF camp, Lalgola (Murshidabad district of West Bengal, 9 November 2011).

234 The A.D.G. of the BSF Eastern Command, Bansidhar Sharma, pointed towards the miscommunication over language as a reason for the failure of the BSF to successfully curb cross-border smuggling practices. Parya, S. (10 August 2013) BSF Commanders and Constables to Be Given Bangla Lessons for Improving Public Relation. *Bartaman*. [Online] Available from: http://bartamanpatrika.com/archive/2013/august/100813/content/sb.htm. [Last accessed: 30 August 2013].

235 Staff Reporter. (25 March 2013) Daulatpurey tarunder proshikhshan BSFer. *Ananda Bazar Patrika*. [Online] Available from: www.anandabazar.com/25mur2.html. [Last accessed: 17 September 2013].

236 Islam regards alcohol as the root of several social problems and misery, including crime, mental illness, despicable behaviour, broken homes, etc. and, thus, prohibits its consumption.

237 Interview with a BGB official at New Sripur BGB camp, Debhata border (Satkhira district of Bangladesh, 12 February 2012).

238 Bangladesh is a Muslim-majority state.

239 Interview with Rashid Hossein, resident at Lalgola (Murshidabad district of West Bengal, 8 November 2011).

240 'বি এস এফ যেহেতু চীন বা পাকিস্তান বর্ডার এ বেশি বীরত্ব দেখাতে পারেনা, ওদের যত বীরত্ব বাংলাদেশ বর্ডার এ. ইন্ডিয়া কোনদিন নিজের বর্ডার পলিসি পাল্টাবে না কারণ ওটা ইন্ডিয়ার একটা ভালো দর কষাকষির জায়গা. বাংলাদেশের ৩ দিকেই তো ইন্ডিয়া বর্ডার।' (Just because BSF cannot exercise its power along the Pakistan or China border, it expresses all its prowess along the Bangladesh border. India will never change its border policy with Bangladesh since it is a good negotiation table for India. Bangladesh shares a border with India on its three sides.) Interview with Bijon, journalist with a Bengali daily in Jessore town (Jessore district of Bangladesh, 16 February 2012).

241 Interview with a BGB officer at New Sripur BGB camp, Debhata border (Satkhira district of Bangladesh, 12 February 2012); even the BGB face the same routine of

216   Gendered practices

staying away from their family during their postings in the border areas. But the sheer length of the border areas in India and the comparatively weak manpower of the BSF force the BSF border guards to undergo longer phases of posting and separation from their families. Distances between the outposts and their home villages/cities also mean that the BSF border guards take longer time to travel between the two (unlike Bangladesh, where the distance and the travel time between the two are often not much, given the size of the state). This prevents the higher officials of the BSF from accepting leave requests from the BSF.

242 A number of de-addiction sessions, yoga sessions and seminars are being held in order to help the border guards get rid of such addictions. *Uttar Vang Prahari Samachar Patrika*. (March 2013). 5(15).

243 A poem by Rakesh Kumar Sharma of 48 Battalion BSF named 'Sharab samaj ko kar rahi kharab' (Alcohol Wearing Out The Society) speaks about how alcohol consumption becomes an obstacle in the path of 'serving the nation' and how it has ruined lives of the guards. *Uttar Vang Prahari Samachar Patrika*. (December 2012). 4(14). Available from: http://nb.bsf.gov.in/magazine/magazine_dec2012.pdf.

244 Commander Rahul Vatsayan of 93 Battalion, BSF, speaks about 'Jawano mein badti atmahatiya ki prabriti' (Increasing suicidal tendencies among the Jawans) in *Uttar Vang Prahari*(March 2013), where he quotes Rashtrakavi Ramdhari Singh Dinkar's poem on soldiers serving the nation, in order to inspire the BSF border guards to see the brighter side and the bravery associated with 'serving the nation', 'shedding blood for the nation' and 'protecting the nation's people'. He also cites issues such as separation from family and long duty hours as reasons for the alarming rate of suicides among BSF *jawans*.

245 Staff Reporter. (28 February 2010) BSF jawan atmaghati Bongaon-e. *Ananda Bazar Patrika*. [Online] Available from: www.anandabazar.com/archive/1100228/28south5.htm. [Last accessed: 17 September 2013].

246 The paramilitary border force of Bangladesh, since its inception in 1971, was known as the Bangladesh Rifles (BDR). BDR has nearly 67,000 soldiers stationed across the country. After Bangladesh gained independence from Pakistan in 1971, the East Pakistan Rifles was renamed as Bangladesh Rifles. The BDR is under the Home Ministry, but the army plays a major role in staffing, training and directing the force. In Bangladesh, BDR has been considered as a nationalistic force because it had revolted against the Pakistani army during the Liberation War. But it is also a fact that BDR soldiers carried out rebellions in 1972 and 1991. But due to limitation of BDR laws, those responsible for the mutinies could not be punished and thus those incidents failed to discourage BDR members from carrying out future revolts. On 25 February 2009, the BDR faced yet another mutiny during the celebration of the annual BDR week in its headquarters in Pilkhana, Dhaka. The mutiny broke out following a clash between a BDR officer and an army officer, catalysed by complaints of the BDR against the BDR chief. The central armoury of the BDR headquarters was looted. Many army officers, the BDR chief and few civilians were killed in the mutiny. The mutiny spread to other BDR posts around the country. The mutiny was eventually controlled by the army. The mutineers were tried in fast track courts. There has been a major overhaul in the organisation of the BDR, including a renaming. The BDR henceforth came to be called Border Guards Bangladesh. Restrictions on the access to and use of weapons by the BGB have also been imposed. Kumar, A. (2009) The BDR Mutiny: Mystery Remains but Democracy Emerges Stronger. *Journal of Defence Studies*. 3(4). pp. 103–117.

247 'বি জি বি-র কু-এর পর একটু উইক হয়ে গেছে. ছোট বাচ্চাদের মত. সবার দোয়ায়ে থাকে যেন. এখন আসতে আসতে উঠে দাঁড়াচ্ছে।' Interview with a BGB official at Goga camp, Sharsha (Jessore district of Bangladesh, 15 February 2012).

248 Ibid.

249 Ibid.

250 Interview with a BSF official at Shikarpur BSF camp (Nadia district of West Bengal, 21 October 2011).
251 Interview with Nikhil Bagdi and Hirak Kanti Munshi, residents of Mathurapur and Dinhata (South Dinajpur district and Cooch Behar district of West Bengal, 24 January and 16 March 2012, respectively).
252 *Uttar Vang Prahari Samachar Patrika*. (July–December 2013).
253 *Bagher Garjan*. (October–December 2012). 26.
254 Ghosh, S. (13 October 2009) Shaktipujoye mela mukhor Changrabandha. *Ananda Bazar Patrika*. [Online] Available from: www.anandabazar.com/archive/1091013/13uttar3. htm. [Last accessed 17 September 2013]; Basak, B. (25 October 2009) Chhatpuja upalakshe Mahananda nadir dhare upche pora bhir. *Ananda Bazar Patrika*. [Online] Available from: www.anandabazar.com/archive/1091025/uttarbanga.htm. [Last accessed: 17 September 2013].
255 Biswas, G. (4 January 2013) Shesh bikeley footballey muchhlo shimanter kanta. *Ananda Bazar Patrika*. [Online] Available from: www.anandabazar.com/4mur4.html. [Last accessed: 17 September 2013]; *Uttar Vang Prahari Samachar Patrika*. (March 2013). 5(15).
256 *Bagher Garjan*. (January–March 2016).
257 *Bagher Garjan*. (April–June 2016).
258 The original poem in Hindi is named *Safarnama* (The Journey), and is composed by Rajeev Vatsaraj, 2nd-in Command, 194B Battalion, BSF. *Uttar Vang Prahari Samachar Patrika*. (March 2012). 4(11). Available from: http://nb.bsf.gov.in/magazine/Mar_2012.pdf.
259 Interview with a BSF official in Shikarpur BSF camp (Nadia district of West Bengal, 21 October 2011).
260 Interview with a BSF official in Ashridoho BSF camp (Murshidabad district of West Bengal, 8 November 2011).
261 Interview with Riazul Mondol, resident of Balurghat (South Dinajpur district of West Bengal, 24 January 2012).
262 *Uttar Vang Prahari Samachar Patrika*. (March 2012). 4(11).
263 Interview with a BSF official in BRC-pur camp (Nadia district of West Bengal, 22 October 2011).
264 Staff Reporter. (14 April 2010) Mela batil. *Ananda Bazar Patrika*. [Online] Available from: www.anandabazar.com/archive/1100414/14uttar10.htm. [Last accessed: 17 September 2013].
265 Staff Reporter. (15 April 2010) Milan Melai bhir. *Ananda Bazar Patrika*. [Online] Available from: www.anandabazar.com/archive/1100415/15sil7.htm. [Last accessed: 17 September 2013].
266 The word used for surveillance in this context is *shak*, a Hindi term that means suspicion. *Bagher Garjan* (October–December 2012). 26.
267 'অষ্টমীর দিন জল ছত্র করেছিল. সেখানে লেখা ছিল 'পরিচয় পত্র নিয়ে ঘুরবেন।' (The BSF had arranged for drinking water kiosks during *Durga Puja*. They had it written there: 'please carry your identity proofs with you'.) Interview with Gourab Sarkar, resident of Hili (South Dinajpur district of West Bengal, 25 January 2012).
268 Staff Reporter. (24 June 2017) Eid-e dekha hobe na? Udbege dui Bangla. *Ananda Bazar Patrika*. [Online] Available from: www.anandabazar.com/district/nodia-murshidabbad/two-bengal-is-worried-over-meeting-in-this-eid-1.633010?ref=nodia-murshidabbad-new-stry. [Last accessed: 17 July 2017].
269 Staff Reporter. (22 February 2017) Bhashar abeg muchhe dilo katatarer bera. *Ananda Bazar Patrika*. [Online] Available from: www.anandabazar.com/district/uttarbanga/everyemotion-removed-in-international-mother-language-day-1.568339. [Last accessed: 17 July 2017]; Bhattacharya, A. and Maitra, S. (22 February 2017). Ekusher manch-e miloner sur dui Banglar manusher.*Ananda Bazar Patrika*. [Online] Available from:

218 *Gendered practices*

www.anandabazar.com/district/dhaksinbanga/north-south-24-paraganas/india-ban
gladesh-harmony-at-petrapole-on-international-mother-language-day-1.568355.
[Last accessed: 17 July 2017].
270 Interview with a BSF official in Shikarpur BSF camp (Nadia district of West Bengal, 21 October 2011).
271 Foucault, M. (1977) *Discipline and Punish: The Birth of the Prison* (trs. Alan Sheridan). London: Penguin. p. 137
272 Foucault, 1977, p. 236.
273 Donnan, H. and Wilson, T.M. (1999) *Borders: Frontiers of Identity, Nation and State.* Oxford: Berg. p. 129.
274 Lefebvre, H. (1991) *The Production of Space.* Oxford: Blackwell.
275 Soja, E. (1996) *Thirdspace.* Cambridge: Blackwell.

6   Conclusion

'Borderlanders hardly think of themselves as living in the margin. The borderland is the centre of their world'[1] – says Willem van Schendel in the conclusion of his seminal work on the Bengal borderland. This expression aptly defines the basic premise of the preceding chapters where border narratives along the West Bengal-Bangladesh border have been used as evidence to highlight the overwhelming presence and centrality of the border in the lives of the border people. Border narratives have also been used as evidence to highlight the production of a spatial consciousness which results from years of negotiating this overwhelming reality of the borderland by the people living across it.

Borders as delimitations of the sovereign powers of the state have evolved historically – from the flexible porous nature of the feudatories of middle age-Europe through their role as marked demarcations of nations following the Treaty of Westphalia (1648), to their later *avatars* as delimitations of the sovereign powers of modern-day state systems. The nature of the study of borders has, likewise, evolved from political to geographical and, eventually, sociological, ethnographical and economical discourses. Each border around the world has a unique story to tell. The stories contribute in their own ways towards the larger discourse on borders, offering new perspectives to understand their uniqueness.

The preceding chapters have looked at some of the inherent, but not always tangible, aspects of one of the most interesting and complex international borders in the world – the border between West Bengal (India) and Bangladesh. The research had set out to:

- Look at the evolution of border narratives as a spatial phenomenon.
- Examine how certain social, cultural, political and economic narratives are modified by the spatial specificity of the border to crystallise into a spatial narrative.
- Understand if such everyday border narratives question predominant statist definitions of inclusion, exclusion, legal, illegal, citizenship, rights, etc.
- Understand if such years of production of border narratives transform into a spatial consciousness, which has been termed here as a *border consciousness*.

The overarching theme of the evolution of border narratives and the creation of a *border consciousness* have been discussed as sub-themes like narratives of

220 *Conclusion*

livelihood, geographical specificities, ethno-social identities and gendered prac-tices. The narratives obtained in the course have been knit together under the larger discourse of a spatial narrative. Interviews with border residents across a wide spectrum of class, caste, gender, religion, profession have been used to high-light the everyday border narratives.

R. D. Sack has rightly observed that the content of a territory can be manipu-lated and its character designed simply by controlling access to it through bound-ary restrictions.[2] But this gives half of the story. Entirety is brought about only when we look at the manipulation and negotiations of the people who populate the territory and survive the control regime. The cynicism produced as a result of this negotiation decides the everyday practices of these people – practices that the states are inclined to regard as subversive.[3] A conflict of interests between the state and the border people occurs at the border, where both the state machinery (embodied in the administrative officials and the border guards) and the civilians are driven by a common sense understanding of life at the border. The perceptions rarely coincide, creating conflicting patterns of statehood, citizenship, legality, etc.

Experience-centred narratives

Human action and experience, according to Paul Ricoeur, always has a narrative structure.[4] Thus, experience-centred everyday forms of narratives have been cho-sen as the basis of analysis because they bring out the spontaneous and real nature of the experiences of the people rather than secondary materials, most of which look at such narratives from a statist perspective, consider such narratives as mere security issues of the state or highlight certain specific crises of the border like smuggling or trafficking as an issue of border management. The 'small stories'[5] of border life 'may concern unfolding, anticipated, imaginary, habitual and indefi-nite events and states, as well as past, singular "events"; they may also involve repeated content or themes spread out across interviews or other data'.[6] But they are the narratives which reveal the 'naturally-occurring' stories and the natural language of expression.[7] Most importantly, they pay 'attention to the "social" in its most microsocial versions, as well as in its wider, cultural variants'.[8] Experience becomes part of consciousness,[9] especially over a long period of time. Hence, such experience-centred narratives have been used as evidence in the study of the *border consciousness* along the stipulated border. And in this, language and use of specific words/phrases have played an important role.[10] The responses of the interviewees have been kept intact in order to keep their articulation as authentic as possible. This explains why certain phrases, words or sentences spoken by the interviewees, despite sounding vague or incongruous, have been cited in their original forms.

Narrator and listener

The convergence of the divergent emotional, cognitive and social life of the nar-rator and the listener (me) has often been difficult in the process of understand-ing and interpreting the narratives. Moreover, certain parts of the narratives,

Conclusion   221

especially the ones to do with anxieties, desires, etc., almost always 'remain outside the narrative',[11] no matter how rigorous the process of recording and analysing the narratives is. 'The factual details of "lived life" obtain an emotional aspect in the "told story", which constitutes the underlying emotional experience that the narrator goes through in negotiating the lived experiences'.[12] These emotions cannot be expressed clearly by the teller nor can the listener do complete justice to such expressions. Despite these drawbacks, experience-centred everyday narratives have been the primary foundation of this research for understanding the evolution of border narratives over a period of time and their crystallisation into a spatial consciousness.

Temporality

The choice of experience-centred everyday narratives as support for my arguments has also to do with the aim of the research to capture this evolution of border narratives beginning from the Partition and the creation of the border in 1947. The period following the Partition has been crucial in the transformation of cultural identities of the Bengali people into a border people and in crystallising their narratives into a border consciousness. The everyday narratives almost always capture the essence of time. Corinne Squire, Molly Andrews and Maria Tamboukou have aptly observed: 'Time, psychically processed, is thought to make us into subjects through its articulation in narrative. Transformation is also assumed to be integral to narrative, in the story itself, in the lives of those telling it; even in researchers' own understandings of it'.[13] This explains the choice of such small stories as the basis for the study of the reproduction of border space and the evolution of border consciousness over a long period of time of about six decades.

Cognition and scales

Cognitive behavioural patterns of the border people along the West Bengal-Bangladesh border, including their own perceptions of inclusion-exclusion, inside-outside, their restricted mobility or significance of their particular territorial location, also have a significant role to play in the evolution of the spatial consciousness. My own experiences during field studies opened my eyes to the cognitive (dis)orientation of the borderland when I ended up confusing which side of the border I was on at a particular time, given my continuous movement across it over a period of six months.[14] This experience was, in fact, a strong hint towards the kind of cognitive disorientations that the border people, negotiating the border over years, might have to deal with.

Neil Brenner's (2001) idea of scalar structuration helps in explaining such cognitive patterns of perception and negotiation. It, in fact, helps in the understanding of the convergence of varying and conflicting spatial perceptions of the state, the border guards and the border civilians along the space of the border. That 'processes of scalar structuration are constituted and continually reworked through everyday social routines and struggles'[15]is amply witnessed in the border areas.

222   *Conclusion*

The process becomes all the more tangible in a 'partitioned geography',[16] as is the case with the West Bengal-Bangladesh borderland where politics of scale comes into play in the societal structuration processes – involving a web of ethnic, religious, social, political and economic ties across the border. The enclaves, *Chars*, *Ghoj*, riverine borders constitute examples of such scalar structuration and cognitive disorientation apart from the general spatial disorientation brought about in the borderland areas during the post-Partition years of displacement, migration and resettlement along the newly-formed border.

Life-cycle approach

The 'life-cycle' approach of borders suggested by Willem van Schendel and Michiel Baud[17] provides useful tools for understanding the evolution process of the West Bengal-Bangladesh border from its genesis to its present form, which, in the process, provides tools for understanding the evolution of *border consciousness*. The six stages of evolution of the border suggested by them are embryonic, infant, adolescent, adult, declining and defunct. The characteristic features laid out for each of them help us in understanding the stage that the various parts of the West Bengal-Bangladesh border is in, as well as highlighting its overall 'coming of age'.[18] The changing form and nature of the border at various phases of its evolution affect the patterns of negotiation practiced by the border people. The negotiation between the state, the border guards and the border civilians changes according to the quiet/harmonious, unruly, half-unruly or rebellious nature of the borderland, depending on the phase of life-cycle that the border is in.[19] This, in turn, affects the everyday practices and, hence, the psyche of the people.

Unquestionable acceptance of the reality of the border by the people who live in the borderland[20] is, probably, what each stage leads to, though the socio-cultural milieu and politico-economic factors of different borders affect the stages differently.[21] The impact of a certain stage can also have diverse effects on its people depending on their socio-political positioning in social hierarchy. While it strengthens some, it disempowers others.[22] Accordingly, certain practices in border areas might characterise a nascent stage of the border while certain others might seem like a result of a matured border. The preceding chapters have tried to highlight certain features which focus on such diverse effects that the bordering process has on its people.

Border identity

The identity of a 'border people' is produced by a modification of the various other primary and secondary identities – of that of ethnic, religious, gendered, economic – into a larger spatial identity. The identity narratives of the civilians as well as the border guards feed into this larger identity paradigm.[23] In fact, some of the narratives of the border guards do not just reveal their sense of identification as a border people (*border man*),[24] but also their assertion of their roles as protectors and patriarchs of the sovereign limits of the state.[25]

Conclusion 223

The undeniable projection of the border as a meeting space for both states by the state officials also, in a way, forms part of the evolutionary stages of the border where the disruptive effect of the Partition and the consequent formation of the border is seen to come full circle, having moved through stages of illicit links and networks, to its current stage of state-backed projects of relinking the broken ties. Jointly-administered border *haats*, relinking the road/rail/waterways, joint river actions,[26] joint celebration of Language Day and joint surveillance in preventing fundamentalist forces[27] across borders are some of the examples of the evolution of the border from a disruptive force to a matured stage of interlinked dependence under state control.

Identification/dis-identification

There is often a 'tendency to confuse the sharing of a culture with the sharing of an identity'.[28] Border narratives often challenge the notion of an intended politico-cultural homogeneity that the bounded space of the state within a demarcated border is meant to attain. The Bengal border is a fine example of the dilemma of identification/dis-identification that the border dwellers face in the light of their interactions with fellow countrymen and the people across the border. The similarity in a national identity between the border dwellers and their non-border brethren often loses relevance in the wake of their daily interactions, intended or otherwise, with those across the borderline. In most cases, this sense of identifica-tion[29] with the border people on the other side is brought about by the daily exigencies of survival, livelihood, security, etc. The ethno-cultural similarity of the people on both sides of the Bengal border makes this border even more complex. They share their 'crisis of belonging' with those on the other side rather than those living away from border areas.[30] They are, as Homi K. Bhabha puts it, 'estranged unto themselves – in the act of being articulated into a collective body',[31] result-ing in a collective mentality, a unique existence. The 'collective mentality' is what constitutes the spatially unique consciousness of being a 'border people' which is often way more overwhelming in its manifestation than any other social, religious or political identity. Dis-identification is more a process of 'distanc-ing oneself from a certain identifying character' and less of an 'opposite of the process of identification'.[32] The border creates an invisible yet strong boundary between the border and non-border people on both its sides. Because of its spatial uniqueness, life and living strategies of the border and non-border people differ vastly, of which the non-border people are rarely aware. 'The very word "border" evokes a Bangladesh-like feeling and indicates a distanced existence from the Indian mainland',[33] is how a border civilian on the West Bengal side expresses this sense of dis-identification. For the non-border people, border was and still remains a romanticised space of dystopia and nostalgic pining for the lost home and hearth – images which barely reflect the reality of a border existence.

Dis-identification, as Jose Esteban Munoz suggests, is a 'strategy of resistance against dominant paradigms of identity'[34] – not in the form of a counter-stance but rather as a positive action,[35] enabling one to understand this unique mentality

224   *Conclusion*

as something not limited to traditional binaries.[36] Border mentality and milieu is, thus, much more than a mere reaction to state-centric narratives; it is a discourse in itself, often spontaneous in origin and as important in understanding the nuances of state-building as are the state-centric narratives. While still being attached to history in terms of being consequential to the historic event of Partition, border culture evolves its own politics of resistance, as Suzanne Bost very aptly puts it. This (border culture) 'transcends its potentially tragic origins and enables resistance to hegemony, a critique of imperialism, and powerful reinterpretations of self and culture',[37] while simultaneously questioning the role of the state as the political and social container.[38] Availability of telecommunication networks of each state on the other side,[39] and the larger spectrum of cross-border practices in general, put the state's sovereign presence at the borders to test.

The idea of the centrality of the border in the life of the 'borderlanders', as propounded by Van Schendel,[40] also finds resonance in the sense of identification between the border people on both sides and their virtual dis-identification from those 'mainlanders' for whom the borderland symbolises a marginal space – a periphery.

Significance of this work

The book, primarily, is a contribution to the recent studies on borders, more specifically South Asian borders. But the point of intervention lies in its focussing on the territorial predicaments of a borderland – not in terms of bilateral affairs and political discourses between two states, but in trying to unearth how local narratives of class, caste, gender, religion, economy operate within the spatial specificity of the borderland in creating a spatial consciousness (*border consciousness*) and a spatial community (*border people*). In the backdrop of capital flow and a seeming blurring of economic and cultural borders between states, studies as this one, as aptly expressed by Joachim Blatter, 'offer useful insights into contemporary processes of state spatial restructuring and the changing operations of borders, boundaries, and territories in global capitalism'.[41] It puts forth the changing nature of the border from being the 'front lines' of sovereign states to socioeconomic 'contact zones' for neighbouring societies.[42] And it shows that the process of evolving into contact zones do not occur through any organised resistance or conscious acts of subversion but happens spontaneously, through everyday survival practices. And it is this 'everydayness' of the practices that makes it difficult for the states to either gauge, discipline or control them. It might make sense for the states, in such cases, to take the lives and practices of the border dwellers into account while framing the regulations and policies for administering their borderlands. The designs of the state and the demand of the so-called mainland people for securing the borders and making them impermeable need to consider the 'everyday transnationality'[43] of the lives of the border people. Borderlanders, as Van Schendel puts it, are active partners in the re-territorialisation of states[44] and, hence, as important as any other part of the state as decisive factors in the discourses of state-building.

The sheer range of media coverage of border issues in West Bengal and Bangladesh hints at the ways states choose to address or ignore their borders. Border

Conclusion 225

questions are state concerns for both India and Bangladesh. This means that any decisions regarding the borders need to be ratified and passed by the parliaments of the states. Moreover, the border guards of both India and Bangladesh are centrally deployed paramilitary forces. Bangladesh does not have a provincial governance structure, unlike India, which has a central government and separate state (provincial) governments in its 28[45] odd states. The central government in Bangladesh addresses situations in any of its borders, be it with India or Myanmar. However, India prioritises its borders according to the sensitivity associated with them, which thus makes the Pakistan and China borders more important strategic concerns than the Bangladesh one. The Bangladesh border has become the concern of the provincial governments of West Bengal, Assam, Meghalaya, Mizoram and Tripura over the years. The central government in India concerns itself with the Bangladesh border only when it becomes a national issue related to security, terrorism, etc. The recent debates over the enclave exchange or the ones regarding the use of the Bangladesh border for terrorist activities are examples. It is no wonder that border issues of the India-Bangladesh border are far more frequently addressed in the Bangladesh national and regional media than in the Indian media, especially the national media. Regional media is seen to report Bangladesh border issues in West Bengal, Assam and other Indian provinces with which Bangladesh shares a border. But the national media hardly reports Bangladesh border issues unless it is of national importance. Thus, while border disputes between West Bengal and Bangladesh affect the electoral agendas of the central government of Bangladesh, they only affect the electoral agendas of the provincial government of West Bengal in India.[46] Even if issues like providing asylum to a particular religious denomination find a place in the agenda of the Parliamentary elections in India, they are only a miniscule portion of the list of agendas of the political parties contesting the elections. It also explains the disengagement of the non-border people about border areas, stemming from a lack of knowledge and awareness about the same.

Instead of being considered merely as a transition zone, or even a crush zone between centres of sovereign territorial power, borders need to be considered in their own right.[47] The smaller stories of the borders need to be considered as the missing links between the grand narratives of state building, transnational linkages and globalisation discourses – a phenomenon that Ranajit Guha calls *statism*.[48] These smaller stories of the everyday lives of a marginal people are often 'drowned in the noise of statist commands'.[49] But it is these stories which form the missing links between statist discourses, while also providing us with 'valuable clues as to the magnitude and limitations of the most powerful mental construction of the present-day world, the nation-state'.[50] Border narratives, thus, demand our attention. This book is a response to the call.

Notes

1 Van Schendel, W. (2005) *The Bengal Borderland: Beyond State and Nation in South Asia*. London: Anthem. p. 363.

226   Conclusion

2 Sack, R.D. (March 1983) Human Territoriality: A Theory. *Annals of the Association of American Geographers.* 73(1). p. 59.

3 Chatterji, J. (February 1999) The Fashioning of a Frontier: The Radcliffe Line and Bengal's Border Landscape, 1947–52. *Modern Asian Studies.* 33(1). p. 236.

4 Ricoeur, P. (1991) Life in Quest of Narrative. In Wood, D. (Ed.). *On Paul Ricoeur: Narrative and Interpretation.* London: Routledge. pp. 28–29.

5 Bamberg, M. (2006) Stories: Big or Small: Why Do We Care? *Narrative Inquiry.* 16(1). pp. 139–147; Freeman, M. (2006) Life on 'Holiday'? In Defence of Big Stories. *Narrative Inquiry.* 16(1). pp. 131–138; Georgakopoulou, A. (2007) *Small Stories, Interaction and Identities.* Amsterdam: John Benjamins.

6 Andrews, M., Squire, C. and Tamboukou, M. (Eds.). (2009) *Doing Narrative Research.* London: Sage. p. 8.

7 Ibid. pp. 8–9.

8 Ibid.

9 Squire, C. (2009) From Experience-Centred to Socioculturally-Oriented Approaches to Narrative. In Andrews, Squire and Tamboukou, 2009, p. 48.

10 Ibid. p. 9.

11 Ibid. p. 10.

12 Ibid. p. 52.

13 Ibid. p. 11; Ricoeur, P. (1984) *Time and Narrative.* Chicago: University of Chicago Press.

14 During my field studies, I would often be asked by interviewees, onlookers and any curious passers-by about my identity and background, like family, marital status, etc. In one such incident in the South Dinajpur district of West Bengal, I, along with three more persons (locals showing me around) was asked by a BSF constable about our identities. After hearing about the details of the other three (in which cities/towns in India their parents and husbands lived, etc.), the BSF constable asked me where I was from, to which I answered 'Kolkata'. After asking about my marital status, he asked me where my husband lived to which I promptly answered: India (instead of specifying the city). The answer was spontaneous and left me wondering why exactly I had said that. The other three companions as well as the BSF official were by then laughing and thinking that this was my way of withholding details of my family. They thought, as they said later, that the answer meant, 'he lives somewhere in India. . .how does it matter?' But I realised that the answer was a spontaneous outcome of my cognitive disorientation. For a moment, I thought I was on the Bangladesh side of the border and, thus, replied India instead of mentioning the name of the specific city, which is what I do on the West Bengal side.

15 Brenner, N. (2001) The Limits to Scale? Methodological Reflections on Scalar Structuration. *Progress in Human Geography.* 25(4). p. 604.

16 Smith, N. (1993) Homeless/Global: Scaling Places. In Bird, J., Curtis, B., Putnam, T., Robertson, G. and Tickner, T. (Eds.). *Mapping the Futures: Local Cultures, Global Change.* New York: Routledge. pp. 87–119.

17 Van Schendel, W. and Baud, M. (1997) Toward a Comparative History of Borderlands. *Journal of World History.* 8(2). pp. 223–225.

18 *Embryonic*: Clear borderlines are yet not distinguishable but where two or more frontiers tend to close into, and sometimes clash with each other; *Infant*: Exists just after the borderline has been drawn. Pre-existing social and economic networks are still visible, and people on both sides are still connected by kinship links. National identities are still vague. Possible disappearance of the border still looms large among the borderlanders; *Adolescent*: The border is an undeniable reality, though its genesis is still recent. Many people remember the period before it existed. Economic and social relations are beginning to be confined by the existence of the new border but old networks have not yet disintegrated and form powerful cross-border linkages; *Adult*: Social networks now implicitly accept and follow the contours of the border. Cross-border relations are

Conclusion 227

increasingly viewed as problematic. New cross-border networks such as smuggling are based on the acceptance of the border. The border has become an unquestionable reality in the lives of the borderlanders; *Declining*: Emergence of new supra-border networks are no longer seen as a threat to the state. The border gradually withers away, either peacefully or sometimes through violent contestations; *Defunct*: Border is abolished and physical barriers between the two sides are removed. Border-induced networks are gradually replaced by new ones. Van Schendel and Baud, 1997, pp. 223–225.

19 Ibid. pp. 227–229.

20 Ibid. p. 224.

21 Jean Brunhes and Camille Vallaux have named such borders 'dead' borders because of their unchanging nature over a substantial period of time. The focus, for Brunhes and Vallaux, has been on the unchanging, stagnant nature of the border. But the idea of unquestionable acceptance of the border in the minds of the borderlanders has been used in the context of the West Bengal-Bangladesh border more with regard to the overwhelming spatial reality of the border in the lives of the border people and less with regard to its form and nature. Thus, contrary to the idea of Brunhes and Vallaux, the border is very much a 'lived experience' of the border people along the West Bengal-Bangladesh border, rather than being dead. Brunhes, J. and Vallaux, C. (1921) *La geographie de l'histoire*. Paris: Felix Alcan. Quoted in Van Schendel and Baud, 1997, p. 224.

22 Van Schendel, 2005, p. 378.

23 River erosion is a usual occurrence in the West Bengal-Bangladesh border rivers, which affects the lives of both the civilians as well as the border guards. In recent river erosion incidences in river Padma, houses of border civilians and border outposts of the BSF border guards have been washed away. The civilians and the border guards were in equal need of relief and support from the state. Staff Reporter. (20 August 2013) Farakka bhanganey mukh feralo shech daptar. *Ananda Bazar Patrika*. [Online] Available from: www.anandabazar.com/20mur4.html. [Last accessed: 16 September 2013]; Staff Reporter. (22 August 2013) Padma bhanganey trosto shimantabashi. *Ananda Bazar Patrika*. [Online] Available from: www.anandabazar.com/22mur3.html. [Last accessed: 16 September 2013].

24 Chief Commander Omendra Singh of 151 Battalion writes about the 'Challenges of Border Man' in the BSF journal Bagher Garjan, South Bengal Frontier, BSF (October-December 2012). p. 6, where he points out the duties of the 'border man' (BSF) along the West Bengal-Bangladesh border and also the challenges that he faces along said border, including tackling smugglers and dealing with fence issues, as well as negotiating with non-cooperative civilians.

25 The author of the original Hindi poem, 'Mere baraso dus bhai', is Deputy Commander Onkar Nath, 104 Battalion, BSF. *Uttar Vang Prahari Samachar Patrika* (March 2013). 5(15). Available from: http://nb.bsf.gov.in/magazine/March_2013.pdf.

26 Moitra, S. (10 March 2010) Holo jautha samiksha, sighrai suru hochhe Ichhamati samskaar. *Ananda Bazar Patrika*. [Online] Available from: www.anandabazar.com/archive/1100310/10jibjagat1.htm. [Last accessed: 17 September 2013]; Staff Reporter. (11 March 2010) Hritajaubana Ichhamati r dai bartai par r bashinda der uporeo. *Ananda Bazar Patrika*. [Online] Available from: www.anandabazar.com/archive/1100311/11jibjagat1.htm. [Last accessed: 17 September 2013].

27 Moitra, S. (4 March 2013) Shahbag andoloney achhi, barta dilo epar bangla. *Ananda Bazar Patrika*. [Online] Available from: www.anandabazar.com/4pgn1.html. [Last accessed: 17 September 2013].

28 Vila, P. (Ed.). (2005) Border Identifications: Narratives of Religion, Gender, and Class on the U.S. Mexico Border. In Earle, D., Campbell, H. and Peterson, J. (Eds.). *Inter-America Series*. Austin: University of Texas Press. p. 4.

29 Feghali, Z. (2011) Re-Articulating the New Mestiza. *Journal of International Women's Studies*. Special Issue. 12(2). pp. 61–74.

30 Ibid. p. 72.

228   *Conclusion*

31   Bhabha, H. (2007) *The Location of Culture*. London, New York: Routledge. p. 33.
32   Feghali, 2011, p. 72.
33   Interview with Bilal, farmer and resident at Basirhat (North 24 Parganas district of West Bengal, 17 January 2012).
34   Feghali, 2011, p. 72.
35   Ibid.; For a detailed understanding of Munoz's idea, see Munoz, J.E. (1999) *Disidentifications: Queers of Color and the Performance of Politics*. Cultural Studies of the Americas, Volume 2. Minneapolis, London: University of Minnesota Press.
36   Feghali, 2011, p. 72.
37   Bost, S. (2003). *Mulattasand Mestizas: Representing Mixed Identities in the Americas, 1850–2000*. Athens, London: University of Georgia Press. p. 20.
38   Taylor, P.F. (2003) The State as Container: Territoriality in the Modern World-System. In Brenner, N., Jessop, B., Jones, M. and Macleod, G. (Eds.). *State/Space: A Reader*. Malden, Oxford: Blackwell. p. 107.
39   Rakshit, R. (17 April 2010) Simante BSNL sangket mele na, bhorsha Bangladesh. *Ananda Bazar Patrika*. [Online] Available from: www.anandabazar.com/archive/1100417/17desh6. htm. [Last accessed: 17 September 2013]; Use of Bangladeshi SIM by border civilians on the West Bengal side and vice versa is a common occurrence along this border.
40   Van Schendel, 2005, p. 363.
41   Brenner, Jessop, Jones and Macleod, 2003, p. 14.
42   Ratti, R. (1993) Spatial and Economic Effects of Frontiers: Overview of Traditional and New Approaches and Theories of Border Area Development. In Ratti, R. and Reichman, S. (Eds.). *Theory and Practice of Trans-Border Cooperation*. Basel: Helbig and Lichtenhahn. pp. 23–54.
43   Van Schendel, 2005, p. 379.
44   Ibid. p. 385.
45   On 30 July 2013, the ruling Congress party resolved to request the Central Government to make steps in accordance with the Constitution of India to form a separate state of Telengana (which will be the 29th state of the Republic of India) – an elaborate process to be completed in 122 days or at least four months. The proposal is still to be approved by the Parliament and the President of India before the new state is officially formed.
46   Staff Reporter. (20 July 2013) Dhruto shimanto chukti cheye chap Dhakar. *Ananda Bazar Patrika*. [Online] Available from: www.anandabazar.com/20bdesh1.html. [Last accessed: 5 September 2013]; Staff Reporter. (23 July 2013) Sholshimanto chukti dhruto rupayoney chap dichhey Dhaka. *Ananda Bazar Patrika*. [Online] Available from: www. anandabazar.com/23bdesh4.html. [Last accessed: 5 September 2013]; Roy, R. (21 July 2013) Padma jagchhe, flood shelter-I lokhhyo vote-er Nirmal Char-er. *Ananda Bazar Patrika*. [Online] Available from: www.anandabazar.com/archive/1130721/21mur1. html. [Last accessed: 5 September 2013]; Roy, R. (22 July 2013) Vote-e nei, tobu Char Meghna tei mon porey Mohishkundar. *Ananda Bazar Patrika*. [Online] Available from: www.anandabazar.com/22mur2.html. [Last accessed: 5 September 2013]; Das, R. (30 July 2013) Chhitmahaler issue te Trinomool ke lal card dekhalen voter-ra. *Samakal*. [Online] Available from: www.samakal.net/print_edition/details.php?news=17&view= archiev&y=2013&m=07&d=30&action=main&menu_type=&option=single&news_ id=359419&pub_no=1484&type=. [Last accessed: 5 September 2013].
47   Van Schendel, 2005, p. 366.
48   Guha, R. (1996). The Small Voice of History. In Amin, S. and Chakrabarty, D. (Eds.). *Subaltern Studies IX: Writings on South Asian History and Society*. New Delhi: Oxford University Press. p. 1.
49   Ibid. p. 3.
50   Van Schendel and Baud, 1997, p. 242.

Bibliography

Print sources: books and articles

Agamben, G. (1995) *Homo Sacer: Sovereign Power and Bare Life* (trs. Daniel Heller-Roazen). Stanford, CA: Stanford University Press.

Agamben, G. (2005) *State of Exception* (trs. Kevin Attell). Chicago, London: University of Chicago Press.

Aggarwal, R. (2004) *Beyond Lines of Control: Performance and Politics on the Disputed Borders of Ladakh, India.* Durham: Duke University Press.

Agnew, J., Mitchell, K. and Toal, G. (Eds.). (2002) *A Companion to Political Geography.* Oxford: Blackwell.

Ahmed, I. (Ed.). (2002) *Memories of a Genocidal Partition: The Haunting Tales of Victims, Witnesses and Perpetrators.* Colombo: Regional Centre for Strategic Studies.

Aigner-Varoz, E. (Summer 2000) Metaphors of a Mestiza Consciousness: Anzaldua's Borderlands/La Frontera. *Melus.* 25(2). pp. 47–62.

Alvarez, R.R. Jr (1995) The Mexican-US Border: The Making of an Anthropology of Borderlands. *Annual Review of Anthropology.* 24. pp. 447–470.

Amin, S. and Chakrabarty, D. (Eds.). (1996) *Subaltern Studies IX: Writings on South Asian History and Society.* New Delhi: Oxford University Press.

Anderson, B. (1983) *Imagined Communities.* London: Verso.

Andrews, M., Squire, C. and Tamboukou, M. (2009) *Doing Narrative Research.* London: Sage.

Annual Report 2009. Jessore: Rights Jessore.

Anti-Trafficking Programs and Promoting Human Rights: A Grassroots Initiative (2002) Sponsored by Royal Danish Embassy. Jessore: Rights Jessore.

Anzaldua, G. (1987) *Borderlands/La frontera: The New Mestiza.* San Francisco: Aunt Lute Books.

Asiwaju, A.I. (Ed.). (1985) *Partitioned Africans: Ethnic Relations across Africa's International Boundaries, 1884–1984.* London: C. Hurst & Co.

Bagher Garjan (October–December 2012). 26.

Bagher Garjan (January–March 2016).

Bagher Garjan (April–June 2016).

Bagher Garjan (July–September 2016).

Bamberg, M. (2006) Stories: Big or Small: Why Do We Care? *Narrative Inquiry.* 16(1). pp. 139–147.

Bandyopadhyay, A. (1971) *Nilkantha Pakhir Khonje.* Calcutta: Karuna Prakashan.

230   *Bibliography*

Bandyopadhyay, S. (1997) *Caste, Protest and Identity in Colonial India: The Namasudras of Bengal, 1872–1947*. Surrey: Curzon Press.

Bandyopadhyay, S. (27 March–2 April 2011) Who are the Matuas? *Frontier: The Citizenship Issue*. 43(37).

Banerjee, P. (2010) *Borders, Histories, Existences: Gender and Beyond*. New Delhi: Sage.

Banerjee, P. and Basu Ray Chaudhury, A. (Eds.). (2011) *Women in Indian Borderlands*. New Delhi: Sage.

Banerjee, P., Basu Ray Chaudhury, A. and Bhaduri, A. (2010) Bengal-Bangladesh Border and Women. *Policies and Practices*. 36. Kolkata: Mahanirban Calcutta Research Group.

Beteille, A. (1992) *Society and Politics in India: Essays in a Comparative Perspective*. New Delhi: Oxford University Press.

Bhabha, H. (2007) *The Location of Culture*. London, New York: Routledge.

Bhasin, A.S. (Ed.). (2003) *India-Bangladesh Relations: Documents, 1971–2002*. Volume 1–5. New Delhi: Geetika Publishers.

Bhattacharjee, J. (July 2013) *India-Bangladesh Border Management: The Challenge of Cattle Smuggling*. Special Report, Observer Research Foundation. 1.

Bird, J., Curtis, B., Putnam, T., Robertson, G. and Tickner, T. (Eds.). (1993) *Mapping the Futures: Local Cultures, Global Change*. New York: Routledge.

Biswas, A. (1982) Why Dandakaranya a Failure, Why Mass Exodus, Where Solution? *The Oppressed Indian*. 4(4). pp. 18–20.

Bose, N.K. (1968) *Calcutta: A Social Survey*. Bombay: Lakshmi Publishing House.

Bose, P.K. (Ed.). (2000) *Refugees in West Bengal*. Calcutta: Calcutta Research Group.

Bost, S. (2003) *Mulattas and Mestizas: Representing Mixed Identities in the Americas, 1850–2000*. Athens, London: University of Georgia Press.

Brenner, N. (2001) The Limits to Scale? Methodological Reflections on Scalar Structuration. *Progress in Human Geography*. 25(4). pp. 591–614.

Brenner, N., Jessop, B., Jones, M. and Macleod, G. (Eds.). (2003) *State/Space: A Reader*. Malden, Oxford: Blackwell.

Brighenti, A.M. (2010) On Territorology: Towards a General Science of Territory. *Theory, Culture and Society*. 27(1). pp. 1–21.

Burchell, G., Gordon, C. and Miller, P. (Eds.). (1991) *The Foucault Effect: Studies in Governmentality*. Chicago: University of Chicago Press.

Butalia, U. (1998) *The Other Side of Silence: Voices from the Partition of India*. New Delhi, London: Penguin.

Catudal, H.M. (1979) *The Exclave Problem of Western Europe*. Tuscaloosa: University of Alabama Press.

Chakravorty, S., Milevska, S. and Barlow, T.E. (2006) *Conversations with Gayatri Chakraborty Spivak*. London: Seagull Books.

Chakrabarti, P.K. (1990) *The Marginal Men: The Refugees and the Left Political Syndrome in West Bengal*. Kalyani, West Bengal: Lumiere Books.

Chakrapani, C. and Kumar, S.V. (Eds.). (1994) *Changing Status and Role of Women in Indian Society*. New Delhi: M.D. Publications.

Chatterjee, N. (1992) *Midnight's Unwanted Children: East Bengali Refugees and the Politics of Rehabilitation*. Ph.D. dissertation (unpublished). Brown University.

Chatterjee, P. (2004) *The Politics of the Governed: Reflections on Popular Politics in Most of the World*. New York, Chichester, West Sussex: Columbia University Press.

Chatterjee, P. and Finger, M. (1994) *The Earth Brokers*. London: Routledge.

Chatterji, J. (1994) *Bengal Divided: Hindu Communalism and Partition, 1932–1947*. Cambridge: Cambridge University Press.

Bibliography 231

Chatterji, J. (1999) The Fashioning of a Frontier: The Radcliffe Line and Bengal's Border Landscape, 1947–52. *Modern Asian Studies*. 33(1). pp. 185–242.

Chatterji, J. (2007) *The Spoils of Partition: Bengal and India, 1947–1967*. Cambridge: Cambridge University Press.

Chattopadhyay, K. (1986) *Tebhaga Andolaner Itihas*. Kolkata: Progressive Publishers.

Clad, J.C. (Summer 1994) Slowing the Wave. *Foreign Affairs*. 95. pp. 139–150.

Clark, R.S. (1977) *Fundamentals of Criminal Justice Research*. New York: Lexington Books.

Colburn, F.D. (Ed.). (1989) *Everyday Forms of Peasant Resistance*. Armonk, London: M.E Sharpe.

Coleman, M. (2009) What Counts as the Politics and Practice of Security, and Where? Devolution and Immigrant Insecurity after 9/11. *Annals of the Association of American Geographers*. 99(5). pp. 904–913.

Cons, J. (May 2012) Histories of Belonging(s): Narrating Territory, Possession, and Dispossession at the India-Bangladesh Border. *Modern Asian Studies*. 46(3). pp. 527–558.

Cons, J. (2012) Narrating Boundaries: Framing and Contesting Suffering, Community, and Belonging in Enclaves along the India-Bangladesh Border. *Political Geography*. [Online] Elsevier. pp. 1–10. Available from: http://dx.doi.org/10.1016/j.polgeo.2012.06.004.

Cons, J. (2016) *Sensitive Space: Fragmented Territory at the India-Bangladesh Border*. Seattle, London: University of Washington Press.

Cooper, F. (2001) What Is the Concept of Globalisation Good For? An African Historian's Perspective. *African Affairs*. 100. pp. 189–213.

Das, P. (2012) *Drug Trafficking in India: A Case for Border Security*. IDSA Occasional Paper No. 24. New Delhi: Institute for Defence Studies and Analysis.

Diener, A. and Hagen, J. (Eds.). (2010) *Borderlines and Borderlands: Political Oddities at the Edge of the Nation-State*. New York: Rowman Littlefield.

Donnan, H. and Wilson, T.M. (Eds.). (1994) *Border Approaches: Anthropological Perspectives on Frontiers*. Lanham, London: University Press of America.

Donnan, H. and Wilson, T.M. (Eds.). (1998) *Border Identities: Nation and State at International Frontiers*. Cambridge, NY: Cambridge University Press.

Donnan, H. and Wilson, T.M. (1999) *Borders: Frontiers of Identity, Nation and State*. Oxford: Berg.

Downs, R.M. and Stea, D. (1977) *Maps in Minds: Reflections on Cognitive Mapping*. New York, London: Harper & Row.

Earle, D., Campbell, H. and Peterson, J. (Eds.). (2005) *Inter-America Series*. Austin: University of Texas Press.

Eiland, H. and Jennings, W. (Eds.). (2003) *Walter Benjamin: Selected Writings, Vol. 4, 1938–1940*. Cambridge: Harvard University Press, Belknap Press.

Eilenberg, M. (2010) Negotiating Autonomy at the Margins of the State: The Dynamics of Elite Politics in the Borderland of West Kalimantan, Indonesia. *South East Asia Research*. 17(2). pp. 201–227.

Feghali, Z. (2011) Re-Articulating the New Mestiza. *Journal of International Women's Studies*. Special Issue. 12(2). pp. 61–74.

Fernandes, W. and Ganguly Thukral, E. (Eds.). (1989) *Development, Displacement and Rehabilitation*. New Delhi: Indian Social Institute.

Festinger, L. (1962) *A Theory of Cognitive Dissonance*. Stanford, CA: Stanford University Press.

Foucault, M. (1977) *Discipline and Punish: The Birth of the Prison* (trs. Alan Sheridan). London: Penguin.

232   Bibliography

Fraser, B. (2006) *Bengal Partition Stories: An Unclosed Chapter* (trs. Sheila Sen Gupta). London: Anthem.

Fraser, N. (1990) Rethinking the Public Sphere: A Contribution to the Critique of Actually Existing Democracy. *Social Text*. 25/26. pp. 56–80.

Freeman, M. (2006) Life On 'Holiday'? In Defence of Big Stories. *Narrative Inquiry*. 16(1). pp. 131–138.

Freitag, S.B. (1989) *Collective Action and Community: Public Arenas and the Emergence of Communalism in North India*. Berkeley, Oxford: University of California Press.

Ganguli, S. (1988) *Purba Pashchim*. Calcutta: Ananda Publishers.

Gellner, D. (2014) *Borderland Lives in Northern South Asia*. New Delhi: Orient Blackswan.

Georgakopoulou, A. (2007) *Small Stories, Interaction and Identities*. Amsterdam: John Benjamins.

Giddens, A. (1985) *The Nation-State and Violence*. Cambridge: Polity.

Giroux, H. and McLaren, P. (Eds.). (1994) *Between Borders: Pedagogy and the Politics of Cultural Studies*. New York: Routledge.

Glassman, J. (August 1999) State Power beyond the 'Territorial Trap': The Internationalisation of the State. *Political Geography*. 18(6). pp. 669–696.

Gramsci, A. (1971) *Selections from the Prison Notebooks* (trs. Quintin Hoare and Geoffrey Nowell Smith). London: Lawrence and Wishart.

Guha, R. (1988) *Selected Subaltern Studies*. Oxford: Oxford University Press.

Guha, R. (Ed.). (1989) *Subaltern Studies VI: Writings on South Asian History and Society*. New Delhi: Oxford University Press.

Guha, R. (1997) *A Subaltern Studies Reader, 1986–1995*. Minneapolis: University of Minnesota Press.

Gupta, C. and Sharma, M. (2008) *Contested Coastlines: Fisherfolk, Nations, and Borders in South Asia*. New Delhi: Routledge.

Gupta, D. (Ed.). (1991) *Social Stratification*. New Delhi, Oxford: Oxford University Press.

Hameed, S., Hlatshwayo, S., Tanner, E., Türker, M. and Yang, J. (2010) *Human Trafficking in India: Dynamics, Current Efforts, and Intervention Opportunities for the Asia Foundation*. Stanford: Stanford University Press.

Hanks, P. (Ed.). (1971) *Encyclopedic World Dictionary*. London: Hamlyn.

Hossain, M. (1991) *Agriculture in Bangladesh: Performance, Problems and Prospects*. Dhaka: The University Press Limited.

Islam, S.S. (May 1984) The State in Bangladesh under Zia (1975–81). *Asian Survey*. 24(5). pp. 556–573.

Jalais, A. (23 April 2005) Dwelling on Morichjhanpi: When Tigers became 'Citizens', Refugees 'Tiger Food'. *Economic and Political Weekly*. pp. 1757–1762.

Jalal, A. (1985) *The Sole Spokesman: Jinnah, the Muslim League and the Demand for Pakistan*. Cambridge: Cambridge University Press.

Jamwal, N.S. (January–March 2004) Border Management: Dilemma of Guarding the India-Bangladesh Border. *Strategic Analysis*. 28(1). pp. 5–36.

Jerome, R. (Ed.). (2001) *Conceptions of Postwar German Masculinity*. Albany: State University of New York Press.

Jones, R. (July 2009) Geopolitical Boundary Narratives, the Global War on Terror and Border Fencing in India. *Transactions of the Institute of British Geographers*. 34(3). pp. 290–304.

Jones, R. (August 2009) Sovereignty and Statelessness in the Border Enclaves of India and Bangladesh. *Political Geography*. 28(6). pp. 373–381.

Jones, R. (September 2011) Dreaming of a Golden Bengal: Discontinuities of Place and Identity in South Asia. *Asian Studies Review*. 35(3). pp. 373–395.

Bibliography   233

Jones, R. (2012) Spaces of Refusal: Rethinking Sovereign Power and Resistance at the Border. *Annals of the Association of American Geographers*. 102 (3). pp. 685–699.

Kaiser, R. and Nikiforova, E. (September 2006) Borderland Spaces of Identification and Dis/location: Multiscalar Narratives and Enactments of Seto Identity and Place in the Estonian-Russian Borderlands. *Ethnic and Racial Studies*. 29(5). pp. 928–958.

Kala, S. and Grimshaw, D.J. (Eds.). (2011) *Strengthening Rural Livelihoods: The Impact of Information and Communication Technologies in Asia*. New Delhi: Practical Action Publishing.

Kalir, B. and Sur, M. (Eds.). (2013) *Transnational Flows and Permissive Polities: Ethnographies of Human Mobilities in Asia*. Amsterdam: Amsterdam University Press.

Kaplan, C., Alarcon, N. and Moallem, M. (Eds.). (1999) *Between Woman and Nation: Nationalisms, Transnational Feminisms, and the State*. Durham, NC: Duke University Press.

Karan, P.P. (1966) The India-Pakistan Enclave Problem. *The Professional Geographer*. 18(1). pp. 23–25.

Kaul, S. (Ed.). (2001) *The Partitions of Memory: The Afterlife of the Divisions of India*. New Delhi: Permanent Black.

Kaur, N. (8–21 June 2002) The nowhere people. *Frontline*. 19(12).

Kohli, A. (1996) Can the Periphery Control the Centre? Indian Politics at the Crossroads. *The Washington Quarterly*. 19(4). pp. 115–127.

Kumar, A. (October 2009) The BDR Mutiny: Mystery Remains but Democracy Emerges Stronger. *Journal of Defence Studies*. 3(4). pp. 103–117.

Kumar Rajaram, P. and Grundy-Warr, C. (Eds.). (2007) *Borderscapes: Hidden Geographies and Politics at Territory's Edge*. Minneapolis: University of Minnesota Press.

Lahiri-Dutt, K. and Samanta, G. (2013) *Dancing with the River: People and Life on the Chars of South Asia*. New Haven, London: Yale University Press.

Lefebvre, H. (1991) *The Production of Space* (trs. Donald Nicholson-Smith). Oxford: Basil Blackwell.

Lionnet, F. (1989) *Autobiographical Voices: Race, Gender, Self-Portraiture*. Ithaca, London: Cornell University Press.

Lugones, M. (Autumn 1992) On Borderlands/La Frontera: An Interpretive Essay. *Hypatia*. 7(4). pp. 31–37.

Mallick, R. (February 1999) Refugee Resettlement in Forest Reserves: West Bengal Policy Reversal and the Marichjhapi Massacre. *The Journal of Asian Studies*. 58(1). pp. 104–125.

Martinez, O. (1994) *Border People: Life and Society in the U.S.-Mexico Borderlands*. Tucson: University of Arizona Press.

Mayer, T. (Ed.). (2000) *Gender Ironies of Nationalism: Sexing the Nation*. New York: Routledge.

Menon, R. and Bhasin, K. (1998) *Borders and Boundaries: Women in India's Partition*. New Delhi: Kali for Women.

Misra, S. (2011) *Becoming a Borderland: The Politics of Space and Identity in Colonial Northeastern India*. New Delhi: Routledge.

Mohanta, B.K. (2011) Tusu Festival of the Kudumis of Northern Orissa: Origin and Causes. *Journal of Sociology and Social Anthropology*. 2(1). pp. 23–29.

Montgomery, Sy. (1995) *Spell of the Tiger*. Boston: Houghton Mifflin.

Morris, R.C. (Ed.). (2010) *Can the Subaltern Speak? Reflections on the History of an Idea*. New York: Columbia University Press.

234 *Bibliography*

Munoz, J.E. (1999) *Disidentifications: Queers of Color and the Performance of Politics.* Cultural Studies of the Americas, Volume 2. Minneapolis, London: University of Minnesota Press.

Nandy, A. (1983) *The Intimate Enemy: Loss and Recovery of Self under Colonialism.* New Delhi: Oxford University Press.

Newman, D. (April 2006) The Lines that Continue to Separate Us: Borders in a Borderless World. *Progress in Human Geography.* 30(2). pp. 143–161.

Newman, D. and Kliot, N. (Eds.). (2000) *Geopolitics at the End of the Twentieth Century: The Changing Political Map.* London: Frank Cass & Co.

Newman, D. and Paasi, A. (April 1998) Fences and Neighbours in the Post-Modern World: Boundary Narratives in Political Geography. *Progress in Human Geography.* 22(2). pp. 186–207.

Ohmae, K. (1990) *The Borderless World.* New York: Harper Collins.

Ohmae, K. (1995) *The End of the Nation State.* New York: Free Press.

Paasi, A. (1996) *Territories, Boundaries and Consciousness.* New York: John Wiley & Sons Ltd.

Paasi, A. (1998) Boundaries as Social Processes: Territoriality in the World of Flows. *Geopolitics.* 3(1). pp. 69–88.

Paasi, A. (1999) Boundaries as Social Practice and Discourse: The Finnish-Russian Border. *Regional Studies.* 33(7). pp. 669–680.

Pal, M. (Ed.). (2011) *Nijer Kothaye Marichjhapi.* Kolkata: Gangchil.

Pandey, G. (2001) *Remembering Partition: Violence, Nationalism and History in India.* Cambridge: Cambridge University Press.

Pathak, A. (2002) *Law, Strategies, Ideologies: Legislating Forests in Colonial India.* New Delhi: Oxford University Press.

Prescott, J.R.V. (1968) *The Geography of State Policies.* London: Hutchinson & Co.

Prescott, J.R.V. (1978) *Boundaries and Frontiers.* London: Croom Helm.

Purcell, G. (2006) *India-Bangladesh Bilateral Trade and Potential Free Trade Agreement.* Dhaka: World Bank Office.

Rabbani, M.G. (2005–2006) Stateless in South Asia: Living in Bangladesh-India Enclaves. *Theoretical Perspectives: A Journal of Social Sciences and Arts.* 12 & 13. Dhaka: Centre for Alternatives.

Ramlow, T.R. (Fall 2006) Bodies in the Borderlands: Gloria Anzaldua's and David Wojnarowicz's Mobility Machines. *Melus.* 31(3). pp. 169–187.

Rath, N. (1996) *Women in Rural Society: A Quest for Development.* New Delhi: M.D. Publications.

Ratti, R. and Reichman, S. (Eds.). (1993) *Theory and Practice of Trans-Border Cooperation.* Basel: Helbig and Lichtenhahn.

Ray, R.K. and Ray, R. (1975) Zamindars and Jotedars: A Study of Rural Politics in Bengal. *Modern Asian Studies.* 9(1). pp. 81–102.

Ray, S. (2009) *Handbook of Agriculture in India.* New Delhi: Oxford University Press.

Reeser, T.W. (2010) *Masculinities in Theory: An Introduction.* Malden, MA: Wiley-Blackwell.

Ricoeur, P. (1984) *Time and Narrative.* Chicago: University of Chicago Press.

Robinson, G.W.S. (1959) Exclaves. *Annals of the Association of American Geographers.* 49(3). pp. 283–295.

Roy, H. (2012) *Partitioned Lives: Migrants, Refugees, Citizens in India and Pakistan, 1947–1965.* New Delhi: Oxford University Press.

Bibliography   235

Sack, R.D. (March 1983) Human Territoriality: A Theory. *Annals of the Association of American Geographers*. 73(1). pp. 55–74.

Samaddar, R. (Ed.). (1997) *Reflections on Partition in the East*. New Delhi: Vikas Publishing House.

Samaddar, R. (1999) *The Marginal Nation: Transborder Migration from Bangladesh to West Bengal*. New Delhi: Sage.

Scott, J.C. (1998) *Seeing Like a State: How Certain Schemes to Improve the Human Condition Have Failed*. New Haven, London: Yale University Press.

Scott, J.C. and Tria Kerkvliet, B.J. (Eds.). (1986) *Everyday Forms of Peasant Resistance in South-East Asia*. Library of Peasant Studies, No. 9. London: Frank Cass & Co.

Sears, A. and Cairns, J. (2010) *A Good Book, in Theory: Making Sense through Inquiry*. Ontario: University of Toronto Press.

Sengupta, D. (2016) *The Partition of Bengal: Fragile Borders and New Identities*. New Delhi: Cambridge University Press.

Sengupta, M. (2003) *Bishadbriksha*. Kolkata: Subarnarekha.

Sevellart, M. (Ed.). (2007) *Michel Foucault: Security, Territory, Population, 1977–1978*. New York: Palgrave Macmillan.

Shapiro, M. and Alker, H. (Eds.). (1996) *Challenging Boundaries: Global Flows, Territorial Identities*. Minneapolis: University of Minnesota Press.

Shewly, H.J. (2013) Abandoned Spaces and Bare Life in the Enclaves of the India-Bangladesh Border. *Political Geography*. 32. pp. 23–31.

Sikdar, R.K. (1982) Marichjhapi Massacre. *The Oppressed Indian*. 4(4). pp. 21–23.

Sikdar, S. (2008) *Dayamayeer Katha*. Kolkata: Gangchil.

Sills, D.L. (Ed.). (1968) *International Encyclopedia of the Social Sciences*. Volume 5. New York: Free Press.

Simon Commission. (1929) *Indian Statutory Commission: Selections from Memoranda and Oral Evidence by Non-Officials (Part II)*. Reprinted 1988. New Delhi: Swati Publications.

Smith, L.T. (1999) *Decolonising Methodologies: Research and Indigenous People*. London: Zed Books.

Sobhan, F. (Ed.). (2005) *Dynamics of Bangladesh-India Relations: Dialogues of Young Journalists across the Border*. Dhaka: The University Press Limited.

Soja, E. (1989) *Postmodern Geographies: The Reassertion of Space in Critical Social Theory*. London, New York: Verso.

Soja, E. (1996) *Thirdspace*. Cambridge, MA: Blackwell.

Spivak, G.C. and Butler, J. (2010) *Who Sings the Nation-State? Language, Politics, Belonging*. London, New York, Calcutta: Seagull Books.

Talbot, I. and Singh, G. (Eds.). (1999) *Region and Partition: Bengal, Punjab and the Partition of the Subcontinent*. Karachi: Oxford University Press.

Tuathail, G.O. (1996) *Critical Geopolitics*. London: Routledge.

Tuathail, G.O. (1999) Borderless Worlds? Problematising Discourses of Deterritorialisation. *Geopolitics*. 4(2). pp. 139–154.

Uttar Vang Prahari Samachar Patrika. (March 2012). 4(11).

Uttar Vang Prahari Samachar Patrika. (December 2012). 4(14).

Uttar Vang Prahari Samachar Patrika. (March 2013). 5(15).

Uttar Vang Prahari Samachar Patrika. (July–December 2013). 5(17).

Uttar Vang Prahari Samachar Patrika. (June 2014). 6(18).

Van Houtum, H. (Spring 2000) An Overview of European Geographical Research on Borders and Border Regions. *Journal of Borderlands Studies*. 15(1). pp. 57–83.

236 *Bibliography*

Van Houtum, H., Kramsch, O. and Zierhoffer, W. (Eds.). (2005) *B/ordering Space*. Aldershot: Ashgate.

Van Schendel, W. (2001) Working through Partition: Making a Living in the Bengal Borderlands. *International Review of Social History*. 46. pp. 393–421.

Van Schendel, W. (February 2002) Stateless in South Asia: The Making of the India-Bangladesh Enclaves. *The Journal of Asian Studies*. 61(1). pp. 115–147.

Van Schendel, W. (2005) *The Bengal Borderland: Beyond State and Nation in South Asia*. London: Anthem.

Van Schendel, W. and Abraham, I. (Eds.). (2005) *Illicit Flows and Criminal Things: States, Borders, and the Other Side of Globalisation*. Bloomington: University of Indiana Press.

Van Schendel, W. and Baud, M. (1997) Toward a Comparative History of Borderlands. *Journal of World History*. 8(2). pp. 211–242.

Verma, S.B. (2005) *Status of Women in Modern India*. New Delhi: Deep & Deep.

Vinokurov, E. (2007) *A Theory of Enclaves*. Lantham, MD: Lexington Books.

Walker, R.B.J. (1993) *Inside/Outside: International Relations as Political Theory*. Cambridge: Cambridge University Press.

Whyte, B. (2002) *Waiting for the Esquimo: An Historical and Documentary Study of the Cooch Behar Enclaves of India and Bangladesh*. Melbourne: University of Melbourne Press.

Wood, D. (Ed.). (1991) *On Paul Ricoeur: Narrative and Interpretation*. London: Routledge.

Yeung, H. (September 1998) Capital, State and Space: Contesting the Borderless World. *Transactions of the Institute of British Geographers*. 23(3). pp. 291–309.

Young, R.J.M (1995) *Colonial Desire: Hybridity in Theory, Culture, and Race*. New York: Routledge.

Yudice, G., Franco, J. and Flores, J. (Eds.). (1999) *Cultural Studies of the Americas 2*. Minneapolis, London: University of Minnesota Press.

Zaman, N. (1999) *A Divided Legacy: The Partition in Selected Novels of India, Pakistan, and Bangladesh*. Dhaka: The University Press Limited.

Online sources

Acquired Territories (Merger) Act 1960. Available from: www.constitution.org/cons/india/shed01.htm#FIRSTSCHEDULE.

Agriculture in South Asia, The World Bank. Available from: http://web.worldbank.org/WBSITE/EXTERNAL/COUNTRIES/SOUTHASIAEXT/EXTSAREGTOPAGRI/0,,contentMDK:20273764~menuPK:548214~pagePK:34004173~piPK:34003707~theSitePK:452766,00.html.

Asian Human Rights Commission. Available from: www.humanrights.asia.

Awasthi, A.P., Safaya, C., Sharma, D., Narula, T. and Dey, S. (2010) *Indo-Bangladesh Fence Issue*. Centre for Civil Society. Research Project by CCS Fellows. Available from: http://ccsindia.org/nolandsman/.

Bangladesh Bureau of Statistics, Ministry of Planning, Government of the People's Republic of Bangladesh. Available from: www.bbs.gov.bd/home.aspx.

Border Guards Bangladesh, Ministry of Home Affairs, Government of the People's Republic of Bangladesh. Available from: www.bgb.gov.bd/.

Border Security Force, Ministry of Home Affairs, Government of India. Available from: www.bsf.nic.in/.

Census of India 2001, Ministry of Home Affairs, Government of India. Available from: www.jsk.gov.in/projection_report_december2006.pdf.

Census of India 2011, Ministry of Home Affairs, Government of India. Available from: http://censusindia.gov.in/.

Bibliography   237

Cheruvari, S. (2006) *Changing Lives in the Brick Kilns of West Bengal*. Report for UNICEF India. Available from: www.unicef.org/india/child_protection_1736.htm.

Cooch Behar Merger Agreement 1949. Available from: http://coochbehar.nic.in/htmfiles/royal_history2.html.

Dinhata Jute Tobacco Co. *Indiamart*. Available from: www.indiamart.com/dinhata-jute/profile.html.

The Dowry Prohibition Act 1961, Ministry of Women and Child Development, Government of India. Available from: http://wcd.nic.in/act/dowry-prohibition-act-1961.

The Foreigner's Act 1946. Available from: http://mha.nic.in/pdfs/The%20Foreigners%20Act,%201946.pdf.

Hindu Marriage Act 1955. Available from: http://lawcommissionofindia.nic.in/reports/report205.pdf.

Human Rights Watch. Available from: www.hrw.org.

The Indian Forest Act 1927, Ministry of Law, Government of India. Available from: http://chanda.nic.in/htmldocs/elibrary-new/e%20Library/Indian%20Forest%20Act,%201927.pdf.

The Indian Penal Code 1860, Council of the Governor General of India. Available from: http://ncw.nic.in/acts/THEINDIANPENALCODE1860.pdf.

Management of Indo-Bangladesh Border. Available from: http://mha.nic.in/pdfs/BM_MAN-IN-BANG(E).pdf.

Ministry of Home Affairs, Government of India (www.mha.nic.in/)

Mirza, T. and Bacani, E. (2013) Addressing Hard and Soft Infrastructure Barriers to Trade in South Asia. *Asian Development Bank South Asia Working Paper Series*. No. 16. Available from: http://sasec.asia/web/images/sasec/pdf/Addressing_Infra_Barriers_to_Trade_in_SA.pdf.

Molla, H.R. (2011) Embankment of Lower Ajoy River and Its Impact on Brick-Kiln Industry in Central Bengal, India. *International Journal of Research in Social Sciences and Humanities*. 2(2). Available from: www.ijrssh.com/webmaster/upload/Oct_2012_Hasibur%20Rahaman%20Molla.pdf.

Odhikar (www.odhikar.org)

Patel, R.P. (2000) *Submission to WHOs Tobacco Free Initiative on FCTC Framework Convention on Tobacco Control*. All India Bidi Industry Federation. Ahmedabad. Available from: www.who.int/tobacco/framework/public_hearings/F2000196.pdf.

Pradan (www.pradan.net)

Tinbigha: Agreements and Verdicts. Available from: http://coochbehar.nic.in/htmfiles/tinbigha_contd.html.

Transport of Animals Rules 1978. Available from: http://pashudhanharyana.gov.in/html/pdf%20&%20downloads/AH%20Acts/15_The%20Transport%20of%20animals%20rules,%201978.pdf.

UK Border Agency (www.ukba.homeoffice.gov.uk)

West Bengal State Election Commission (www.wbsec.gov.in/)

The World Bank (http://web.worldbank.org)

Newspapers: (print and online version)

Bengali

Anandabazar Patrika (www.anandabazar.com)
Bartaman (www.bartamanpatrika.com)
BBC Bangla (www.bbc.co.uk/bengali/)
Dainik Ittefaq (www.ittefaq.com.bd/)

238 *Bibliography*

Ebela (www.ebela.in)
Ei Samay (www.eisamay.com)
Ganashakti (www.ganashakti.com)
Prothom Alo (www.prothom-alo.com/)
Samakal (www.samakal.net)

English

Asia Times Online (www.atimes.com)
Banglanews24.com (www.banglanews24.com)
Business Standard (www.business-standard.com)
The Daily Star (www.thedailystar.net)
Deccan Herald (www.deccanherald.com)
The Economic Times (www.economictimes.indiatimes.com)
The Financial Express (www.thefinancialexpress-bd.com)
Headlines India (http://headlinesindia.mapsofindia.com)
The Hindu (www.thehindu.com)
Hindustan Times (www.hindustantimes.com)
IBN Live (www.ibnlive.in.com)
The Independent (www.theindependentbd.com)
The Indian Express (www.indianexpress.com)
India Today (http://indiatoday.intoday.in)
Infochange (www.infochangeindia.org)
News Wala (www.newswala.com)
Open Magazine (www.openthemagazine.com)
Tehelka (www.tehelka.com)
The Telegraph (www.telegraphindia.com)
The Times of India (www.timesofindia.indiatimes.com)
Zeenews.com (www.zeenews.india.com)

Blogs and social forums

Hindu Samhati. Available from: http://hindusamhati.blogspot.co.uk/2008/04/hindu-samhati-exhbition-thakurnagar.html. (blog)
Mystery of Marichjhapi. Available from: http://marichjhapi-mystery.blogspot.co.uk/. (blog)
The New Horizon (http://horizonspeaks.wordpress.com) (blog)
Pakistan Defence (forum) (www.defence.pk)

Index

accomplices 177
adhiars 101
Adversely Possessed Territories 102
agriculture 7, 31, 127, 144, 152, 158
Amra Bangali 148

Bangabhumi 148; *Bangalistan* 148
Baruni Mela 150
belonging ix, 159, 161, 162, 223
Bengal border i, viii, 1, 5, 18, 29, 167, 196, 223 *also see* border
Berubari question 95, 96, 98
border civilians 5, 11, 30, 38, 48
border consciousness 20, 70, 99, 150, 168; spatial consciousness i, 18, 21, 168, 203
border districts 8, 13, 24, 36, 40
border economy 54, 62
border fence 9, 34, 186, 190
border guards i, 5, 7, 8, 9, 16 *also see* border security forces
border i, viii, ix, 1, 3, 6, 7, 8, 16, 18, 20, 29, 30, 34
border identities 1 *also see* identity
border narratives i, 12, 14, 16, 21, 70, 123, 166, 167, 193
border roads 9, 25, 192
border rules 6, 18, 30
border security forces 9
border-crossings 48, 108, 123, 201
borderlanders ix, 6, 70, 224, 226, 227; borderland people 4
borderline viii, 4, 9, 31, 43, 188; boundary line 62, 9, 92 *also see* zero point
Boundary Commission 2, 3, 92, 93, 96
boundary-making viii, 3

caste 6, 11, 21, 124, 141, 142, 148; identities i, 142, 148, 153, 166, 167
Chars 4, 7, 20, 56, 124, 125, 128

Chhitmahals 90, 92 *also see* enclaves
citizens 6, 35, 36, 94, 100, 104, 105, 106, 113, 117; citizenship 3, 6, 20, 21, 93, 94, 99, 104, 105
civilians i, 5, 6, 11, 16, 21, 47
class 148, 153, 165, 220
Cognitive 115, 220, 221; cognitive disorientation 222
common sense i, 29, 31, 70, 168, 203, 220
contraband 41, 45, 48, 53, 62, 125
control regime 19, 201, 220
Coolies 40, 41
counter-enclaves 90, 110; counter-counter-enclaves 90
cross-border 5, 7, 16, 30, 38, 51, 55, 57, 68, 184, 201
cross-border mobility 5
cultural outcastes 148; *cultural outsiders* 148

Dandakaranya 143, 144, 149
dhoor 47
disputed territories 20, 90, 119
double-bordering 34
drugs 41, 45, 46, 63, 193

enclave 4, 20, 90, 92, 94, 96, 110, 117; enclave dwellers 93, 98, 107, 108, 122
enclave people 98, 104, 105, 106, 107, 119, 122; enclave population 94, 99, 107
ethnicity 21, 148, 149; ethno-cultural ix, 141, 223
exclave 90
experience i, 14, 61, 220
experience-centred i, 14, 220

fenced-out 31, 32, 34; fencing 9, 35, 68, 99, 179
Forest Preservation Act 144

240 *Index*

gender 13, 21, 124, 177, 181; Gendered
practices 177
gendered narratives 21, 177, 202, 203
Ghoj 20, 124, 126, 127, 128, 179, 222

haats 51, 52, 53, 64, 65, 102, 223
hijras 63, 64, 193, 194
Hindu-majority districts 2
Human Rights 11, 119, 121, 191, 196

identification 104, 111, 201, 222, 223, 224;
dis-identification 223, 224
identity i, ix, 6, 9, 16, 67, 99, 110, 157, 203,
222, 223
illegal 6, 7, 29, 35, 37, 45, 156
illegal migrants 38, 49, 152, 156, 165;
illegal livelihood practices 45, 45, 50,
161 *also see* livelihood practices
inclusion 4, 20, 34, 96, 112, 115, 124, 221
India-Bangladesh enclaves 92, 99
Indian nation 3
infiltrators 6, 36, 152, 156, 165
interdependent borderland 6, 30

labourers 32, 38, 39, 41, 52, 67, 105, 127,
160, 183, 185
land ports 7, 38, 40, 41, 42, 67, 70
lethal weapons 54, 67, 195, 196, 199
life-cycle 30, 222
linemen 47, 48, 60
livelihoods 1, 6, 19, 30, 36, 67, 156, 160;
livelihood practices 13, 20, 29, 31, 44,
45, 69

mainlanders viii, 4, 6, 125, 224
majority 2, 3, 4, 156, 199
marginal spaces 141
marginality 3, 17, 21, 141, 158, 166
Marichjhapi 142, 144, 145, 149, 152, 156,
157
materiality 30, 126, 149
Matua 150, 151, 153
migrants 5, 6, 49, 125, 141, 165
minority 3, 4, 62

Namasudra 94, 141, 143, 154, 156, 157,
161, 166, 167
narratives i, viii, 1, 11, 12, 14, 17, 19, 21,
70, 94, 118, 150, 167, 168, 177, 220,
222, 224, 225
nation-state 225
negotiation 62, 70, 99, 165, 166, 222
networks 5, 10, 29, 68, 223

Nikhil Banga Nagarik Sangha 148
No-Man's Land 9, 187

partition i, 1, 115, 124, 152, 199, 223
patriarchs 192, 193, 222
patriotism 3, 163, 198
peripheral subjectivities 12
perpetrators 168, 177
physical abuse 178, 181, 188, 196, 197, 198
proxy citizens 104

refugees i, 1, 6, 125, 141, 142, 144, 150, 181
riverine border 9, 43, 44, 56

scalar structuration 34, 221, 222
security ix, 4, 8, 15, 20, 36, 53, 98, 187,
195, 196, 220, 225
sexual abuse 177, 181, 184, 202
smugglers 7, 46, 51, 54, 63, 109, 161, 188,
189; smuggling 9, 16, 41, 43, 47, 48, 54,
59, 61, 68, 193 *see also* trade
social administration 111
social justice 111
socio-cultural viii, 1, 16, 17, 21, 141, 177
spatial disparities 90; spatial identities 1
state machinery i, 13, 17, 19, 70, 126, 145,
220
statelessness 4, 93, 111, 123, 125, 126
statism 225; statist 68, 166, 191, 219, 220,
225
subalternity 17, 70, 123, 167
surveillance mechanisms 13, 41, 48, 67,
165, 177

territorial 2, 3, 19, 34, 68, 90, 92, 149, 152,
187, 225 *also see* territory
territorial attachment 118; territorial
detachment 118
territory 1, 3, 36, 90, 104, 112, 117, 148, 220
thirdspace 17, 69, 167, 203
Tinbigha Agreement 97; *Tinbigha* Corridor
97, 115, 117, 118
trade 5, 7, 41, 50, 51, 55, 64, 183 *also see*
transactions
trafficking 12, 46, 181, 182, 183, 184, 186,
220
transactions 7, 52, 60, 107, 117
transterritorial 104

Vaishnava 150, 151
victims 41, 68, 104, 106, 149, 168, 184, 185

zero point 34, 35, 117, 187, 188